FAMILY EXPER
PRESS A
A LESSE

"An eye-opening and enormously provocative look at the historical forces that have trapped modern women in a daily grind of trying to reconcile motherhood and work in a country with one of the highest divorce rates and weakest family support systems of any industrial nation.... The author has provided a framework for a women's movement that will address the most pressing daily concerns of working women's lives." —Judy Mann,
Washington Post

"Scholarly, controversial appraisal of the women's movement and its shortcomings....Hewlett argues that the women's movement forgot someone special: mother." —*People*

"An important, thoughtful book, both insightful and courageou; —American Library Associati

"Sylvia Ann Hewlett is an economist and mother who written a trenchant, well-researched economic analysis of en in America that could become the *Feminine Mystique Female Eunuch* of the eighties...Hewlett's analysis is fa ing. It speaks in terms of statistics, and the statistics are both unassailable and astounding...America has the highest divorce rate in the world and the fewest societal supports for mothers and children....*A Lesser Life* presents a concrete vision of a revitalized feminism that puts children squarely at the head of all other national priorities. Is America ready for this vision? I hope so." —Erica Jong, *Vanity Fair*

"Makes a strong case that misguided modern feminism has worked to the disadvantage of most American women." —*Los Angeles Herald Examiner*

more...

"Her concern for working women is genuine. And this book is the best description I've seen of the difficulty women face in trying to do it all, without visible means of community support."
—*Houston Chronicle*

"More than an eloquent plea for the plight of working mothers, a *cri de coeur* for the working mother, whose maternal function seems to have been bypassed in the struggle for equality."
—*John Barkham Reviews*

"An excellent analysis of the employment problems of women. The book comprises a skillful blending of personal experience, case studies and scholarship."
—Ray Marshall,
Secretary of Labor, 1976–80

"The first book to explore feminism's current identity crisis."
—*Toronto Sun*

"A remarkably fine book...passionate and skillfully argued, it accurately describes the plight of so many young women in our society."
—Jerome Kagan, Professor of Psychology,
Harvard University

"Both a scholarly and deeply moving achievement."
—*Memphis Commercial Appeal*

"Poignant and damning...a breakthrough book on the plight of the family in America today."
—F. Forrester Church, Minister,
All Souls Unitarian Church, NYC

"Required reading. Passionate and totally convincing, this book will change the direction of the women's movement and galvanize our policy makers."
—Albert Shanker, President,
American Federation of Teachers,
AFL-CIO

more...

About the author

Sylvia Ann Hewlett is vice-president for economic studies at the United Nations Association and a member of the Council on Foreign Relations. She was born in South Wales, Britain, and at age seventeen won a scholarship to Cambridge University. After graduating she was awarded a Kennedy Scholarship at Harvard University, and went on to complete her Ph.D. in economics at London University. Between 1974 and 1981 she was assistant professor of economics at Barnard College, Columbia University. She is the recipient of a Cambridge University Research Fellowship and a Lehrman Institute Fellowship. Her published works include *The Cruel Dilemmas of Development* (1980), and articles in *Foreign Affairs, Harper's* and *The New York Times*. Ms. Hewlett lives in New York City with her husband and four children.

A Lesser Life

The Myth of Women's Liberation in America

Sylvia Ann Hewlett

WARNER BOOKS

A Warner Communications Company

Warner Books Edition
Copyright © 1986 by Sylvia Ann Hewlett
Afterword copyright © 1987 by Sylvia Ann Hewlett
All rights reserved.
This Warner Books edition is published by arrangement with
William Morrow and Company, Inc., 105 Madison Ave., New York, NY 10016

Warner Books, Inc., 666 Fifth Avenue, New York, NY 10103

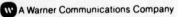 A Warner Communications Company

Printed in the United States of America
First Warner Books Printing: March 1987
10 9 8 7 6 5 4 3 2

Library of Congress Cataloging-in-Publication Data
Hewlett, Sylvia Ann, 1946-
    A lesser life.
    Reprint. Originally published: New York: W. Morrow,
©1986.
    Bibliography: p.
    Includes index.
    1. Feminism—United States. 2. Women—United States—
Social conditions. 3. Women—United States—Economic
conditions. I. Title.
[HQ1426.H457 1987]   305.4′2′0973   86-23367
ISBN 0-446-39122-0 (pbk.) (U.S.A.)
        0-446-38512-3 (pbk.) (Canada)

For Richard

Acknowledgments

For me this is a special book in that it represents a unique coming together of the personal and the professional. It therefore gives me particular pleasure to acknowledge the extensive help I have received from family, friends, and colleagues.

My greatest debt is to my husband, Richard Weinert. This book could not have been written without his constant support, which spanned the gamut from intellectual to domestic. He read all six drafts of the book and was my most rigorous and most constructive critic. Even more important, over the course of the last three years he has spent numerous evenings and weekends cooking meals and looking after the children so that I could work. If every career woman had such a partner, much of this book would be redundant.

A special word of thanks is due to our children—Shira, Lisa, David, and Adam. They helped me out with daily doses of love and were generous enough to be proud of a mother who sometimes worked too hard and too long. Besides which, it was their births and their childhoods that prompted the questions that lie behind this book.

I am also indebted to many others. I have depended on my editor, Pat Golbitz, for her fierce commitment to the book, which sustained me through the agonies of redrafting. My agent, Molly Friedrich, contributed generous amounts of time, judgment, and friendship. Few authors receive such wholehearted support and I am deeply grateful.

My greatest intellectual debt is to Betty Friedan, Lenore Weitzman, and Sheila Kamerman. Their ideas—and their scholarship—inform the arguments in this book and I am pleased to pay tribute to their work.

Over the last three years I have relied on the encouragement of my colleagues at the Economic Policy Council. I would like to express my appreciation to: Robert O. Anderson, Doug Fraser,

Acknowledgments

Charles Barber, Ray Marshall, Jack Sheinkman, Henry Kaufman, John Sweeny, Alice Ilchman, Albert Shanker, Ed Luck, Dan Burton, and Rose Carcaterra.

I would also like to thank Elizabeth Jakab, Joyce Kozloff, Charles Perrow, and Benjamin Kalman for thoughtful comments on early drafts of the book, and Margie Simmons for sharing her time and expertise. Pam Laber, Judy Farrell, Marthe Abraham, and Marie Sauveur provided invaluable assistance throughout the life-span of this project; and Wendy Atkin, Kathryn Bregman, Roy Brown, Frances Beinecke, Tru Helms, Abby Hirsch, Helen Knight, Ruth Spellman, Thelma Weinert, and Marcia Welles gave generous amounts of support and affection. I thank them all.

I also wish to acknowledge all those people I interviewed. Business leaders, journalists, government officials, and hundreds of working parents in five different countries gave freely of their time and their energy. In a critical sense they made this book possible and I am grateful.

Finally, my heartfelt thanks go to my parents, Vernon and Jean Hewlett. Before it became fashionable, they taught me to strive for both a career and a family, and any success I have found is grounded in their unconditional love.

New York City
September 1985

Contents

— 1 —
Introduction

"How'm I doing?" is the question New York City's Mayor Ed Koch uses as a battle cry in his campaigns. Ask it about American women—how're we doing?—and the answer is likely to be a re-working of the old cigarette ad: We've come a long way, baby, but we still have a long way to go. Broaden the question a little, and ask how American women are doing compared with European women, and the response is likely to be a touch smug: Maybe things aren't perfect here, but we're certainly light-years ahead of women in Europe.

But are we? I once thought so. I grew up in Britain, and, like most Europeans, viewed American women with awe and respect. They were, after all, the most powerful and liberated women in the world.

My view reflected the conventional wisdom. For two centuries America has been seen by its own citizenry and by foreigners as a land where women are born free, where they enjoy a degree of freedom and independence unparalleled in the rest of the world. In the early nineteenth century French aristocrat and social critic Alexis de Tocqueville pointed to the superiority of American women. "I have nowhere seen women occupying a loftier position," he wrote in 1830.[1] In more recent times women in the United States have had the benefit of many more civil rights and much more education than their contemporaries elsewhere. And as if to clinch the matter, there is the women's movement, which has been so much more vocal in America than in other countries. The prominence of feminism in the United States is seen as visible confirmation of the advanced status of American women.

When I arrived at Harvard University as a graduate student at the end of the 1960s, I felt doubly lucky. Not only had I come to America—to immigrants always the land of opportunity—but I felt that I was destined to be part of that golden generation of women who were going to find a place in the sun. By the early 1970s the women's movement was maturing, doors were being flung open, and the barriers to professional achievements for women were falling. I felt confident I could have it all: career success; marriage; children. A few years later, when I actually dealt with the problems of bearing and raising children while building a career, I learned what most women learn: It's damn tough. In fact, it was (and is) much tougher than I had expected given the popular image of the new superwoman—strong, efficient, cheerful, working, raising her kids, having it all.

While living here, I stayed in close touch with my sisters in Britain, two of whom were also working and having children around the same time I was. They didn't seem to have as hard a time as I. At first I thought this was most likely due to differences in type of job, career ambitions, life-styles, and so on. But as time went on, I began to wonder.

So I decided to look into it. And the more I looked, the more shocked—and dismayed—I became. For despite all those new female M.B.A.'s, M.D.'s, astronauts, and TV anchorpersons, modern American women suffer immense economic vulnerability. They have less economic security than their mothers did and are considerably worse off than women in other advanced countries.

Way back in the 1950s a traditional division of labor gave women a substantial degree of financial security. Maybe many were stuck in bad marriages, but the man did go out every day and earn enough to support his family. In exchange the woman ran the home and brought up the children. With the sexual revolution and liberation this all changed. Divorce became common—in fact, it became three times more common—and women could no longer count on marriage to provide the economic necessities of life.

This, of course, is a worldwide trend, but the rate of divorce in the United States is now two to twenty times higher than in other rich nations, and the degree of financial insecurity and injury women suffer as a result of divorce is far higher in America than anywhere else in the world.[2]

Accompanying the breakdown of traditional marriage in the late sixties and seventies was a dramatic rise in the proportion of women who worked. This was part cause, part consequence. The weakening of traditional roles forced women into the labor force, while the fact of working and earning salaries enabled more women to free themselves of the bonds of traditional role playing.

Again, this was part of a larger trend; throughout the advanced world women have entered the labor force at an extremely rapid rate in recent years. How have they fared in the workplace? It is fairly well known that working women in the United States earn approximately 64 percent of the male wage and that this earnings gap holds true for corporate executives as well as for retail clerks. But it is less well known that the United States has one of the largest wage gaps in the advanced industrial world and is one of the few countries where the gap between male and female earnings hasn't narrowed over the course of the last twenty years.

The plain truth is that modern American women, liberated or not, have little economic security as wives and mothers, or as workers. They are squeezed between the traditional and modern forms of financial security to an extent which is unknown in other societies.

Our mothers sought, and the majority of them found, economic security in marriage, but that avenue no longer offers any such guarantee. Because of stagflation, higher rates of unemployment, and much higher rates of divorce, men can no longer be relied upon to be family breadwinners—at least not over the long haul. The escalating divorce rate is a critical factor because with divorce men generally relinquish responsibility for their wives and often for their children. Thus the breakdown of marriage massively increases the disparity between male and female incomes.

In *The Divorce Revolution,* Stanford sociologist Lenore Weitzman shows that after divorce the standard of living of the ex-husband rises 42 percent while that of the ex-wife (and her children) falls 73 percent.[3] Since alimony is paid in only 5 to 10 percent of divorces, and since two-thirds of custodial mothers receive no child support from ex-husbands, millions of women end up bearing complete financial responsibility for raising the children of divorce.[4] Partly because of this economic fallout of divorce, 77 percent of this nation's poverty is now borne by women and their children.[5]

But perhaps modern women neither need nor want the security of traditional marriage. After all, conventional wisdom tells us that today's liberated women should be able to find their economic salvation in the marketplace. Yet in the workplace there continue to be highly unequal rewards for men and women. American women earn 64 percent of the male wage,[6] this despite the fact that they have had as much education as their male counterparts—unlike women in other countries, who generally lag behind men in educational attainment. The earnings gap between men and women has not narrowed in five decades and shows no sign of doing so in the future. A female wage is often inadequate to provide a woman, let alone a family, with the bare necessities of life. Getting a job does not necessarily lift a single woman or a divorced mother out of poverty.

In Western Europe, by contrast, women have a much better shot at economic viability. Marriage remains a considerably more dependable institution than in America, and therefore, traditional forms of economic security mean more. The divorce rate in the United States is now double that in Sweden, Britain, and Germany; triple that in France; and twenty times as high as in Italy.[7] On the work front, wage gaps in Europe have been closing, and women's wages relative to men's are now 2 to 30 percent higher than in the United States.[8]

But that's not all. These other advanced democracies have also instituted family support systems, such as paid maternity leaves, child allowances, subsidized day care, and free health services, all of which considerably ease the lives of working parents.[9] In contrast, more than 60 percent of working mothers in the United States have no right to maternity leave, and recent social spending cutbacks have reduced even further the low level of public support for child care.[10] These problems of childbearing and child rearing are critical as 90 percent of women have children at some point during their lives.[11]

In other words, while women in other countries have better maintained the security of marriage and have steadily improved the material conditions of their lives—by narrowing earnings differentials between men and women and increasing the scope of family support systems—women in this country are becoming more and more vulnerable. Despite their legendary claims to power and privilege, American women actually face a bad and deteriorating economic reality.

The *Wall Street Journal* put its finger on the nub of the problem when it described my generation of American women in the following terms: "Aglow with talent and self-confidence, young women who came of age in the early 1970s breezed through college, picked up their law degrees and MBA's and began sprinting up the corporate ladder."[12] There was only one snag: These same women found their careers "sabotaged by motherhood."[13] Although most of these women chose joyfully to become mothers and would have a hard time seeing their babies as saboteurs, the *Journal* hit the nail on the head.

The problem centers on a clash of roles. Those of us who reached maturity in the 1970s were expected to clone the male competitive model in the labor market while raising our children in our spare time. Compounding this double burden were gratuitous psychological pressures, because we were also expected to raise these children according to wildly inflated notions of motherhood. In essence, I belonged to that "lucky" generation of superwomen who got to combine the nurturing standards of the 1950s with the strident feminism of the 1970s. But as many of us discovered when we struggled to bear and raise children midcareer, the rigid standards of the 1950s "cult of motherhood" are impossible to combine with the equally rigid standards of our fiercely competitive workplaces. Mere mortals such as I end up trapped between the demands of the earth mothers and the hard-nosed careerists, and because these demands are incompatible and contradictory, we are ultimately unable to satisfy either. Neither hired help nor supportive husbands can insulate working mothers from these antagonistic pressures.

My own difficulties led me to pose the central questions of this book. How did the most independent and best-educated women in the world come to have the least good conditions of life? And why has the American women's movement failed to deliver on these critical economic fronts?

To help me better understand this great American paradox, I decided to look closely at four Western democracies: Britain, France, Italy, and Sweden; all nations that have produced better conditions of life for the majority of their female citizens. I studied these countries in depth, spending time in each and talking to ordinary men and women as well as to scholars and cabinet ministers, in an effort to understand how and why these countries have done better for their women than our nation has. I chose these particular countries because they represent a range of political values; I wanted to examine traditional Catholic societies as well as secular welfare states. But despite their differences, all these countries are affluent Western democracies and constitute a legitimate peer group with which to compare America. I also chose them because I knew them well. I grew up in Britain, I have lived and worked in both France and Italy, and I have done research in Sweden. This firsthand experience enabled me to interpret the mass of data I collected.

As well as understanding these problems I wanted to develop some practical policy measures capable of improving the situation in the United States. So I decided to turn directly to some major players in the American economy. Since 1981 I have been director of the Economic Policy Council (EPC), a powerful private-sector think tank made up of business leaders, labor leaders, economists, educators, and policy analysts. Each year the council launches two study panels each of which explores a major economic problem and comes to a set of policy recommendations. I persuaded the EPC that family life in this country was in the midst of revolutionary change and that this was throwing off problems that had major economic as well as social implications. In 1983 we set up a policy panel chaired by Alice Ilchman (president, Sarah Lawrence College) and John Sweeney (president, the Service Employees International Union), and funded by the Ford and Rockefeller foundations. Its mission was to investigate the problems facing working parents in this country and to recommend policy measures that would help resolve these problems. Other members of the panel included former President Gerald Ford, Steven Ross (chairman of Warner Communications), and Katharine Graham (chairman, the Washington Post Company).

This exercise I thought would produce realistic solutions, not pie in the sky. The panel members, while sympathetic to the problems in hand, were not professional do-gooders but hardheaded members of the establishment who had a firm grip on economic and political reality. In addition, because many of them were men, my panel would not be yet another group of concerned women sitting around talking to the converted. I wanted to find out what could be done in present-day America, not what might be done in utopia.

2

A PERSONAL VIEW

Up until the time I had children, I was profoundly confident of my ability to find fulfillment in both love and work. Having grown to maturity on the crest of the modern women's movement, I expected nothing less. In the early seventies women were rapidly breaking down the male monopoly on career achievement, and I, like millions of educated men before me, was encouraged to believe that I could build a successful career *and* lead a rich personal life. When the political activists of my generation told me that American women had never had it so good, I believed them; when they told me I could dictate my terms to life, I believed that, too.

It is hard to remember how bright and shining the future seemed in those years. For me it seemed particularly dazzling because of the dreary hopelessness of my early life. I was raised with five sisters in a narrow-minded, unemployment-ridden mining community in South Wales. My father was a struggling teacher who was (in the absence of sons) intensely ambitious for his six daughters. Although we were brought up in straitened circumstances—no refrigerator, telephone, television, or car—we were encouraged to think big and, above all else, get ourselves an education. And most of us put together enough effort and determination to do precisely that. But it was a hard, lonely struggle, and my memories of childhood and adolescence are grounded in a harsh reality. At age seven my most valued skill was an ability to peel potatoes very fast; I got lots of practice since we ate them for supper every evening. At age fourteen I was a social outcast because neither my wardrobe (none of us sisters ever had new clothes; we wore other families' castoffs) nor my career aspirations enabled me to fit into the local working-class scene. But hard work and doggedness paid off. At age seventeen I won admission to Cambridge University and went off to start a successful academic career at this elite institution.

In 1967 I won a graduate fellowship to Harvard University and sailed across the Atlantic to the country that to me, as to so many other immigrants, had always been the Promised Land. I was not disappointed. The Great Society was then in full swing; America was eradicating poverty and urban decay. The younger generation was repudiating the materialism of middle-class life and working up a great cleansing anger over the immorality of the Vietnam War. Blacks and women were beginning to claim their birthright as free and equal human beings. I still recall the exhilaration I felt being in the right place at the right time— America in the latter part of the twentieth century. I was destined to be part of that special generation of women who were going to reap the benefits of all this progressive social change. While I could not quite believe that the world was at my feet, it seemed clear that the barriers to professional achievement for women were falling. We were now allowed to join the mainstream and compete on equal terms with men for power, status, and material rewards. At the very least, I thought, I was not condemned to repeat my mother's life and see my best years slip away in endless domestic drudgery.

In the early seventies I returned to England to complete my Ph.D. at the London School of Economics, but in 1974 I decided to make my home in America and accepted my first professional appointment as assistant professor of economics at Barnard College, Columbia University. Two years later I got married, and in 1977, at the age of thirty-one, I had my first baby. Lisa was a very wanted child, and I was profoundly happy to have a beautiful, healthy daughter. However, the first few months of her life turned out to be a difficult period, full of frustration and failure. First of all, I was trying to breast-feed. But since my teaching job at Barnard, a prestigious women's college, offered no maternity leave (paid or unpaid), I had to be back at work within ten days. Despite an immense effort, I failed to combine my demanding job with breast-feeding. When my milk supply dried up and I reluctantly had to substitute bottle for bosom, I felt that I could not now bond adequately with Lisa, that I had flunked the first test of motherhood.

More serious challenges soon followed. As a conscientious new mother I read the child-rearing manuals and found, to my dismay, that much of the experts' advice was incompatible with a professional existence. Most books simply assumed that the mother was available to her child sixteen hours a day. Besides physical care, there were such complex duties as "architect or designer of the child's world and daily experiences" and "consultant, someone to provide constant advice and assistance to the child."[1] Only by fulfilling these roles could a mother ensure an adequate start in life for her child. I failed to find any child-rearing book that expended more than two pages on the problems of the working mother; most experts were more or less hostile. Benjamin Spock told me that unless a mother absolutely must work, it makes no sense for her to "pay other people to do a poorer job of bringing up [her] children,"[2] while Berry Brazelton argued that "two mothers are not as good as one" and urged mothers to delay their return to work.[3] I felt that Brazelton should have a word with my employer. Burton White was a little more generous, grudgingly conceding that work is permissible if a mother arranged "her work hours to overlap with the child's nap time."[4] But Lisa, as is the habit of many babies, napped briefly and erratically. White, a committed professional himself, clearly had not tried collapsing his work schedule into an unpredictable three-hour day—his wife had stayed home to look after their four children.

I found my first brush with the child-rearing experts an undermining experience, but I remained determined to qualify as a good mother. Had I not succeeded in other, more difficult spheres? Every minute I was not actually in my office or in class, I earnestly took care of my child, trying to compress into early morning, lunchtime, and evening hours the elaborate responsibilities of motherhood. At the same time I was striving to be especially conscientious on the job, staying late, taking work home, and generally assuming extra duties. My great fear was that given my new maternal role, I would no longer be seen as a committed professional.

A typical working day when Lisa was three months old went like this: I was up at 5:00 A.M. to feed and change Lisa (she was a very small child, and it took months before she would sleep through the night). From 6:00 to 8:00 A.M. was a precious period when I tried to cram in all kinds of "quality time," attempting to "lay the foundations of intelligence" in my three-month-old child, in the way suggested by Burton White in *The First Three Years of Life*.[5] As well as the more obvious things, like encouraging Lisa to kick, gurgle, and coo, I was supposed to move her about the house in an infant seat, do complicated things with steel mirrors (just seven inches from her face),[6] devise simple toys from cooking utensils to encourage her to use her "hands as tools,"[7] and train her sight by teaching her to follow a dangling ring "with successive fixations" of her eyes.[8] This latter test could easily be flunked by the mother, for if the ring "is moved too suddenly, or is left static too long, the visual attention of the infant will flag."[9] Poor Lisa, her infancy must have been rather arduous; I certainly didn't allow her to just lie around being a baby.

My husband, Richard, came on duty about 7:00 A.M., made breakfast for everyone, and cleaned up. At 8:00 A.M. our part-time baby-sitter arrived, and by 9:00 A.M. I was teaching a class. I tried to cram all my work responsibilities into the morning and early-afternoon hours, often going home at lunchtime, bringing Lisa into the college for 12:00 to 1:00 P.M. department meetings, and relegating my own lunch to a sandwich, eaten on the run. From 3:30 to 6:00 P.M. was "quality time" again with Lisa. From 6:00 to 8:00 P.M. I coped with dinner and laundry while Richard put Lisa to bed; then, from 8:00 P.M. to midnight, I ground away at my research. I had taken on a major writing assignment in addition to my normal job responsibilities since I felt pressure to prove to my colleagues that I was still a full-blooded professional worthy of consideration for tenure. I crammed all this work into the later evening hours so that it would not encroach on my time with Lisa. As a result, I was always desperately short of sleep.

I had further complicated matters by electing to employ a baby-sitter part time rather than full time. I did this partly to save money and partly because I did not want to be accused of handing my baby over to a stranger. As a result of this part-time baby-sitting arrangement, any lunch-hour work commitment plus those that happened to fall after 3:30 P.M. had to be undertaken with Lisa *in tow*. It is hard to exaggerate how wrenching it is to try to carry out work responsibilities with a baby in attendance. Simple tasks like dictating a letter or meeting with students become impossible if there is a fussy (and often messy) baby in the room, and colleagues were simply not amused if Lisa started to wail or filled her diaper in the middle of a meeting. Although to a nonparent these chaotic scenes seem to verge on the farcical, living through them was truly a nightmare, and I cannot now understand how I endured the constant physical and psychological stress of trying to combine motherhood and career in this way.

When Lisa was four and a half months old, I capitulated and hired a full-time baby-sitter. I did this not out of any consideration for myself or Richard (though by this stage both of us were wretchedly tired) but because I was encountering tremendous disapproval and hostility at work and I knew that I could not take Lisa to my office any longer. The final straw was a note I found on my desk that spring. It was from a colleague down the hallway, and it read: "Dear Professor Hewlett, I would like to point out that we, at Barnard, are not running a creche but a college." I was surprised and hurt; weren't we supposed to be providing role models for our women students? But I was also cowed. I never took Lisa to work again except for the annual Christmas party.

A word on why I was dependent on private baby-sitters. When Lisa was born, I made inquiries about what child care was available on campus. I discovered that the only program offered by Barnard College was for toddlers. This program cost just under $1,000 a year and took children ages eighteen to thirty months for two hours two mornings a week. I did not think I could use it even when Lisa was old enough since the program required that mothers attend with their kids for the first six weeks of class! I remember being a little surprised. The toddler program was clearly not designed for the women who worked at Barnard College; we needed day care, not another set of responsibilities. Maybe the program was meant for the nonworking wives of male faculty members.

When I look back on this situation several years later, I realize that only one other person in my department had ever actually had a baby and that I was surrounded by people (many of them women) who, for one reason or another, had opted not to embark on conventional family lives. Any thoughts I may have had about this being an unusual state of affairs are dispelled by a look at the statistics. By age forty 90 percent of all women have had children, but among professional women (who are, after all, fewer than 10 percent of all working women) the story is different. Surveys of lawyers, business executives, and other professionals show that less than half the career women of my generation have had children.[10] In many cases work pressures seem to have ruled out the possibility. These same women often tend to resent working mothers, viewing their struggles to bear and raise children as an illegitimate effort to have their cake and eat it.

My sister Helen, who lived in Manchester, England, and taught in a secondary school, also had a baby in 1977. I was surprised to learn that she was entitled to an eight-month maternity leave, six months of it on full salary. At the time I didn't know anything about policies in other countries, and after thinking about Helen's situation for a while, I decided that it must be some sort of special deal. I saw Great Britain as being rather backward on women's issues and decidedly "unliberated." Why, English people still talked about manpower and chairmen when they referred to women and weren't even self-conscious about doing it! I could not imagine that progressive America had anything to learn from the Old World. In spite of all my American advantages, however, it was clear that I had not been able to cope successfully with the dual roles I had so joyfully undertaken. Instead, I had lost the precious beginnings of my daughter's life in a fog of desperate exhaustion. This was, I felt, a personal failure on my part. I knew there had to be a way to be superwoman and succeed on all fronts. I just hadn't been able to find it yet.

Two years later, in 1979, I attempted to have a second child. From the very beginning this second pregnancy was difficult. I was more than usually nauseated, I swelled up at an alarming rate, and I experienced frightening bouts of cramping. My obstetrician calmly and authoritatively told me not to worry, everything was in order. I found it hard to believe him, and at the end of the third month I sought a second opinion, carefully selecting a senior woman obstetrician at a New York City teaching hospital, who, I felt, would take my apprehension seriously. The consultation did not turn out as I had hoped. The doctor examined me quite brusquely, and afterward, when we were seated in her fancy Fifth Avenue consulting room, she glanced at her watch and told me that she had only two minutes to spare. I tried to assemble my thoughts and blurted out some of my worst anxieties: that I was feeling much too uncomfortable for this stage in pregnancy, that I was frightened by the intermittent cramping, and that I was fearful that I might miscarry. The doctor smiled condescendingly and said that she was sure everything was normal and that since I seemed to be getting a little obsessed with this pregnancy, "why don't you take up swimming or maybe even a little gentle jogging to take your mind off your aches and pains?" Surprised and offended, I made one last stab. Did she think I should cut back on my work load during the remainder of my pregnancy? "Good heavens, no!" she said heartily. "This isn't the nineteenth century!"

A few weeks later the sonogram I had in connection with amniocentesis (a test carried out on older pregnant women to detect any chromosomal abnormalities in a fetus) showed that I was carrying twins. While Richard and I were delighted with the news, I now felt somewhat justified in my forebodings. I did some reading and found out that twins were often born dangerously early. Back I went to my calm male obstetrician and asked again: Should I stop working or at least cut back to part time? "Not at all, my dear, college teaching isn't hard labor." He pinched my cheek and sent me home. I was immensely depressed; I yearned for some authority to tell me to take time off and concentrate my energies on growing those babies. Despite reassurances from the doctors, in my gut I felt that this pregnancy was in trouble. I talked it over *ad nauseam* with Richard, who gently encouraged me to follow my instincts. If I was so worried, I should stop working.

But it wasn't that simple. Since I appeared to have no legitimate medical problem, I could not request a leave of absence; I would have to resign. Ten years of hard, grinding work had gone into the acquiring of my present job. It would be extremely difficult to replicate it since the academic job market was shrinking. Besides, I was only eighteen months away from being considered for tenure at Barnard College. Could I really give up the possibility of lifetime job security? I agonized but finally decided to stick with my career. The truth was that without external validation of physical problems with the pregnancy, without a doctor's approval, I could not throw in my job. I simply did not have the courage to take the decision into my own hands and deliberately destroy my professional prospects. I did not take the woman doctor's advice and start jogging, but I did try to stamp down my worries and concentrate on coping with the tasks in hand, which included a two-year-old child, a full-time job, and a painful and malfunctioning body.

Later that year, on November 17, at about 6:30 P.M., I was sitting in my office in a state of total exhaustion. Earlier that afternoon I had given a seminar to the assembled faculty, a rather tension-ridden event where I exposed my most recent research to the critical comments of my colleagues. This seminar was extremely important because it marked the beginning of my tenure review and would help decide whether I was eventually promoted or let go. I was slumped in my desk chair, trying to summon up enough energy to go home, when water began to trickle down my legs. My mind was a little befuddled, and at first I didn't know what it was. Then, as the trickle turned into a stream, I realized in horror that my waters had broken, that it was much too early to go into labor (I was in the sixth month of pregnancy), and that this might mean the death of my two babies. By now my boots were filled with water and a great puddle was spreading across my office rug. I stumbled out into the corridor and, discovering that no one was in the building except me, made my way, dripping, shivering, and sobbing, across the cold dark campus to Broadway. I hailed a cab and asked to be driven to Lenox Hill Hospital.

Hours later my now grim-faced male obstetrician told me that if my body did not go into contractions, and if the amniotic fluid replenished itself, I had a very small chance of saving the babies. The more probable outcome was that over the course of the next forty-eight hours I would spontaneously go into labor and the babies would be born. Given their age and size (about one and a half pounds each), they would have no chance of survival.

I spent two days in limbo, lying flat on a hard hospital bed, sick with fear and praying to some ill-defined deity for the lives of my children. Then the technicians did a sonogram, and to my great joy not only were the babies alive, but they were floating around in what seemed like plenty of amniotic fluid. But on the morning of the third day I awoke to find something strange and hard protruding from my vagina. It was an umbilical cord, and it was lifeless. No blood pulsed through the lifeline to the baby; it was stiff and dry like a withered stalk. One of the children was dead. I frantically rang the bell for a nurse, and everything started happening at once. Interns, residents, and stretchers arrived, and I was rushed to the delivery floor. "What are you doing?" I cried. "The other baby is still alive, and I want to keep it inside me!" One of the doctors on duty patiently explained that they had no option but to induce labor. With a dead baby in my uterus there was considerable danger of maternal infection. Both babies had to be delivered. One was dead; the other would die. I hit my head against the steel railing of my bed and screamed at them not to touch me. It was Richard who finally persuaded me that I had no choice. We could have more babies, he said, but there was only one of me.

Later that morning I started a "normal" fourteen hour labor. I screwed up my eyes and plugged my ears so that I would not see or hear my dead and dying children be born—but I felt them warm and wet against my thighs. Although my obstetrician claimed that a natural (i.e., undrugged) labor was quicker and safer, to my dying day I will never understand why he couldn't or wouldn't knock me out with anesthesia for the birth. I should have been spared such gratuitous agony.

Afterward, for quite a long time, life was truly hard to bear. First, there were the physical ironies. My breasts swelled up hard and hurtful, full of milk for my dead babies. Several weeks later my breasts were still leaking milk, providing a constant reminder of my loss. But I needed no reminder. I mourned my children with an intensity that frightened me. In addition to my grief, I was coping with an overwhelming sense of responsibility. Night after night I lay awake going through various scenarios in my head. I found at least four or five ways in which I thought I might be directly to blame. If only I had given up work, I would not have miscarried. If I had sought a third medical opinion, I might have found a doctor who could have saved the pregnancy. Or if I had chosen an obstetrician attached to a teaching hospital, perhaps one of the babies could have been saved by access to a "state of the art" neonatal unit. I was riddled with guilt; I had failed to protect my babies and therefore had no pity on myself. For a while I believed that I was living proof of the conservative wisdom that women could not have both careers and babies.

As I gradually recovered and my life became happier, the dreadful sense of blame ebbed away. In retrospect it seems that I will never know for sure why I miscarried, but I now believe it would probably have happened even if I had given up my job.

My anguish during that dark winter of 1979–80 prompted me to do some reading and thinking about pregnancy. I discovered that my case was not unique. Twenty percent of all pregnancies end in miscarriage, and for older women, who have often waited many years to start a family, miscarriage is almost always profoundly upsetting. In an interview obstetrician Alan Berkeley of New York Hospital told me that in his practice many older patients who experience a miscarriage go through such anguish that they often redefine their lives (resign their jobs, change the pace of their lives, move to the suburbs) in order to decrease the likelihood of losing another pregnancy.[11] If one adds to the toll of mis-

A Lesser Life

carriage the difficult burdens of infertility—and one out of seven couples has serious problems conceiving[12]—it becomes obvious that childbearing in the latter part of the twentieth century is far from being an easy or automatic process, whether or not the mother is in the labor force. However, I was beginning to realize that for many working women the problems of pregnancy are compounded by the indifferent and often harsh attitudes of institutions and employers. Modern superwomen are meant to have children on the side, "on their own time," and the less said about the matter, the better. In this country there is little appreciation of the fact that having children is a societal imperative as well as a private choice, that children are a nation's collective future. In America children tend to be defined as private consumption goods. If working women choose to have them, then it is up to them to cope, as best they can, on their own.

The reaction at work to my loss of the twins ran true to form. I was allowed two weeks off for the "procedure" (as one colleague called it) and was then expected to resume a full work load. Very few people ever referred to my loss. They found it embarrassing and a little messy, hard to mix with professional small talk. However, two women colleagues from different departments whom I hardly knew did seek me out. Pamela* invited me to meet her for lunch off campus and in a quiet voice (as she glanced around the restaurant to make sure no one else was listening) told me of the day ten years before when she had miscarried in the middle of a lecture. She had left the room trailing blood and fled to the bathroom, eventually depositing a bloody bundle in the trash can. She had never told anyone at work what had happened for fear that her professional image would be compromised. She still dreamed about the baby she had lost and never replaced. She clasped my hand and said in a choked voice that she understood how I felt.

A few days later Susan* came to find me in my office. She had given birth to a stillborn child five years before. That tragedy made her want to reach out to me. Susan's story was chilling. Her stillbirth had been followed by two subsequent miscarriages, and it had taken her four years to give birth to a healthy infant. She

*Pseudonym.

28

had been fired from three different jobs over this period because no institution had been willing to give her a leave of absence to deal with the various pregnancies. Her husband had been unemployed for part of this time, so she had had no option but to try to continue working. Like Pamela, and for the same reason, she had kept her childbearing problems a secret. Susan offered to take over some committee duties for me, and before she left, we held each other and cried. I was deeply touched by these brave and lonely women, each hiding her grief as if she had committed a crime. They were afraid of professional repercussions and ashamed of showing their maternal vulnerabilities in the workplace. By this point I was bitterly aware of the fact that they would have received considerably more sympathy from their colleagues and support from the workplace if, instead of losing a child, they had broken a leg on a skiing vacation.

When I returned to work after losing the twins, my chairperson called me into his office and, after offering his condolences, got straight to the point. He strongly advised against my getting pregnant again until the tenure issue had been resolved (and that decision was still more than a year away). He implied that he would not be able to answer for the consequences should I be so headstrong and emotional as to get pregnant before then. But I was past caring whether I was endangering my prospects for tenure. I had finally decided to follow my instincts, and what my instincts told me was that I desperately needed to replace my babies. Two months later I became pregnant again.

This time I sought out a specialist in high-risk pregnancy. In my third month I was sewn up—that is, my cervix was secured with stitches to minimize the chance of another miscarriage. For the remainder of the pregnancy I was under strict medical orders. I could carry out most of the basic functions of my job but was not to take on anything stressful or physically taxing. It was an immense relief to be able to "take things easy" now that I had the imprimatur of a higher medical authority. I spent much of those months semihorizontal on a daybed in my office. Students and colleagues came to me, not vice versa. My son, David, was born prematurely, but alive and well, at the end of the seventh month. Richard and I were overjoyed; it was, even with the additional problems of coping with a premature baby, the happiest of endings. As usual I had to return to work quickly, this time two weeks after the birth, and the expectation was that I should perform as though I did not have a family care in the world.

By now I had become deeply perturbed by the difficulties of combining a career with childbearing in this liberated society of ours. My concern was especially acute because I knew that I was a privileged person. Seventy percent of today's women in the labor force work out of economic necessity; they are single, widowed, divorced or are married to men who are either unemployed or earn less than $15,000 a year.[13] I was not poor, black, or single, and I had an abundance of marketable skills. What happened to working mothers who were more vulnerable than I?

As for me, why had I gone on working if I was so bent on having children? I was, after all, married to a man who was able to support all of us.

There were some obvious reasons. I loved my job. I was good at it, and working made me feel useful and effective. But there were other, much more powerful reasons. I knew from looking around me that professional women who took a few years off to have children rarely made it back "on track" and often spent their mature years in second-rate jobs. Did I really want to be someone else's research assistant when I was forty-one? My own institutions, Barnard College and Columbia University, seemed to have an abundance of female instructors and assistant professors but few in the more senior tenured ranks.[14] Most faculty women seemed to fall by the wayside in their thirties as they struggled, unsuccessfully, to both raise a family, and live up to the competitive pressures of their profession.

I was also afraid of divorce. Richard and I had a strong and loving marriage; but I knew the statistical odds (at least half of all marriages fail), and I had too many friends who had been left not only jobless and poverty-stricken but literally "holding the baby" in the aftermath of divorce. I had endured too much economic insecurity in my childhood to want to expose myself (and my children) to that kind of risk. Stories about the sad plight of displaced homemakers distressed and frightened me. My future in terms of both job satisfaction and earning power seemed to depend on sticking with my career during my thirties, and my job was also my only insurance in case of divorce.

In the wake of my childbearing experiences I decided to form a committee with other junior faculty women to press for the adoption of a maternity policy at Barnard college. We had modest demands—a two- to three-month leave, a small reduction in the teaching load during the first year of a child's life, and the ability to stop the tenure clock during the same period—but we failed to get our policy through the college administration.[15] The policy was never defeated *per se;* it was simply allowed to die. My committee kept on meeting, and we kept on getting our draft policy back for revisions and additional information, and nothing ever happened. It was like petitioning a brick wall.

Our biggest surprise was to find that the feminists on the faculty disapproved of maternity policies. To comprehend our astonishment, it is necessary to understand that Barnard College was and is a national bastion of women's rights. The college is understandably proud of its Women's Center (with its rape crisis center, its abortion counseling service, and its steady stream of national and international visitors); its annual "The Scholar and the Feminist" conference, which produces some of the finest feminist scholarship in the country; and its fierce determination to remain independent of Columbia University precisely because it thinks that Barnard stands for values that are important to women and that these values (and the academic programs these values spin off) would be swallowed up if the college were to merge with the larger university. Barnard College is one of the few elite colleges to have an undergraduate major in women's studies, and there is a powerful group of feminist scholars on the faculty who teach in this program and are active at the Women's Center. In our naïve way we thought that all this emphasis on women's rights and feminist values had to translate into concrete support for the working mothers on the faculty. It did not.

Many of my feminist colleagues did not have children and were less than enthusiastic about families. Indeed, one of them publicly accused me of trying to get a "free ride" when I spoke out at a meeting for a college maternity policy. Didn't I understand that if women wanted equality with men, they could not ask for special privileges? She and her (childless) colleagues were passionate in their insistence that liberated women should strive to replicate the career patterns of men—to become male clones.

In the event, the Barnard Women's Center gave very lukewarm support to the proposed maternity policy. The director of the center (who was personally supportive) apologetically explained to me that maternity leave was a divisive issue among feminists. If this was the other side of the coin of liberation, I thought, heaven help the working mother. It was clear our sisters wouldn't.

By 1980 my difficulties in having children mid-career had made me a less idealistic and less ambitious woman. I had become aware of an enormous gap between the aspirations of modern women and the practical reality of their lives. Despite the achievements of the women's movement, my generation was a long way from being able to combine work and family life in the way that is taken for granted by the majority of men. As a social scientist I began to want to understand better the contradictions that so adversely affect the lives of American working mothers. For a while this new interest of mine was no more than a hobby. I was preoccupied with the care of two small children and my work as an academic economist. However, I was able to do a certain amount of research and traveling and discovered (to my amazement) that most Western democracies have made more progress in helping women shoulder their dual burden than we have in liberated America. I became determined to discover why this was so. Several years later, when I became director of the Economic Policy Council and obtained some funding to set up a policy panel on women and work in America, I finally found myself in a position to push these questions further. All of which led to this book.

By the early eighties my experience had already led me to one important conclusion: Women of my age in America are at the mercy of two powerful and antagonistic traditions. The first is the ultradomestic fifties with its powerful cult of motherhood;

the other is the strident feminism of the seventies with its attempt to clone the male competitive model. Both these traditions can be found in other industrialized societies, but in these other contexts they are pale reflections of the American prototype. Only in America are these ideologies pushed to extremes. An American woman trying to fulfill the demands of both traditions is obviously in something of a dilemma. It is not easy to be simultaneously the earth mother-goddess and the hard-bitten, hard-nosed corporate executive or fireperson. And her attempt to manage both roles is further undermined by the fact that American society, having produced the strongest and most antithetical dual roles for women, has left them with the weakest support systems with which to mediate these roles. Successive administrations have repeatedly failed to provide the maternity leaves and child-care facilities so taken for granted by working parents in other advanced countries.

Just trying to meet the demands of the cult of motherhood can prove to be an almost impossible task. Take, for example, the ways in which modern American mothers are expected to give birth without drugs and to breast-feed. The earth mother-goddess "American-style" has her roots in the fifties, but the countercultural rebellion and feminism both added to the burdens of this role.

The highly domestic women of the 1950s were encouraged to glory in the specialness of being female, particularly in the unique ability of women to bear children and suckle their young. According to Betty Friedan, "they were told to choose with free intelligence to have babies, to bear them with proud awareness that denied pain, to nurse them at the breast, and to devote mind and body to their care."[16] In the 1960s the flower children of the counterculture added their own special brand of earthiness. Rebelling against the life-styles and the values of affluent Middle America, they led the return to a more natural state. College-educated young women of this period abandoned foundation garments and makeup, ate macrobiotic foods, and stopped shaving their legs and their armpits. Natural childbirth and breast-feeding were emphasized as part of this back-to-nature trend.

In the seventies feminists latched onto natural childbirth as a way in which women could assert control over their bodies. They rhapsodized about birth being the ultimate "whole body orgasm" and hammered away at the need for women to reclaim this precious experience from the space age technology of male obstetricians. Most of us were persuaded to believe that real women give birth naturally and without pain.

Why did the earth mother syndrome become so influential in America? Natural childbirth, for example, had been pioneered in Europe. The great leaders in the field—Grantly Dick-Read, Fernand Lamaze, and Frederick Leboyer—lived and practiced in England and France.[17] But it was in the United States that the movement found exceptionally fertile ground in which to plant its ideology. The ultradomesticity of the 1950s and the radical chic of the 1960s joined with the new feminist desire to glory in woman's ability to control her own body, to produce new standards and new pressures for modern American women.

My own experience was typical. During my first pregnancy Richard and I took Lamaze classes, faithfully immersing ourselves in the techniques and philosophy of the natural childbirth movement. We absorbed the message that modern obstetrical practices were at best unnecessary and at worst a conspiracy on the part of the male medical establishment to deny women the "great experience" of birth. Specifically I was told to avoid using pain-killing drugs during labor. A healthy woman undergoing normal childbirth would only detract from her own experience and the well-being of her baby by using such crutches. After all, if my head were in the right place, I would be able to cast out fear and use the simple techniques of natural childbirth to reduce the pains of labor to "mild discomfort." Surely I was enough of a woman to face this!

Fired up by such a worthy cause, I interviewed obstetricians until I found one who was suitably gung ho about natural childbirth. When my due date came, I went into labor right on schedule. And that was about the only thing that happened according to plan.

I remember it clearly. At noon on November 8 (I was about four hours into labor and had just been admitted to the hospital) I began to experience serious pain. I was startled and a little apprehensive. This wasn't supposed to be happening. It would probably stop soon, I thought. Instead, it got worse. Richard wanted to help, but since I was hooked up to a whole set of machines, the only way he could get near me was to kneel on the floor and lean over a bunch of wires to put his arms around me. Thus encouraged, I tried very hard "to think about daisies and pant like a dog" in the way I had been taught in my Lamaze class.[18] But things got steadily worse. When I entered the second "accelerated" stage of labor (during which the uterus acts like a piston to propel the baby out), the pain became so intense that the puffing and panting went by the board and I lost all semblance of control. For seven excruciating hours pain invaded and devastated every intimate part of my body. Each contraction lasted an average of a minute and a half and hit at thirty-second intervals. I groaned and I writhed, and as each contraction crested, my cries of pain turned into a long, continuous shriek. By early evening I had had it with nature and was thoroughly disgusted with all those male advocates of painless childbirth. I implored Richard to get some help. I no longer cared what kind of drug was administered as long as it was strong enough to produce relief from the appalling pain. At some level I was also very frightened. Normal labor was supposed to result in mild discomfort; obviously, in my case, something had gone horribly wrong. Perhaps the baby was coming out the wrong way or had a grotesquely swollen head.

Richard summoned the obstetrician. He was not at all worried. He was, however, disapproving. Couldn't I pull myself together? After all, I was seven centimeters dilated, and I had to hang in there for only another two to three hours. His sole concession to my pain was to allow the nurse to administer a little Demerol. It did not help; it merely sent me to sleep between contractions. I awoke, every minute or so, in the middle of the racking pain at the height of a contraction and with no time to brace myself. I could not bear any more, and after a particularly cruel contraction I implored Richard to get me knocked out.

But our obstetrician was fast losing patience with both of us. After disgustedly surveying his screaming patient, he called Richard out into the corridor and stated baldly, "Your wife is hysterical. It is my judgment that much of her behavior is an attempt to impress you. If you leave the room, she will calm down and begin to cooperate in her delivery." He then quoted a phrase or two from Nietzsche, intending to underline the moral weakness of women.

Richard practically spat at him and decided to take matters into his own hands. He found the hospital's anesthesiologist, browbeat the obstetrician into giving a (grudging) consent, and arranged for me to be given an epidural (a local anesthetic which cuts out all sensation in the lower abdomen but leaves the rest of the body unaffected).

Within minutes I was a different person. The incredible, unbearable pain just drained away. I became calm and reasonable, even joyful. The epidural left me completely conscious and with a great deal of control over my body so that when the time came, I was able to help push my baby out. Lisa was born pink, noisy, and beautiful. Back in my room the three of us celebrated the splendid moment of birth with a bottle of champagne.

Of the thirteen women in my natural childbirth class, three had cesareans, and seven of the remaining ten (myself included) had unexpectedly painful experiences. All seven of us succumbed to some type of medication and remembered their birth experiences as dominated by agonizing pain. Only three of the thirteen had been able to deliver their children according to the Lamaze blueprint, and subsequently many of us had to deal with bouts of depression. At some level we truly believed that we were the weaklings that had failed.

When I was calm enough to look back at Lisa's birth with some objectivity, I was amazed at how completely I had swallowed the natural childbirth trip with all its unrealistic expectations. I thought that I had learned the Lamaze techniques so well that I would not be one of your ordinary run-of-the-mill women whose pain would be "greatly reduced"; I would be one of your superwomen whose pain would be "totally eliminated." In retrospect it all sounds a little nutty, but the pressures for women of my generation to prove their womanhood by giving birth without drugs and without pain were and are quite intense.

For more than a decade "experts" in the natural childbirth movement have told us that "with proper training of husband

and wife over 90% of mothers neither need nor ask for drugs"[19] and that "a mother who has had any medication is mentally confused, 'drunk' from drugs and not to be trusted with the baby."[20] So asserts Dr. Robert A. Bradley, natural childbirth enthusiast and author of the well-known book *Husband-Coached Childbirth.* He even claims that the use of medication in labor produces "shortened attention span and memory, inability to handle stress, impaired reading ability and hyperactivity" in children.[21] He proudly describes the son of one of his patients: "Now 13 years old, Greg has won a spelling contest. His keen memory is undoubtedly related to his unmedicated birth and to being breastfed immediately by his mother."[22] However, there is, as even Dr. Bradley admits, *no scientific proof of any connection between medication during childbirth and subsequent child development.*[23] The object of most of his writing seems to be to shame women into undergoing natural childbirth.

The natural childbirth movement in other countries has been much less stringent in its demands on women for ideological purity and has focused much less on a drug-free "birth experience." For example, at London's Westminster Hospital the standard natural childbirth course gives a realistic appraisal of the role of pain-killers in labor and spends as much time teaching prospective parents how to care for the child once it is born (feeding schedules, bathing techniques, and medical care) as it does on pregnancy and childbirth. All of which would seem to leave both mother and father better prepared for actually having a child.

What most new wave enthusiasts in America forget is that modern medicine got into the business of childbirth in the first place because the bearing of children through the ages has been an appallingly hurtful and dangerous experience for women. In Genesis we are told that "in sorrow thou shalt bring forth children,"[24] and until the medical advances of the last century this dictum held true.

The proponents of natural childbirth have a great deal to say about the good old days. Traditional peasant societies are seen through a rosy, nostalgic haze as cultures where women, supported by a midwife and a community of other women, dropped their babies simply and easily on the earth. This was the golden age before the advent of the medical establishment conspiracy, a time when women had complete control over their bodies. An appealing image, but unfortunately historical reality was a good deal less attractive.

For example, in seventeenth- and eighteenth-century Europe not only was infant mortality appallingly high—children had only a 50 percent chance of living until they were twelve months old—but women had a 10 percent chance of dying in childbirth and a 20 percent chance of being permanently injured by the incompetent interference of untrained midwives.[25] As historian Edward Shorter has put it, ". . . the actual midwives of traditional Europe intervened furiously in the natural process of birth. Constantly tugging and hauling at the mother's birth canal, at the infant's head and at the placenta, they were captives of a folkloric view that the best midwife is the one who interferes most."[26] Common procedures included puncturing the sac of amniotic fluid with a (dirty) fingernail, a practice that greatly increased the likelihood of life-threatening maternal infection.

In contemporary primitive societies pregnant women are almost invariably malnourished and overworked as well as prey to fear and superstition. In some tribal societies the laboring woman is forced to swallow live crabs[27]; in others she is merely suspended from the ceiling by a bamboo rope.[28] But whether the superstitions of the culture are gentle or harsh, it is impossible to escape the terror induced by the fear of death—for oneself or for one's child. Infant and maternal mortality figures for present-day peasant societies are as bad as for premodern Europe. If having a child entails risking one's own life, or if the newborn child has only a 50 percent chance of living, it is hard to approach the experience of birth with joyous anticipation. For anyone who has lived in poor, backward parts of the third world and seen at close range the misery endemic in these societies, it is difficult to swallow the chic literature of the natural childbirth movement with its romantic vision of the "good old days" and the "noble savage."

Yet the power and pervasiveness of an ideology can sometimes overcome even firsthand experience. I myself was a research economist in West Africa and Latin America for periods of time in my early twenties and worked with very poor people—the Ewe tribe of the Volta delta and the shantytown dwellers of Recife and Natal. Yet because this slice of my life preceded marriage and children, I somehow was not able to integrate this experience with the ideology of the natural childbirth movement in America. It was only in retrospect that I was able to put the two together.

Along with natural childbirth, the earth mothers of postwar America have emphasized the importance of breast-feeding. Once again the ideological pressures to prove one's womanhood through this natural act are impressive. When Lisa was born, I, along with millions of other new mothers, read Karen Pryor's classic *Nursing Your Baby*. It told me that "a good nursing relationship is valuable, perhaps essential for the emotional growth of the infant, and possibly of the mother as well"[29] and that breast-fed infants are happier because they have more affectionate mothers "who were naturally more apt to breastfeed."[30] Since the emotional as well as the physical well-being of my child seemed to be at stake, I became extremely anxious to breast-feed Lisa. It never occurred to me (then, at any rate) to question any of the experts' assumptions.

But as was the case with childbirth, breast-feeding, albeit a natural act, also turned out to be more difficult and painful than I had anticipated. My first problems resulted from the fact that I left the hospital twelve hours after Lisa's birth. My gung ho obstetrician came to see me the morning after the birth, slapped me on the back, and told me I was as right as rain and, of course, I should go home immediately. One result of my precipitous departure from the hospital was that I failed to learn any of the relevant breast-feeding techniques from the nursing staff. Over the course of the first days of Lisa's life I had (in sequence) cracked nipples, massive engorgement of both breasts, and mastitis (a painful staph infection of the breasts). Such a collection of aches and pains might have forced a less committed mother to succumb to the dreaded bottle, but I had absorbed the teachings of the feminine mystique and just knew that breasts were best. I gritted my teeth and soldiered on. Things went from bad to worse when, out of necessity, I went back to work ten days after birth. Karen Pryor and the other experts warned me of the dangers of skipping too many breast-feedings until the baby was three months old and the milk supply firmly established. Sound advice, but extremely difficult to put into practice if you happen to be working. (In the latest edition of her book Pryor spends a mere one and a half pages on the problems of working women).[31] If I was to survive the working day, I simply had to delegate one of the nighttime feedings to my willing husband, and often, despite my constant rushing between home and office like a headless chicken, I missed a daytime feed as well. I tried all the conventional ruses (pumping my breasts in the ladies' room, drinking beer, and eating potatoes), but my milk supply gradually and remorselessly dried up. I felt that I had failed again, failed my baby and failed myself. If only I had been better organized or less selfishly concerned with sleep, I could have or should have been able to do it all.

The difficulties involved in feeding my second child made my first experience pale by comparison. By this time I was both more exhausted and less ideological. However, since David was premature and allergic to formula, there were medical reasons that made breast-feeding advisable. The logistics were formidable. David was so small and immature that he both required frequent feeding and couldn't suck very well. The recommended solution to these problems was to pump my breasts and feed him the breast milk through a special preemie nipple at two-hour intervals. But pumping my milk and then feeding David took close to an hour. Unless I could speed up the pumping process, just feeding my baby threatened to consume half of all my time. The obvious solution was to get an electric pump. A few days before I returned to work (two weeks after birth), Richard telephoned the New York branch of La Leche League and asked if we could rent an electric breast pump. (La Leche League is a group founded in 1956 which advocates and supports the cause of breast-feeding.) At first the woman who answered the phone at the league could not have been more helpful. She asked concerned questions about David's birth weight and digestion problems and was just getting into feeding schedules and how best to use an electric pump when Richard let slip that one reason I needed this equipment was that I was about to return to work. The conversation turned icy. In hostile tones she told Richard that the league disapproved of nursing mothers working and, as a matter of policy, would neither rent nor lend us any equipment.

Richard and I were stunned, appalled, and, finally, outraged. How could this group of self-righteous women deny help to a frail infant (David at this point weighed under five pounds) on the ground that they disapproved of the mother's work commitments? But I swallowed my indignation. David *needed* this equipment. I called them back. I was not choosing to return to work so soon, I explained meekly; rather, it was that I was forced to return if I wanted to keep my job. The ladies found this argument irrelevant. Anyone who was interested in keeping her job was obviously not worthy of their attention.

In the end, after much searching around, we rented an electric breast pump from a medical equipment store. The proprietor was interested only in a modest rental fee and asked no questions about maternal work commitments or family values.

When I look back at my breast-feeding experience, I can see that it involved many of the same pressures as natural childbirth. In both cases I was driven to attempt the impossible by experts imbued with a zealot's faith in complete motherhood. This ideology clearly grew out of the fifties. The earth mothers of this ultradomestic era had every reason to elaborate maternal responsibilities, in particular the roles of childbearing and breast-feeding. These are, after all, the only functions that are unique to women. But while complete motherhood may have been harmless in an era when most American women with young children stayed at home, it can be downright pernicious in an era such as ours. In the modern world it collides with the demands of a rigorous and inflexible world of work, where there are few concessions to maternal roles, natural or not. Today millions of mothers in America do not stay at home; they work, mostly because they have to. In 1984, fully 48 percent of children under one year old had mothers in the labor force.[32] The majority (more than 60 percent) of these women have no right to time off for pregnancy or childbirth.[33] Moreover, given the inadequacies of public child care in this country, women with small children are under constant domestic stress. It is hard enough for them to arrange and pay for decent child care without, in addition, being made to feel guilty about failures to perform on the natural childbirth and breast-feeding fronts.[34] One professional woman I know still worries about the fact that she gave birth to her son by cesarean section. Her chief consolation, several years later, is that "at least I breast-fed Jason until he was sixteen months old. I made up to him for my failure to give birth naturally."[35] However, she paid a high price for her breast-feeding commitment. She had to give up a career she loved and replace it with a variety of temporary, low-paying jobs.

The degree to which the child-rearing professionals continue to be out of touch with reality is astounding. For example, a widely read manual on breast-feeding, *The Complete Book of Breastfeeding* by Marvin Eiger and Sally Olds, devotes fewer than two pages to the working mother.[36] The advice it does offer is both patronizing and irrelevant. We are told that "nursing couples" (this is a term which in breast-feeding manuals refers to mothers and infants; fathers are left out in the cold) are homebodies who require a lot of rest and need to pamper themselves. My favorite passage is one which states that however ecstatic the nursing couple, "the time will come when you want to go out and do things. Once the baby is three to four weeks old, there is no reason why you can't get out for an occasional visit with friends or a trip to a drive-in movie."[37] When my babies were three or four weeks old, I was already (albeit reluctantly) back at work, and the thought of putting my baby in the car and driving off into the sunset (or New Jersey, as the case may be) in search of that perfect recreation for the "nursing couple"—the drive-in movie—struck me as simply absurd. Richard didn't think much of the idea either.

The complications attendant on and following David's birth had prompted me to do some soul-searching about my goals and the manner in which I was trying to accomplish them. It was very clear to me that my children came first. However, I still wasn't reckless enough (or courageous enough!) to throw in the sponge with my career. However, I did make a decision to cut down on the amount of work I did for my job, even though I realized this might imperil my tenure chances. I stopped volunteering for extra duties within the department, I resigned from some optional college committees, and I temporarily gave up any attempt to do research. In addition, if David and Lisa were sick, their needs took precedent over any work responsibility. In short, I established my priorities in much the same way as any working mother does. I continued to fulfill the basic functions of my job and was conscientious in fulfilling my obligations to colleagues and students, but I systematically eliminated extra work effort in order to save some of my best energies for my children. I was ruthless in sticking to this compromise, and by and large I was at ease with my decision.

It is a good thing I felt comfortable with my decision because when David was six months old, I was turned down for tenure at Barnard College, Columbia University. Everyone was surprised, especially since I had in the end been unanimously recommended by my department and by the Appointments and Tenure Committee of Barnard College. It was the final committee, the Ad Hoc Committee of Columbia University, that turned me down. No one will ever know why since this committee meets in secret and gives no reasons for its decisions. I can't help suspecting that it had something to do with my struggles to bear and to rear children while holding my job. There were student demonstrations and faculty appeals; but the decision stuck, and I was given notice.

Quite unexpectedly there was a happy ending, which is not the usual case in situations like these. Within weeks of the tenure decision I received several job offers, and I moved into a policy position—directing the Economic Policy Council. The new position actually turned out to be well suited to my abilities and was both more lucrative and more flexible than academe. Apart from this practical fallout, I also coped with the massive psychological rejection of having failed to get tenure (seven years' hard work down the drain!) with a considerable amount of equanimity. It was, after all, so very, very much less painful than losing the twins.

My problems following Lisa's birth had prompted feelings of depression and failure. I viewed my inability to perform my diverse roles with ease as my fault, the result of my own inadequacy. Somehow I simply hadn't been able to measure up. After the loss of the twins and David's premature birth, with all the special agonies that followed, I started to become angry. It seemed clear that the stresses of this exceedingly difficult period had little to do with my shortcomings but rather were a result of the attitudes of our society. I came to the bitter conclusion that at least some of my anguish had been unnecessary. Why had I been told that childbirth did not hurt? Why had I felt so much pressure to breastfeed? Why wasn't I entitled to maternity leave? And why did the commonplace complications of pregnancy have so little legitimacy in the workplace?

Becoming a working mother seemed to elicit the worst from all sides of society. It was as if I had entered some kind of forbidden no-man's-land where every hand was turned against me and women like me. My place of work, supposedly an enlightened institution, had established its rules and regulations as if childbearing and rearing had no place in the life of a professional woman. My feminist colleagues were opposed to any kind of maternity policy because in their view, such policies smacked of special privileges in an era when liberated women were supposed to be behaving exactly like men in the labor market. My earth mother "sisters" at La Leche League, on the other hand, were prepared to deny me (and my premature infant) the use of equipment they had available because I was not, in their eyes, taking motherhood sufficiently seriously and devoting all my time to nursing my baby. Obviously the demands of these two groups of women were mutually incompatible; taken together, they guaranteed failure for mere mortals like me.

In most other modern societies working mothers are not put under these special and exaggerated pressures. For example, French and English mothers often prefer to breast-feed their babies, but they do not feel that their womanhood is at stake if they fail to do so. Nor does anyone else. Even more important, working mothers in Europe take for granted a set of societal support structures which enable them to choose to breast-feed if they so desire. Free and extensive postnatal care; a statutory right to generous maternity leaves; provisions for breast-feeding time during the working day—all these rights and services are built into the fabric of European society.

Not only does contemporary America provide few of these support systems in comparison with other industrialized countries, but it also does rather badly in comparison with its own recent history.

A case in point concerns my former employer. After my failure to get a maternity policy approved at Barnard College, I did some research into the history of the college and discovered that more than fifty years ago, in 1932, the trustees adopted a maternity policy which offered a woman faculty member expecting a child the right to "a leave of absence for half a year on full salary or for a full year on half salary."[38] Reporting on this new policy in the fall of 1932, Virginia Gildersleeve, the dean of Barnard College, said, "One of the most perplexing problems thrust upon women by the economic and social changes of recent years has been the necessity of combining marriage, motherhood and careers. It is of the greatest importance that our teachers should be normal and interesting human beings with as full and rich lives as may be. Neither the men nor the women on our staff should be forced into celibacy, and cut off from that great source of experience, joy, sorrow and wisdom which marriage and parenthood offer."[39] For these reasons, Dean Gildersleeve was "much gratified by the enlightened and progressive action of the trustees in passing a maternity policy."[40]

Fine-sounding, noble thoughts, and we recognize them immediately since we heard them expressed so many times in the 1970s. The policy initiative is less familiar. Barnard's maternity policy seems to have lapsed in the late 1940s, and my own efforts to establish a similar, though considerably less generous policy in the late seventies failed. Indeed, the committee I formed has only just completed its work, for it took until the summer of 1985 to get a minimal maternity policy readopted by Barnard College.

My professional history is clearly not an isolated case. Most women in academe have found it impossible to progress to the senior ranks of their profession, and at least at Barnard things seem to have gotten worse rather than better in recent years. When I interviewed at Barnard College in the fall of 1973, there were three tenured professors in the economics department, all of them women. Two were about to retire; the third remained to become chairperson of the department. During the period 1973–84 four female assistant professors (myself plus three others) were turned down for tenure. During this same time span a man was brought in from Stanford University (where he did not have tenure) and given tenure at Barnard College.

But that is not the end of the story. Since the department remains undertenured, plans are now in motion to bring in another man—this time from Harvard University (where he does not have tenure)—and this man will be given a tenured appointment at Barnard. In addition, the department is confident that its next internal candidate for tenure (a man) will be given tenure during the academic year 1985–86.[41] In short, over the course of thirteen years (1973–86) the economics department at Barnard College will go from having 100 percent of its senior faculty women to having 25 percent of its senior faculty women.[42] The odd thing is that this shift to male domination in the economics department bridges a decade of militant feminism at Barnard College.

Barnard College—because it is a college for women—is a particularly distressing example of what are national trends. In its 1982–83 report from more than 2,500 institutions of higher education the American Association of University Professors concluded that "after a decade of affirmative action women have achieved very little . . . at Harvard women are only 4.2% of full professors; at Princeton 3.2%, at Stanford 2.6%, and at Yale, 3.9%."[43] This situation cannot be blamed on a scarcity of qualified women; the pipeline is full of women. Almost a third of the pool of Ph.D.'s are women, and more than a quarter of junior faculty nationwide are women.[44] At least some of these women do not make it to the top of their profession because they have the audacity to become mothers and proceed to raise children in a work environment that makes few concessions to maternal roles. Since they were busy earning their Ph.D.'s in their twenties and need to bear children before their biological clocks run out, many of these women are constrained to raise their families in their thirties. Many—perhaps a third—have to deal with complications of miscarriage, prematurity, and infertility without missing a beat on the work front, and even those who are blessed with easy pregnancies find raising children—in the absence of subsidized day care and other support structures—an immensely strenuous activity. The end result is that professional women with children find their energies hopelessly stretched in their mid-thirties, precisely the time when academic careers (and many other careers) are either made or broken. In short, these women fail for much the same reasons as I did.

One final comment on my profession: Even if a woman is lucky enough to be promoted in academe, she is unlikely to be paid as much as her male colleagues. The salary picture in the Barnard economics department is instructive. In the fall of 1984 the department had two tenured members, a woman and a man. They had similar publication records and similar reputations in their respective fields. In some ways the woman was senior to the man because she was a few years older and had held a tenured position longer than he. Yet she was paid $45,000 a year and he was paid $59,000 a year.[45] Barnard's commitment to equal rights for women seems to be largely a verbal accomplishment. It is not allowed to interfere with the economic facts of life. But in this respect the college merely mirrors the nation.

PART A

---·~~·---

Between the Devil and the Deep Blue Sea

People tell us that American women have never had it so good. And we believe them. After all, we can see the changes. Our city streets are full of confident career women, complete with M.B.A.'s, business suits, and briefcases. And we hear the differences. The language of the nation has changed. Even the most establishment of men talk carefully about chairpersons and have learned how to pronounce *Ms.*

But these first-level impressions are misleading. For a lucky few the 1970s did constitute the decade of liberation. Doors were flung open, and young, privileged women beat a noisy path into the male worlds of medicine, law, and corporate management. But the vast majority were left behind to cope with deteriorating economic and social realities. The economic reality is that most women still earn very little on their own, and the social reality is that contemporary women are more likely to be on their own.

American women are locked into a no-win situation. They have lost the guarantees and protection of the past—marriage has broken down as a long-term and reliable source of financial security—and at the same time they have failed to improve their earning power as workers in the labor market, for the wage gap between men and women is as wide and as stubborn as it ever was. Modern women are squeezed between the devil and the deep blue sea, and there are no lifeboats out there in the form of public policies designed to help these women combine their roles as mothers and as workers. For the United States has the least adequate family support system in the Western world.

The bottom line is that American women (and often their children) are in bad shape. They are squeezed between the modern and the traditional forms of economic security to an extent which is unknown in other countries. Women elsewhere simply do better, as wives and mothers and as workers.

3

THE ECONOMIC
FALLOUT OF DIVORCE

Once upon a time women could rely on marriage to provide a financially secure way of life. Leaving aside emotional issues such as, Did the married couple really live happily ever after?, it is clear that marriage used to be a practical division of labor. The husband directed his best energies to building a career, while the wife worked hard at creating a home, an occupation which she saw as a lifetime career. For our grandmothers and even our mothers this was a reasonably safe arrangement. Some marriages may not have been "made in heaven," but most of them were enduring and provided a better standard of living for women than paid employment.

But times have changed. "In 1940 there was 1 divorce for every 6 marriages, while in 1980, there was 1 for every 2 marriages,"[1] and demographers predict that two out of every three new marriages will end in divorce.[2] While marriage used to be a safe bet, for today's women it cannot be relied upon to provide lifetime job security.

Up until six years ago Julie Davenport* was a traditional home-

*Pseudonym.

maker. For two decades she had been a dedicated wife, mother, and housekeeper. She was proud of her accomplished children and proud of the prosperous life she had built with her husband, Bill. For fifteen years, ever since the children were born, they had lived in a five-bedroom house in Chappaqua, an affluent New York suburb. It was a good life. They had a live-in maid and a part-time gardener and took two vacations a year. In the winter they skied at Vail, and in August they rented a house on Martha's Vineyard. Julie owned a Blackglama mink and had her dark blond hair streaked at Kenneth's.

In the fall of 1978, one day shy of their twentieth anniversary, Bill Davenport announced to Julie that he had fallen in love with another woman and wanted a trial separation. Two days later Bill moved out, leaving her with two teenage children. As Julie put it, she felt as though she had been "tossed on the scrap heap."

By the spring of 1979 Bill had stopped paying the bills. He now wanted a legal separation and a divorce. Julie was reluctant, so his strategy became, in Julie's words, "If I cut her off and starve her, she will settle for anything." Six months later Julie, hounded by debt collectors and unable to keep up the mortgage payments on the house, went to court, and Bill was ordered to pay the costs of running the house plus support payments of $325 a month.

For the next two years the Davenports fought over the terms of the separation agreement. Although Julie hired an expensive lawyer, she failed to prove that Bill had any assets other than their house, but she did establish that he earned $120,000 a year in his management consultancy business. They settled in 1981. Julie got the house, which she immediately sold. After she had paid off the mortgage and some back debts, she cleared $90,000. She was also awarded $26,500 a year in child support and maintenance until their youngest child left for college—an event which was just two years down the road. Under New York's amended divorce laws Julie was not entitled to long-term alimony.

Today, at age forty-nine, Julie lives in a one-bedroom rental apartment on West Eighty-third Street in Manhattan. She is strapped for money, tired, lonely, and bitter.

In 1983 support payments stopped, and since she could not live on $10,000 a year (the interest income on her profit from the house), Julie returned to nursing—a profession she had prepared herself for some twenty-five years ago. She now holds a job at Mount Sinai Hospital. She works rotating shifts (one-third nights, one-third evenings, and one-third days) and earns $20,000 a year. She now fervently wishes that "as a young woman I had trained for a career that is decently paid, but I never imagined I would have to support myself nursing."

Bill, meanwhile, has remarried and is living with his twenty-eight-year-old wife and new baby in an elaborate house in Saddle River, New Jersey. Julie estimates that his income is now in the $150,000 range, and with that, she says with angry emphasis, "he is able to buy not only the latest-model wife but also our children." For the last year Julie and Bill's two children have elected to spend most of their vacation time with their dad. "Who can blame them?" says Julie. "Their father has a pool, a tennis court, and a stay-at-home wife who cooks gourmet meals. . . . He also has a large house so they can have their own rooms when they stay with him. Why, at my place they have to sleep in sleeping bags on my living-room floor and are often alone evenings because of my shift work."

Despite her troubles, Julie is an appealing woman—slim, attractive, and obviously capable. I asked her about the men in her life. She looked startled, then amused. "You obviously don't know what the market is like for single women my age. Believe it or not, there are about four of us to every one of them [eligible men], and those that exist are looking for sprightly young blondes. No man I know is interested in a used wife with stretch marks on her belly and slightly sagging breasts."

Julie is convinced that the good part of her life is over, although she probably has another thirty years to live. As she points out, "my ex-husband is going to get richer and richer and will spend his middle age in comfort surrounded by a growing family. I, on the other hand, am going to get poorer and more lonely. I've lost my partner, my house, my friends, my status, and even my children. I have nightmares about being old, poor, and arthritic, and it's all because I did what I was supposed to do and spent my best years being a loyal and loving homemaker. It's not my fault that the rules changed mid-game. I guess I feel cheated."[3]

A Lesser Life

* * *

Julie Davenport's case is not unusual. Indeed, by the standards of the modern world her story is not even particularly pathetic. Under the amended divorce laws she was rather well treated. After all, she got the house and an impressively high (if short-term) maintenance award. In addition, Julie is a trained nurse and was able to find a job. Our social landscape is littered with "displaced homemakers" in much worse shape than Julie.

Displaced homemaker is a term coined in the mid-1970s to describe some of the more poignant victims of the breakdown of traditional marriage—former full-time homemakers who have lost their sources of income and self-esteem through divorce (or, in some cases, widowhood).[4]

A typical displaced homemaker is fifty-two years old and has invested two to three decades in her home and family. "She has barely finished eighth grade, has high blood pressure, varicose veins, gynecological problems, little stamina and her self-confidence is in shreds."[5] The U.S. Labor Department estimates that there are anywhere from 4 to 15 million displaced homemakers in contemporary America.[6] Estimates are vague because displaced homemakers fall through the cracks of society. There are no societal safety nets for them, as there are for other needy segments of the population, and thus no reason why the federal bureaucracy should make an accurate estimate of their number. Little is being done for them. Because homemaking is an unpaid job, homemakers do not qualify for unemployment compensation; usually they aren't old enough to collect Social Security; and if their children are over eighteen, they are not eligible for AFDC (Aid to Families with Dependent Children). But what of alimony, the traditional unemployment insurance of marriage? Has alimony gone the way of the trolley car and the thirty-five cent subway fare?

Folk wisdom about divorce in the United States has it that alimony provides divorced women with meal tickets for life. According to one famous legal opinion, alimony converts "a host of physically and mentally competent young women into an army of alimony drones who neither toil nor spin and become a drain on society and a menace to themselves."[7]

A *Doonesbury* comic strip published in the *San Francisco Chronicle* sums up the conventional wisdom. In it a pollster asks a middle-aged wife why she voted against the Equal Rights Amendment:

Woman: I guess it was the alimony issue—ERA would have eliminated alimony! The way I see it, alimony has a very important deterrent value—it keeps families together.
Pollster: It does?
Woman: Sure, take us for example—Morris and I don't have the greatest marriage in the world. We're not proud of the fact, but we live with it. And one of the reasons we live with it is *alimony*! If Morris didn't have that threat hanging over him, he'd probably walk right out of here, without leaving me a red cent!
Husband: It's true—I probably would.[8]

The California couple in the cartoon did not seem to realize three facts: that by the mid-1970s only 15 to 17 percent of divorce cases in that state involved alimony payments (or, to use the correct California term, spousal support payments) to the ex-wife;[9] the amount of money involved in these payments was modest (median award $209 per month);[10] and in only a third of these cases was the alimony award open-ended (until death or remarriage). Indeed, two-thirds of the awards had a median duration of less than three years.[11] In reality, alimony is no longer much of a deterrent for a dissatisfied husband.

Over the last fifteen years two things have happened to the divorce laws in this country which have served to undermine the economic position of divorcing women. Most states have enacted some version of no-fault divorce, and most have adopted equitable or equal division of property laws. The main practical effect of these amendments has been to drastically reduce alimony as a source of long-term income maintenance for the divorcing wife.

Alimony has always been rather less common than folklore would have us believe. One study finds that as early as 1919 alimony was awarded to only 32 percent of divorcing women.[12] It seems that for most of this century alimony has been a prerogative of the affluent classes. Only well-off ex-husbands were required to pay alimony. Despite this qualification, middle- and upper-class women who had been left by their husbands found that alimony did provide a measure of financial security in the wake of divorce. All this changed with the advent of no-fault divorce.

Frances Leonard, an attorney in Oakland, California, for the national Older Women's League, describes the pre-1970 "fault" system: "In the old days women had a marriage contract unless it was broken through adultery, abandonment or cruelty. If her husband wanted out of the marriage she could strike an economic bargain with him—i.e., you support me and I'll give you a divorce. The impolite word for this is blackmail. Nobody feels that it was a good system, but it helped place a value on the marriage contract."[13] This became more difficult when either party could sue for divorce without cause.

In 1970 California became the first state to enact a no-fault system of divorce, and over the last fifteen years most states have followed suit. In the early days no-fault divorce was thought to improve women's lot. It was embraced by feminists in the first heady days of women's liberation as the enlightened path to singleness. No longer would marital breakup lead to a public and perhaps humiliating airing of grievances.

But experience has shown that no fault is a bad economic bargain for women because it tends to reduce alimony as well as acrimony. For example, in California it has triggered a drop in the "overall frequency of alimony awards"[14] and a noticeable "decrease in the percentage of open-ended awards and an increase in 'transitional awards.' "[15] According to Judge Leander Foley of Milwaukee, lower settlements follow naturally, if not inevitably, from no fault. "Because fault finding required negotiation," he says, "it benefitted the nonfaulting party which was generally the woman. The husband had to *give* in order to get the divorce. It somehow resulted in a fairness. He had to give more than he would have otherwise."[16]

Judge Barteau of Indianapolis describes the effect of no fault in Indiana: "We don't have alimony any more. We have limited spousal maintenance for two years. It's pretty drastic. In a no fault, if a husband wants a divorce, he gets it. If there aren't any minor children and she's a 45-year-old empty nester who's accumulated no property, she ends up with nothing. It's a tragedy."[17]

As states have moved toward no-fault divorce, they have also moved toward equitable division of property laws. These cut even deeper into an ex-wife's long-run financial security.

New York State is a case in point. In 1980 it became the forty-first state to amend its divorce laws so as to provide for the "equitable" distribution of property acquired during the marriage. It replaced the common-law principle that awarded property to the spouse who held title to it, no matter that the division might seem unequal or that the titleholding spouse might seem undeserving. Many women's groups originally supported equitable-distribution legislation on the ground that wives would be awarded a more equal share of the property, but at least some feminists are now ruefully admitting that "the [new] law is primarily a device to deny women alimony."[18] True, wives now have a slightly better shot at a fair division of property, but the new laws have eliminated alimony, replacing it with something called mainte-nance—a temporary award designed to help wives (or, in rare cases, husbands) get back on their feet.

And even on the property front wives are not doing all that well. A study analyzing twenty-six of the first equitable distribution cases decided by the courts in New York State found that seventeen favored the husband, seven were ambiguous, and two were prowife.[19] *Segal* v. *Segal* is an example of a prohusband case.

Sandra and Lenny Segal* had been married for twenty-five years when in 1978 he left her for his new girlfriend (who was the same age as his eldest daughter). Lenny had made it big in Sandra's father's company, and by the time of the separation he was earning a six-figure income and held considerable assets in addition to their house, which was in both their names. Sandra, who had spent her adult life being a wife and mother, knew that the divorce settlement was critically important to her. She had no skills and no track record in the labor market; how could she land a job, let alone earn a living? So she borrowed money from her parents and hired an expensive lawyer. He advised waiting for passage of the new divorce laws, telling her, "You will get a fair deal out of equitable distribution." She took his advice, but it didn't help. In the spring of 1984, after a long and messy court fight and a re-

*Pseudonyms.

57

volving door of expensive lawyers, accountants, tax experts, and economists, Sandra's divorce was settled. She was awarded half the house which the judge instructed her to sell immediately, and $100 a week in maintenance. She was not awarded legal fees or any other costs, and her bills for the divorce proceedings totaled $65,000. Sandra was desperate. She took the only job she could find, working as a retail clerk in a fashion store owned by a friend. She now earns $15,500 a year and is expected to work Saturdays.

In the divorce hearings Sandra's expensive lawyers and accountants had produced evidence (proof, she thought) that Lenny had at least $600,000 in stocks and bonds. The judge dismissed the evidence on the ground that it was insufficient. Her lawyers also produced evidence that Sandra's parents had paid the original deposit on the house and argued that the house was rightly hers. The judge decided that "in-law help" was irrelevant to the question of ownership. Her lawyer hired an economist to ascertain what her services as a homemaker had been worth over those twenty-five years. The economist constructed elaborate flow charts and testified that Sandra had performed $230,000 of work for her husband over the years. The judge was thoroughly contemptuous of this exercise. He tossed the charts aside, saying they were not worth the paper they were written on.

Sandra, an elegant, poised woman, can hardly control her voice when she talks about her divorce judgment. "You know, he [the judge] had the gall to tell me that in mid-life both my ex-husband and I were starting new lives and new careers. He [Lenny] was setting up a new real estate venture, while I was starting a new job in retail business. He forgot to mention that Lenny is working with thirty years of business experience and six hundred thousand dollars of capital he got out of my father's company. My 'new career,' on the other hand, will barely keep me above the poverty level. To imply that we have an equal shot at earning a living is a parody of the real situation." Sandra paused and then added, "They may have changed the laws, but they sure haven't changed the judges."[20]

Three aspects of equitable distribution are particularly negative for women.

First of all, the burden of proof is on the partner who doesn't hold title to the marital property. This is almost always the woman. If a wife can't prove the existence of an asset or can't prove she deserves a share in the asset, she doesn't get a share in the asset. Obtaining such proof means hiring accountants, appraisers, tax and pension specialists, and, of course, a very good lawyer. The cost of contesting a divorce has therefore escalated—$60,000 or $70,000 is now not an unusual amount—and obviously many wives do not begin to have access to that kind of money. In short, the spouse with the "deep pocket"—most often the man—gets to dictate what an equitable division of property looks like.

Secondly, and more fundamentally, the vast majority of divorcing couples own few assets, and even if the property is divided in an equitable manner, it does not mean as much to the woman as alimony.[21] According to Manhattan matrimonial lawyer Benjamin Kalman, "in such a situation the wife-mother may well get the house, but that is all she gets, and many may then have nothing for everyday living expenses."[22]

Finally, a great deal of discretion is left in the hands of the judge. According to a 1983 report published by a task force of the New Jersey Supreme Court, judges make an assumption that divorced women often remarry and thus regain lost economic ground.[23] In fact, women remarry significantly less often than men do. Judges also assume that women can get good jobs and earn decent salaries. As we shall see in the next chapter, they don't. Judges also consistently "overestimate the earning power of women who have been out of the job market for many years" and fail to appreciate the "particular employment problems of the displaced homemaker."[24] Not only are judges unaware of how much women earn in the labor market, but according to the New Jersey study, they also systematically underestimate the cost of feeding and clothing a family. This is because "judges do not do the grocery shopping and are not really aware of the cost of items."[25] It seems that the judge that ruled on the *Segal* v. *Segal* case had a mind set that was typical of his profession.

The bottom line is that a decreasing minority of divorced women get any kind of income support after the breakdown of marriage. No-fault divorce seems to have increased the economic vulnerability of wives, and so has the move to equitable-distribution laws. Today fewer than 14 percent of divorced wives nationwide are awarded alimony (commonly referred to as maintenance or spousal support). Most of these wives are awarded alimony on a temporary basis, and many never collect what they are entitled to. In a 1980 survey of maintenance orders only a third of the women collected the full amount of the court-ordered support, another third collected less than the full amount, while the final third "never received a penny of the support ordered."[26] In summary, *fewer than 10 percent of ex-wives actually collect any alimony payments.*

Despite these facts of life, the alimony myth dies hard. Even in sophisticated circles it is commonly believed that ex-wives are often freed from worldly cares while their former husbands struggle to support them. Even lawyers and judges who should know the most about divorce because their specialty is matrimonial law "seem genuinely to believe that the majority of all divorced women are awarded alimony."[27] In one study ninety-two matrimonial attorneys in Los Angeles County estimated that two-thirds of all currently divorcing women get alimony.[28] They were, of course, way off the mark.

One result of these misconceptions is that women often have unrealistic notions about life after divorce. Divorce lawyer Benjamin Kalman told me that "women still enter my office with completely distorted conceptions of what they are entitled to. . . . Some wives are still capable of saying to an absconding husband, 'I will take you for everything you have plus your testicles, which I want handed to me on a silver platter.'" Kalman paused for a moment and then said, "Frankly I don't see husbands' being taken for a ride. . . . The law, in its operational effect, overwhelmingly favors men."

I asked Kalman why the myth was so persistent. "People get these ideas from *Dallas* and from Hollywood, where a few starlets have gotten large settlements and their hotshot lawyers have publicized the cases in the popular press. Palimony is a good example. A lawyer on the West Coast made a big splash with the *Lee Marvin* case, and everyone's girlfriend started to imagine she could cash in. Not so. The great majority of palimony cases have no legal basis and are thrown out of court."[29]

The Economic Fallout of Divorce

Scholars in the field seem to agree with Kalman. In one study sociologists Lenore Weitzman and Ruth Dixon came to the conclusion that "the persistence of the alimony myth is largely due to the visibility of middle- and high-income divorce cases."[30] The publicity surrounding these cases encourages everyone to believe that wives are left in the lap of luxury after divorce.

Last time I was in a suburban supermarket I picked up a copy of a popular tabloid called *Globe*. The headline read GLEN CAMPBELL: MY LOVES COST ME $7 MILLION.[31] It told the story of how Campbell had been forced to settle $7 million on two ex-wives. This story may be typical of Hollywood, but it has nothing to do with the reality of divorce for ordinary American women.

So far we have been talking about the plight of ex-wives. What happens when these ex-wives also happen to be the mothers of small children?

Rose Barroso* separated from her husband six years ago, when her son, John, was five years old. Although she had worked as a secretary before marriage, she had spent her married life at home looking after the household, her husband, and her child. In 1979 at the time of the divorce Rose was awarded child support but no alimony, and after the separation she found a job as a waitress. The job was hard, unpleasant, and badly paid ($3.50 an hour with no fringe benefits; her weekly salary was $122.50 before taxes). Its only saving grace was that the hours were 6:00 P.M. to 1:00 A.M., which allowed Rose to look after her child and do her domestic chores during the day. Her sister, who lived in the adjacent building, came over for a few hours every evening to bridge the gap between the beginning of Rose's job and John's bedtime. Rose repaid her sister by looking after her sister's child on weekends. In 1982 Rose took a new job as a secretary in the local high school. It is not as badly paid as her former job (she now earns $12,000 a year), and it does provide some health and retirement benefits (John has had bronchitis quite a lot recently, and health coverage has become essential), and since Rose works an 8:00 A.M. to 3:30 P.M. day, she can be with her child when school lets out.

Rose's ex-husband is supposed to contribute $200 a month in

*Pseudonym.

child support according to the terms of the separation agreement, and most of the time he does pay on time. He also sees John regularly for a few hours each weekend, and every other week John sleeps over at his father's house on Saturday night.

Rose's greatest concern is money. She and John barely survive on what she makes plus the child support, and she hates it that her son has to do without many things he needs. However, she says, "For another few years I am stuck. Until John is older, it is useless to look for a better job because that would mean longer hours and a longer commute; he is too young to become a latch-key kid and spend hours on his own until I come home from work." Rose does not think that her separation agreement was particularly unfair. Her ex-husband is more reliable than most divorced men she knows. However, she did point out that his income is now slightly more than double hers, and he has only himself to look after.[32]

Rose is right to think that her ex-husband is more responsible than most divorced men. The financial profile of most single mothers is bleak. Most of them are worse off than she is. At least part of the problem is the irresponsibility of divorced fathers.

In 1983 children from households headed by single women constituted almost a quarter of the entire population of children, but they made up a half of all poor children.[33] Divorce can depress a single mother's income as much as 70 percent, and since nine out of ten children of divorce live with their mothers, the children suffer accordingly. Shockingly few divorced men help support their children. According to a 1982 Census Bureau survey, 41 percent of custodial mothers are not awarded any child support in the first place, and of the 5 million single mothers who are legally due child support, only a third receive the full amount. A further third collect a small proportion of the award, and the remainder collect nothing.[34] Indeed, *60 percent of divorced fathers contribute nothing at all to the financial support of their children.*

Custodial mothers who do receive child support average $150 a month, a sum which is clearly not enough to make a great deal of a difference in the modern world.[35] In a Michigan study a sample of 163 fathers, who were placed under court-ordered support obligations following their divorces, was followed over a period of ten years. After the first year only 38 percent were in full conformity with their obligations and 42 percent had refused to pay. By the end of the tenth year the percentage in full compliance had dwindled to 13, whereas 79 percent were making no payments at all.[36]

One particularly shameful finding of the research in this field is that most divorced fathers can afford to comply with the court orders and are able to live quite well after doing so. In other words, most divorced fathers cannot plead poverty; *the money is there.* The data show that if an ex-husband earns $40,000 a year, he is as unlikely to pay child support as one who earns $14,000 a year.[37]

A poignant example of the low priority the legal system and divorced men attach to their children is contained in a survey of child-support practices in Denver. This study found that two-thirds of the fathers were ordered by the courts to pay less for child support than they reported paying on monthly car payments. While most were current on their car payments, more than half were delinquent in their child-support payments.[38]

In recent years there have been a variety of attempts, at both the federal and the state level, to grapple with the problem of delinquency in child-support payments (which has reached record levels; in 1984 unpaid child support totaled $4 billion). In August 1984 Congress passed the Child Support Enforcement Amendment, which requires states to set up a system for withholding money from the paychecks of parents whose support payments are a month or more overdue.[39] While this act is helpful, it fails to provide the custodial parent with an income while the state goes after the delinquent parent.[40] Besides, even if all child-support awards were collected on time, a larger problem would not be solved. The plain facts are that the level of awards is low and falling[41] and that only 59 percent of custodial mothers are awarded child support in the first place. Our present system of child support is simply not capable of going far to meet the real long-run costs of raising a child. Estimates of how much this costs range from $71,000 to $160,000.[42] In the wake of divorce most of these expenses are picked up by single mothers.

* * *

Abby's relationship with her ex-husband is, unfortunately, more typical than that of Rose. Abby Gaynor* is a schoolteacher with two children, Ben and Jessica, aged twelve and eight. When she and her husband divorced in 1979, Abby thought that finances would be tight but possible. Her teaching job paid $23,000 annually, and although she had no alimony, she had been awarded $650 a month in child support—$7,800 a year. Although her living expenses were high because she lived in New York City, she estimated that these two sources of income would just be enough to enable her and her children to get by. There was only one problem: Her ex-husband did not pay child support most of the time. By the fall of 1983 he was in arrears by $20,000. Abby says, "It is difficult to know which is worse: Bob's financial irresponsibility or his failure to maintain contact with the children." Since the divorce he has never taken the children for a complete day. As Abby puts it, "he says he can't think of things to do with them." During this entire four-year period the older child, Ben, slept over twice at his father's house, and the younger child, Jessica, slept over three times. The pattern is that every now and then Abby's ex-husband will call and ask to see the children for a few hours. Sometimes he doesn't call for months. Despite the financial and emotional difficulties his behavior has caused them, Abby never tries to prevent the children from seeing their father. "His relationship with them is very imperfect, but he is the only father they will ever have and they need to know him," she says.

For the first two years after the divorce Abby's financial position was precarious. During this time she took a second job, working vacations, weekends, and sometimes evenings for a collection agency. Her economic problems were finally resolved last year when she remarried. Two salary checks enable the family to live comfortably once again. Abby feels extremely fortunate. In her experience divorced women with dependent children often fail to find second husbands.[43]

Abby's perceptions are accurate. Older divorcées, particularly those with dependent children, are casualties of a marriage squeeze.[44] The plain fact is there are many more available women than available men.

*Pseudonym.

The Economic Fallout of Divorce

According to a 1984 study, "after age 24, the prospects for women [finding a mate] deteriorate rapidly, with the odds in favor of men growing from a 20% male advantage at 25–29 to an advantage over 13 times greater by age 60–64."[45] At ages forty to forty-nine (Julie Davenport's age-group) "there are fewer than three suitable men available for every 10 college-educated women."[46] All these glum statistics boil down to a remarriage rate for divorced and widowed men which is twice that of women in the twenty-five to forty-four age bracket, while in the older age bracket, forty-five to sixty-four, the remarriage rate for men is four times the rate of women that age.[47] According to the Bureau of the Census, only 18 percent of divorced women eventually remarry.[48]

There are several reasons for this imbalance. First, men's tastes for younger women leads most divorced men in their forties to remarry women significantly younger (ten plus years) who have never been married rather than divorcées in their forties. Secondly, the fact that women live, on average, nine years longer than men creates a shortage of men in the older age brackets and dramatically reduces the number of potential mates for middle-aged women. Thirdly, baby-boom-generation women, now in their thirties, are particularly disadvantaged because the group of men immediately their senior is much smaller—a result of the low birthrates of the depression and war. These women have an even smaller pool of older men to draw upon.

If divorced women derive little financial security from ex-husbands, and if divorcées in their thirties and forties are unlikely to remarry, it becomes obvious that women like Sandra Segal may have no choice but to seek economic salvation in the labor market. Indeed, the new divorce laws instruct them to do precisely this.

The new litany tends to be: Any woman who wants to can get a job and be self-supporting. Therefore, she doesn't need any long-term supplement to her income. In a recent legal decision a Florida appellate court denied a forty-eight-year-old housewife's request for continued alimony (she had been divorced for two years) with this statement: "In this era of women's liberation movements and enlightened thinking . . . the woman is as fully equipped as the man to earn a living and provide for her essential needs."[49]

But as we shall see in the next chapter, the earning capability of divorced women is low. Not only is a divorcée faced with the lower wage rates typical of women's jobs (and the median wage of year-round full-time women workers is only $14,479), but often she is going back into the labor force after years (sometimes decades) spent being a full-time homemaker. It is extremely hard to get a job if you are older and inexperienced. If you have any skills, they are likely to be obsolete in the modern workplace. If you are lucky enough to get a job, it's likely to be low-level, badly paid, and have few prospects for advancement. Add to this the fact that many divorced women (60 percent) are single parents. Inadequate and expensive child care provides further constraints on the kind of employment a divorcée can get or accept. All these factors severely depress her earning capability at a point in life when her ex-husband usually is rising rapidly in his career.

Contemporary divorce laws supposedly have the goal of equal or equitable treatment. And "most judges appear to view the law's goal of equality as a mandate for placing an *equal burden* of support on men and women whose position and capacity for support are, by virtue of their experience in marriage, typically *unequal.*"[50] Many ex-wives are simply not equipped to bear an equal burden. If they are older or if they have young children, they are severely handicapped in a job market which already discriminates heavily against women.

All the evidence demonstrates that in the economic arena divorced women—and their children—fare extremely badly, while divorced men do considerably better. A study by Stanford sociologist Lenore Weitzman shows that just one year after divorce the standard of living of the ex-husband has risen 42 percent while that of the ex-wife—and often her children—has fallen 73 percent.[51] According to Weitzman:

> [D]ivorce is a financial catastrophe for most women: in just one year they experience a dramatic decline in income and a calamitous drop in their standard of living. It is difficult to imagine how they survive the severe economic deprivation: every single expenditure that one

takes for granted—clothing, food, housing, heat—must be cut in one-half or one-third of what one is accustomed to. . . . It is not surprising that divorced women report more stress and less satisfaction with their lives than any other group of Americans.[52]

Other studies show similar results. For example, the 1983 New Jersey Supreme Court study cited earlier found that "divorce portends long term, deepening poverty for a large proportion of women and their custodial children."[53] Conversely, the study showed that the economic status of divorced men "appears to follow a normal upward course with increasing age and experience.[54]

The economic consequences of divorce for women seem to be particularly severe in the United States. The American divorce rate is far and away the highest in the world. It is currently twice that of Sweden, Britain, West Germany, Canada, or Australia—other affluent democracies culturally similar to the United States—and three to twenty times higher than the Catholic nations of Western Europe (France, Italy, and Spain).[55] Moreover, not only is divorce much less prevalent in other advanced countries, but in these other countries its impact is softened by social policies expressedly designed to lighten the load on single parents. As one Norwegian woman explained:

[E]veryone knows that divorced parents need more money and more social support because of the additional pressures involved in raising children as a single parent. . . . So, as soon as I got divorced *my income went up:* both the local and national government increased my mother's allowance, my tax rate dropped drastically as I was now taxed at the lower rate of a single head of household, and my former husband contributed a significant sum for child support. . . . It also helped to have the possibility of 24 hour day care and a husband who was willing to take some of the responsibility for parenting during the week.[56]

These support policies for divorced mothers are not limited to the welfare states of Scandinavia. In France a newly divorced woman is eligible for a special Social Security payment for a year after divorce or until the youngest child is three; reimbursement for children's health expenses; a family allowance; a variety of special tax deductions; and government retraining programs which pay 90 percent of the minimum wage.[57]

Many European countries (e.g., Sweden and West Germany) have instituted a system whereby the government guarantees the custodial parent (usually the mother) a minimum child-support payment. If the noncustodial parent (usually the father) fails to come through with child support, the government steps in, pays the mother the minimum amount, and then tries to collect from the father by such mechanisms as attaching his salary. The European system has a major advantage over the 1984 Child Support Enforcement Amendment in that it guarantees a base income for custodial parents and their children.[58]

In view of the economic distress visited on the majority of divorced women, it is disheartening to see how unrealistically their problems are portrayed in the popular culture. In the novels, plays, and films dealing with the "older" (over thirty-five) woman who gets divorced, reality is generally kept firmly at bay. For instance, in the film *An Unmarried Woman* Jill Clayburgh, abandoned by her husband, continues to live with her child in a large and lavish apartment on Manhattan's Upper East Side. She appears to have no financial anxieties whatsoever. Every day she blithely takes an extremely long taxi ride down to her part-time job in a funky Soho art gallery which couldn't possibly pay enough to cover even her cab fare. Her greatest dilemma is deciding whether to spend August in New York searching for her true identity or in Vermont with new boyfriend Alan Bates, risking her precarious new independence. Would that all newly divorced women faced such problems!

As we have seen, most divorced women are overwhelmed by the grim economic consequences of marital breakdown. Not only do women bear the direct costs of divorce—their own standard of living takes a nose dive—but they also bear almost all the costs and take almost all the responsibility of raising the children of divorce. A recent study by Furstenberg at the University of Pennsylvania finds that *49 percent of children in the custody of their mothers do not see their fathers at all.*[59] It is easy to see how the pressures on mothers in the immediate aftermath of divorce can become so intense that "parenting breaks down and becomes inconsistent and erratically punitive. The kids start acting out, the result is often a battle for survival. One divorced mother said that the constant harassment was 'like being bitten to death by ducks.' "[60] It is hardly surprising that these women find it difficult to hold down a job, let alone build a career.

4

THE WAGE GAP

Say the words *modern working women,* and our minds immediately conjure up images of superwomen, those female anchorpersons and executive vice-presidents so beloved by the media. Barbara Walters, Mary Cunningham, and Sherry Lansing are our modern heroines, and the press would have us believe that the underbrush is full of glamorous career women with six-figure incomes.

Fortune magazine runs a spread on vivacious Linda Taylor. A graduate of Harvard's Business School, Linda is in her mid-thirties and on the fast track. She has just been promoted to chief investment officer of the United Mine Workers' $2.3 billion pension and health fund and now earns more than $100,000 a year. Linda is also the mother of three children. To keep her household running smoothly, Linda employs a staff of three—housekeeper, nanny, and weekend substitute (who takes over housekeeping and child care on Saturday and Sunday). The annual payroll of Linda's domestic staff totals $27,000.[1]

Forbes has a story on dynamic Lorraine Mecca. Five years ago this enterprising thirty-four-year-old former English teacher invested $25,000 from her divorce settlement in her fledgling Micro D Inc. of Fountain Valley, California—a wholesale operation that sells computer software. In the first nine months of 1983 Micro D had sales of $50 million and a net of $859,000. The company went public in July 1984, raising $25 million. Lorraine is now a wealthy woman.[2]

Would that Linda and Lorraine were representative of working women in our society. Unfortunately reality is a lot less glamorous. Despite the enormous expansion of the female labor force in recent years—the number of women working has doubled since 1960—there has been little improvement in women's economic position.[3]

Only 7 percent of employed women in America work in managerial positions, and only 10 percent earn more than $20,000 a year.[4] Three-quarters of American working women continue to be employed in traditional "women's jobs" and spend their time waiting on tables, typing letters, cutting hair, emptying bedpans, and cleaning offices. Most are badly paid. In 1984, 1 out of every 4 women earned less than $10,000 a year when working full time.[5] In many cases, some women's salaries fail to lift them above the poverty line, and this produces much hardship in a day and age when women's wages no longer constitute pin money. Today 45 percent of working women are single, divorced, separated, or widowed and have no option but to take prime economic responsibility for themselves (and often their children). The low earning power of women helps explain why 35 percent of single mothers fall below the poverty line.

A critical measure of how well women are doing in the labor market is the wage gap, which is the difference between male and female earnings. The wage gap in America is extremely wide and has not shifted in fifty years.

In 1939, when Franklin D. Roosevelt was president, *Gone with the Wind* was awarded the Academy Award as best picture, and Joe DiMaggio won the batting title, women earned sixty-three cents to a man's dollar.[6] Presidents have come and gone, *Gone with the Wind* is on cable TV, and DiMaggio is a legend. But women's earning power hasn't changed much. Today women earn sixty-four cents to a man's dollar (August 1985 figure released by the Bureau of the Census).[7] We have women astronauts and women vice-presidential candidates—indeed, fully 45 percent of the U.S. labor force is now female—but despite all these changes, the gap between male and female earnings is as wide as it was half a century ago.

In 1984 the median earnings of women who worked full time year-round was $14,479, while similarly employed men earned $23,218.[8] A woman with four years of college still earns less than a male high school dropout.

Mary Engle works at the Ms and His Unisex salon in Pennsauken, New Jersey, mostly cutting hair. She is single and twenty-six years old and has been working at the salon on Center Street for eight years, ever since she finished her training at the Maison de Paris beautician school in Haddonfield, New Jersey.

With salary and tips she earns about $10,000 a year, the average wage for a female hairdresser of her age with a high school diploma. Average, that is, for a woman, not average for a man.[9]

According to 1980 census data female hairstylists between ages twenty-five and thirty-four earn $3,677 less than male hairstylists of similar age and educational background. Female hairdressers between ages thirty-five and forty-four earn $7,603 less than their male counterparts.

Engle's wage-earning experience is mirrored in virtually every occupation. Male lawyers between the ages of twenty-five and thirty-four earn, on average, $27,563 a year; the figure for female lawyers is $20,573. Bus drivers average $15,611 if they are men but $9,903 if they are women. As for retail salespersons, males average $13,002 a year while females average $7,479 a year.[10] We seem to have eliminated sexist terminology without doing anything about economic inequality.

The wage gap pursues women into old age. There are 16 million women over sixty-five years old in the population. In 1982 their median income was $5,365, compared to $9,188 for men.[11] It seems that if you are a woman, you have a 60 percent shot at being poor in old age, and since women live on average to be seventy-nine, old age can last a long time. The main reason for the disparity between the incomes of elderly men and women is that the jobs women hold are rarely good enough to qualify them for private pensions, only 11 percent of women over sixty-five collect pensions.[12]

The Wage Gap

One deeply disturbing fact is that the wage gap in America is wider—and more stubborn—than in other advanced industrial countries. As British economist Peter Sloane describes it, "in most countries for which data are available the average gender wage differential narrowed significantly during the 1970s"; only in the United States did the sex wage differential "remain fixed as if through some divine law."[13] For example, in Sweden, where women are among the highest-paid in Europe, women earned just over 81 percent of male earnings in 1980, up from 71 percent in 1970.[14] And in Britain, where women are among the lowest-paid in Europe, women's wages as a percentage of men's increased from 54 percent in 1970 to 66 percent in 1982.[15] This narrowing of the gap between male and female earning power can be seen in most advanced democracies. In Italy women's wages as a percentage of men's wages increased from 74 percent in 1968 to 86 percent in 1982; in West Germany women's wages rose from 69 percent in 1968 to 73 percent in 1982; in France they rose from 76 percent in 1964 to 78 percent in 1982; and in Denmark they rose from 74 percent in 1968 to 86 percent in 1982.[16] Traditional Catholic societies as well as Scandinavian welfare states have made more progress than we have on this critical front.

The low earning power of American women workers is particularly surprising when one takes into consideration the educational picture. American women are the best-educated in the world. Of current four-year college students 52 percent are female, and half of all master's degrees and a quarter of all professional degrees go to women. Indeed, the average woman worker is now slightly better educated than the average male worker, having completed a median of 12.65 years of schooling, compared to 12.57 for men.[17] In other countries women continue to lag behind men in educational attainment. In Britain women make up only 39 percent of students in higher education, in Italy the figure is 41 percent, and in France it is 45 percent.[18] One would therefore expect the wage gap in these countries to be wider, not narrower. All of which adds to the mystery of why American women do so badly in the workplace.

Perhaps the biggest surprise is that elite women are not closing the economic gender gap. Census data show that more women hold executive and professional positions than ever before—the percentage of managerial jobs held by women rose from 14.5 percent in 1960 to 28.9 percent in 1980[19]—yet over these two decades, when executive women made such impressive numerical gains, the wage gap between men and women executives actually widened. In 1960 women managers earned 58 percent of the male wage; in 1980 they earned 55 percent.[20] Women are simply not making it into upper management; they remain heavily concentrated in the lower half of the corporate pyramid. According to Barbara Everitt Bryant, a senior vice-president at the Market Opinion Research Company in Detroit, women make up about 50 percent of entry management and 25 percent of middle management. But although business began recruiting and promoting women in substantial numbers in the early 1970s—far enough back to give them time for considerable career advancement— they account for only a tiny percentage of upper management. Estimates are in the 1 to 2 percent range.[21] There seems to be a revolving door for women at the bottom of the managerial career ladder.

A final piece of depressing news is that the difference between starting salaries for men and women has widened in recent years. Gordon Green, a demographer at the Bureau of the Census, has found that the wages of white women entering the job market were 3 percentage points farther behind comparable white men in 1980 than they were in 1970. This is "despite the growth of affirmative action and educational gains by women."[22]

A favorite indoor sport among economists is debating the reasons behind the wage gap. Those on the liberal left of the discipline emphasize the fact that women are paid less because they are discriminated against; those on the conservative right stress that the home and family responsibilities of women depress their earnings potential.[23]

Discrimination against women in the labor market shows up in a variety of ways. The most overt kinds of discrimination occur when a woman is paid less than a man for doing the same job, or when a qualified woman is denied access to a job or promotion to a better job on account of her sex. These forms of discrimination have been illegal since the passage of the Equal Pay Act in 1963 and Title VII of the Civil Rights Act in 1964. This does not mean that these types of discrimination have disappeared completely but progress has been made, and many previously male fields have been opened up to women. For example, between 1962 and 1982 the proportion of women among engineers rose from 1 to 6 percent; among mail carriers, from 3 to 17 percent; among physicians, from 6 to 15 percent; and among bus drivers, from 12 to 47 percent.[24]

Another and less obvious form of discrimination occurs when women are segregated into a pink-collar ghetto of low-paying jobs. These jobs are not necessarily low-skilled, but for a host of social and political reasons they are almost always low-paid. In the first place, women's occupations have often been overcrowded because of legal and social restrictions on the jobs open to women. Secondly, women's jobs have generally not been organized by trade unions, and this has weakened the earning power of these jobs. Thirdly, employers have gotten away with paying women less because many of them were, and to some extent still are, secondary wage earners within the family. Finally, women workers have often interrupted their work to bear and raise children. All these factors have depressed wages in women's fields. So powerful are these factors that any field dominated by women is almost guaranteed to have low wages. Indeed, there are certain occupations in America that used to be dominated by men and used to be well paid until women took them over.

For example, a century ago most clerical workers in the United States were male. They earned about twice as much as blue-collar workers. Today 80 percent of all clerical jobs are held by women, and the average wage is far below that of blue-collar work. In fact, in the modern economy a secretary with eighteen years' experience earns less than a parking lot attendant. A similar story can be told about bank tellers. Before the Second World War bank tellers were male, and the jobs they held were prestigious and well paid. Today, as we all know, this occupation is dominated by women, and bank tellers have lost both status and earning power.

Despite the changes of recent years, the United States labor market is still largely segregated by sex. In 1982, 50 percent of employed women worked in only 20 occupations—out of the 427 occupations detailed by the United States Department of Labor.

More than half of all employed women worked in occupations which were 75 percent female, and 22 percent of employed women were in jobs that were more than 95 percent female.[25] Women still account for 99 percent of secretaries, 97 percent of typists, and 96 percent of all registered nurses.[26]

Contrary to popular opinion, the entry of women into professional and blue-collar jobs has *not* reduced the overall degree of segregation. This is because the movement of a few women into predominantly male jobs has been overwhelmed by a flood of new women workers into predominantly female jobs. In other words, for every woman entering a traditionally male field such as law or auto mechanics, there are several women entering traditional women's fields.

Over the last two years there has been an increasingly vigorous attempt to combat this more subtle form of discrimination—the segregation of women into low-paying occupations—by applying the principle of equal pay for jobs of comparable worth. The argument is that women have been "segregated into job classifications on the basis of sex, and as a result, are paid less than employees in historically predominantly male classifications which require an equivalent [amount] of skill, effort and responsibility."[27] The strategy is to conduct job evaluations, measure the value of different jobs to the employer, and come up with a numerical rating for each. If a secretary is rated the same as a plumber, then both jobs should command the same pay. Currently a score of states and municipalities are under pressure from public employee unions to pay women in low-paying occupations more by applying the principle of comparable worth.

One of the first comparable worth cases was in San Jose, California. In 1981 municipal workers in this city went on strike for nine days to enforce a job evaluation study that demonstrated that certain occupations dominated by women were underpaid. In the end the city provided $1.5 million in pay adjustments to reduce this form of group discrimination.

Another early case was in the private sector. In 1981 the International Union of Electrical Workers (IUE) sued the Westinghouse Corporation for operating with a pay scale that relegated all women workers to the lowest pay grades. The union won, a new job evaluation was undertaken, and women were distributed through the pay scale in a way which reflected the value of the work they did.[28]

Perhaps the most important legal decision came at the end of 1983, when a federal judge ordered the state of Washington to pay its women workers $800 million in back pay and wage increases on the basis of a comparable worth evaluation. Judge Jack Tanner ruled that the state practiced "direct, overt and institutionalized" discrimination against its women employees.[29] The Washington State ruling triggered scores of cases, and by the end of 1984 litigation was pending across the nation. In numerous states and municipalities public-employee unions are seeking to upset traditional pay patterns that discriminate against women.

Comparable worth has been called the civil rights issue of the 1980s, and it is already a political football—supported by liberals, opposed by conservatives. In the 1984 election campaign it was endorsed by the Mondale-Ferraro ticket and opposed by the Reagan administration. The Democratic leadership of the House of Representatives has endorsed "equal pay for work of comparable social value," while Reagan appointee Clarence M. Pendleton, Jr., chairman of the U.S. Civil Rights Commission, has called comparable worth "the looniest idea since 'Looney Tunes' came on the screen."[30] William Bradford Reynolds, assistant attorney general for civil rights, is currently opposing the principle of comparable worth in the courts.

Liberals see comparable worth as the best way of producing economic justice for women workers who are shunted into the lowest-paid jobs, and they vigorously defend the use of job evaluations to determine the value of a job. "This is done every day by American business and industry," says Eleanor Holmes Norton, a former head of the Equal Employment Opportunity Commission. As she sees it, "women are doing valuable work which just happens to be underpaid because it is done by women."[31]

Conservative critics respond that unlike the job evaluations of individual companies, which are useful internal measures that take into account the forces of supply and demand, comparable-worth plans like the one used in Washington State are not pegged to the market. But many people—including Ray Marshall, economist and secretary of labor in the Carter administration—aren't sure that market forces work with much precision in internal labor markets. "If you compare the predominantly male profession of engineer with the predominantly female profession of nurse, you find there is a shortage of both but the market's response is different. The wages offered to engineers go up, while nurses who will work cheap are imported from abroad."[32]

The cost of raising wages for what have traditionally been women's jobs can be high. The Washington State settlement, if upheld by the courts, would cost an estimated $642 million in back pay and $195 million a year in raises. However, in Minnesota the cost of bringing women up to a comparable level with men was only 4 percent of the payroll, a manageable amount. Another issue raised by opponents is that if comparable worth were applied on any scale to private business, it would increase the wage bill and the cost of production, bringing higher prices at home and hindering the ability of American firms to compete in overseas markets.

All this implies that the principle of comparable worth is not going to be accepted quickly or easily in the U.S. labor market.

If occupational segregation is important in explaining the wage gap,[33] the other critical explanatory factor is the heavy load of family responsibilities borne by most working women.

Women attain much less seniority and earn much less money than men whatever occupation they are employed in. As a woman you don't have to be a waitress or a secretary to be badly paid; you don't even have to be discriminated against. You can attend the best professional schools, you can be hired by the most prestigious firms, and you can be treated the same as a man but still find that over a lifetime it is easy to earn a fraction of the amount earned by male contemporaries. The fact is most women bear weighty home and family burdens and need more than equality with men if they are to attain equal earning power in the marketplace. They need job protected maternity leave, child care, flextime, and specially tailored career ladders.

Susan Fischer* works three-fifths time as a program officer at a private foundation in Washington. She is 39 years old, earns

*Pseudonym.

$23,000 a year, and lives quietly with her husband and two small children in suburban Maryland. It's a pleasant enough life but not one that will set the world on fire.

I first met Susan some ten years ago. At the time she was single and fiercely ambitious. I remember being impressed by her professional zeal and by the fact that her recent book on trade policy had just won a coveted prize awarded by the American Economic Association. Susan dreamed of being the first woman president of the Council of Economic Advisers, and many people thought that she had a shot at realizing her ambition.

In her early thirties Susan got married, and over the course of five years she bore two children. Gradually her career options narrowed. Looking back, Susan sees two critical decision points. "Just after I became pregnant with Anthony [her first child], Carter won the election and I was asked to go to the National Security Council to work on East-West trade questions. Saying no was one of the hardest things I have ever done. Imagine the excitement of actually working in the White House, being involved in some of the most difficult trade problems of the decade. But the decision was cut-and-dried. Of course I couldn't do it. I knew I wanted to take a six months' leave when my first child was born, and if I had accepted that job, it would have meant making a total commitment—sixty hours a week and no time off." Susan paused and said reflectively, "You know, that first pregnancy not only ruled out working at the National Security Council, it also cost me the job I was in. The organization I worked for allowed you to take a six-month unpaid leave for childbirth but did not guarantee your job back. In the event, they filled my position when I was on leave." Susan's expression became almost bitter as she remembered this period of her life: "I tell you it is not much fun hitting the job market with a new baby at home, but Robert [her husband] was still in graduate school and earning peanuts. I had to find a new job.

"Four years later I was faced with another tough set of choices. I had changed course and was now working at a research foundation; the hours were regular, and I found it fitted in with family life much better than policy work." Susan smiled. "But you know me, I am ambitious and, I suppose, capable, and soon I was made a vice-president. In the early part of 1980 the president of the foundation announced his intention to retire in eighteen months time, and it suddenly hit me that if I went all out for it, I could probably land his job. But Robert and I had just made the decision to have a second child, so instead of working for a promotion, I became pregnant and took a ten-week maternity leave.

"I was careful to take a short leave so as to not jeopardize my job. But this time I ran into another problem. We could not find decent child care. I tried hiring a full-time baby-sitter. I even brought over from Europe an old-fashioned nanny, but no one lasted more than a month. I guess we live too far out in the suburbs to attract live-in help. I then tried day care but found that the only center that would accept a three- or four-month-old infant was forty miles away. Even if I had been willing to do all that driving, it would not have solved the problem of what to do with Anthony at the end of his short school day. In the end we put together a complicated child-care package by combining local part-time sitters with a live-in student. But despite all kinds of organizational effort, the package kept on breaking down. Vanessa would not take her bottle from the new Thursday sitter, or our in-house student decided to take an impromptu vacation. The tension and the guilt were overwhelming. Every time a sitter called me at work I found my hands shaking as I picked up the phone in anticipation of yet another crisis. My concentration became poor, and I just knew that I was not performing well on the job. When Vanessa was eight months old, I cut back to three-fifths time. At least I could now guarantee some quality time for my children.

"The repercussions of going part time were serious, as I knew they would be; why else had I tried so hard to remain full time? I could no longer be an officer of the foundation as they do not allow vice-presidents to work part time. So here I am, almost forty years old and a lowly program officer once again. I suppose I have become downwardly mobile." Susan pulled a face and said with some humor, "The guy they did promote to the presidency now earns eighty thousand dollars a year. When you stack that up against my paltry twenty-three thousand a year, I guess Vanessa comes out to be a pretty expensive baby." Susan's face relaxed into a wide grin. "But naturally her adoring mother thinks she is worth every penny of it."

Susan wanted to add one more thought. "The other day I caught myself thinking about how I will take up the threads of 'my brilliant career' in my mid-forties, when Anthony and Vanessa are launched and don't need me so much. But that is just a pipe dream. No one wants a gray-haired lady on the staff of the National Security Council. Those slots are strictly for up-and-coming thirty-year-olds. I am trying to reconcile myself to reality, which is that I have fallen behind my generation and can never re-create the opportunities I once had. My career is permanently stalled."[34]

A surprising aspect of Susan's story is that she took a total of only eight and a half months' leave for the birth of her children and that for twelve out of the last fifteen years she has worked full time. Yet childbearing has severely compromised her career prospects and her earning power. It doesn't take much to derail a career. A couple of leaves, a stint of part-time work will do it. Susan's story accurately reflects the mechanisms through which women—even well-qualified ambitious women—fall behind in the job market.

Some convincing research in the field (much of which has been done by conservative "human capital" theorists) links earning power to the lifetime work histories of men and women.[35] According to this view, the wage gap can best be explained by the fact that working women bear a double burden—in the home and in the labor force. Domestic responsibilities, particularly those associated with child rearing, interrupt and limit women's careers, permanently depressing female earning power. In the words of economist Solomon Polachek, the lower earnings of women are due to "the division of labor within the family. . . . It is the wife who is shackled with the family responsibility, and it is the wife who forgoes wages and job opportunities to take on these responsibilities."[36]

The typical woman drops out of the labor force for nine years.[37] There are signs that this period is shortening as more and more mothers of small children stay in the labor market, but recent census data show that women are three times as likely as men to have their careers interrupted, and only 36 percent of currently employed women have worked continuously since leaving school.[38]

Human capital theorists argue that the wage gap can be largely explained by these interruptions that mark women's work lives. For example, when Polachek compares the difference between the reentry wage—the wage a woman earns when she comes back into the labor force after a period of not working—with the wage she would have received had she stayed in the labor force, he finds that he can explain 50 percent of the wage gap. Indeed, when he adds in the assumption that women will train less precisely because they expect to spend less time in the labor force, he claims to account for close to 100 percent of the wage gap.[39] Polachek is not alone in stressing the depressing effect of interruptions on women's earnings. Other studies find that occupational tenure accounts for 25 to 44 percent of the wage gap.[40] It seems that a two- to four-year break in employment lowers average earnings by 13 percent while a five-year break in employment lowers average earnings by 19 percent.[41] Economist Eli Ginsberg goes so far as to say that "a continuous work history is almost a prerequisite for high or even good achievement."[42]

Various kinds of circumstantial evidence lend support to theories that link the wage gap to women's family responsibilities. First, wage levels for women vary dramatically according to family status. Never-married women have complete wage parity with never-married men, while the wage gap between married men and women is extremely large. On average, *married women earn less than half the earnings of married men.* The number and spacing of children also affect the wage differential. Women with large families, with children spanning a broad age band, have the lowest wages of all.

Secondly, a greater proportion of single and childless women—with continuous work histories—are in professional, technical, and administrative "male" jobs. Indeed, more than 50 percent of the women in top management positions are childless. In contrast, married women with children crowd into low-paying "women's" fields. These women tend to have large gaps in their work histories.

In the third place, black men do a great deal better in the labor market than women, whether they are white or black. In 1981 white women earned 60 percent of the male wage while black men (who have two years less schooling than white men and women) earned 69 percent of the wage for all men.[43] Since black men continue to be discriminated against in the labor market, the only way to explain these figures is to assume that the family responsibilities borne by women exert such a strong downward pressure on earnings that they outweigh even the disadvantages of being black. Gender seems to be a more powerful handicap than race in the labor market.

Finally, there is evidence drawn from the pattern of earnings over the life cycle. Age-earning profiles for men and women demonstrate the severely depressing effect of child rearing on female earnings. When women enter the work force in their late teens and early twenties, they earn somewhat less than men, but for a few years they do experience a fairly rapid rate of wage increase. However, in the twenty-five to thirty-four age bracket (the main childbearing years) their earnings fall way behind that of men. Note in Figure 1 how female earnings dramatically level off during these years especially for high school graduates. In other words, when one compares women's age earnings profiles with that of men, it becomes obvious that women miss out on the rapid upward mobility men typically experience in their late twenties and thirties. At this critical stage of most career paths, women have children (or at least 90 percent of them do), and given inadequate (or no) maternity leave and the paucity and expense of child-care facilities, the majority of working women are forced to make drastic compromises in their work lives. Some leave the labor force for a number of years; others take third-rate jobs with short hours and little responsibility close to home. Economist Lester Thurow puts the problem succinctly: "The years between 25 and 35 are the prime years for establishing a successful career. These are the years when hard work has the maximum payoff. They are also the prime years for launching a family. Women who leave the job market completely during those years may find that they never catch up."[44]

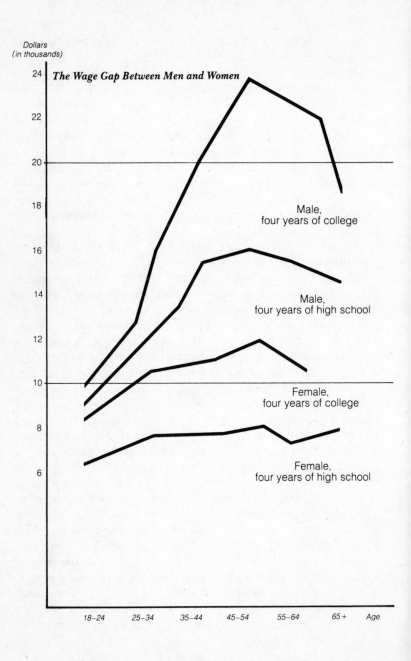

Dollars
(in thousands)

The Wage Gap Between Men and Women

Male,
four years of college

Male,
four years of high school

Female,
four years of college

Female,
four years of high school

18–24   25–34   35–44   45–54   55–64   65 +   Age

Thus, because of children-related handicaps, most women—even highly educated ones—fail to take off into careers in their thirties. And when they are able to resume the all-out commitment necessary for career advance (usually around the age of forty), the structure of the labor market makes it extremely difficult, if not impossible, for them to get back on track.

Susan Fischer's case is not unusual. Her experience is typical of women trying to combine a career with raising a family. Forty-five percent of women returning to part-time jobs after having children "find themselves moving down the occupational ladder into jobs which are worse paid or duller than those they had before their children were born."[45] The consensus seems to be that interruptions, even if few and of short duration, exert a substantial downward pull on women's earning power.

The legal profession, which has more women than other elite occupations, is an interesting example of how family responsibilities continue to limit women's careers and their earning power. Women have clearly come a long way. More than a century ago, in 1873, the United States Supreme Court ruled that a young woman named Myra Bradwell was not constitutionally entitled to practice law. In his opinion Justice Joseph P. Bradley wrote: "The natural and proper timidity and delicacy which belongs to the female sex evidently unfits it for many of the occupations of civil life. The paramount destiny and mission of women are to fulfill the noble and benign office of wife and mother. This is the law of the Creator."[46] Columbia University did not admit its first woman law student until 1928, and as late as the mid-1960s only 5 percent of the class was female.

By 1984 almost 50 percent of law school students were women, as were 30 percent of associates at private law firms. But only 5 percent of partnerships in these firms were held by women.[47] Women lawyers are still not making it to the centers of power, money, and prestige.

A study of the seventy-one women of the Harvard Law School's class of '74 by Jill Abramson and Barbara Franklin sheds some light on why this is so.[48] As they describe it, "entering the job market when they did, at the height of the women's movement and armed with Harvard Law degrees, these women probably stood a better chance of finding success than any other group of women in the country. They certainly hoped to do as well as the 478 men in their class."

Nine years later the results were startling; 23 percent of the women from the class were partners at law firms, compared with 51 percent of the men, although roughly equal percentages started out in private practice. For most, partnership decisions have already been made (they were faced in the 1981–83 period). Abramson and Franklin find that for many of these women lawyers there is a definite trade-off between family responsibilities and career advancement.

Carolyn Lewis Zeigler, an associate in the litigation department of a New York law firm, is a case in point. "When I hit thirty," says Ms. Zeigler, "I said to myself, Gee, it's time." That was three years ago, and soon afterward Zeigler became pregnant with her first child, a daughter. Now she is pregnant again. She has worked part time, usually three days a week, since the birth of her first child, and she anticipates keeping a part-time schedule until her second child turns three. She sees no way of carrying the full load of a fifty-hour workweek while her children are little. Zeigler's decision to be a part-time lawyer has had a profound effect on her career. She has not made partner; indeed, she will not even be considered for partnership until she returns to work on a full-time basis. She is now earning a fraction of what her male contemporaries earn. Her career is on hold.

Katherine Reed is another example. Ms. Reed joined the New York firm Proskauer, Rose, Goetz & Mendelsohn in the mid-1970s. She did not stay long, for she found that the pace of work ruled out any kind of private life, let alone the possibility of husband and children. "Proskauer did not discriminate," says Reed. "Everyone was forced to work an eighty-hour week." She eventually switched to the legal department of a large corporation. This represented a step down in career terms because the potential financial rewards are lower. The biggest attraction of the new job was an 8:00 A.M. to 6:00 P.M. working day.

Of the forty-six women Abramson and Franklin interviewed from the class of '74, nineteen have children. These women found that in all spheres of legal work—private firms, government, legal aid, and corporate in-house—"balancing maternity leaves and part time work with career advancement has proved difficult, and the demands of family life are one of the most common reasons cited by women who have left high powered jobs." In addition, many of the women lawyers who do not have children strive to arrange their work lives so as to leave open the possibility of finding mates and having a family.

The conclusion of this study was that "few of the women in Harvard's law school class of '74 turned out to be superwomen. They found that they could not stay on the fast track and develop satisfying personal lives."[49]

The conventional wisdom used to be that the thousands of women entering the legal profession just have not had the time to make their way up through the ranks to partnership. Senior partners at law firms are fond of pointing out that they are hiring a veritable flood of women fresh out of law school; as soon as these women put in the necessary seven to nine years as associates, they say, there will no doubt be a flood of women partners.

It does not seem to be happening that way. True, a great many women are being hired as associates, but a far greater percentage of them seem to be leaving the fast track after four or five years than do their male counterparts.[50] Some are "let go" or "passed over" by the firm. Others like Carolyn Zeigler and Katherine Reed go part time or turn to less demanding jobs—in teaching, in government work, or on corporate legal staffs—to create more time for themselves or their families.

The career trajectories of the class of '74 make for a better understanding of the census figures cited earlier in this chapter: Male lawyers aged twenty-five to thirty-five earn $27,563 a year, while their female counterparts earn $20,573. Even the best-trained and most ambitious professional women find that they have to make considerable career sacrifices—in terms of both status and salary—in order to have a family.

As we have seen, economists have advanced powerful arguments to support the theory that career interruptions wrought by homemaking and childbearing explain at least half the wage gap between men and women. Polachek takes this theory further and argues that much of the low earning power of women is caused not by employers discriminating but by "the more implicit and subtle forms of societal discrimination taking place within the family."[51] In less elegant language, working women are still stuck with most domestic chores, and this severely limits how well they can do in the labor market.

Looking after a home and a family is still an enormously time-consuming activity. According to one study, a good home life for a family of four takes about sixty hours of nurturing work per week.[52] That work may have been more physically strenuous in the past but never more complex. Homemaking in our modern industrial society includes the management of extensive relationships with stores, banks, schools, hospitals, and government offices as well as housekeeping and child care. It involves seeing that thousands of personal needs are met. The five-year-old needs a booster shot or a costume for the school play, camp applications have to be filled out for the seven-year-old and name tapes need to be ordered, an appointment must be set up with the kindergarten teacher to explain Johnny's stammering problem, and 300 family snapshots are waiting to be put into albums. Sometimes relationships with stores, schools, or government offices are fraught with problems. If the new car is a lemon, if the grade-school teacher can't discipline the children, if the Social Security benefit is late, or if a credit card is lost or stolen, "then the stressful nature of the homemaker's brokering work between home, market and state is exacerbated."[53]

Over the last fifteen years there has been a great deal of talk about men taking on more household responsibility. Magazines have discovered a "fathering boom," and films such as *Kramer vs. Kramer* and *Mr. Mom* have tried to convince us that modern men develop intimate nurturing relationships with their children. And it is true, some men have taken on considerably more housework and child care. I have interviewed men who take care of their children by day and work factory shifts at night, and my own husband takes 50 percent of the responsibility for our children. But in the aggregate this increased participation by men does not add up to very much. Recent studies show that American men still do less than a quarter of all household tasks, and that married men's average time in family work has increased by only 6 percent in twenty years despite the massive shift of women into paid employment.[54] One survey finds that the work week of American women is twenty-one hours longer than that of men.[55] Indeed, economist Heidi Hartmann claims that men actually demand eight hours more service per week than they contribute.[56]

Philip Blumstein and Pepper Schwartz sum up the contemporary situation in their 1984 book *American Couples:*

> Working wives do less housework than homemakers but they still do the vast bulk of what needs to be done . . . even if a husband is unemployed he does much less housework than a wife who puts in a 40 hour week. . . . This is the case even among couples who profess egalitarian social ideals. . . . While husbands might say they should share responsibility, when they break it down to time actually spent and chores actually done, the idea of shared responsibility turns out to be a myth.[57]

Joseph Pleck hits the nail on the head when he describes "men's characteristically low level of family work" as one of the key problems of contemporary life.[58]

An insurmountable obstacle to increased male responsibility for housework is the absence of men in many households. Any small progress that has been made in recent years toward raising the consciousness of concerned husbands and fathers has been canceled out by the inroads of divorce. Approximately 50 percent of the children borne in the early 1980s will go through a divorce, and 90 percent of these children will end up living with their mothers. As we saw in the last chapter, custodial mothers pick up nearly all the physical and financial responsibilities of rearing the children of divorce.

Nora Ephron in *Heartburn* displays a jaundiced, if amusing, view of how much women have actually achieved on the household division of labor front. As she describes it, in the 1970s it was fashionable to sit down with your husband and draw up a list of household duties in order to divide them equally: "This happened in thousands of households, with identical results: thousands of husbands agreed to clear the table. They cleared the table and then looked around as if they deserved a medal. They cleared the table and then hoped that they would never again be asked to do another thing. They cleared the table and hoped the whole thing would go away. And it did."[59]

Ephron may have been bitter because her own husband left her when she was pregnant with her second child. Unfortunately her experience is not unique.

The division of household labor between men and women seems stubbornly resistant to change, and part of the problem is that women earn so much less than men. Married women when working full time earn less than half the wages earned by married men, and when you weigh in part-time workers, employed wives contribute only 26 percent of the family budget. In view of this asymmetry it is hardly surprising that men have picked up so little domestic responsibility. It still makes economic sense for a family to put the husband's job first. When a parent has to leave the work force in order to take care of a child, it usually costs the family less for the mother to stay at home than for the father. But this is a vicious circle. As we have seen, by "interrupting" her career, the mother permanently lowers her earnings potential.

A raised consciousness on the part of a man is not enough. Many husbands have the best of intentions when embarking on family life. Over the long haul goodwill is often defeated by the economic facts of life. As French feminist Simone de Beauvoir put it some thirty years ago, "Many young households give the impression of being on a basis of perfect equality. But as long as the man retains economic responsibility for the couple, this is only an illusion."[60] You cannot expect to change behavior without first changing the economic logic on which this behavior is based. In *American Couples* Blumstein and Schwartz demonstrate that "money establishes the balance of power in relationships," and according to them, this shows up most crudely in who does what in the household.[61]

For women the wage gap sets up an infuriating Catch-22 situation. They do the housework because they earn less, and they earn less because they do the housework. The only way to break this vicious circle is to develop public policies that support women in their domestic roles so that they can do better in the labor market. Doing better in the labor market has to include limiting those interruptions that so severely depress women's earnings.

The Wage Gap

High-quality, subsidized child care would enable many women to take fewer years out of the labor force when they have children and thus pay a smaller penalty in terms of a lower wage when they reenter (remember a two- to four-year break in employment lowers average earnings by 13 percent while a five-year break in employment lowers average earnings by 19 percent). Indeed, generous maternity leaves with rigorous job-back guarantees would enable many women to bear children without paying any penalty at all in terms of earning power or seniority. In short, public policies that support women in their efforts to bear and rear children would go a long way toward narrowing the wage gap. And once the gap between male and female earnings narrows significantly, the household division of labor may well shift. It seems that an equal sharing of housework and child rearing between men and women will await the day when a woman's job is as important to the household economy as a man's.

Over the last twenty years a great deal of energy has been channeled into devising ways of improving the economic position of women. In the 1960s and 1970s policy was aimed at getting rid of overt discrimination. Title VII of the Civil Rights Act and Executive Order 11246 were used to sue firms that had unfair hiring practices or paid unequal wages for equal work. And much was accomplished as barriers fell and professional and blue-collar jobs were opened up to women. In the 1980s the main policy thrust seems to be utilizing the concept of comparable worth to tackle occupational discrimination—the segregation of women in low-paid jobs. But all this activity on the antidiscrimination front has had little effect on women's earning power.[62]

This effort to eliminate discrimination in the job market is seriously limited because it has failed to deal with women's double burden. Unless women get some relief from their domestic responsibilities, they will continue to fare badly in the labor force. Such relief seems a long way away.

America's family support system is shamefully weak and shrinking, e.g., subsidies for child care have been cut by 21 percent since 1980. In our society having a baby is viewed as strictly a private matter. Fewer than 40 percent of working women have any maternity coverage, and in most cases such coverage is very limited.[63] And this is despite the fact that 48 percent of babies under one year old have mothers in the labor force.

The only federal provision for maternity leave is contained in the 1978 Pregnancy Disability Amendment to Title VII of the Civil Rights Act which decrees that an employer can no longer fire a worker *solely* because she is pregnant. But since "the law is based on nondiscrimination [it] names no special benefits associated with childbirth."[64] A pregnant woman is merely eligible for the same fringe benefits as workers with other disabilities. This seems to boil down to the right to use temporary disability insurance for pregnancy.

Unfortunately this provision is less useful than it might be because federal law *does not require employers to provide disability insurance.* In fact, only five states (California, Hawaii, New Jersey, New York, and Rhode Island) require disability coverage. Thus the 1978 act, which was touted as "solving" the maternity leave problem for American women, is a dead letter in forty-five states of the Union. Even those women lucky enough to live in the right states might still not be covered by disability insurance. For example, in New York State, government workers, farm workers, and workers in firms with fewer than fifteen employees all are excluded from the disability insurance requirement. And what does this much talked-about disability coverage amount to? A few (usually six to ten) weeks of partial wage replacement at the time of a normal pregnancy and delivery.

If some 40 percent of working women have some disability coverage for pregnancy and childbirth, what provision do they have for care of the infant during the first months of life? It is shocking but true that "our laws are silent about any period of time a mother or indeed a father may wish to be at home to care for an infant child."[65]

The shortcomings of the Pregnancy Disability Amendment as a national maternity policy seem obvious, yet it is all we have. Unlike other countries, pregnant women in the United States are not guaranteed leave from employment for a specific length of time at childbirth and therefore have no right of job protection if they do take some unpaid leave. Employers still routinely fire women if they take even a short leave of absence to have a baby.

According to Arkie Byrd, attorney for the Women's Legal Defense Fund in Washington, D.C., "It happens every day . . . and outside of sexual harassment, the largest number of employment discrimination cases handled by the Fund involve pregnancy."[66]

In addition, the United States does not guarantee health coverage to women for their own medical expenses or that of their newborn children at the time of birth. Since one-third of single women and one-quarter of married women have no health insurance, childbirth can be a very expensive proposition (costs range between $1,000 and $3,000). And even if women have some coverage for the medical expenses of childbirth, it is rarely comprehensive. None of the 100-odd working mothers I interviewed were completely covered for the expenses of childbirth.

The best maternity policies in the United States are to be found in large corporations as part of their employee benefits package. In a 1981 survey of 250 large corporations, 88 percent reported offering some type of maternity leave.[67] The median length of maternity leave in these corporations is twelve weeks (six weeks' paid leave, six weeks' unpaid leave), and in most cases these leaves carry job protection guarantees. The most generous employers tend to be banks, financial institutions, and insurance companies, and the least generous employers are in the retailing sector. A few companies have exceptionally good policies (by American standards); for example, the Aetna Life and Casualty Company offers pregnant women employees as much as six months' leave at 60 to 100 percent of salary.[68]

As good as some of the best corporate policies are, one should not lose sight of the fact that fewer than a quarter of American working women are employed by large corporations. For the vast majority there is no substitute for a statutory maternity policy that guarantees certain essential rights and benefits to working women when they give birth. In the modern world women often cannot simply chuck their jobs in when they have children; they desperately need to continue working to support themselves and their growing families. (Besides, their future earning power is affected by how much time they take off and whether this time is defined as job-protected leave or time out of the labor market.) It constitutes "cruel and unusual punishment" to present women workers with the choice of either losing their jobs or leaving their newborn children in the hands of (often inadequate) caretakers. This is precisely the choice that faces more than half of America's working women. No other advanced industrial country forces this choice on its female citizens.

Carmen Santos* is a medical secretary, and for the last four years she has worked for a large teaching hospital in New York City. When I interviewed her, she had a twenty-one-month-old child and was six months pregnant with her second child. At the birth of her first child Carmen's disability insurance replaced two-thirds of her salary for a period of six weeks. She originally planned to go back to work when her child was three months old and had been told that her job was secure. Despite these assurances, Carmen was fired one week before she was due to go back to work. Her union made sure that she was first in line for any new job that opened up, and five months later she found a job at the same salary in another department of the medical school. However, Carmen lost seniority in the job switch. In her new job she is defined as a "new hire" and is not entitled to paid vacation for six months and cannot vest in the pension plan for another two years. In her old job Carmen had built up considerable seniority—i.e., she had the right to three weeks' paid vacation and had been participating in the pension plan for a year. "It's a pity about the paid vacation," Carmen said wistfully. "It would have helped to tide us over the next six months."

When her next child is born, Carmen plans to take another three months off. She would prefer to take less time, but the neighborhood woman who does the bulk of the baby-sitting will not take babies younger than three months. Carmen is keeping her fingers crossed and hoping that this time she will get her job back immediately. Family finances are precarious. Together she and her husband earn $27,000 a year. Her husband's income alone is not enough to cover the basic expenses of food, shelter, and transportation. Carmen *has* to work.

In one respect Carmen feels that she is fortunate. Her medical plan is very comprehensive (it was negotiated by her union), and out-of-pocket expenses for the birth of her first child amounted to

*Pseudonym.

only $300. She knows many couples who faced bills of thousands of dollars when they had a child. I told Carmen that America was the only advanced country that didn't completely underwrite the medical costs of childbirth. She didn't believe me.[69]

Gail Tobias* is a writer. For the last six years she has been one of the principal writers for a TV soap opera. In late 1983, at the age of thirty-five, Gail became pregnant with her first child. Gail's employer had no provisions for maternity leave in place, and so after extensive negotiation it was arranged that Gail should work right up to when she went into labor and then take two and a half weeks off for the delivery. One and a half weeks of this comprised Gail's paid vacation time; the other week was defined as leave at half pay. In the event, Gail had a difficult labor and eventually delivered her child by cesarean section. She therefore found it particularly difficult to be back on the job so soon after the birth. In Gail's words, "I don't know how I lived through those first weeks back at work. I was exhausted and in pain from the surgery. I could hardly drag myself around. The worst thing was the lack of sleep. Annie woke to be fed at least three times a night, and by midday I was ready to kill for sleep. But somehow I had to work—and to smile and pretend to my boss that I didn't have a family care in the world." Gail is convinced that she would have lost her job had she taken additional time off. "I'm in a very competitive field, and they would have filled my slot easily and quickly." Since she and her husband have recently bought a house, they could not manage without her salary. Gail's poor maternity coverage extended to medical costs. She estimates that $1,800 of the childbirth expenses were not covered by medical insurance.[70]

The experiences of many European women I interviewed throw Carmen's and Gail's struggles into sharp relief. Take Susan Arnbom who works as a secretary in Stockholm and has three children, ages eight, three, and two. When each of her children was born, Susan was entitled to nine months' paid leave at 90 percent of her salary plus a six-month job-protected, but unpaid, leave. Since her two youngest children were born within a year of

*Pseudonym.

each other, she chose to merge her maternity leaves into a consecutive two-and-a-half-year period. Her husband was also eligible to share parental leave with her, and he took a four-month leave at the time of the birth of their first child.[71]

Or consider Annette Laborey, a program officer at a cultural foundation in Paris. Annette is married with two children, aged seven months and two years. At the birth of each child she was entitled to and took a three-month leave at full pay. She was also entitled to a two-year unpaid leave. She took part of this leave when her first child was born, but when she had her second child, she decided to go back to work at the end of the three-month paid leave. "With two children we needed my salary more, besides there was an excellent crèche [public child-care facility] just around the corner from home, so day care presented no problem."[72]

The United States is the only industrialized country that has no statutory maternity leave. One hundred and seventeen countries (including every industrial nation and many developing countries) guarantee a woman the following rights: leave from employment for childbirth, job protection while she is on leave, and the provision of a cash benefit, to replace all or most of her earnings.[73]

As we can see from Susan Arnbom's case, Sweden is particularly generous in its maternity policies. Since 1975 this Scandinavian country has provided a parental leave of nine months at the birth of a child which can be taken by either parent. It replaces 90 percent of earnings up to a specified maximum, protects seniority on the job, maintains fringe benefits, and, most important, guarantees that a parent can go back to the same or a similar job.[74]

Italy has a package of benefits typical of the European Economic Community (EEC). A pregnant woman is entitled to five months' paid leave at 80 percent of her wage, followed by a further six months at 30 percent of her wage. Her job is held for both time periods. A woman is also allowed to stay away from work when her child is ill up until the child is three years old. In addition, a woman worker is entitled to two years' credit toward seniority each time she gives birth to a child.[75]

Britain, which is parsimonious by European standards, has an

Employment Protection Act (enacted in 1975 and improved upon by the Employment Protection [Consolidation] Act of 1978 and the Employment Act of 1980) which provides: paid time off from work for prenatal care; six weeks' paid maternity leave, during which time 90 percent of earnings are replaced; and the right to leave work six weeks before a child is born and to return to work at any time before a child is twenty-nine weeks old and to be reemployed on terms "not less favorable than those applicable if she had not been absent."[76] Many employers in Britain, particularly those in the public sector, provide additional maternity benefits to their employees.

It is interesting to note that the British maternity provisions (which are on the low end of the European scale) have been instituted during a period of public spending cutbacks and increasingly conservative policies. Even Prime Minister Margaret Thatcher has had to recognize that in a world where more and more women are in the labor force, pregnant women and newborn babies need protection, and the state is the only entity able to guarantee such protection. In this area private-sector initiatives are not enough. British women see their maternity benefits as critically important. Ruth Spellman, who works at the National Economic Development Office in London, put it this way: "I cannot imagine how I would have dealt with those first months of my son's life without the provisions of my maternity leave. The Employment Protection Act is as important to women as gaining the vote. It makes it possible for you to keep your job without shortchanging your kid."[77]

I called a friend in London in the fall of 1983 to talk about a conference we both were attending. She was not in her office, so I called her at home—rather apologetically since I thought she might be home from work because she was ill. "Oh, don't worry," Judy said breezily. "I feel fine. I am at home because I just started my maternity leave. I actually won't be in the office until June, and I'm glad you called here because I wanted to talk to you about the paper I am writing for the manpower conference." My initial reaction was interesting. I couldn't figure out what she was talking about. Why, her baby wasn't due for another six weeks, and June was seven months away! Despite the fact that I had done a great deal of research on maternity policies, and I knew that Britain, in common with the rest of Europe, had long statutory maternity leaves, I still couldn't absorb the fact that someone I knew—a committed, driven professional—was taking an eight-month leave to have a baby and was not the slightest bit guilty or defensive about it. Rather, she took it completely for granted. As Judy said later in the conversation, "It's my right. It is every woman's right." She paused and said reflectively, "It's not even a big deal for employers. How many children am I going to have anyway? One or perhaps two. Fourteen months' leave is very little considering that I will spend forty-odd years in the labor force." My conversation with Judy made me realize how little help we American women expect to receive from public policy or from employers and how low our expectations are.[78]

Over the course of the last fifteen years most advanced industrial countries have undergone major economic and social changes which have resulted in a dramatic rise in the number of women working. In 1984, 63 percent of American women, 59 percent of British women, 77 percent of Swedish women, and 55 percent of French women were in the labor force.[79] In all these countries a variety of "push" factors have propelled women into paid employment. Rising divorce rates, inflation, stagnant real incomes, growing unemployment rates in male blue-collar occupations, and the heightened career aspirations of modern women—all are factors which have pushed women into employment. On the "pull" side of the equation is the changing occupational base of advanced countries as economic activity increasingly tilts toward services. Business services (which range from word processing to cleaning offices), health care services (in hospitals, nursing homes, and social welfare agencies), and food catering services have all expanded enormously in recent years in both Western Europe and North America. Two-thirds of the new jobs in these areas of the economy have gone to women. This has not happened by accident. As Marvin Harris has pointed out, women provide "a literate and docile" labor pool and are therefore desirable candidates for the information- and people-processing jobs thrown up by modern service industries.[80]

The Wage Gap

Women are joining the European work force at much the same rate and for much the same reasons as in America. But there is one major difference. In Europe working women are supported by an elaborate (and in most cases expanding) family support system which is a major factor behind their improved earning power. It is no coincidence that the country with the most developed benefits and services for working women—Sweden—is also the country with the smallest wage gap, while the country with the least developed benefits and services—the United States—is also the country with one of the largest wage gaps.

Working women in this country bear the full brunt of the double burden because the United States does less than any other advanced industrial nation to provide support systems for families. And it is not just the advanced welfare states of Scandinavia that provide maternity leave, family allowances, and child care. Traditional Catholic nations such as France and Italy and conservative governments such as that of Britain are all doing much more than we are to provide benefits and services for working mothers. Most American women who work are hard pressed in their attempts to raise a family while continuing to hold down a job. Compounding these difficulties is the high rate of divorce, which has substantially lessened male participation in child rearing. These facts are a root cause of the large and persistent wage gap in America.

Policy has floundered while economists have debated the reasons behind the wage gap. The liberal left of the discipline emphasizes discrimination, particularly the more subtle forms which segregate women in a pink-collar ghetto. Economists on the right wing of the discipline stress the ways in which family responsibilities limit the earning potential of women.

This debate is often acrimonious because the left and the right have very different views of policy. Liberals press for rigorous enforcement of antidiscrimination legislation while conservatives tend to say that since women "choose" to have families and "choose" to limit their careers, low female wages are a result of individual choice and should not be interfered with by government (a line of argument which is bolstered by right-wing faith in free markets).

But these two explanations of the wage gap are not antagonistic; they complement each other. Women's careers are heavily conditioned and constrained by marriage and child rearing. Precisely because of this conditioning and these constraints, many women opt for low-paying jobs in the pink-collar ghetto. Being an elementary-school teacher does provide a good fit with maternal responsibilities, and a secretarial position is easy to replace if you are expected to follow your husband to a new city. Remember Rose Barroso from Chapter Three? She found that being a school secretary jibed well with being a single parent because she finished work the same time as her son got out of school. She took this job despite the low pay because she did not want her child to become a latchkey kid.

On the policy front, both family support measures and antidiscrimination efforts are needed if women are to improve their earning power significantly. In the first place, family support systems are needed so that women can take better advantage of opportunities in the labor market. For the right-wing argument is a little silly. Of course, women "choose" to have families but they do not also "choose" to do all the child care or "prefer" low-paying jobs. If working women had job-protected maternity leave, subsidized day care, and flextime, they would then be better able to seek out high-paying jobs.

Secondly, since women do encounter discrimination in the workplace, vigorous antidiscrimination efforts should continue. Particularly important is the discrimination that ensures low wages for traditional jobs in the pink-collar ghetto.

The bottom line seems to be that working women need more than equal treatment. In the 1970s it was thought that all you had to do was outlaw discrimination and break down the barriers so that women could fully participate in the labor market. And these battles are clearly important in the struggle for equal opportunity. But swimming in the mainstream and taking your chance doesn't produce equality of result if you are picking up 75 to 85 percent of all household responsibilities. Equal treatment in the workplace has to be supplemented by family support systems if women are to improve their economic position.

Superwoman, eighties-style

*"So where do we spend this Thanksgiving? Your father's place, your
mother's place, my mother's place, or my father's place?"*

The modern family, The New Yorker, *November 1979*

The classical family of Western nostalgia: **Walking to Church,** *Norman Rockwell, 1953*

Everyone backs the ERA, New York City, November 1975

First ladies support the ERA, Houston, November 1977

Anti-ERA rally led by Phyllis Schlafly, the White House, Washington, D.C., September 1977

A lone anti-ERA demonstrator, August 1976

*Rosie the Riveter contributes strength and confidence to
the war effort, Norman Rockwell, 1943*

Wifely Duties, *Norman Rockwell, 1960*

5

CHILDREN:
THE OTHER VICTIMS

American women aren't the only ones squeezed between the devil and the deep blue sea; their children are right there with them. The breakdown of traditional marriage and the failure of women to achieve significant earning power in the labor market are factors which severely affect the well-being of today's children who are increasingly dependent on their mothers.

As a result of high rates of divorce, one-quarter of all children are being raised—and largely supported—by their mothers. Indeed, it is estimated that 40 to 50 percent of children born in the late 1970s will spend part of their youth in female-headed households. This is a large part of the reason why increasing numbers of children are growing up in poverty. Although women (particularly mothers) have entered the labor force in unprecedented numbers both as a cause and as a consequence of marital breakdown, few of them can ever expect to earn an adequate "family" wage. The average income of single mothers is $9,000 a year. In fact, the majority (57 percent) of female-headed households are poor. [1]

Children who grow up in poverty are at risk in all kinds of ways: Their health is poorer, their life expectancy is shorter, their educational prospects are dimmer, and they are more often the victims of abuse and neglect than children growing up in adequate material circumstances. Child abuse has increased right along with the children-in-poverty figures, and is perhaps the most painful illustration of the consequences of neglecting our children. In New York City a 1983 task force reported an increase of 140 percent in the incidence of child abuse between 1974 and 1982.[2] In all, forty-five states have seen an increase in reported cases, and in most of these states this increase has been accompanied by a cutback in child abuse prevention programs.

The net result: Today in child-centered America about 1 million children are abused and neglected, more than 44,000 are sexually abused, and 5,000 children die each year as a result of severe physical maltreatment.[3] Children are not doing well in contemporary America, and our public policies seem to be making the situation worse, not better. In 1983, 22 percent of all American children fell below the poverty line, as opposed to 14 percent just ten years ago.[4] Statistics such as these caused Representative Barney Frank (Democrat, Massachusetts) to remark that Ronald Reagan seems to believe that "life begins at conception and ends at birth."[5]

Early on the Sunday morning of September 26, 1982, as his brothers looked on and an upstairs neighbor heard his cries, Shawn Nicely was beaten to death. He was three years old. His killers were his own mother and father.

The Essex County medical examiner attributed Shawn's death to a combination of injuries, including internal hemorrhage, a laceration of the liver, and lacerations and contusions of other internal organs. The medical examiner also found a recent break in Shawn's right arm, one newly fractured rib, three previously fractured ribs, hemorrhaging on the tongue, bruised gums, a slight swelling of the brain from repeated blows to the head, and old scars on the buttocks, thigh, and upper back. All these injuries proved to be more than a small boy could take. At his death Shawn Nicely stood thirty-six inches tall and weighed thirty-one pounds.

Shawn's parents have since been convicted and jailed, his

mother, Renée Nicely, for murder, and his father, Allen Bass, for manslaughter. Behind the courtroom verdicts is the story of Shawn Nicely and his twenty-one-year-old parents, who began having their children at the age of fifteen and who never married. In jail for the murder of her second child, Renée Nicely wrote Shawn a poem:

> I wish I knew who he was because his life was so dim.
> Who gave him to me? And why did he suffer so?
> The things I used to do to him,
> Tell me why? I don't know.
>
> I wish he was alive again
> But he was freed from sin.
> He would have ended up like me,
> But now he's free.
> He reminded me of myself when I was small.
> I hated that life so, I would recall.
>
> Shawn, could it be, was given to me
> So I could forget the way it used to be.
> Don't feel bad, I had it hard just like you.
> Bad thing is: I lived, you didn't make it through.
> You're lucky, you know, God took you away.
> I wish it was me killed on that Sunday.

Renée Nicely's childhood was also marked by poverty, parental strife, and physical abuse. She dropped out of high school to have her first child, and by the time she was twenty she had three children under five. With no skills, no husband, and no access to child care she was trapped on welfare and existed on a meager AFDC income. Depressed, hopeless, and angry, she took out her frustrations on her most vulnerable child, perpetuating and deepening the grim cycle of poverty and abuse.[6]

If 1 million children are the victims of abuse and neglect, a great many more suffer the consequences of poor-quality child care. Hundreds of thousands of preschoolers and 2 to 5 million schoolchildren spend large chunks of their parents' working days either unsupervised or in highly inadequate care situations.[7] As a result, the physical and psychological well-being of these children is often imperiled. A point which was brought home in the summer of 1984, when sex abuse scandals at child-care centers across the country shocked the nation.

Today more than 50 percent of the mothers of preschool children work, in contrast with 12 percent in 1950, and *48 percent of mothers with children under one year of age now hold jobs,* up from 24 percent in 1970.[8] Since most of these women work out of economic necessity, they cannot afford to buy high-quality child care on the private market, where, when it is available, it can cost anything from $80 to $200 per child per week. Research shows that many mothers resort to a patchwork of informal arrangements, which typically involve relatives and friends as well as paid help. Many of these arrangements are inadequate for the child, and almost all of them produce a great deal of stress and anxiety for the parents.

Jeremy Morenzi is thirteen months old and despite his youth already leads a very complicated life. He has two older brothers, and in order to meet basic family expenses, both his parents work. His mother, Debbie, teaches in a nursery school in New York City, and it is she, who has a more flexible job than his father, who orchestrates Jeremy's day.

At 8:00 A.M. every weekday Debbie takes Jeremy to Mrs. Hopkins, an elderly neighbor, whom she pays $30 a week for "watching" Jeremy in the mornings. Mrs. Hopkins is sixty-eight years old and is a cautious, kindly woman who takes her duties seriously. Because she is too old and clumsy to run around after a toddler, she keeps Jeremy in an old crib with some toys rather than let him loose in the apartment. As Mrs. Hopkins explains it, "this way he cannot come to any harm." At noon Debbie picks Jeremy up, feeds him lunch, and takes him to school with her. She teaches a small group of four-year-olds in the afternoon and finds it possible to keep an eye on Jeremy at the same time. However, once again Jeremy is confined, this time in a playpen, so that he does not disrupt the activities of the older children. At 2:45 P.M. Debbie drops Jeremy off at either her friend Linda's house or her friend Nancy's house and catches a bus to her second job—teaching in an after-school program at a private school. Three days a week Jeremy spends these late-afternoon hours with Linda, and two days a week with Nancy, playing with the children of his mother's friends. At 5:45 P.M. Debbie picks him up on her way home. Debbie repays Linda and Nancy for this afternoon baby-sitting by looking after their children on the weekends.

Jeremy is too young to reflect on the pros and cons of his daily schedule, but his mother is unhappy, particularly about the mornings. "I know Mrs. Hopkins doesn't have the energy to look after a toddler properly," she says, "but what can you find for thirty dollars a week? At least I know that he is safe." Debbie believes that her choices are a direct result of family finances. Ideally she would have liked to take some time out of the labor market and look after Jeremy herself, but without her salary (small as it is) she and her husband could not cover rent, utilities, and food. For the same financial reasons Debbie feels that she is locked into second-rate child care; "the good child-care situations I know about cost between a hundred twenty-five and two hundred dollars a week, which is simply out of the question for us." Debbie, a thoughtful and well-educated woman, said that she couldn't understand why nothing had been done to provide affordable child care to ordinary working families like her own. Everyone she knew was tortured by this issue. "The women's movement seems to have won a lot of rights for gays, and this is well and good, but the women I talk to are in worse shape than they were ten years ago."[9]

Jeremy is luckier than many children: He has two parents. As we saw in Chapter Three, the United States has by far the highest divorce rate in the Western world. Of children born in the late 1970s 40 to 50 percent will live in single-parent homes for part of their childhood; in 1970 the figure was 11 percent.[10] The majority of children from "broken homes" live with their mother. Take Jenny.

It is 7:30 in the morning and Jenny* is getting her own breakfast. She climbs onto a kitchen stool in order to reach the cabinets.

*Pseudonym.

A Lesser Life

Carefully she takes the cornflakes down from a shelf, holding the box with both hands because one hand isn't big enough to fit around the container. As she stands at the counter spooning dry cereal into her mouth (the household has run out of milk), she makes herself a jam sandwich for lunch and stuffs it into her knapsack. Jenny would like to have breakfast with her mom, but according to this eight-year-old, "my mom doesn't have to be at her job until ten, and since she worked overtime last night, she needs to get as much sleep as she can."

Jenny tiptoes into her mother's bedroom to kiss her good-bye. Jenny's mother is taking a course at the local community college after work today, and she sleepily tells Jenny that she won't be home until late. "Just make yourself a sandwich, and I'll try to be home by your bedtime. If I can't make it, I will call you." Jenny is disappointed and a little scared at the prospect of spending another long afternoon and evening on her own, but she bites her lip and stops herself from complaining. She knows that her mother is desperately trying to stay abreast of the mortgage payments and the food bills, and scared as she is by dark, lonely evenings, she is even more frightened by the notion that they might have to sell their home. Jenny looks at the clock, realizes that it is getting late, and hurries out the door to catch the school bus.

Jenny didn't used to get up all alone. When her father was still home, he often got up with her and they had a big breakfast of cereal, eggs, and toast before he went to work and she went off to school. Her mother didn't work then and always packed her lunch for her the night before. More important, her mother was home when she got back from school and could be counted on to make a snack for her, help her with her homework, and generally keep her company. The best time of the day was when Daddy came home from work and the three of them had dinner together. But all that has changed now. Her father has moved out, and Jenny sees him erratically, maybe twice a month. Even the small amount of time she has with her father is strained because her parents are fighting about overdue child-support payments. If Jenny's father is gone, so is her mother much of the time.

Jenny is just one of many children of divorce who essentially lose both parents. The father has left; the mother, depressed and anxious about financial matters, is concentrating on making it in a tough labor market.[11]

The sorry but remediable truth about divorce is that much of the anxiety that follows it is centered on money. As one authority has put it, the most detrimental aspect of the absence of fathers from one-parent families headed by women is "not the lack of a male presence but the lack of a male income."[12] Two-thirds of divorced fathers cease to support their children, forcing mothers to assume the entire financial burden for both themselves and their children. This economic pressure, in turn, means that these mothers have less time for child care.

Children cannot successfully handle too many changes. In a widely respected study English psychiatrist Michael Rutter demonstrates that while children are able to absorb a single stress with no appreciable risk, as they are subject to additional stresses, such as moving, changing schools, mothers going out to work, and new (and often imperfect) child-care arrangements, the adverse effects of divorce begin to multiply.[13]

It was eighteen months since her parents' separation, and twelve-year-old Laura was not coping well. In her new school she was cutting classes and refusing to do her homework assignments. She was also increasingly hostile toward her father; just last Saturday she had stormed out of his house at lunchtime and refused to go back despite the fact that she was supposed to spend the entire day with him. Laura's mother was worried but also a little puzzled; after all, "Laura dealt with the immediate aftermath of the separation very constructively." A few weeks later Laura finally unburdened herself to a sympathetic teacher. As she saw things, it was not her parents' divorce that was upsetting her but rather the new apartment and the new school. In order to save money, her mother had sold the family home, and she and Laura had moved into a small apartment on the other side of town. Laura felt depressed and humiliated by her new situation. "I despise the tacky furniture and the tiny rooms, but most of all, I hate sharing a bedroom with my mother," she declared passionately. Laura also desperately missed her friends and her teachers in her old school; "I feel stranded. Since I am the only new kid in the seventh grade, no one will ever want to know me." Laura blamed her father for her newly reduced circumstances and was very angry with him: "He has lots of money. Why he just spent Christmas in Vermont skiing. Mom and I, on the other hand, have to pinch and scrape and live in this mean little apartment."[14]

If mothers had more adequate incomes after divorce, many of these negative changes could be avoided. Part of the problem is the nonpayment of child support by divorced fathers. Only a third of all fathers liable for child support comply with the terms of the awards, and a third pay nothing at all.[15] But even more important is the low earning power of working women. In 1984 one quarter of working women, when working full-time, earned less than $10,000 a year.[16] For such women getting a job is not a route out of poverty. As the Catholic bishops described the situation in late 1984, "hundreds of thousands of women both hold fulltime jobs and are still poor."[17]

The public provision of high-quality and affordable care emerges as central to any solution to the problems facing children whether these problems involve parental abuse, divorce, or working mothers. Experts agree that if poor parents had ready access to free day care, there would be a dramatic reduction in child abuse with its terrible toll. Child deaths associated with abuse fall off dramatically after age six, indicating that troubled parents can do better by their children once the children are out of the home for part of the day. The New York City task force cited earlier in this chapter found that 60 percent of fatalities arising from child abuse occur among children less than two years of age.[18] In a similar, though less chilling, vein, the negative repercussions of divorce for children would be mitigated by access to high-quality subsidized child care. The question of how to care for her children often constitutes *the* major unresolved problem for a newly single mother, and inadequate alternative care often prevents her from earning enough money to put the household back on its feet.

Karen, a black divorced mother I interviewed, recalled with horror the years when her two children were preschoolers. "When

George left me, the kids were eighteen months and three years old. I tried so hard to hold a job down, not only for the money but because I liked my work as a legal secretary, and it was a way of rebuilding my self-respect after the separation." Despite her determination, Karen was fired from three jobs—for arriving late, for absenteeism, and for bringing her youngest to work with her on two occasions. The basic problem was that her baby-sitting arrangements kept breaking down. "I lived in Brooklyn at that time, and I couldn't find day care. I wasn't eligible for subsidized care since I was working, and I could not afford the private day-care centers." Karen resorted to a multiple arrangement package comprising her sister-in-law (who covered the mornings) and a neighbor and local teenager (who split the afternoons). Karen paid a small wage to the neighbor and the teenager but repaid her sister-in-law in kind by looking after her two-year-old nephew on the weekends. But Karen's child-care package was subject to recurrent crises. Her sister-in-law moved away and left her with no one to take care of the baby in the mornings (this was the point at which she tried taking her baby to work), the neighbor was always getting sick, and Karen had to fire the teenager for negligence: The three-year-old fell out of the first-floor window while she was baby-sitting. Karen will never forget the phone call she got at work from the hospital emergency room saying that her child had had an accident; fortunately it turned out not to be very serious. After the accident Karen gave up her struggle and went on welfare until her youngest was old enough for public kindergarten. "It was the only way to be sure that my kids were safe."[19]

But the day-care problem is obviously not limited to single mothers. *All* working mothers, even if they have husbands and decent salaries, need better access to quality child care if the next generation is not to be shortchanged. The United States has a large deficit in child-care facilities at *every* economic level. As Annice Probst, executive director of the Preschool Association in New York, has put it, "The system simply fails many people. There is insufficient care for low-income families, there are middle-income families who have trouble paying the full cost of care, and there is a shortage of quality centers at any price."[20]

It is extremely difficult to obtain an accurate picture of child care in America because there is no systematic collection of data at the national level. However, experts in the field are agreed that hundreds of thousands of preschool children spend the working day in poor-quality care, and somewhere between 2 and 5 million schoolchildren ages six through thirteen are without adult supervision for several hours each day because both parents are working.[21] The child-care deficit is most severe for infants and toddlers. This is because mothers of very young children have entered the labor force at a particularly rapid rate in recent years. Of mothers with children under one year of age, 48 percent now hold jobs, and since a minority of these women are entitled to maternity leave, many of them need to find substitute care for their children from a very early age.

For young children (six weeks to three years) there are four types of care in general use. In the first place, there are family day-care homes which account for more than 40 percent of the child care used by employed mothers.[22] Family day care generally comprises informal arrangements whereby a neighborhood woman cares for several children in her own home. Only a small proportion of this kind of care is licensed—estimates are in the 10 percent range—and a very small number of family day-care plans are subsidized by the government.[23] The cost of family day care ranges from $40 to $70 per week per child, and the standard of care is very uneven. However, this is the only kind of care most parents can afford.

Remember Carmen Santos from Chapter Four? Carmen is a medical secretary and works for a large teaching hospital in New York City. She had, when I interviewed her, a twenty-one-month-old child and was five months pregnant with her second. Carmen went back to work eight months after the birth of her first child, placing the baby with a family caretaker—a neighbor who looked after seven children in her own home. Carmen quickly became disillusioned with this arrangement. When she picked up her son, she often found him propped up in an infant seat in front of a television set, hungry and dirty. After a desperate search Carmen found another child minder who takes in fewer children and seems to have higher standards of care. Unfortunately the new person lives thirty minutes away from Carmen's home and forty-five minutes away from her place of work. This considerably lengthens Carmen's working day, but she thinks that it is well worth the extra commute to get a better situation for her baby. Carmen investigated other options but found that the only local day-care center was full and that a private baby-sitter would have been three times as expensive as informal family care—well beyond her budget. As it is, the $55 per week she pays the child minder consumes a third of her take-home pay. Carmen continues to be worried about the quality of care provided by the child minder. Her recurrent nightmare is that her son will be involved in a bad accident. "After all, none of these women are licensed or have any training, and who knows what kind of neglect my child might be exposed to."[24]

Secondly, there are day-care centers, which provide approximately 10 percent of the child care used by working mothers. Half these centers cater to poor, usually single-parent families and are publicly subsidized. These have been severely affected by the Reagan budget cuts. Title XX funding, which supports these day-care centers, has been cut by 21 percent since 1980.[25] The other half are private day-care centers, which supply an upper-middle-class market and can cost anywhere from $80 to $200 per week per child.

For-profit child-care chains, with branches all over the country, have grown significantly in the last year or so. For example, Kinder-Care Learning Centers, Inc., which is the largest, now has 850 centers in forty states.[26] These establishments cater to an affluent clientele (middle-class, professional) and are aggressive commercial enterprises. They have been criticized for being more concerned with making money than with the quality of the care they provide. It does seem that in the interests of keeping costs down these child-care chains pay their staff such low wages (their teachers are paid, on average, $7,000 per year) that there is a very high rate of labor turnover, which cannot be beneficial for the children in their care. According to a report of the National Council of Jewish Women, one-half of all for-profit preschools provide inadequate care, and as a group they are less good than nonprofit centers.[27]

Thirdly, some professional and upper-middle-class women (perhaps 5 percent of all working women) choose to employ full-time baby-sitters in their own homes. This arrangement costs between $120 and $250 per week. Although this kind of money is high for child care, it certainly isn't high as a wage, which is why private baby-sitters are often new immigrants with few skills and little education.

Finally, there are the packages of multiple informal arrangements, where parents piece together a mixture of their own time, relatives' time, neighbors' time, and paid help to provide enough child care to get through the working day. Many working parents resort to this desperate juggling act when they cannot find high-quality day care or, more usually, when they simply cannot afford it. Approximately a third of all children under three with working parents are cared for in such a package. Remember the nursery-school teacher Debbie and her thirteen-month-old son, Jeremy, whom we met at the beginning of this chapter? Her package of child-care arrangements comprised Mrs. Hopkins (paid help), herself, and Linda and Nancy (neighbors). The disadvantages of this kind of solution are that the child is subject to many different caretakers, the quality of care is erratic, and juggling all these arrangements is always very stressful for the parents concerned, especially since they can easily break down. Karen, the single mother we described earlier, was clearly not able to make her package work and was forced to give up her job and go on welfare until her children were old enough to attend school. The advantage of packaged arrangements is, of course, that the cost is low (in Debbie's case $30 per week for Mrs. Hopkins; in Karen's case $40 per week split between the teenager and the neighbor), and it is therefore the only feasible solution for many working parents. In her survey research in Westchester County, Sheila Kamerman found that a package comprising relatives, neighbors, and paid help was the most common child-care solution. "More than half of the preschool children experience 2 or more types of care each week and half of these are exposed to 3 or 4 types of care during a routine week."[28] All this adds up to a great deal of strain for parents and children.

A variation on the multiple arrangement package occurs when parents manage without any paid help by working different shifts and relying on relatives to fill in the gaps.

Eileen is a registered nurse currently working twenty-four to thirty-six hours a week on private duty. When I interviewed Eileen, her daughter was twenty-two months old. Prior to the birth of her child Eileen was working in a large teaching hospital. She was entitled to a three-month leave of absence but, in the event, failed to go back to her job because she was unable to find affordable child care despite an intensive search. Eileen needed to work; her income was essential to maintain an adequate family standard of living. She therefore began private-duty nursing, working nights and weekends. By coordinating her hours with her husband's shifts and her mother's and mother-in-law's days off from work, she always had a family member available to look after the baby. From Eileen's perspective, this family package is far from ideal: The baby rarely sees her parents together, the parents rarely see each other, and sometimes Eileen doesn't see her baby for a three-day stretch as the child is left at one or the other of the grandmothers' houses for a long weekend while the parents cope with their shift work. The other problem is that these arrangements will probably limit their family to one child. As Eileen puts it, "none of us could deal with this crazy schedule if there were more than one [child]."[29]

Quality child care for three- to five-year-old children is slightly easier to find, but only if you have a high enough income to pay for both nursery schooling and considerable additional baby-sitting. Nursery school enrollment has doubled over the last decade, and 35 percent of three- and four-year-olds now attend nursery school.[30] Unhappily for low-income working parents, more than 90 percent of nursery schools are private, and tuition costs range from $1,500 to $3,000 per year. Another severe disadvantage is that most of these schools are in session for only three hours a day, a schedule which does not begin to cover normal working hours. For women with jobs, nursery school has to be part of a more complicated and more expensive package.

Another problem is that nursery schools remain geared to enriching the development of the children of at-home mothers, and many stubbornly refuse to adapt their schedules so as to also provide convenient child care for modern working parents. The tradition of regarding the nursery school as a positive experience and day care as an unpleasant necessity dies hard. We have a segregated system: (insufficient) public day care for low-income families, private part-time nursery schools for the affluent, and "potluck for those families who fall into neither category."[31] We still tend to think of day care as a cheap custodial operation for the poor, not to be confused (or combined) with education.

When my son, David, started nursery school in the fall of 1983, his schedule was as follows:

Week 1.	School hours.	9:00 A.M. to 10:00 A.M.
Week 2.	School hours.	10:00 A.M. to 11:30 A.M.
Week 3.	School hours.	9:00 A.M. to 11:00 A.M.
Week 4.	School hours.	9:00 A.M. to 12:00 noon

In short, it took this particular nursery school almost a month to work up to the full program of three hours a day. This schedule has been in place for twenty years and is based on the premise that since nursery school is the first time the child and the mother are separated, it is necessary to ease them into the school routine very gradually. This assumption is out of date. Two-thirds of the mothers of children in David's class worked, and all the easing-in process did was create enormous problems for us working parents as we struggled to put together a patchwork of extra baby-sitting in the morning hours. David, who at age three was an old hand at group care situations, couldn't understand why he was being sent home so early.

I did ask the school for one concession: Could we drop our child off a little early between 8:30 and 8:45 A.M.? This would enable either me or my husband to bring David to school before going to work. The school administrator I talked to dismissed this suggestion out of hand, telling me condescendingly that "this nursery school organizes its program for the benefit of the children, not of the parents." It is obviously to the child's advantage to be taken to school by a parent rather than by a casual baby-sitter hired for the purpose of getting a child to school precisely at 9:00 A.M. It is also extremely nice for the parent to be able to take a child to his or her first school. What this reaction really shows is how deeply our schools disapprove of working mothers—despite their numerical dominance!—so much so that they make it gratuitously difficult to match school schedules with the working day.

Over the last two years I have kept a log of when the schools of my children have requested my presence—for conferences, for special assemblies, for birthday celebrations—and the favorite time slots are 10:45 A.M. and 2:30 P.M. It is hard to think of less convenient times for a working mother (or father) to take a couple of hours out of the office.

Because of the expense of nursery schools and the short duration of the nursery-school day, many working mothers (almost half) keep their children in family care until they are old enough to go to public school (either kindergarten or first grade).[32] There has been a significant (and welcome) expansion in public kindergarten over the last few years, but since most kindergartens are half day, they pose many of the same scheduling problems for working parents as nursery schools. This leads us into the whole question of the mesh between our schooling system and the world of work.

In 1983 the National Commission for Excellence in Education released its now-famous report on the American educational system entitled *Nation at Risk*. Part of the explanation given in this report of why the United States is witnessing "a rising tide of mediocrity" in education is the fact that American children spend so little time in school; our school year is about 25 percent shorter than that typical of other advanced countries. In Britain and other industrial countries it is not unusual for high school students to spend eight hours in school 220 days per year. "In the US by contrast the typical school day lasts 6 hours and the school year 180 days."[33] In the 1950s and 1960s the nation probably didn't suffer too much from this abbreviated school year. After all, mothers were available to supervise homework, to chauffeur children to enriching after-school activities, and to look after children during the long school vacations.

Today's working parents who think that they have solved their child-care problems because Bobby and Jane are finally old enough for public school are faced with a decade of trying to deal with those hours before and after school (7:30 A.M. to 8:30 A.M., 3:30 P.M. to 6:00 P.M.), those nine to twelve weeks of vacation in the summer time, and other sundry holidays. No one knows for sure how working parents cope with their children over this long haul, but only a tiny fraction of schools offer after-school or before-school programs. It is estimated that between 2 and 5 million schoolchildren ages six through thirteen are latchkey kids—that is, they return home every day to empty houses because both parents are working.[34] Sometimes they spend their time with friends or siblings, but the fact is they are without adult supervision for several hours each working day. In a recent survey of working parents 23 percent admitted that they regularly left their children alone.[35]

Many children find the experience of being latchkey kids negative—full of fear, loneliness, and conflict. According to one study, approximately 25 percent of latchkey children have experienced serious problems coping with self-care. "Fear levels were high enough to cause hiding, sleeplessness and nightmares. Isolation was intense enough to cause depression or strong feelings of rejection. The responsibility placed on them was overwhelming enough to cause bitterness, resentment and anger."[36]

Tracy grew up in Danbury, Connecticut, with her parents and sister. She lived in a nice house in a neighborhood considered safe. At age five, when she started school, her mother returned to work. Tracy was expected to care for herself from the time she arrived home from school at 3:15 P.M. until her mother arrived at 5:30 P.M. Tracy's sister, who was seven years older than she, went to a private school across town and arrived home after their mother.

On the face of it, Tracy's experience was uneventful. During the thirteen years she had to care for herself there was never any reason for her to call the police or even a neighbor for that matter. She was well behaved and followed her mother's rules. But although Tracy was physically safe, she had a difficult time dealing with the experience. "I felt shortchanged. Mom cared enough to stay home when my sister was little, but she didn't care enough to stay home with me."

Tracy was also very frightened staying alone. "The house seemed so large and was full of shadows in the late afternoon. There were lots of small, unexplained noises, and I would turn on the TV to block them out." Because she was so afraid, Tracy spent a great deal of time playing in closets, where she felt safe. Even though her parents were home in the evening, Tracy was often too frightened to go to sleep at night and suffered from insomnia and nightmares.[37]

Our educational system makes life extremely difficult for working parents. No attempt is made to mesh school hours with work hours, and many school administrators either ignore or are actively hostile to the constraints that jobs impose on mothers. It would be a relatively simple process to make a few changes in the educational calendar. For example, lengthening the school year and the school day would considerably ameliorate the burdens of working parents. It would also enhance the lives of their children. More hours of schooling would both upgrade educational performance and ensure that children were left unattended for fewer hours of the week.

In the late 1960s and early 1970s there was a major legislative push to provide day care and preschool for America's children. It was supported by, among others, the American Federation of Teachers, led by Albert Shanker, who thought that both day care and preschool should be undertaken by the public school system. As Shanker saw it, the declining birthrate left the country filled with underutilized school buildings and qualified teachers without jobs. It therefore made a lot of sense to put these resources to work in providing desperately needed child care.[38] Unfortunately the Comprehensive Child Development Act of 1971 was vetoed by President Richard Nixon, and the family services bill of 1975 failed to get through Congress. Shanker's ideas were never realized.

Thus the world of work and the educational system remain particularly incompatible in America. Children spend 25 percent fewer hours in school than their European counterparts, while employed adults have much shorter vacations than European workers. Nations such as France and Sweden provide their workers with five weeks of paid vacation plus public holidays each year, while West German workers average more than four weeks off a year. Indeed, among the member countries of the EEC the standard minimum vacation is four weeks.[39] In America, on the other hand, workers average two weeks of vacation plus holidays each year, and about 20 percent of workers (many of them women) have no right to paid vacation.

How did this situation come about? Limited vacation time in the United States seems to be a function of our rigorous work ethic and our free-market system, which has little tolerance for social benefits or for state interference in private-sector activities. Originally the school year in the United States was developed on an agricultural calendar when America was largely a nation of farmers. As the country became more urban, families (or, more precisely, mothers) were expected to span the gap between the work and the school day, filling in with supervised play, piano lessons, Little League practice, Boy Scouts, etc. This arrangement, which places a considerable educational burden on mothers, works only when women are able and willing to stay out of the labor force in large numbers. It obviously is not working today. The gap between the school and the work day—a gap which is much wider in America than in Europe—merely serves to increase the miseries of millions of latchkey kids.

Europe also has an agrarian past (indeed, a quarter of the French and the Italian populations still work on the land), but in modern times education has been defined by both governments and citizens as a serious business to be undertaken by professionals in the schools, not by amateurs at home. This approach has been reinforced by the fact that European countries have not been as affluent as the United States and therefore have not been able to afford to keep so many young people at school until their mid-twenties. Thus there is a more rigorous approach to education at the primary and secondary levels which requires long hours of schooling.

But America is no longer top dog in the economic universe. Several European countries have higher per capita incomes than the United States, and this country can no longer afford to take

Children: The Other Victims

such a haphazard approach to education. This is especially true since a critical component of our system supplied by at-home mothers is much less available now than in the past.

What are other advanced industrial nations doing to meet the needs of working parents and their children? In most of these countries, even the most progressive, there is a lag between the demand for and the supply of public child-care facilities. This is because women have entered the labor force at an extremely rapid rate in recent years, just as they have in America. It has been hard for governments to keep pace with the changing social and economic realities. However, the services that are in existence are considerably more elaborate than those available here. And many European governments are committed to trying to catch up with demand as quickly as possible—which is a good deal more than can be said for the United States.

We met Susan Arnbom in Chapter Four. Susan works as a secretary in Stockholm, Sweden. She is also the mother of three children ages seven, three, and two. During the working day Susan's eldest child, Eric, is in public school, which gets out at 4:00 P.M.; he then attends an after-school program at the same school. The younger two are enrolled in a government-sponsored day-care center. The fee for this program is income-adjusted, and Susan pays the same for her two children as she would for one. The day-care center is located in the apartment complex where Susan and her family live and is open from 7:00 A.M. to 6:00 P.M. The center has an enrollment of twelve children, who are supervised by four adults. The facilities are bright, airy, and well equipped.[40]

Approximately one-third of all children under seven years old in Sweden are in some form of public child care.[41] The options range from municipal day-care mothers (who care for three to four children in their homes and are paid for and licensed by the municipalities) to various types of day-care centers. A further third of Swedish children under seven are cared for privately, most commonly by unlicensed day-care mothers who take children into their own homes. Priority in allocating public day-care places is given to single mothers and low-income families.[42]

Child care in public day-care centers is of very high quality.

The centers are generally open ten to twelve hours a day five days a week. Costs are paid by the federal government (50 percent), municipal government (40 percent), and parental fees (10 percent). Fees are charged on an income-related basis; e.g., a parent earning $500 a month or less may leave a child nine hours a day five days a week for as little as $16 a month, while parents earning $1,325 or more a month would pay $122. This fee includes three hot meals a day plus snacks.[43]

In France out-of-home child care is taken for granted partly because of the long history group care has in this nation; the first child-care centers were started in the early nineteenth century. In modern times the *écoles maternelles* (free public nursery schools) have been accepted as a given since the 1950s and have enrolled nearly all three- to six-year-olds ever since that time. Since these preschools have short hours, *Haltes-garderies* (part-time day-care centers) have been set up to make up the difference in hours between the preschool day and the average work day. Parents can pay for meals and supplemental care at these centers, which are often attached to the *écoles maternelles.*

Crèches, or day nurseries, care for children six months to three years. While the actual cost of crèche care per child is about $100 a week, parents pay on an income-adjusted basis, and parental fees can range anywhere from $15 to $50 a week. The remainder is paid for from a variety of municipal and national funds. The crèches are generally open from 7:00 A.M. to 7:00 P.M. five days a week. The quality of care is excellent, and there are very long waiting lists for places. Some of the excess demand is filled by publicly licensed *nourrices,* who charge approximately the same as the crèche, or else by private *nourrices,* who can be very much more expensive. In addition, grandmothers still play an important child-care role in France.

In 1980 the French Ministry of Education estimated that 35 percent of two-year-olds, 90 percent of three-year-olds, and 100 percent of four-, five-, and six-year-olds were enrolled in crèches and in the public preschools.[44]

In Italy the public provision of day care and preschool is a recent development. However, by 1980 nearly 70 percent of three- to six-year-olds were attending nursery schools.[45] Most of these are run by private nonprofit and church organizations, although there are increasing numbers of public nursery schools. Public preschools are free; private preschools charge income-related fees, which are kept low through large government subsidies.

Day nurseries for under threes are also predominantly privately run. Free state-run nurseries are increasingly available and now serve 10 to 25 percent of this age-group. Relatives also continue to play an important child-care role in Italy.[46]

Most advanced industrial countries (welfare states such as Sweden and Denmark, traditional Catholic countries such as France and Italy) have made considerable progress toward providing public or publicly funded child care. This has been done to ease the lot of working parents, primarily mothers, but it has also been done to ensure their nation's future prosperity. For example, by the end of the 1970s France was spending more than 4 percent of its gross national product on subsidies to preschool children, not because French society is gung ho about women's rights (France, in fact, is very traditional in its attitudes toward women) but because French policy makers consider these expenditures a good investment in the nation's future.[47] The French logic is impeccable: If government neglects the needs of two- and three-year-olds, it is likely to create expensive problems later; after all, it is possible to pour all kinds of public money down the drain at the primary- and secondary-school levels if preschoolers are allowed to suffer. Many governments recognize that the quality of their human resources is directly linked to facilitating a decent start in life for children. Only America is decreasing public support for children. Since 1980 an additional 3 million children have fallen into poverty, 700,000 poor children have been struck from the Medicaid rolls, and 200,000 have lost their day-care subsidies.[48]

There is a substantial body of research (ironically, much of it undertaken in the United States) demonstrating that "more than half of intelligence measured at age 17 develops before age 5."[49] The preschool years are the ones in which general learning abilities develop more rapidly than at any other period. According to psychologist Benjamin Bloom, "failure to develop appropriate achievement and learning in these years is likely to lead to continued failure throughout the remainder of the individual's school career."[50] Reinforcing this viewpoint is the work of Martin Deutsch, which shows that higher intelligence scores are found among children who have preschool experience compared to those whose initial contact with school was in first grade.[51] Finally, the research of Katrina de Hirsch demonstrates that many "intelligent but educationally disabled children ... would not have required help had their difficulties been recognized at early ages. . . . Early identification would have obviated the need for later remedial measures."[52]

Some of the most persuasive evidence of the positive effects of early-childhood education comes from the Perry Preschool Project of Ypsilanti, Michigan. This program began in the 1960s and closely tracked the lives of 123 impoverished black children, half of whom were given one to two years of high-quality preschool education. Researchers have found that the children with the preschool experience, now in their late teens, stay in school longer, have better earnings prospects, are less involved in crime, and get pregnant less often than their peers who began school later. Their lives appear to have been changed for the better, and so has their community, in terms of lower crime rates, lower expenditures for special education, welfare, and criminal justice proceedings, and higher tax revenues from the participants' earnings. The administrators of the Ypsilanti project took the unusual step of trying to calculate the net rate of return of their program and estimated that the benefits of the program amounted to seven times the cost.[53]

The results are also in from a larger project. Between 1961 and 1970, 750 black children in New York City took part in early-education programs. They were enrolled at the age of four and continued to receive enrichment classes through the third grade. A recent follow-up study shows that half those in the enriched group have obtained jobs (double the proportion for a comparison group), and about 60 percent have graduated from high school (in contrast with 40 percent for the comparison group).[54] It seems that early-childhood education pays off for society by producing more productive citizens and preventing major public-welfare expenditures in later years.

Children: The Other Victims

Mayor Ed Koch was so impressed by the results of these projects that he is proposing a citywide prekindergarten program to be phased in, starting in September 1986. "This program will be costly," said Koch in his 1985 State of the City address, "But dropouts cost even more in both human and financial terms, and the expense lasts a lifetime. Let's get our young people on the right track and keep them there."[55]

Children have always been our collective future, but this statement is particularly true today, when the economic facts of life make us particularly vulnerable to a shortfall in the quality of our human resources. The U.S. economy is moving into an era of intense international competition. In the latter half of the 1980s and in the 1990s maintaining our domestic and international markets in the face of fierce competition from low-cost producers (Japan, South Korea, Brazil, Mexico) is going to become ever more difficult. We have no chance of keeping our competitive edge (let alone bettering it) without increasing both our rate of productivity growth and the quality of the products we make. Both these goals are critically dependent on the caliber of the next generation of workers. America is not doing well on this front.

The deterioration in our educational system is such that the National Commission for Excellence in Education was prompted to comment that "if an unfriendly foreign power had attempted to impose on America the mediocre educational performance that exists today, we might well have viewed it as an act of war."[56] Today 13 percent of our seventeen-year-olds are functionally illiterate, and the average achievement of high school students on most standardized tests is lower than it was twenty-five years ago.[57] All this has extremely negative implications for the quality of our future labor force. However, it is difficult to blame all these problems on a deterioration in the formal educational system. On the contrary, in recent years there has been a sharp rise in inputs to the system, teacher-pupil ratios have risen, and there has been an even sharper rise in real expenditures per child (5 percent a year during the 1960s and 1970s).[58] Perhaps our schools have been failing our children not because they have lacked resources but because they are not making up for the deficit on the home front! Half of all preschool children in this country are in some

131

type of out-of-home care because their mothers are working, and at least 50 percent of these children (one-quarter of the total) are in highly inadequate care situations, which compromise their chances for achievement—at school and ultimately in the labor market. The idea of investing in young people is not foreign to this country—America spends more public money per capita on education than many Western European countries[59]—but to date we have had a blind spot with regard to day care and preschool and find it difficult to see that investing in child care and child health may be as important as investing in high school and college.

The official position of the Reagan administration is that child care is the responsibility of the family and the private sector, that government has no business "interfering" with child rearing. Well, as we have seen, the family is having a hard time coping. As for the private sector, despite some tax incentives that make child-care benefits more attractive, American businesses have done little to demonstrate that they are willing to play a central role in filling the child-care vacuum. In a 1983 survey of 374 companies conducted by Catalyst (a women's advocacy organization), only 1 percent reported having on-site child care, and a further 1 percent provided some type of subsidy for child care.[60] More recently, child-care expert Dana Friedman estimated that fewer than 550 employers nationwide have on-site child-care centers.[61] Half these centers are at hospitals; the others tend to be in large corporations specializing in high-technology products. Both these sectors report difficulty in recruiting skilled women, and the day-care programs are obviously intended as a lure for them.

There seems to be far more talk than action on the child-care front by corporations. And some corporations don't even indulge in the talk. For instance, in the food industry, which is one of the largest employers of women in the United States, management does not believe that a company should know or even ask about its employees' child-care arrangements. According to one analyst, "there is no point in even discussing employer assisted child care options with these employers."[62] Since most women work in unskilled, low-paid sectors of the economy (like the food industry) and are easily replaced, their employers have little incentive to provide for their needs. As one might predict, it is mostly those companies desiring to recruit qualified women that actually commit resources to child care.

It is time the U.S. government recognized the fact that it makes economic as well as humanitarian sense to invest in the health and well-being of small children. Only then is a nation able to make the most of its chief asset, people. Neglecting children triggers direct costs: welfare charges, hospital charges, and court and imprisonment charges. In recent years we have become penny-wise and dollar-foolish, saving a few dollars on food subsidies for pregnant poor women and then spending $40,000 to $100,000 of public money to care for each underweight preemie that is born to many of these same women.[63] But besides incurring these direct costs, by neglecting our children we are compromising the educational standards and future productivity of our nation. After all, America faces an even bigger challenge in this sphere than Western Europe does. Because our divorce rate is enormously high, our family structure is much weaker than that typical of many Western European nations, and still, we continue to do so much less for our children. If our government cares about America's children or about the long-term economic health of the country, massive changes need to be made in our child-care policies.

One political deterrent any president faces is that children do not vote, and it needs courage and vision for a politician to respond to the needs of a constituency that is so powerless in the political arena. Back in 1969 Richard Nixon declared before Congress that "so crucial is the matter of early growth that we must make a national commitment to providing all American children an opportunity for healthful and stimulating development."[64] However, Nixon quickly discovered that there was precious little political capital to be made out of supporting child care, and in 1971 he vetoed the Comprehensive Child Development Act, the only such act to pass Congress in the postwar period.

While children don't vote, their mothers and fathers do. It is time that parents realized that they have a legitimate claim on government as far as programs for their children are concerned and that they organize to press this claim. It is no secret that elderly people have considerably improved their economic position in recent years because they have organized and used their collective vote to win concessions from politicians. The beleaguered parents of America should do the same. Providing for the needs of our children should be part of our national agenda.

It is strange that as a nation we do much more for our senior citizens than we do for our children despite the fact that our future depends on these children. In 1983 there were "nearly four times as many children living beneath the official poverty line as there were senior citizens in such need."[65] It is also true that in recent federal budgets elderly people have received four times as much money (mainly through Social Security and Medicare) as children.[66] Isn't it time we reordered our priorities? One quarter of the spending on the elderly goes to households with incomes over $30,000 per year. It may well be that Shawn Nicely and Jeremy Morenzi need help more urgently than middle-class senior citizens.

In May of 1985 President Reagan spoke in eloquent terms of his deep regard for American family life: "I believe the worth of any economic policy must be measured by the strength of its commitment to American families, the bedrock of our society. . . . There is no cultural institution as enobling as family life. And there is no superior, indeed, no equal means to rear the young."[67] Let our President make good on this commitment to families with young children.

When we think of childhood, our mental images rarely include physical abuse, latchkey children, or single parenthood. Our culture has been called child-centered, and our poets and novelists have seen childhood as a paradise, a time of innocent family fun. John Betjeman describes it as "the peace before the dreadful daylight starts of unkept promises and broken hearts."[68] Many of our classic storybooks begin, as *The Railway Children* begins, with a description of an ideal family situation:

> They were just ordinary suburban children, and they
> lived with their Father and Mother in an ordinary red-

brick-fronted house, with colored glass in the front door, a tiled passage that was called a hall, a bath-room with hot and cold water, electric bells, french windows, and a good deal of white paint, and "every modern convenience."

Mother was almost always there, ready to play with the children, and read to them and help them to do their home-lessons. Besides this she used to write stories for them while they were at school . . . and she always made up funny pieces of poetry for their birthdays and for other great occasions, such as the christening of the new kitten, or the refurnishing of the doll's house, or the time when they were getting over the mumps.

These three lucky children always had everything they needed: pretty clothes, good fires, a lovely nursery with heaps of toys, and a Mother Goose wall-paper. . . . They also had a Father who was just perfect—never cross, never unjust, and always ready for a game.[69]

For many of us this kind of family is no more than a contemporary dream. Way back in the 1950s, half of all American families comprised a breadwinning husband, a dependent homemaking wife, and two or more children. Today this "classical family of Western nostalgia"[70] constitutes a mere 6 percent of the population.[71] We are more likely to see it pictured on a box of cornflakes than in our own lives. Yet our public policies still assume that children grow up in such families and have no unmet needs.

PART B

❦

The Women's Movement

American women are caught between the devil and the deep blue sea. They can no longer rely on marriage to provide financial security for themselves or their children, and at the same time they have failed to acquire significant earning power in the labor market. The consequences of this double squeeze are exacerbated by our nation's staggering dearth of family support structures.

The major problem occurs when women with the roles of mother and worker attempt to combine them, as more of them increasingly have to do. It was all very pleasant being an American "supermom" when all the traditional props were in place (breadwinning husband, suburban ranch house, two kids, dog, and station wagon), and it is now possible to become a successful career woman, provided one has the right educational credentials, has stayed on track, and has been sensible enough not to have children. But putting these roles together is an invitation to failure.

Many of us try, feeling, as I did in the mid-1970s, that in this brave new world women as well as men should be able to find fulfillment in both love and work. And most of us fail. For a few privileged women such as myself, failure may not be dramatic. Rather, it surfaces in painful trade-offs, underachievement, and hundreds of small, disappointing compromises. But for many women failure can, all too easily, result in hard, grinding poverty. The mechanism is simple. One's marriage breaks up—or one's husband is laid off—and all those traditional props disintegrate. Women are left earning a lousy wage in a highly inequitable job market with no adequate way of looking after their children.

But what of the women's movement? We have just gone through more than a decade of militant feminism. Why has this not succeeded in upgrading the economic conditions of women's lives?

The answer is that American feminists have emphasized formal equality and have encouraged women to enter the world of work on male terms. Modern liberated women are supposed to clone the male competitive model, even to the extent of wearing gray flannel suits and little string ties. The last thing most American feminists would admit is that working mothers might just need special concessions to give them a shot at equal opportunity. Compare this to Sweden, where Anna-Greta Leijon, the current minister of labor, believes that "women need a plethora of special benefits and services in order to compete on an equal basis with men in the labor market."

Forty years ago Eleanor Roosevelt opposed the ERA not because she espoused a traditional role for women, but because she thought that this legislation might make it more difficult to create the support structures women need to carry their double burden in the home and in the workplace. It is hard to know whether she was right because to date we have neither the ERA nor the support structures.

6

IMAGE AND REALITY

Americans are condescendingly sure that women in this country are much better off than women elsewhere.

In a *New York Times* Op-Ed piece in December 1983 American writer Kati Marton smugly reports:

> It's good to be home. After nearly six years abroad, I am struck first of all by what a good time it is to be a woman in America. Speak not to me of a gender gap. I have lived for the past four years in London. I now feel a surge of new life akin perhaps to what a ghetto child might experience contemplating an endless expanse of green space. . . .
>
> The country I have just left is light years away from all of this. Life for a woman in Britain can be an energy-sapping experience.[1]

Energy-sapping or not, if you are interested in increasing your earning power or trying to have a child while working, British women are in better shape than their American sisters.

New York Times correspondent R. W. Apple, back in the States after many years overseas, is astonished by American women "whose role has changed out of all recognition in a single decade." He confesses to being gripped "by the sight of female forest rangers, female bulldozer operators and female partners in hundreds of law firms all across the country."[2] Apple obviously has not read the studies which document how and why women are not making partner in the law firms across the country.

These New World women, who, everyone is agreed, are the most liberated in the world, actually face major economic handicaps. As we now know, they have to cope with fallout of the highest divorce rate and the largest earnings gap (between male and female earnings) in the advanced world. The female experience in backward, "energy-sapping" Europe is a whole lot easier to deal with, at least if one focuses on the material conditions of life. American women are long on image and short on substance.

Our perception of the powerful American woman has undoubtedly been shaped by the modern women's movement, which has been larger, noisier, and more visible in the United States than in any other country in the Western world. Remember those heady days in 1969, when feminists stormed the Atlantic City beauty pageant? Dumping padded bras, curlers, girdles, false eyelashes, copies of *Playboy* and *Family Circle,* and steno pads into a "freedom trash can," they placed a Miss America crown on the head of a live sheep and sang:

> Ain't she sweet,
> Making profit off her meat.[3]

Later that year members of the Women's International Terrorist Conspiracy from Hell (WITCH for short) disrupted a fashion show for brides by singing (to the tune of the Wedding March):

> Here come the slaves,
> Off to their graves.[4]

In August 1970, 10,000 feminists marched along Fifth Avenue

and Kate Millett declared, "Today is the beginning of a new movement. Today is the end of millenniums of oppression." The same summer 1,000 women marched in Boston, and 2,000 in San Francisco. In Miami women smashed crockery at a "liberation garden party" while in Philadelphia's Rittenhouse Square feminists prepared themselves for the struggle by taking free open-air karate lessons. Back in New York City's Duffy Square, Mary Orovan made the sign of the cross at a ceremony honoring Susan B. Anthony, intoning, "In the name of the Mother, the Daughter, and the Holy Granddaughter, Ah-Women. Ah-Women," while the crowd waved placards reading REPENT, MALE CHAUVINISTS, YOUR WORLD IS COMING TO AN END.

All very stirring stuff, and in some important ways the women's liberation movement has managed to reconstruct the language and the consciousness of this nation. There has been an impressive increase in personal and sexual freedom for women, the career aspirations of elite women have been permanently raised, and there has been a dramatic rise in the number of women lawyers, doctors, and managers. But if women are allowed to be ambitious in this new liberated age, and if they have become free not to have children, the fact remains that they have not made a dent in the wage gap, and many are increasingly unable to reconcile motherhood with their professional aspirations. In short, very little of this feminist agitation has boiled down to policies that help women deal with the concrete realities of their daily lives; for the majority, these realities center on reconciling motherhood with a job.

The European experience has been different. In some ways European women seem to have made much less progress than their American counterparts. As Kati Marton correctly points out, there are fewer women executives in the City of London than on Wall Street, and British men still find it difficult to get their tongues around the term *Ms.* But despite the fact that European society has not reconstructed its consciousness, many Western European countries have instituted generous maternity leaves, pushed ahead with public child care, and made considerable progress in closing the gap between male and female earning power. It is also true that there are more women in high public office in these countries than in the United States.

Why has the experience of European women been so very different from that of women in this country? Part of the explanation lies in the goals and objectives of feminism there and here.

The central emphases of the American movement have been on equal rights and on sexual freedom. Most American feminists have stressed the importance of acquiring an equal set of legal rights and of achieving control over one's body. The assumption has been that once women possess the same rights as men and can choose not to have children, they achieve true equality of opportunity and are able to compete for jobs, income, and power on the same terms as men.

For a century and a half much of the energy of American feminism has been channeled into the struggle to win formal equality of rights between the sexes. In the nineteenth and early twentieth centuries the main goal was to win the right to vote; in the modern period the central struggle has been over the Equal Rights Amendment (ERA). Modern feminists have added abortion and birth control rights to the core agenda. Eleanor Smeal (president of the National Organization for Women from 1978 to 1983 and reelected in 1985) underlines these priorities in her 1984 book, *Why and How Women Will Elect the Next President,* in which she lists the ERA and abortion as the two most important issues for contemporary American feminists.[5]

In Europe various groups of social feminists have conceived the problem of the female sex quite differently. For them, it is not woman's lack of legal rights that constitute her main handicap, or even her lack of "reproductive freedom." Rather, it is her dual burden—in the home and in the work force—that leads to second-class status. The goal of the social feminists has therefore become one of lightening this burden by instituting family support systems —many of which were described in Chapters Four and Five— that make this dual role less oppressive for women. Their conviction is that because women are wives and mothers as well as workers and citizens, they need special compensatory policies if they are to accomplish as much as men in the world beyond the home.

Equal rights are seen as only a small part of the story. As Anna-Greta Leijon, the current Swedish minister of labor, points out, "If children cannot receive good care while their parents are away working, the right to work becomes illusory for most women."[6]

One thing is immediately apparent: These contrasting visions of the female problem place a very different weight on the issue of motherhood. American feminists have generally stressed the ways in which men and women should be equal and have therefore tried to put aside differences. This has led them to sidetrack issues of motherhood. When it comes to the special functions of women in the bearing of children, there has been a tendency to focus on reproductive freedom and the right to choose *not* to have a child since that is what would permit women to approximate men. The critical problems of having children or of being a mother are ignored or downplayed.

Social feminists, on the other hand, have placed motherhood center stage. The essence of the female problem, in their view, is to reconcile the demands of childbirth and child rearing with those of the workplace and the wider community. They believe that men and society at large should provide systematic support to women in recognition of their dual role as mothers and workers. The logic of this view is simple and compelling. Ninety percent of women have children, and in the absence of support structures it is precisely during the childbearing years that women fail to make the grade in the career struggle. In Chapter Four, when we examined wage differentials in the American economy, we found that the earnings gap between the sexes widened considerably when men and women reached their late twenties and thirties. Women simply fall behind in the job market when they bear and raise their children, and they rarely catch up.

Of course, not all American feminists have been equal rights enthusiasts and not all European feminists have concentrated on material realities. Social feminists have played a small role in the United States, and equal rights advocates have been present in Europe. But it is true that the overwhelming preoccupation of the American women's movement has been on equal rights and reproductive freedom, while the central focus of most European feminists has been on the material conditions of life, specifically on the support structures necessary to reconcile women's maternal and labor force responsibilities.

This difference between feminists, between the equal rights enthusiasts and those that stress material realities, is more than a theoretical distinction, for these two groups of feminists have very different policy agendas. A recent furor in California over maternity leave highlights the clash between these two visions of feminism.

In the summer of 1984, just after Geraldine Ferraro had been selected as the vice presidential nominee at the Democratic National Convention in San Francisco, the *New York Times* ran an article entitled "Maternity Leave: Is It Leave Indeed?" It told the story of Lillian Garland's fight both to have a baby and to keep her job:

> Miss Garland, a receptionist at the California Federal Savings and Loan Association here [in Los Angeles], gave birth to Kekere Yuri Latik Gamer on February 12, 1982. The delivery was by Caesarean section, and Miss Garland's doctor certified that she would be medically able to go back to work on April 21st. But when Miss Garland presented herself at the bank, ready to resume work, she was told her job had been filled—and there were no openings for her.
>
> "I just felt faint, I was cold all over," said Miss Garland. "It never occurred to me that I might lose my job because I'd had a child. I was in total shock. I don't think a woman should have to choose between having a baby and having an income."
>
> Things got worse for Miss Garland after she lost her job: lacking income, she was evicted from her apartment, and had to sleep on a woman friend's couch. Without resources to care for the baby, she lost custody to the child's father.
>
> Finally, Miss Garland called California's Department of Fair Employment and Housing for help. The lawyers there told her that what Cal Fed had done was

illegal. Under the department's interpretation of a 1979 California law, every woman is entitled to up to four months' unpaid leave, without losing her job, for medical disability caused by pregnancy or childbirth. But Cal Fed—joined by the California Chamber of Commerce and the Merchants and Manufacturers Association, an employers' group with 2,900 members employing about 3 million workers—decided to use the Garland case to challenge the law.

Requiring employers to give disability leave to pregnant women, they argued, is a form of sex discrimination singling out women for preferential treatment. If disabled men do not have the right to reinstatement, they said, neither should women who have just had babies.

Federal District Judge Manuel L. Real, in a March 21 ruling, accepted that argument and declared the California law null and void. The case is now on appeal to the United States Court of Appeals for the Ninth Circuit, and more than 200 pending cases like Miss Garland's—that is, cases of women whose pregnancy cost them their jobs—are frozen in the Fair Employment Department. Many legal observers believe the question is ultimately headed for the United States Supreme Court.

Throughout the nation, the Garland case has set off a bitter debate. . . . The issue is whether the law must always treat men and women the same, or whether the law, and the business community, should accommodate the unique childbearing capacities of women workers. . . . The idea offends many employers. "I don't believe that picking out a small select group of people and giving them preferential treatment is a good thing," said Richard E. Bradley, vice president of the Merchants and Manufacturers Association.

Dianne Feinstein, the Mayor of San Francisco, supports this reasoning. "What we women have been saying all along is we want to be treated equally," she said, shortly after Judge Real struck down the California law. "Now we have to put our money where our mouth is. What we were asking was to create a special group of workers that, in essence, is pregnant women and new mothers. I just don't happen to agree with that. *I don't think the work market has to accommodate itself to women having children.*[7] (my italics)

Most women's rights groups are siding with Cal Fed and against Miss Garland. For starters, the American Civil Liberties Union and the National Organization for Women (NOW) have filed briefs supporting equal treatment.

Does Mayor Feinstein realize that the U.S. is the only advanced democracy that doesn't provide paid maternity (or parental) leave as a matter of national policy? Today 117 nations, including Britain, France, Italy, West Germany, and Canada, have no trouble accommodating the workplace to women having children. These other nations believe that allowing mothers to recuperate from childbirth, allowing infants to spend the first few weeks of their lives with their mothers or fathers, and producing circumstances in which working women feel able to become mothers, is actually good for society—and for the economy.

Does Mr. Bradley realize that we are not talking about a small, select group of people? Women constitute 53 percent of the population and 45 percent of the American labor force. As we have noted before, 90 percent of these women will have children, and most of them have no option but to try to hang on to their jobs during their childbearing years.

Does Lillian Garland realize that many feminists think that she should not have had the right to take a maternity leave and get her job back? That they think that she has less right to a leave for childbirth than if she were incapacitated in a skiing accident? After all, anyone can have a skiing accident, but only women can have babies, so if you apply the principle of equal treatment, skiing accidents qualify and childbirth doesn't. It is my guess that if she knew where NOW stands on this issue, she would pass up feminism and throw equal rights out of the window—along with the ERA.

Does NOW realize that women are not men? It is true, only women can have babies; it is both the privilege and the responsibility of the female sex. To ignore this biological difference, as many American feminists chose to do, is to commit a double folly. In the first place, it ensures that most women will become second-class citizens in the workplace. For *without public support policies few women can cope with motherhood without hopelessly compromising their career goals.* Secondly, society has to suffer. For a child cannot be compared with a new car or a vacation, some private consumer good that a woman can choose to spend resources on if the fancy strikes her. The decision to have a child is both a private and a public decision, for children are our collective future. If we fail to create decent conditions for the bearing of children, and if we deprive these children of parental contact in the first few weeks of life, we will pay a huge price in the future. As we saw in Chapter Five, neglected children grow into problem-ridden, unproductive adults.

Providing maternity leave does require treating women differently from men. So be it. Surely we should strive for equality of opportunity rather than for some rigid application of equal treatment.

Eleanor Roosevelt once said, "Women are different from men, their physical functions are different, and the future of the race depends upon their ability to produce healthy children."[8] Because of this belief in the importance of motherhood, Mrs. Roosevelt was indifferent to women's suffrage and was a lifelong opponent of the Equal Rights Amendment (ERA). She thought that if men and women had to be treated equally, it would undermine the protective laws she and other social reformers had sought for women in the workplace—factory safety standards, minimum wage laws, a forty-eight-hour workweek, elimination of night work, and exclusion from dangerous work.

Mrs. Roosevelt was so irritated by the equal rights emphasis of mainstream American feminists that she refused to be labeled a feminist herself. The fact that she avoided the term doesn't, of course, mean that she didn't act like a feminist a good deal of the time. She thought women were every bit as capable as men. As Gloria Steinem said in a recent tribute, Eleanor Roosevelt "did a great deal to support women as individuals in private life, in the

Democratic Party and in the Roosevelt Administration."[9] But perhaps the lesson we should learn from the life of this great woman is that feminism should not be equated with equal rights and that sometimes women have to be treated unequally if they are to have a fair deal as mothers and workers. This broader conception of feminism has had a larger following in Europe than in the United States, and because of this, feminism has been a more constructive force in Europe than in America.

7

EQUAL RIGHTS VERSUS SOCIAL BENEFITS

The equal rights theme in American feminism goes back to the beginning of the movement some 150 years ago. It is a strong thread, which binds together the early agitation for women's rights in the 1830s and 1840s, the suffrage movement of the late nineteenth and early twentieth centuries, and the women's movement of the 1960s and 1970s. Dominating each of these periods was a consistent and overwhelming concern with formal equality of rights between men and women.

There is a curious similarity between the nineteenth and twentieth centuries. The earliest feminists demanded a range of legal rights—property rights, child-custody rights, and divorce rights. Then, from the Civil War to 1920, the focus gradually narrowed to a single issue: the right to vote. With the rebirth of feminism in the 1960s the focus widened once more to encompass a large range of sexual, civil, and economic rights. But in the 1970s and early 1980s American feminists once again narrowed down their focus to a single issue: the Equal Rights Amendment. As former Congresswoman Bella Abzug has pointed out, "the ERA became the heart and soul of the contemporary women's peaceful revolution, with its quest for equality and economic justice, it was the legal bedrock on which all other changes were to be inscribed."[1]

The first battle was won, women were enfranchised in 1920; but contrary to expectations, women did not change the conditions of their lives by virtue of the fact they could now vote. The second battle was lost; the ERA has not been ratified. This defeat was due in large part to the opposition of women who saw, quite accurately, that the ERA did not address the central problems of their lives.

The initial period of feminist activity coincided with the beginning of industrialization. In the 1830s and 1840s the textile mills, food-processing factories, shoe factories, and other nascent industries of the Northeast attracted large numbers of women workers, including the celebrated mill girls who migrated to Lowell, Massachusetts, to work in the textile plants. Historian William Chafe underlines the importance of industrialization as a trigger for feminist agitation: "Although the industrial revolution did not directly cause feminism, it provided the context for the first collective assault on traditional ideas about women's place."[2] In the new industrial order working women were even more exploited than they had been in the agricultural production process. While pioneering women were often accorded rough equality with men, in the new factory system women often worked as hard as men for half the male wage rate.

At the same time more affluent women were beginning to resent their second-class status. The antislavery movement provided the catalyst. Many middle-class women were active in the abolitionist movement, which defined slavery as a religious abomination and a national disgrace. But what was the condition of these slaves? They could own no property and indeed themselves were treated as property. They had no legal rights to their own children, no right to vote, no right to payment for the work they performed for their masters, no redress against abuse or violence, and no access to education, skilled work, or independent social status of any kind. It could scarcely have escaped the attention of the married women working for abolition that despite their relative comfort and security, precisely the same restrictions applied to them. A key consciousness-raising moment was the exclusion of women from effective participation in the World Anti-Slavery Convention in London in 1840.

The women's rights movement was formally launched in 1848, at a convention in Seneca Falls, New York, organized by Elizabeth Cady Stanton and Lucretia Mott. The resolutions adopted by the Seneca Falls Convention were based on the principle that "woman is man's equal, was intended to be so by the Creator, and the highest good of the race demands that she should be recognized as such."[3] This convention and the subsequent public debate called for a broad range of new rights and freedoms for women. Stanton, Susan B. Anthony, Lucy Stone, and other activists demanded equal rights for women in marriage, education, industrial employment, and politics. Radical in sentiment and small in numbers, these early feminists had only limited influence on public policy.

A later wave of nineteenth-century feminism attracted widespread support but for a much more limited goal: the vote. Ever since the Seneca Falls Convention, suffrage had been a central demand of feminist activists. In the last two decades of the nineteenth century the right of women to vote was turned into a respectable and legitimate political issue. Instead of presenting the vote as an assault upon the family and traditional ideas of "woman's place," feminists increasingly portrayed it as a means of bringing women's natural moral and spiritual concerns to bear upon government. The rationale for enfranchising women shifted from Stanton's natural rights argument that men and women were equal and therefore citizens with identical claims to a demand for suffrage which rested on female righteousness. Women deserved the vote not because they were equal to men but because they were virtuous, maternal, devout, sober, and respectable. In the words of Jane Addams, it was a way for women to become the housekeepers of the nation.[4]

Stanton herself was impatient with the single-mindedness and conservatism of the late-nineteenth-century feminist movement. Refusing "to sing suffrage evermore," she continued to advocate labor unions for women workers, divorce reform, and birth control.[5] She even went so far as to publish *The Woman's Bible,* which attacked traditional church teachings on the status of women.

Stanton paid for her heresy. Suffragists feared that Stanton's radical feminism would damn their chances for success, and to avoid the Stanton stigma, they isolated and ignored her. They turned Anthony's home into a shrine and named the Nineteenth Amendment after her despite the fact that Stanton had proposed women's suffrage three years before Anthony joined the feminist movement; indeed, Anthony did not even attend the Seneca Falls Convention. Later generations, unaware of Stanton's role, put Anthony's image on a stamp and a coin.[6]

The battle to win the vote was enormously costly. Feminists abandoned all other policy goals, cultivated conservatism, and devoted fifty-two years to a ceaseless campaign. According to Carrie Chapman Catt, "the women of this country were forced to conduct 56 campaigns of referenda to male voters, 480 campaigns to get legislatures to submit suffrage amendments to voters, 277 campaigns to get state party conventions to include women suffrage planks . . ." and the dreary list goes on.[7] By the time the vote was granted in 1920, the long channeling of feminists' energies into the limited goal of suffrage had exhausted the women's movement. By then many feminists had forgotten what the vote was for.

Those who had assumed that the right to vote held the key to improving women's economic and social position were disappointed by the events that followed their victory in 1920. As Aileen Kraditor has described it, the Nineteenth Amendment, heralded as the catalyst for a virtual revolution in women's status, produced "little tangible progress toward the goal of economic equality."[8] The enfranchisement of women was a political nonevent. Those women who used their vote (and only a third of them did) tended to vote the same way as their fathers or husbands.

Part of the problem was internal to the movement. In the early twenties there was a serious split between equal rights enthusiasts who wanted to push for an equal rights amendment and social reformers who wanted to preserve and expand protective legislation for working women. This schism prevented feminists from putting together a coherent plan of action. Contributing to this impasse was the economic and political climate of the day. During the twenties there was a red scare, and feminists were suspected of being Bolshevik sympathizers, while the decade of the thirties was dominated by the Great Depression. During these grim years questions of economic survival overshadowed women's rights. The net result was that feminist issues faded from the public agenda. It was forty-five years before women became militant again.

The feminist revival of the 1960s and 1970s displayed once more a steadily mounting concern with the equal rights of women. In its early stages the new women's movement had two parts, distinguished by their structure and style. The first was a highly decentralized network of consciousness-raising groups which flourished in the early seventies. Typically these groups lacked any formal structure, they tended to dissolve and re-form frequently, and they focused their energies on personal relationships and sexuality.

The second part of the movement encompassed the national women's organizations and included the National Organization for Women (NOW), the National Women's Political Caucus (NWPC), and the Women's Equity Action League (WEAL). These were set up as formal organizations with elected officers, bylaws, and boards of directors.

When the movement all began in the late 1960s, consciousness raising was intended to politicize the personal aspects of people's lives. But the participants were too privileged, their concerns were too private, and the groups were too ephemeral for them to develop a unified public voice. Besides, the focus was on individual redemption, not on promoting societal change. In the event, consciousness raising prompted emotional and behavioral changes without mobilizing energy for political action.

The consciousness-raising group I belonged to in the 1970s was typical. It met sporadically between the fall of 1975 and the spring of 1977. Sometimes it met as much as twice a month, and once a whole summer went by without a meeting. The membership was also somewhat fluid. In 1975 we started with seven members, but in 1976 three dropped out and four others joined, so that the group remained roughly the same size with a slightly different mix of people for its eighteen-month life-span.

As was the case with many of these groups, mine was essentially a circle of friends. We had three things in common: We lived in Manhattan, mostly on the Upper West Side; we all were professionals struggling to overcome various barriers to career success; and we all were infected with the spirit of women's liberation and saw ourselves as feminists. We were otherwise a diverse group. Our professions ran the gamut from struggling artist to editor to teacher; some of us were married, others were single, and about a third of the women in the group were mothers. Our ages ranged from twenty-eight to fifty-three, and in keeping with such chronological diversity, some of us were just beginning our careers while others among us were established. The guiding purpose of the group was to examine our various attempts to reconcile the personal and the professional sides of our lives and to help one another do a better job of integration.

We had some procedural rules, which we thrashed out at the beginning of our existence as a group. The meetings rotated around the members' homes, and each session had a different lead person. This position also rotated around the group. The job of this lead person was to present an issue or a problem and then to monitor the discussion to make sure that everyone had a chance to talk and that no one became overly critical or judgmental of anyone else in the group. Consciousness raising was, after all, an exercise in supportive interaction.

Our sessions ranged over a great variety of topics from how to integrate stepchildren into one's life to attitudes toward ambition. The focus was overwhelmingly personal; we looked to our relationships, to our childhoods, to our interior worlds to explain our life problems. I remember one session with great clarity.

It was mid-January 1977, and it was Lila's* turn to host the meeting. We all met at her house at 8:30 P.M. for dessert and coffee. Some of us had not been to Lila's home before and were startled at how luxurious it was. She and her immensely successful husband lived in a glorious town house on East Seventy-fourth

*Pseudonym.

Street, just off Park Avenue. It had wonderful fireplaces and paneling and seemed to be full of antiques. The thing that impressed me most was that Lila and her family seemed to occupy the entire five floors (at the time I was living in a hole in the wall in an unfashionable part of the Upper West Side). The group met in the downstairs library. The room was furnished with bottle-green leather couches, kilim rugs, and shelves of books and looked out onto a peaceful, floodlit winter garden. I still remember the scene; it was quite magical.

Lila herself seemed totally incongruous. A pretty but unkempt woman, she simply was not credible as the mistress of this splendid mansion. This particular evening she was wearing an old, shapeless skirt and a creased silk blouse which was much too tight and clearly predated her most recent pregnancy. I was mesmerized by this blouse; throughout the evening the buttons over her bust kept on popping, and Lila kept on fastening them—to no avail.

Our topic for the evening was money: how much we made; how much we would like to make; how we shared money with our partners; whether we felt anxious, dependent, or vulnerable in this sphere and, if we did, what we should do about it.

Joanna,* who was the lead person for the evening, opened the session with "I feel more nervous about this topic than about any other we have covered. I guess people these days are just much more secretive about money than they are about anything else." She cleared her throat and went on rather hesitantly. "I want to begin by making a confession. Last Saturday I was at Bloomingdale's getting some basic stuff for the apartment—you know, sheets and towels, that kind of thing. When I had finished, I peeked into one of those new designer boutiques on the second floor and some mad impulse came over me. I found myself buying this incredibly expensive sequined evening blouse that we couldn't even begin to afford. But that's not the worst of it. I then took it home and hid it in the closet in the spare bedroom so that Bob wouldn't see it." Joanna paused and then let out a long sigh. "How's that for immature, irresponsible behavior?"

*Pseudonym.

A Lesser Life

*   *   *

We all murmured sympathetically, recognizing too readily and a little painfully the scene she described. Molly* pushed Joanna to analyze her behavior a little: "But did you hide the blouse from Bob because you really couldn't afford it—after all, you earn a good salary—or because you had neglected to ask his permission before buying it?"

This hit a chord in Joanna, and she responded eagerly. "That's exactly what I have been asking myself. You know, I think that maybe I can afford the blouse. I just got a raise at Harper and Row [the publishing house Joanna worked for as an editor], and there is enough money left over after my share of household expenses to allow for the occasional extravagance. But you see, Bob still earns twice as much as I do despite the fact he holds a similar position [Bob was an editor at another publishing house], and I feel that I ought to ask his permission before making any major purchase. Every now and then I rebel and end up acting like a child hiding forbidden goodies under the bed."

Lila had been listening intently and decided to join in the discussion. "I really connect with that business of earning less than your partner. Rick* has been so successful recently that he now earns five times more than I do. I work so hard for my thirteen thousand dollars a year [Lila taught music in a private school], yet it hardly pays for the baby-sitter, let alone anything else. Rick hates my splurging on clothes, and I've no self-control in stores, so last winter I just decided never to go into department stores again so that I wouldn't be tempted." Lila paused and smiled triumphantly. "It works! I order all household things by phone, and this way I avoid spending anything on me."

I looked at Lila in amazement. My eye traveled from her creased and ill-fitting blouse (which had popped some more buttons) to the opulent furnishings. Just one of those rugs would have bought Lila a mink coat. "But, Lila," I said, "are you saying that you and Rick can't afford to buy you any clothes?"

*Pseudonym.

156

Lila nodded sadly. "Well, you see the house and the kids pretty much take up everything we earn, and then Rick has to dress well because his position in the corporation demands it. I feel that it is up to me to economize."

The rest of us looked at one another wide-eyed and decided not to push Lila any further just then; we moved on to the next person.[9]

Looking back at this consciousness-raising session, I now think of all the things we did not bring up. For example, why did Joanna's husband, Bob, earn twice as much as she despite the fact that he had a very similar job? Why was Lila's teaching position so badly paid despite her impressive qualifications? Why didn't we focus on these issues and talk about a strategy for helping Joanna and Lila improve their earning capabilities? So much of the guilt and the dependency we were talking about seemed to be triggered by the asymmetry in economic power between these women and their husbands. But we were entirely wrapped up in our own interior worlds and in our relationships. We never thought to go outside—to the public world of institutions and political connections—to explain our problems.

Consciousness raising was the single activity most universally associated with women's liberation in the late 1960s and early 1970s. In fact, for many women, their weekly "rap" sessions constituted their *only* feminist activity. But while consciousness raising was meant to politicize the personal aspects of people's lives, it never quite made that transition. The new awareness seems to have led most commonly to emotional and behavioral changes. As psychologist Phyllis Chesler reports, "Some women started living together; some began living alone for the first time. . . . Some women left their husbands; others began to live with a man. . . . Women stopped giggling and competing with each other for male attention. . . . Some women stopped going to beauty parlors and began to value their time; they needed fewer adornments to 'make up' for being female."[10] There is, however, little evidence to show that the consciousness-raising experience mobilized women to push for public policy change.

The problem is that consciousness raising tends to shift the burden for change away from society and toward the individual woman. It encourages women to look to themselves, or to that small group of women with whom they share consciousness, as the source of their "liberation." In short, consciousness raising is an approach that deemphasizes broad-based social action in favor of personal redemption.

In her best-selling book *The Cinderella Complex* Colette Dowling describes a dramatic collapse of ambition. Her protagonist leaves New York City, where she has just spent four years as a self-sufficient single parent, and goes to live with her three children and her new male friend in a small rural community in the Hudson Valley.

Gradually her ambition ebbs away. She launders, bakes, rakes, mulches, and plays helpmate to her man. She becomes increasingly less motivated and less effective as a writer. By the end of a year she and her children are completely financially dependent on her male friend.

Dowling sees this collapse of independence as a psychological phenomenon. She describes her protagonist as yearning to return to an infantile state of dependency so as "to avoid the strain involved in undertaking an authentic existence."[11] No mention is made of the practical difficulties of being a free-lance writer in a small rural community. Without an office or a library, far removed from the contacts and the network that make up the stuff of a professional writer's existence, it is easy to see that any person (male or female) might become unproductive. Dowling also fails to stress the real burdens of looking after a rambling old house and three children, burdens which don't seem to have been shared by the male friend.

Dowling focuses exclusively on the inner consciousness of her protagonist. The great stumbling block that prevents career success is "the deep wish to be taken care of by others,"[12] which Dowling sees as the chief force holding women down today. Like Cinderella, women "are still waiting for something external to transform their lives."[13] According to Dowling, women have only one real shot at liberation, and "that is to emancipate themselves from within."[14]

Dowling's emphasis on consciousness raising and personal redemption is characteristic of the American women's movement.

She encourages women to get their heads in the right place and look to themselves as the source of their salvation. The material conditions of life or broad-based social change play no part in this vision of women's liberation.

While consciousness raising had little political impact, contemporary feminists have sought policy action through the national organizations and their local chapters. There can be no doubt that the priority of these organizations has been to win equal rights for women.

NOW was formed in October 1966 by Betty Friedan and a few other women activists. It revived and carried forward the nineteenth-century tradition of equal rights feminism, and its stated purpose was "to take action to bring women into full participation in the mainstream of American society *now*, exercising all the privileges and responsibilities thereof in truly equal partnership."[15] NOW had an elite constituency and a liberal agenda. It was populated by middle- and upper-middle-class women, and these women wanted equal educational and job opportunities, equal pay, and the abolition of all legislation which discriminated against women. The initial strategy of NOW was to push the infant Equal Employment Opportunity Commission (EEOC), and to act on sex discrimination complaints being filed under Title VII of the 1964 Civil Rights Act. Another national feminist organization, WEAL, was established in 1970 to advance the cause of women's participation in political parties and in government.

These groups claim success in pursuing equal rights for women in the marketplace and in education, specifically in securing employment and educational opportunities and in gaining access to credit. In the 1960s the effect of these feminist organizations on these areas of public policy was limited. For example, they cannot claim responsibility for the inclusion of sex as a category in Title VII of the Civil Rights Act. The sex provision was inserted by a southern congressman who hoped that such an unreasonable addition would destroy the bill's credibility with his congressional colleagues. When the bill passed as amended, even the staff of the newly created EEOC refused at first to take the sex discrimination provision seriously.

The case for a feminist influence on federal legislation is

clearer after 1970. For example, pressure from women's organizations played an important role in the passage of Title IX of the 1972 Educational Amendment, and in the passage of the 1974 Equal Credit Act. The most conspicuous failure of feminist organizations has been their inability to achieve ratification of the Equal Rights Amendment.

If the dominant goal of the feminist movement has been equal rights, it has attempted to achieve this goal with a two-pronged strategy. First, feminist leaders have tried to protect the purity of the movement by avoiding alignments with interest groups, such as political parties and labor unions, outside the movement. Secondly, they have set themselves the task of uniting sisterhood in independent mass-based organizations, believing that the common bond of gender is enough to hold together a coherent movement.

This strategy has a historical root. Throughout the suffrage campaign feminists followed a policy of organizing outside the major political parties. For example, the National American Woman Suffrage Association (NAWSA), a nonpartisan organization founded in 1890 for the purpose of winning the vote, refused any permanent party alignment, remaining "obdurately non-partisan."[16] While NAWSA supported Woodrow Wilson in 1913 because he appeared sympathetic to their cause, the organization showed its disappointment with the Democratic Congress by organizing campaigns in 1914 and 1916 to defeat Democratic congressional candidates.

Having won the vote, feminists debated the question of whether women should move toward integration into the established parties or maintain their identity as an independent political force. Some prominent feminists within the League of Women Voters (the organizational heir to NAWSA) urged women to become active participants in the Republican and Democratic parties. While a separatist faction advised women against joining parties, arguing that party politics was by nature a corrupt and unsavory enterprise that would force women to abandon their reformist ideals and thereby destroy their unique contribution to politics. As one commentator said in 1922, "A woman who joins one of these parties simply becomes an imitation man, which is to say, a donkey. Thereafter, she is nothing but an obscure cog in an ancient and creaking machine, the sole intelligible purpose of which is to maintain a horde of scoundrels in public office."[17]

Ultimately the league advised women to become nonpartisan and all-partisan; this seemed to boil down to a rejection of the established parties as appropriate vehicles for expressing women's demands. The most active political arm of the feminists became the Women's Joint Congressional Committee, which coordinated feminist lobbying activity for a variety of women's organizations but remained outside the party system.

The effectiveness of this separatist strategy depended on whether women would retaliate at the polls against a politician who was unresponsive to their demands. This threat was used to some advantage in the early 1920s, but feminists' influence on politicians dropped precipitously once it was discovered that electoral retaliation from women was an idle threat.

American women did not rush to participate in electoral politics after 1920, and the speedy realization by male politicians that the women's vote was a myth virtually eliminated feminist influence on policy. At the same time women could exercise little internal influence within the party structure because their separatist strategy had prevented feminists from making inroads into the party organizations. The result: impotence. In 1925 a Democratic committeewoman was able to write in *Harper's Magazine:* "I know of no woman who has a following of other women. I know of no politician who is afraid of the women's vote on any question under the sun."[18]

With the revival of feminism in the 1960s the separatist tradition reappeared. Many of the modern proponents of women's liberation expressed "an overt female separatist viewpoint, which calls for women to isolate themselves from men in order to come to terms with what it means to be female."[19] Just as the black power movement used the slogan *Black Is Beautiful* the women's liberation movement coined the phrase *Sisterhood Is Powerful.* Both slogans were meant to convey a sense of group identity. The term *sisterhood* has been used to promote "female solidarity, respect for women as women, support for all women by women."[20]

Thus present-day feminists have chosen not to form any continuous alignment with political parties, trade unions, or other power blocs, but instead have formed a series of nonpartisan interest groups, the most important of which is the National Organization for Women (NOW). A resolution adopted in 1978 reiterates this organization's position on the issue of separatism: "NOW and its subunits wish to remain independent and free from political party pressure, yet able to endorse individual candidates who support NOW's positions: *Therefore, be it resolved,* that no political party be allowed to use NOW or any subunit of NOW as a vehicle to further its political goals."[21] The policy of endorsing individual candidates has not worked very smoothly or effectively. For example, dissatisfied with President Carter's level of commitment to the ERA, NOW held off and did not endorse him until the last moment in the 1980 election. As a result, this large and influential women's organization failed to mobilize against Reagan, who posed a clear threat to women's rights.

The decision to avoid partisan alliances is directly related to NOW's stated purpose, which is to serve the interests of *all* women regardless of their class, their race, their religious background, their party affiliation, or their sexual preference. Thus radical lesbians, whose participation in NOW is often viewed as a political liability, are welcomed on the ground that women's rights are indivisible. The premise is that all women, no matter how diverse they are in other respects, share the common problems of their sex. Working on this assumption, the NOW leadership has avoided permanent alignments with political parties or any other interest group whose membership and goals are less inclusive than their own.

If feminists were merely seeking to keep public debate on women's issues alive, then the umbrella strategy might be a good one. National conventions of NOW and the other feminist organizations provide excellent platforms from which to dramatize women's grievances. But if the goal is to effect policy change, then the strategy of maximizing the coalition works only for those issues that unite women on the basis of gender alone. Equal rights comes closest to fulfilling this condition. However, as may be seen from the ERA battle, going after equal rights is not a foolproof strategy. Women, after all, do not share a common economic status, religious background, or cultural heritage and therefore do not constitute a coherent class. Their ability to mount a unified campaign for a common goal is consequently limited. For programs the benefits of which are less inclusive than equal rights, the umbrella coalition simply cannot be a very effective pressure group.

An organization like NOW, based on the principle of universal sisterhood among women, faces serious difficulties in promoting programs that benefit only certain groups, such as pregnant women, women who need day care for their children, or retired women. Umbrella organizations are forced to promote many issues at the same time to satisfy their diverse membership, and consequently, resources must be divided among many campaigns. It is also true that a great deal of the organization's energy is spent in group maintenance activities rather than on goal-oriented activities. Struggling to hold the coalition together becomes the leadership's primary task.

At a national conference on "Women and the American Economy" in 1975, Betty Friedan called into question the feminists' strategy of going it alone. She argued that the women's liberation movement she had helped found was only a way station: ". . . the questions we face now cannot be solved by women alone." Women now need to develop economic alliances with "old people, young people, heart-attack-prone executives, trade unionists, Blacks and other minorities."[22] Friedan was essentially arguing that the utility of the separatist strategy was exhausted, and it was essential for the women's movement to develop more functional specialization and align itself with other organizations and institutions.

Such a trend is beginning. The late seventies saw the emergence of a prochoice coalition, linking feminist organizations (NWPC, NOW) to other interest groups (Planned Parenthood, the American Civil Liberties Union) to counteract groups pressuring Congress to limit Medicaid funds for abortions. More recently the Child Care Action Campaign, which was launched by Elinor Guggenheimer in 1983, has sought to align the feminist organizations with groups such as churchwomen, junior leaguers, trade unionists, and child development specialists in an effort to come to grips with the urgent problem of child care in America. It is too early to tell whether these coalitions will be effective in promoting their policy goals.

Emphasizing equal rights via a separatist strategy which unites sisterhood is not the only way of approaching women's liberation. Sweden is a country where the principle of equal rights lost ground to other more concrete issues when the social feminists became a powerful force in the early years of this century.

Swedish social feminists believe that a preoccupation with equal rights is wrongheaded. Their own focus has been on developing support systems for women that allow them to be more effective as wives, mothers, and workers. The view of these social feminists is that women deserve unequal treatment in the labor market. As Anna-Greta Leijon, the Swedish minister of labor, puts it, "We think it compatible with equality that women should now be overcompensated in various ways."[23] She is specifically referring to the elaborate benefits and services that the Swedish government has put in place to ease women's dual role in the labor market and at home.

Another point of contrast between America and Sweden is that Swedish social feminists express little faith in the possibility of changing social conditions by altering individual consciousness, which was, as we have seen, a particular emphasis of the American movement during the early 1970s. One Swedish woman journalist told me, "What good does it do an individual to raise her consciousness if she then cannot find a well-paid job because of the structure of opportunities in the labor market, or because of the lack of child-care services? Getting your head in the right place is not enough if material conditions interfere with your ability to reconcile work and family life."[24] In the opinion of many Swedish feminists, the line of causality runs from the conditions of life to individual consciousness, not the other way around. That is to say, if material reality permits women to become effective wives and mothers *and* productive workers in the world beyond the home, then and only then can they develop their consciousness and fulfill their human potential.

Equal Rights Versus Social Benefits

Swedish social feminists believe that consciousness raising is not just ineffective, but is actually counterproductive. Because it shifts responsibility away from society and toward the individual, it tends to deemphasize political action in favor of highly personal transformation experiences. These self-help solutions to problems—even when they don't work—relieve the pressure on government to seek collective solutions to women's problems. Remember Joanna and Lila? Their consciousness-raising experience encouraged them to seek solutions to problems in their personal relationships rather than in a more public arena.

Swedish women point to a second negative effect of consciousness raising: It breeds divisiveness. An attempt by women's organizations to reconstruct their members' consciousnesses can be guaranteed to generate hostility from women who do not want to be reconstructed. In large measure American feminists have alienated traditional women because they have asked them to alter their values and their identities. Engineering a clash between a "liberated" and a "traditional" vision of the world can obstruct practical policy initiatives. As we shall see when we examine the fight to ratify the ERA, this measure became bogged down by ideological as well as substantive differences.

A final difference between feminism in the United States and in Sweden is the American movement's separatist strategy. In Sweden, by way of contrast, feminists have chosen to work through a women's section established in virtually every party, union, and professional, social, and religious organization in the country. The typical pattern has been for groups of feminists operating within these larger interest groups to press for better conditions for women workers, women lawyers, retired women, or women students rather than to unite and campaign for women as a class. This strategy has been enormously effective. For example, the women's section within the Social Democratic party has persuaded this powerful political force to recognize the special needs of women. This commitment by the dominant political party to equality of economic result has led to the extensive parental leaves and the elaborate child-care facilities that we associate with modern Sweden.

Visitors to Sweden often remark that despite the high visibility of women's issues in the media and in public debate, it is hard to detect a women's liberation movement as such. This is because Swedish feminism is deliberately low-key. The strident tone of the American separatist movement has been avoided. Instead, Swedish feminism has become embedded in virtually all of the country's social, political, and economic organizations.

These distinguishing characteristics of Swedish feminism have their roots in the late nineteenth century, when two branches of women's political activity emerged. Equal rights activists became concerned with advancing women's legal rights, especially property rights, while a group of social reformers tried to improve the living conditions of working women.

The suffrage question was less important to nineteenth-century Swedish activists than it was to American feminists in this period. There seem to be two reasons for this. First was the early preoccupation of Swedish feminists with improving women's material circumstances. To many nineteenth-century Swedish feminists, winning the vote seemed a great deal less important than winning equal property rights and the ability to earn a subsistence wage in factories.

An equally important reason was that in Sweden the issue of the vote for women was subordinated to the issue of universal suffrage. Hence women's interests were bound up with those of larger organizations seeking general universal suffrage, such as the Social Democratic party, formed in 1889 to represent the industrial working class, and the Liberal party, established in 1902 to represent the lower middle classes and urban intellectuals. The battle for the vote was thus a battle that cut across the sexes and was led by the nation's two largest political parties. In the event, universal male suffrage was legislated in 1909 and women received the right to vote ten years later.[25]

Thus the struggle to enfranchise women in Sweden was carried out within the major parties, rather than being fought, as it was in the United States, outside the party system.[26] In Sweden, when universal adult suffrage became a leading political issue, the women's suffrage movement as such faded away. In this way feminism entered the arena of mass politics, and this early integration of women's activists and women's issues into the major parties helped overcome a separatist bias in the original women's movement.

As the twentieth century progressed, social feminists gained ascendancy over equal rights activists in the Swedish women's movement. Significantly they worked not only through political parties but also through labor unions. For example, in 1960 the National Federation of Employers (SAF) agreed with the National Federation of Labor (LO) that women should receive equal pay for equal work, and that all low-paid work should be upgraded.[27] Since that date this policy of solidarity, as it is called, has dominated the wage-setting process and has been largely responsible for the dramatic narrowing of the gap between male and female earnings in Sweden. The Liberal party has argued that such collective bargaining agreements between management and labor do not have the legal force of a national law guaranteeing women's equal rights, but the Social Democrats see legal remedies as only appropriate for elite career women. They do not think that legal measures are effective for ordinary working women, whose interests are best served when they pool their strength in the collective bargaining process. The social feminists continue to place their faith in solidarity wage policies and in improving the already impressive array of Swedish family support policies described in Chapters Four and Five. In the spring of 1984 Anna-Greta Leijon told me that despite the extended economic recession in Sweden and severe budget constraints, "This government intends to press ahead with the rapid expansion of child-care facilities. No issue is more important to our women workers."[28]

Other European countries also have a tradition of groups of social feminists working inside the centers of political power to improve the material conditions of women's lives. In some countries these groups have not called themselves social feminists. Indeed, many of them have felt so alienated by American-style women's liberation that like Eleanor Roosevelt, they have avoided the term *feminist* altogether. But whatever the label, these women's support groups have done much which is of immense practical benefit to women. In the same spirit as the Swedish social feminists, they have concentrated on providing the support structures that women need to fulfill their dual role in the home and in the workplace.

Listen to Anna McCurley, British Conservative Member of Parliament: "Of course I want equal opportunities but I don't like the petulance in this business of 'women's issues'. . . . I find my shrieking sisters a bit of a pain in the neck. I do loathe the idea of being a second-class citizen and I'll do everything to ensure that it is overturned, that legislation is not maintaining the old traditional roles. That's what I'm here to do. But not to bare my bosom about abortion and sexual harassment. I find that very tedious and I don't mind saying that publicly."[29] In this interview, conducted in the fall of 1983, McCurley displays a scornful attitude toward American-style women's liberation, but her policy positions seem quite close to that of many European social feminists.

A dramatic aspect of the British scene is that most progress in the sphere of women's issues has been achieved not by the "shrieking sisters" but by groups of women working quietly and effectively within the bastions of established power. The majority of these women do not regard themselves as feminists, although they have a long and proud history of improving conditions of life for women.

One of the earliest and most influential of these groups was the Women's Cooperative Guild, founded in 1883 and still active today with some 25,000 members.[30] The original purpose of the guild was educational and social. Women were encouraged to form discussion circles and cooperative self-help groups, but by the beginning of this century the guild had developed into a vigorous political organization.

In 1911 the guild was instrumental in obtaining the first British maternity policy which gave working women a thirty-shilling maternity benefit and four weeks of paid leave after the birth of each child. The guild also fought for reform of the divorce laws and was the first women's organization to pass a resolution in favor of legalized abortions (in 1934). Although the guild presidents were educated and middle-class, the members themselves were working-class. (The powerful working-class mother in D. H. Lawrence's book *Sons and Lovers* was a keen participant in guild activities.) As one historian has put it, "the Guild was reformist, but its achievements were of more practical value to working class women than the unrealized and more radical objectives of other [feminist] groups."[31]

Another important organization in this early period was the Women's Labour League, founded in 1906. The League concentrated on "the economic side of the women's question."[32] Some of the many issues which the league took up during the early decades of the twentieth century were: the compulsory provision of school meals, medical inspection and treatment of schoolchildren, the establishment of baby clinics, and the provision of free milk to expectant and nursing mothers.

The guild and the league greatly influenced official thinking in these areas. A 1908 government report pointed to the importance of a mother's care to the survival of her child and emphasized the responsibilities of government to both mothers and babies: "The children of the State are the business of the State; if it neglects that business there is nothing that will atone."[33]

In recent decades these women's pressure groups have remained strong and have continued to focus on the material conditions of life. However, in the late sixties these established groups were joined by the more radical feminists of the women's liberation movement. In Britain some of the radical feminists are linked to socialism through the international socialist movement and the Workers Revolutionary party. Others in the radical camp derived their focus—on equal rights, on consciousness raising, on problems of sexuality—from new wave American feminism. However, in Britain, unlike America, "the voice of the new movement was first heard not from the intellectual radical community but from the working class."[34]

In the early spring of 1968 a group of fishermen's wives began to organize in the port city of Hull. Under the leadership of Liz Bilocca, a fisherman's wife, they set up a committee to improve safety conditions on the trawlers. Middle-class women joined the confrontation, and a women's liberation group was formed. In

June of the same year women sewing machinists at the Ford Motor plant at Dagenham staged a three-week strike for equal pay, and in London bus conductresses demanding the right to become bus drivers went on strike. This outburst of industrial militancy among working women shook up the complacent trade union movement.[35] A union committee called the National Joint Action Committee for Women's Equal Rights was established to press for more energetic action. Shortly afterward an equal pay bill was piloted through the House of Commons. It was supported by the Trades Union Congress (TUC) and the Labour party and became law in 1970.

While American-style radical feminists have conditioned the debate in Britain—by writing books, by keeping women's issues in the limelight—concrete changes have been brought about by the established women's groups working within the political structure. "Organizations like the National Council of Labour Women, the Child Poverty Action Group, the National Council for Civil Liberties and the TUC Women's Congress between them [have taken up] most of the legal and egalitarian issues which in America required separate and more specifically feminist pressure groups."[36] As was the case in Sweden, the most effective women support groups in Britain are embedded within the established centers of political power—specifically the parties and the unions—not in separatist feminist organizations.

One especially effective group is the Women's Rights Unit of the National Council for Civil Liberties (NCCL), which was set up in 1973. It consists of a small group of women, some paid and full time, others part time and voluntary, who have access to the lawyers and research facilities of the council. The Women's Rights Unit has a large number of affiliates in the trade unions and in the Labour party and has many local branches. Over recent years it has been concerned with equal pay for work of equal value and sex discrimination in the marketplace, particularly with regard to part-time and home workers (the majority of whom are women). Britain now provides more training courses aimed at encouraging women to enter male-dominated occupations than any other country.[37]

The National Labour Women's Advisory Committee, a division within the Labour party, is another active women's group in Britain. The Labour party has worked hard to attract women voters and likes to be seen as the woman's party. In 1974, together with the TUC, it drafted the influential "Charter for Women," which was eventually incorporated into the 1975 Sex Discrimination Act.[38] More recently, in the winter of 1983, it spawned the sex equality bill, which proposed paternity leave as a right for all new fathers and sought to mandate proportionate equal pay for part-time workers and home workers.[39] This bill was narrowly defeated in Parliament, and the Labour party intends to introduce it again.

Even Margaret Thatcher and the Conservative party have been qualified supporters of women's rights. For example, Thatcher backed the equal pay bill of 1970, and in 1980 her government expanded maternity leave benefits (see discussion in Chapter Four). However, it should be remembered that the massive public-sector cutbacks that have dominated her years in office have reduced the support structures available to women and children.

The Italian approach to women's issues is similar to that of Britain. There is a long tradition of women's support groups working within the trade unions, the political parties, and the church. For example, as early as 1902 women workers were guaranteed a leave of absence after childbirth and time off from the job to nurse their babies.[40] Legal rights have come much more slowly. Italian women only won the right to vote in 1945, and it was 1970 before divorce became legal.

Since the Second World War two of the most important women's support groups in Italy have been the Union of Italian Women (UDI), a semiautonomous outgrowth of the Communist party, and the Italian Women's Center (CIF), which is linked to the Christian Democratic party. These two political pressure groups have pursued a variety of reforms to improve the material basis of women's lives. The 1971 Law on the Rights of Working Mothers is a case in point. Under this law it became illegal to fire a woman during pregnancy or during the first year of her child's life; maternity leave was extended to five months with 80 percent of the wage replaced; mothers were given the right to stay away from work when a child is ill up until the child is three years old; and mothers were given two years' credit toward a variety of seniority rights each time they gave birth.[41]

The UDI and CIF were also largely responsible for the passage of the 1971 legislation which created 3,000 public nursery schools and an extensive network of public day-care centers. But perhaps most important was their sponsorship of the 1975 Family Charter, which gave extensive economic rights to wives. This law provides for common ownership of all family property by husband and wife, and it recognizes unpaid farmwork and housework as an economic contribution to family income for inheritance purposes and in the event of separation or divorce.[42] (As we saw in Chapter Three, in practice, New York's equitable distribution laws do not recognize the unpaid work of wives as an economic contribution to marriage.)

As in Britain, these women's pressure groups are not self-consciously feminist. These groups fight for concrete rights, benefits, or services for women; they are motivated by material needs and tend to be politically conservative. In Italy they are both conspicuous and active. Abby Laber, who lives and works in Ferrara, tells of the support services this northern Italian city (population 150,000) offers to working women: "For starters there is the local branch of the UDI. This provides an extensive library; a feminist newspaper which is geared to women's concerns; a drug abuse program; and a three-person legal aid office which offers help in all kinds of areas—divorce, wife abuse, adoption, abortion, you name it." Abby paused for a moment, then added, "The odd thing is, Ansalda Sirolli, who runs the branch, does not like to be called a feminist. She told me that she has a normal life and a family and that this precludes a militant attitude toward men or an experimental life-style. I guess in Italy most feminists are thought to be pretty radical."

According to Abby, other valuable services for women are provided by the *consultori* (health clinics that provide free gynecological, obstetrical, and pediatric care to women and their children). But most important of all are the subsidized day-care centers and nursery schools. "These have expanded very rapidly since the early 1970s," says Abby, "and they're great; they make all the difference to working women. A quarter of all the babies in the city and half of all three- to five-year-olds are now in these programs. They are very popular."[43]

In Italy the term *feminist* is reserved for the post-1968 women's liberation movement, inspired by the political radicalism of the late sixties and new wave American feminism. The MLD (Women's Liberation Movement) and the Lotta Femminista (Feminist Struggle) were vocal and active in the 1970s but are less so now. The MLD has been particularly concerned with issues of sexual and personal freedom—divorce, abortion, and nonsexist education. These radical feminists have sometimes worked against, or shown no interest in, legislation that promised to improve the material conditions of women's lives. As Daniela Colombo said in an interview, "the feminist movement has been more interested in abortion and sexuality than in work and family issues."[44] To take an example, feminists failed to support the Family Charter because they didn't like the language of the legislation and because it was not central to their own, highly personal, agenda. Yet, according to one Italian professor I interviewed, "the Family Charter has produced more security for more women than any other piece of legislation in recent Italian history."[45] No wonder the women in the political parties and in the church find it hard to identify with the radical feminists.

It seems clear that feminism in three very different European countries has produced an emphasis on material reality which has been largely missing in America. The social feminists in Sweden and the women's support groups in Britain and Italy have devoted their best energies to improving the material conditions of women's lives. Working within the established centers of power— party, union, and church—these pressure groups have been effective in promoting the benefits and services women need if they are to reconcile their maternal and labor force responsibilities.

Western Europe has also experienced some American-style feminism. Equal rights enthusiasts have retained considerable influence in Sweden's Liberal party, and a preoccupation with consciousness raising and sexual liberation runs through radical feminism in both Britain and Italy. But despite the presence of these typically American preoccupations, the core of European feminism is centered on a practical concern with the concrete conditions of women's lives. This social feminist tradition is almost totally absent in modern America. Nothing dramatizes this more than the issue of maternity leave, which has always been a top priority for social feminists in Europe. Italy developed its first maternity policy in 1902, Britain in 1911, and Sweden in 1939. As we learned in Chapter Four, as of 1983, more than one hundred countries had mandatory maternity policies, which, on average, gave working women the right to five months' paid leave.

The United States presents a stark contrast. It is the only advanced industrial country that still does not have a national maternity policy. The maternity coverage that does exist is so patchy that 60 percent of American working women have no rights to any kind of leave when they bear a child. And as we saw in Chapter Six, in a recent California case, feminists actually lined up against a woman who lost her job when she took a disability leave for childbirth. This is a striking example of how completely American feminism has failed to connect with the material side of life and with motherhood.

In late February 1984 Women in Crisis, Inc. held its fifth national conference. It was called "Women and Power" and was held at the Sheraton Centre in New York City. The opening plenary session was crowded. Carol Bellamy, president of the New York City Council, was the moderator, and the featured speakers were Congresswomen Geraldine Ferraro and Claudine Schneider.

In their opening remarks both Ferraro and Schneider talked about the economic and political power of women, how much they had and where the gaps were. They then talked about what they were doing in Congress to help women. Ferraro was an active supporter of the Economic Equity Act, which was first floated in 1981. The main provisions of this act are pension equity, enforcement of child-support payments, insurance policy fairness, IRAs for homemakers, and bigger tax breaks for child care. It's an important list of demands, which, unfortunately, is not getting very far in Congress.

Equal Rights Versus Social Benefits

In her talk Ferraro concentrated on issues of pension equity, while Schneider focused on equal access to education for women. Bellamy, in a pessimistic mood, received a standing ovation when she presented a shopping list of all the problems facing women: low pay; low job mobility; low levels of representation at the upper levels of business and government. Her conclusion was that things haven't changed that much for women. Bellamy did not go on to offer any solutions; indeed, she didn't even talk about any measures she was supporting that might remedy some of these problems. The discussion was then opened to the floor.

After almost thirty minutes of questions on pension equity, equal pay, comparable worth, and the enforcement of equal opportunity and nondiscrimination laws, I decided that there was a serious gap in the discussion. *No one* had mentioned what is perhaps the fundamental problem of working women's lives: the difficulties inherent in integrating work and family life. The closest the discussion had come to even touching on the subject was a brief discussion of dependent-care tax credits.

So I asked a question: "How can women achieve economic equality without family support structures such as maternity leave, child allowances, and public day care? Only forty percent of working women in this country are entitled to any maternity leave; is there any action being taken in Congress to expand this right? Hundreds of thousands of American preschoolers spend their days in overcrowded dangerous day care; are there any plans to extend the scope of quality public child care?"

Neither Schneider nor Ferraro seemed anxious to respond. After a long pause Schneider volunteered that "there are tax credits for dependent care, and we are working to raise the maximum credit level." I thought to myself: Big deal. If there is no child care available in your neighborhood, tax credits are meaningless, or if you don't earn enough to pay substantial taxes, tax credits are again meaningless. But feeling that I had heard their answer to child care, I decided to push the congresswomen on maternity benefits. So I ran down the long list of Western democracies that provided statutory maternity leave and emphasized how generous and how extensive this leave was. I then asked how the richest nation in the world could be the only country without these benefits for its working women. I waited for an answer, but an awkward silence hung over the dais. Finally Ferraro said rather plaintively, "All I can say is that nothing is being done at the federal level about maternity leave." She then signaled she was ready for the next question and briskly moved on. The next question from the floor was on abortion—what was being done to defend *Roe v. Wade*. Both congresswomen responded eagerly to this question. They were on top of the debate and listed recent court rulings and legislative action with practiced ease.

After the conference I caught Ferraro as she was trying to hurry out. I managed to give her some information about the panel on family policy at the Economic Policy Council. She nodded her thanks and was moving toward the door when she looked back, caught my eye, and said, "Maternity leave? I learned something."

8

WOMEN'S LIBERATION AND MOTHERHOOD

Motherhood is not going out of style. The vast majority of American women are mothers by the end of their childbearing years. In 1980 only 10 percent of all women aged forty to forty-four were childless. Women are having fewer children, and they are having them later, but more women are having at least one child than ever before.[1]

The only exception to this trend are elite professional women (who are such a tiny proportion of all women that they scarcely affect the average picture). Many of these women are single or divorced, and a large proportion remain childless. Surveys of women executives and high-level professionals show that more than half have reached age 40 without having children.[2] In fact, census figures show that 20 percent of all highly educated women (women with graduate training) remain childless.[3] But although elite professional women often do not have children, for many it is not a preferred choice, and some are prepared to go to extraordinary lengths to have a child.

Jenny Windler* is forty-five years old. Up until a year ago she was the executive vice-president of a clothing manufacturing firm in

*Pseudonym.

New York City. She was number three in the firm and, with bonuses, earned $75,000 a year. In 1983 she gave up her job in order to adopt a child.

Jenny explains her decision in the following way: "I have wanted a child for as long as I can remember. I was married for several years in my thirties, but it was an unhappy, restless relationship, and Jon did not want children, so those prime childbearing years passed me by. I guess I just buried myself in work.

"We were divorced in 1978. By that time I was thirty-eight and desperate to have a baby. So I hatched this plan to have a child on my own. I decided to work hard for two more years and accumulate a nest egg so that I could take some time off to be with my child. I then intended to hit the adoption agencies. By then I would be over forty and too old to cope with pregnancy."

Jenny sighed and said with feeling, "It's a good thing I didn't know then how difficult it was going to be." By 1980, when Jenny was ready to adopt her child, she was forty-one years old, much too old to be a prime candidate for adoption. Besides, she was single. On both accounts she was frowned upon by the adoption agencies; in fact, most would not even consider her as a prospective parent. Jenny bent over backward: She was willing to take an Oriental child or a South American child, she was willing to take an older child, and she was willing to spend a lot of money. But two years of exhausting effort went by, and still Jenny failed to find a child. In desperation she got on a plane and went to northern India, where she had been told it might be possible to adopt a child from one of the refugee camps. The adoption struggle took four months and featured court battles and mountains of red tape, but Jenny just refused to budge until she could leave with her new three-year-old daughter.

I asked Jenny how she had dealt with her job during this difficult period. "I coped with the Indian trip by taking a leave of absence from my work," said Jenny, "but when I got back, I realized that Toby needed all of me if she was going to cope with the massive adjustments required of her. So I resigned my job, and right now we are living on my savings." Jenny smiled and added,

"It's a good thing I did give up my job. I couldn't possibly have fitted it in. I haven't even gone to the bathroom by myself in a year. Adopting a three-year-old presents all kinds of special problems." But Jenny didn't seem to mind any of these problems. She looked very content.[4]

Afton Blake is a single woman in her mid-thirties. She is a psychologist and lives in a quiet neighborhood in a house crammed with books and art. In 1981 she decided to have a child by artificial insemination. "It was time to have a child," she says. "I was secure emotionally and not in a steady relationship with a man." She thought first of asking a friend to coparent with her, but she feared that such a setup could turn into an awkward triangle. That left insemination.

She shopped around the sperm banks of California and eventually ended up at the Repository for Germinal Choice. After studying the catalog of donors—with view to picking out traits, values, and characteristics that appealed to her—she chose Number 28. The catalog described Number 28 as having "good intellectual and musical ability, a charismatic personality, and very good looks." As Afton sees it, "he is the kind of man I might have married."

When she started artificial insemination, Afton was lucky and conceived straight away, but two months later she miscarried. Several more months of insemination followed before she conceived again. A year ago Afton Blake gave birth to a healthy boy she named Doron.[5]

Doron joins the 500,000 other children conceived in the United States since 1960 by artificial insemination. It is estimated that 1.5 million more Americans will be created this way by the year 2000.[6] Two-thirds of the women undergoing artificial insemination are single.[7] They want children but have failed to find Mr. Right.

The feminists of the modern women's movement made one gigantic mistake: They assumed that modern women wanted nothing to do with children. As a result, they have consistently failed to incorporate the bearing and rearing of children into their vision of a liberated life. This "mistake" has had serious repercussions.

In the nineteenth century feminists held motherhood in great esteem. As Elizabeth Cady Stanton said in an address to the National Woman Suffrage Association in 1885, "surely maternity is an added power and development of some of the most tender sentiments of the human heart and not a limitation."[8] But these early activists did not feel the need to focus on motherhood as a feminist issue. They tended to take their maternal duties for granted, an attitude facilitated by the fact that they were privileged women in an era when in affluent households most domestic responsibilities were delegated to servants. They therefore devoted little energy to thinking through what support structures women might need if they were to become both mothers and workers.

In the modern period the situation has been much more extreme as many new wave feminists have been openly hostile to both mothers and children. They have identified the family and the biological function of motherhood as the central institutions of male power serving to enslave women in the interests of men.[9] Radical feminists have even envisaged a utopia where childbirth through science could be removed from the domain of women's bodies.[10] Rather than help women cope with their double burden—in the home and in the workplace—modern feminists have encouraged women to avoid both marriage and children.

All five women who organized the Seneca Falls Convention in 1848—Elizabeth Cady Stanton, Lucretia Mott, Martha Coffin Wright, Mary Ann McClintock, and Jane Master Hunt—were married, and all had children. Stanton later wrote of this group that they "were neither sour old maids, childless women nor divorced wives, as the newspapers declared them to be."[11] Even unmarried, childless Susan B. Anthony warmed to the idea of babies. In a September 1857 letter to Stanton she wrote that reproduction was "the highest and holiest function of the physical organism ... to be a *mother,* to be a *father,* is the best and highest wish of any human being."[12] Anthony often found herself holding babies and stirring puddings to allow her friend and collaborator Elizabeth Cady Stanton time out from her large family and write speeches and tracts for the feminist cause.

With the possible exception of Stanton (who found that the bearing and rearing of seven children did get in the way of political activity), these early feminists did not regard motherhood as a burden. Given their middle-class status, the plenitude of servants, and the contemporary hands-off approach to mothering, they did not feel weighed down by their maternal roles. Childbirth itself might have been dangerous, but once the children were born, there were lots of servants to look after them. As we shall see in Chapter Eleven, prior to the 1940s it didn't occur to anyone that children needed the constant presence of their own mothers for several years from birth onward. As Emily Davies put it in the 1870s, "An educated woman of active, methodological habits, blessed with good servants, as good mistresses generally are, finds an hour a day amply sufficient for her domestic duties. Nothing is gained by spreading it over a longer time."[13]

Thus, although these nineteenth-century feminists attached great value to family and children, they did not feel the need to focus on motherhood as a burden that needed to be lightened. Maternal and wifely duties were taken for granted, as were nursemaids and cooks, and the more onerous domestic responsibilities were offloaded on the servant class. It was therefore possible for these early activists to treat children as enjoyable additions to their lives. "A professional woman spending a short time a day in the superintendence of her nursery, and enjoying the society of her children, would find it a means of rest and refreshment."[14]

There was one small group of feminists in this early period who did see housework and child care as a basic cause of women's inequality. These social feminists were most active at the turn of the century, when, under the leadership of Charlotte Perkins Gilman, they defined a "grand domestic revolution" in women's domestic lives. They demanded wages for women's household labor and proposed a transformation in the design of American homes. They developed housewives' cooperatives, kitchenless houses, day-care centers, public kitchens, and community dining clubs.

Gilman's suggestions included purpose-built apartment houses for professional women and their families:

> If there should be built and opened in any of our large cities today a commodious and well-served apartment house for professional women with families, it would be filled at once. The apartments would be without kitchens; but there would be a kitchen belonging to the house from which meals could be served to the families in their rooms or in a common dining-room, as preferred. It would be a home where the cleaning was done by efficient workers, not hired separately by the families, but engaged by the manager of the establishment; and a roof-garden, day nursery and kindergarten, under well-trained professional nurses and teachers, would ensure proper care of the children.[15]

Gilman argued for the communal raising of babies, believing that a child "would benefit and grow up less shy if he spent certain hours a day among other babies, thereby learning that he is one of many." As for the mother, she "will love her child as well, perhaps better, when she is not in hourly contact with it, when she goes from its life to her own life, and back from her own life to its life, with ever new delight and power."[16]

Gilman's novel perspective was influenced by her personal history. She had gone through a divorce and brought up a daughter in difficult circumstances. Because her life had been less comfortable than many other nineteenth-century feminists, she had a firm grip on the difficulties inherent in combining domestic responsibilities with a professional existence. Writing at the peak of the suffrage controversy at the turn of the century, Gilman staunchly maintained that the right to vote was of relatively little importance in improving women's economic position. A more important goal was to develop support services that would ease women's household and child-rearing duties. In her eyes the existence of such services was essential if women were to participate fully in the mainstream of society. In Gilman's eloquent words:

> We have so arranged life that a man may have a home, a family, love, companionship, domesticity and fatherhood, yet remain an active citizen of age and country. We have so arranged life, on the other hand, that a woman must "choose"; must either live alone, unloved, uncompanied, uncared for, homeless, childless, with her work in the world for sole consolation; or give up all world service for the joys of love, motherhood, and domestic service.[17]

But one should not exaggerate the impact of this splinter group. These early social feminists were small in number and hardly made a dent on the consciousness of the day. In the half century preceding 1920 about 5,000 women and men participated in these experiments designed to revolutionize domestic work. Contrast this with NAWSA, which for twenty years had 2 million members. Turn-of-the-century feminist activity was clearly centered on the fight for the vote.

However, despite their low profile, the social feminists did provide an alternative vision of women's liberation which had more in common with European social feminism than did the mainstream American movement with its emphasis on equal rights.

Most of these ideas were lost in the 1920s and 1930s as feminists, particularly the social feminists, came under direct political attack. The years following the First World War were marked by unemployment, strikes, and social unrest. The political climate of the day was brittle and tense, and women's organizations came under heavy fire. It was thought that women might use their newly acquired right to vote to trigger unwelcome social change. The War Department spearheaded the attack in 1919 and 1920 by devising an infamous spider web chart, which represented feminist activities and their organizations as part of a "red web" aimed at destroying America through pacifism and socialism. All the moderate women's groups, including the Young Women's Christian Association, the American Home Economics Association, and the League of Women Voters, were smeared in this campaign. But the social feminists were especially threatening and came in for the heaviest attacks. They were accused of advocating "free lovism," "unnatural motherhood," and "futuristic baby raising."[18]

As early as the 1920s policy makers were considering the strategy of offering male workers the chance to buy small suburban homes on long-term mortgages as a way of achieving greater social and economic harmony. This would both tame male discontent and ensure that women were not tempted to try out dangerous feminist ideas. As one publication of the era put it, "A wide diffusion of home ownership has long been recognized as fostering stable and conservative habits. . . . The man owns his home but in a sense his home owns him, checking his rash impulses."[19] If male workers were to be defined as homeowners, women were to be the home managers and consumers of the new age. This new philosophy was in place by 1931, when President Herbert Hoover convened the National Conference on Home Building and Home Ownership, which was aimed at men "of sound character and industrious habits."[20]

Despite the ambitious plans of the new social conservatives, the Great Depression and another World War intervened, and they had to wait until the late 1940s before circumstances were receptive to their ideas. As I shall describe in Chapter Ten, after the Second World War the suburban flight began in earnest and women became even more grounded in their individual, labor-intensive homes. When women began to rebel in the late sixties, they took for granted the three-bedroom house with a kitchenful of appliances. They knew nothing about the earlier generation of social feminists and their rigorous questioning of the single-family home as an appropriate framework for a liberated woman.

Modern feminists have failed to come to terms with motherhood more thoroughly than their nineteenth-century sisters. The women's liberation movement has not just decided to ignore children; many contemporary feminists have reviled both mothers and babies.

Some feminists rage at babies; others trivialize, or denigrate them. Very few have attempted to integrate them into the fabric of a full and equal life. When Betty Friedan wrote *The Fem-*

inine Mystique in 1963, she described the deep well of frustration faced by homemakers as "the problem that has no name." One might say that *motherhood is the problem that modern feminists cannot face.*

My own experience at Barnard College illustrates this point very well. The college, in refusing to develop a maternity policy, exhibited a profound indifference to the whole issue of reconciling professional and maternal responsibilities—this despite Barnard's reputation as a bastion of women's rights. My colleagues, many of whom were active feminists, were hostile toward such a policy and accused me of trying to "take a free ride." At the time I felt bewildered and betrayed. It was somehow a lot more difficult to take this kind of treatment from Barnard College than from some stronghold of male privilege. After all, if my liberated female colleagues did not think I deserved any time off to deal with miscarriage or premature birth, maybe they were right and I was just being self-indulgent. I have since discovered that their reaction to my predicament was part of a larger trend. The modern women's movement has not just been anti-men; it has also been profoundly anti-children and anti-motherhood.

The book titles of the movement in its early, more radical phase are illustrative: Jill Johnston's *Lesbian Nation,* which declares that heterosexuality is the female form of treason; Germaine Greer's *The Female Eunuch,* which finds an explanation for impotence in being female; Kate Millett's *Sexual Politics,* in which the personal becomes the political and sex is redefined as a power struggle; Kathrin Perutz's *Marriage Is Hell,* which argues that marriage is precisely that; and Ellen Peck's *The Baby Trap,* which reveals how and why babies are incompatible with liberation. The slogans of the day were extraordinary: Marriage was hell, sex was political, coitus was killing, married women were prostitutes, babies were traps, intercourse was rape, love was slavery, families were prisons, and men were enemies.

The 1972 Manifesto of SCUM (Society for Cutting up Men) captures the extreme spirit of the day:

> ... there remains to civic-minded, responsible, thrill-seeking females only to overthrow the government,

eliminate the money system, institute complete automation, and destroy the male sex. . . . It is now technically possible to reproduce without the aid of males (or, for that matter, females) and to produce only females. We must begin immediately to do so. The male is a biological accident: the Y (male) gene is an incomplete X (female) gene, that is, has an incomplete set of chromosomes. In other words, the male is an incomplete female, a walking abortion, aborted at the gene state.[21]

Many groups of radical feminists (e.g., the Redstockings) put out similar statements.

It is well known that the first targets of radical feminist rhetoric were men. According to the Redstocking Manifesto, "*All men* receive economic, sexual and psychological benefits from male supremacy. *All men* have oppressed women."[22] Men were enemy number one, but family, marriage, and children also came under direct attack because they were the mechanisms through which woman's second-class status was perpetuated through time. "Freedom for women cannot be won without the abolition of marriage."[23] However, since women as wives and mothers play a central role in all aspects of family life, they too became prime targets of the movement. To be a nurturing and empathetic mother and to be a loving and supportive wife—the overriding goals of women who grew to maturity in the 1950s—were seen as signs of weakness and inadequacy. These attributes and these roles were to be stamped out in the brave new world of liberated women. The problem with being a woman could not be taken care of by getting rid of oppression or even by destroying the oppressors; it was wrapped up in *being a feminine woman*. In the late sixties and early seventies significant numbers of young feminists rejected the whole package—marriage, motherhood, and children—as a bad life choice for any woman. To be liberated came to mean wiping out all special female characteristics, leaving behind an androgenous shell of abstract personhood. Stripped of their men and their children, these unfettered women could then join the mainstream and clone the male competitive model in the marketplace.

At least some of the new wave feminists were fleeing from the ultradomestic world of the 1950s. Betty Friedan was typical. When she wrote *The Feminine Mystique,* she was struggling to free herself from fifteen years as a suburban housewife, years which featured three children and a failed marriage. Her own salvation was wrapped up in dismissing homemaking as comprising "tasks for feeble minded girls and eight year olds,"[24] and it was to be twenty years before she could look motherhood in the eye again. In her 1982 book *The Second Stage,* written when she was enjoying the pleasures of grandmotherhood, she acknowledges the central role of children and family in women's lives. Then she was able to say that "the failure of the women's movement was its blind spot about the family. It was our own extreme reaction against the wife-mother role."[25]

Gloria Steinem is an example of another genre—the modern feminist leader who has chosen not to have children. This decision is undoubtedly colored by her personal history. In her powerful and touching essay "Ruth's Song," Steinem describes her mother, Ruth, as "a spirited and adventurous young woman who struggled out of a working-class family and into college, who found work she loved." But all this was before "she gave up her career to help my father."[26] Ruth's first bout of mental illness "followed years of trying to take care of a baby [and] be the wife of a kind but financially irresponsible man."[27] Ruth's daughter Gloria has obviously done her best to avoid such traps as marriage and babies, and this is reflected in her feminist perspective. In her 1983 book *Outrageous Acts and Everyday Rebellions* Steinem collects together twenty-seven essays. They represent the best of her writing and are impressively diverse, ranging from a piece on "The International Crime of Genital Mutilation" to a poignant essay entitled "In Praise of Women's Bodies." Aside from the description of her mother's life, not one page is devoted to motherhood, family, or children.

Most of the women who were on the cutting edge of the women's movement in the late sixties and seventies were trying to obliterate those bright and smiling housewife-mothers of the 1950s with their "unique femininity" and their devotion to the bearing and raising of children. They were not impressed by woman's "God given sensationally unique ability to wear skirts."[28] In many instances the doll-like creatures of the fifties did not wear well. During the countercultural rebellion of the 1960s millions of them were tossed on the scrap heap by their husbands and became pathetic "displaced homemakers"; others dealt with the "empty nest syndrome" by the liberal use of Valium and alcohol.

If the lives of our mothers had been less artificial (or more viable), modern women might not have had to rebel so radically. In any event, contemporary feminists "threw the baby out with the bathwater." Twenty-five years of the feminine mystique and a birthrate rivaling that of India meant that anything which smacked of motherhood became anathema to the modern women's movement.

We are often told that those "libbers" alienated ordinary women because of their extravagant rhetoric and behavior. They burned their bras, called respectable men chauvinistic pigs, and ordinary folks tuned out. I don't find this explanation very convincing. Every revolution requires its polemics since oppressors are usually deaf to reasoned whispers. Much more negative than the language of the movement has been the fact that it has alternately ignored, reviled, and lashed out at the most widely shared experience of women (after sex), motherhood. In so doing the movement alienated its main constituency. The great majority of women have children at some point during their lives, and few of these women ever cease to love their sons and daughters. For the majority of mothers their children constitute the most passionate attachment of their lives. It is absurd to expect to build a coherent feminist movement, let alone a separatist feminist movement, when you exclude and denigrate the deepest emotion in women's lives. It is difficult to build a women's movement on an anti-men platform, but it could probably be done. The modern world is, after all, populated with divorcées, widows, gays, and singles, many of whom bear grudges against the male sex. But it is impossible to build a mass women's movement on an anti-child, anti-mother platform.

Despite this logic, modern feminists have not been restrained in their treatment of women with children. The views of feminist Juliet Mitchell are typical. In *Woman's Estate* she describes women with families as inclined to "small-mindedness, petty jealousy, irrational emotionality and random violence, dependency, competitive selfishness and possessiveness, passivity, a lack of vision and conservatism."[29] It is almost necessary to remind oneself that this is a portrait drawn not by a misogynist but by a feminist. Mitchell goes further: If women in families are despicable, the family itself is, "By its very nature . . . there to prevent the future."[30]

Shulamith Firestone developed what was perhaps the definitive feminist view on the subject with her theory of history based on sex itself. According to Firestone, the elimination of sexual classes requires the revolt of women and the seizure of control of *reproduction,* just as the elimination of economic classes requires the revolt of the proletariat and the seizure of the means of *production.* There must be, she says, elimination not only of privilege but also of class distinction and sexual distinction. She goes on to advocate artificial reproduction or at least its option. This would eliminate reproduction by one sex for the benefit of the both. In her schema the dependence of the child on the mother would be replaced by dependence on a small group of adults.

Thus Firestone produces a social framework in which "the tyranny of the biological family would be broken."[31] But her framework implies that women can be freed only by the elimination of motherhood. With the proposal of such a utopian and unrealistic solution the problem is effectively shelved. It becomes a way of not coming to terms with motherhood. Although few feminists are as extreme in their views as Firestone, this tendency to brush motherhood to one side runs through the modern movement.

It is easier to find feminist positions on abortion, rape, the female orgasm, the rights of lesbians, and genital mutilation in the third world than to find out what feminists think about motherhood. In a popular anthology of writing from the women's liberation movement, *Sisterhood Is Powerful,* only one out of seventy-four essays has anything to do with motherhood.[32] One can read an essay on "The Politics of Orgasm" or digest a poem called "Song of the Fucked Duck," but it is difficult to find anything on childbearing or childraising, which are the central issues of most women's lives.

It is important to note that hostility toward children has not been limited to the radical wing of the feminist movement. The mainstream of the women's movement has been indifferent to motherhood and family, and at times this indifference has shaded into antipathy.

For the last fifteen years the national feminist organizations (such as NOW and WEAL) have given top priority to the ERA and abortion. Issues such as access to credit, equal educational opportunities, and getting women elected to political office have constituted a second tier of goals. Child care has been at the bottom of the scale of priorities, and as we saw in Chapters Six and Seven, maternity leave hasn't even made it onto the feminist agenda.

The various platforms of the movement generally include child care, but treatment of this issue is always perfunctory. For example, at the 1977 International Women's Year conference in Houston, child care was hardly touched upon. The burning issues of the conference were the ERA, abortion, and sexual preference.[33] In the thirty-page "National Plan of Action" that resulted from this conference, child care occupied half a page.[34] At other meetings child care has been mixed up with issues of reproductive freedom and control over one's body. For example, the Congress to Unite Women called for the "elimination of all laws and practices that compel women to bear children against their will." This congress also strongly advocated "research in extrauterine gestation."[35] Mainstream feminists have generally treated motherhood as something most women want to avoid.

In an interview, child-care expert Dana Friedman talked to me about the six years she spent in Washington, D.C., lobbying, trying to get various pieces of child-care legislation through Congress. As Dana puts it, "The feminist groups never took the lead on child-care issues. It's not that in the end they didn't sign off on child-care initiatives, but they never put any real effort into this area." Dana paused and then said reflectively, "It's as though they wanted to look good—they didn't want to be accused of not supporting government funding for child care. But they viewed child care as an issue that was too connected to motherhood—too related to the role they were trying to downplay. At the Houston Conference, child care was number fourteen on a list of goals that had fifteen items on it. I think that's a pretty accurate reflection of the importance of child care to feminists—it is priority number fourteen."[36]

Friedan in *The Second Stage* describes how many feminists thought that the 1970 White House Conference on Families was not worth attending. She also talks about the cold silence that greeted her appeal in the fall of 1979 for the women's movement to come to grips with the practical problems of the family.[37]

The issue of women's control over their bodies has enabled some feminists to address and yet to avoid the issue of motherhood. Natural childbirth is a good example of this sleight of hand. In the 1970s it became a rallying point for feminists wanting to seem helpful on the childbirth front but all the while retaining an almost exclusive concern with the female experience. Childbirth became an occasion to glory in one's body and experience self-fulfillment, rather than a time of birthing a child and becoming a mother.

The declared goal of one of the first birth centers set up in California in 1971 was to form "a sisterhood concerned with birth and its process. . . . We are finding out about the natural capabilities of women . . . and have taken our birthright, freedom, and decided for ourselves what our rituals of birth will be."[38] The enthusiasts in the natural childbirth movement are convinced that "Doctors are always enemies of women" and "this is especially true of most obstetricians who elect to play the role of the Father and God to their patients, forcing women into the role of helpless, stupid, ridiculous little girls."[39]

Thus childbirth (like rape and abortion) is reduced to yet another struggle for control over a woman's body or (like sex) is treated as though its only function were to give women a valuable experience. Some of the insights of the natural childbirth movement are valid. Hospital births probably did become too clinical in the middle decades of this century, and women were not consulted enough in the process of labor and birth, but the movement has produced burdens of its own. As I myself found out when I had children, all this emphasis on performing to prove one's womanhood, all this talk about the great "birth experience" can set a woman up for failure, and it almost always obscures rather than facilitates coming to terms with the central issues of parenthood.

Helen* was thirty-one years old when she became pregnant with her first child in 1977, and she and her husband became tremendously involved in giving birth naturally. As Helen put it, "we were so idealistic. Like many of our friends, we believed in women's liberation and felt committed to this movement that was going to allow us to gain control over our bodies and truly experience this great moment in life. The idea seemed so good, so warm, so attractive to give birth naturally, together as a couple."

Helen and Jim went to Lamaze classes, learned that childbirth would not hurt, did their breathing exercises, and chose an obstetrician who could offer a Leboyer delivery. This was the last word in naturalness. It meant that delivery would take place in a quiet, darkened room; that a birthing chair would be used; that the umbilical cord would not be severed immediately; that the newborn baby would be placed on the belly of the mother and allowed to nurse; and that one of the immediate postdelivery experiences of the baby would be to float in a warm tub of water. Helen and Jim were very proud to have found one of the few obstetricians and one of the few hospitals (the Washington Hospital Center) that could offer a Leboyer delivery.

Despite all the joyous preparation and despite all the careful plans, the actual delivery of Helen and Jim's daughter was a traumatic experience.

Helen had an incredibly painful and extremely long labor—thirty hours. Acting on her instructions, the obstetrician administered no drugs and tried desperately to avoid a cesarean section. After twenty-nine hours of labor the baby went into acute dis-

*Pseudonym.

tress, and the delivery scene took on the frantic quality of a real medical emergency. The fetal heart became erratic and actually stopped for a while. The obstetrician used forceps, surgical incisions, anything, to get the baby out. And when Laura was born, she looked blue, battered, and lifeless. The parents were not even told whether their child was a boy or a girl. The baby was snatched away by the medical team and immediately taken to another floor, where the infant intensive care unit was housed. Helen says she will always remember the appalling emotions that swept over her in the immediate postdelivery period: "I felt that I had been butchered, I felt an overwhelming sense of bitterness and betrayal in being cheated out of the greatest experience of my life, and I felt a sense of utter failure." Oddly enough, in this immediate postpartum period, Helen says quite frankly, that she barely thought about Laura. So thoroughly had she absorbed the messages of the natural childbirth movement that the shattering of her own birth experience was uppermost in her mind.

Worry about Laura came later when it was discovered that the baby had a heart problem and, at six months old, had to undergo corrective surgery. The medical experts told Helen and Jim that the heart problem was congenital, that it had nothing to do with the difficult birth. But Helen does not altogether accept this. "Laura had to work so terribly hard to get born, and it was quite clear that this did produce tremendous strain on her heart." She goes on to say regretfully, "If only I had not been so ideological, so committed to avoiding a cesarean, we all might have avoided the dreadful anxiety of those early months of Laura's life."

Helen's retrospective judgment of natural childbirth is terse and to the point: "I now think that it can get in the way of good medical practice. If I were to have another child, I would be more realistic in my expectations and I would not martyr myself for the sake of any cause, however fashionable."[40]

Helen and Jim were left with a sense of bitterness, their birth experience had been "spoiled" by pain, trauma, and a sense of failure. But in a larger sense they were fortunate: Their baby is now a well-developing, loving child, and giving birth to a healthy baby has to be the ultimate point of pregnancy and childbirth.

Even in the modern world anguish and tragedy can surround the birth process. When I lost my twins in the sixth month of pregnancy, and when I faced the physical and emotional problems of prematurity, I thought that I had been singled out for pain. I felt that I should remind God that this was the latter part of the twentieth century and women were supposed to jog through pregnancy and birth their children with joy and ease. I thought that it was only in nineteenth-century novels that women suffered when giving birth to a child. But the miracles of conception and birth can still be fraught for women.

It is true that modern women don't die when giving birth to a child, and babies generally survive the ordeal of being born (although the infant mortality rate is considerably higher in the United States than in Europe). But real problems of infertility, miscarriage, and of birth itself continue to haunt women.

One ironic fact of modern life is that infertility rates are sharply on the rise. The last twenty years have seen a dramatic increase in sexually transmitted disease and an increase in the use of IUDs as a birth-control method. Both factors have served to boost the incidence of pelvic inflammatory disease in women, which in its turn has pushed up the infertility rate.[41] A not so welcome by-product of the sexual revolution!

According to Dr. Alan Berkeley, an obstetrician who specializes in high-risk cases at New York Hospital, "fifteen percent of couples face some serious problem of infertility, and the risks increase significantly with age. The infertility rate for women starts climbing at age thirty, and a forty-year-old woman has a forty percent chance of being infertile." Modern medicine can bring the final infertility rate down to 5 percent, but this is after months of unpleasant tests, procedures, and surgery. In Berkeley's experience most couples don't give up until they have been in treatment for two to three years.

Miscarriage is also an ongoing problem. Today 15 to 20 percent of pregnancies end in miscarriage, an event which many women find difficult to take in their stride. As Dr. Berkeley put it, "miscarriage can be profoundly disturbing, especially for a career woman in her thirties who has waited years for the right time to start a family. After losing a pregnancy, many of these women want a child so badly that they are willing to redefine their lives. Some of them are even willing to throw in their job and go to bed for nine months if this will enable them to carry a child to term."[42] His words brought back to me the desperation I felt when I lost the twins. For me, too, the need to replace those babies temporarily obliterated other aspects of life.

Finally, birth itself is not without its complications. Thirty percent of deliveries in this country are by cesarean section, and although some C sections might be "discretionary," the majority are performed for the safety of either the mother or the baby. For those women who have "normal" vaginal deliveries, many will lose control in labor and experience intense pain. In short, they will fail to live up to the natural childbirth ideal. In Chapter Two I pointed out that only three out of the thirteen women in my Lamaze class experienced childbirth as the easy, joyous event they had been taught it should be.

Thus, for the millions of women who are struggling with the anguish of infertility or miscarriage, or for those who merely "fail" to give birth naturally, the emphasis of the women's movement on the "great experience" of birth can seem like a cruel joke. What many of us modern working women need when we finally get around to being able to have children is concrete support in the problems we face, not another lesson in consciousness raising. Getting your head in the right place is not enough. Today's women need support when they encounter difficulties in childbearing, many require expensive medical care, and all need a clear right to maternity leave. The women's movement has not produced any of these items. Indeed, they hardly figure on the feminist agenda.

Hostility toward mothers and children permeates the American women's movement. The full-time care of a baby is likened to "spending all day, every day, in the exclusive company of an incontinent mental defective,"[43] while pregnancy is described as "the temporary deformation of the body of the individual for the sake of the species."[44] Even Betty Friedan, a moderate in the movement, accuses her generation of feminine fifties women of having a "sick, sad love affair with their own children."[45]

All this prompted a swift and fierce reaction not only from men (who were clearly labeled as enemy number one) but from women. Women might wish to be free, but not of their families. If accepting sisterhood meant abandoning husbands, children, home, love, and nurturing, then they would do without sisters.

If Anita Bryant and Marabel Morgan were feminine cartoons, their adversaries were feminist cartoons, and if there had to be a choice, a great many women preferred the caricature of femininity. For among the half truths and exaggerations that critics of feminism like Schlafly deployed to discredit the feminist position, there were kernels of truth, which the women's movement ignored—to its detriment. Homemaking could be denigrated as an occupation only by belittling millions of women, and by trying to attach to it a market value, feminists cheapened rather than enhanced the value many women believed it had. Marriage might produce new forms of bondage, but it also produced new forms of freedom, while the vaunted independence of the liberated and divorced often turned out to mean loneliness and penury. Children were demanding, but often brought joy and fulfillment and extended rather than narrowed the boundaries of a woman's life. And employment, although it could bestow status in the marketplace, was for most women drudgery that limited rather than extended a woman's opportunities.

In the 1970s all this ideological baggage, this polarization between homemakers and workers, and between mothers and anti-mothers, got snarled up in the acrimonious fight to ratify the ERA.

9

THE ERA: A TEST CASE

When I started my work on the American women's movement, I knew that I had to come to terms with the bruising defeat of the Equal Rights Amendment. I was one of those East Coast liberals who had given the ratification campaign a certain amount of knee-jerk support during the 1970s and early 1980s. I contributed money, signed petitions, did a little canvassing, and nodded approvingly when experts talked about the amendment as a measure that would "establish fully, emphatically and unambiguously the proposition that before the law women and men are to be treated without difference."[1] I frankly couldn't understand how or why it had stirred up such intense controversy, and I couldn't begin to explain why it had been defeated, especially since the opinion polls told me that it had the support of a majority of the American people.

Like everyone else, I heard rumors about Phyllis Schlafly. People told me that although she seemed to be responsible for the failure to ratify the ERA, in reality she was merely a cover for an ugly, well-heeled conspiracy spawned by the lunatic right wing of American politics.

Little did I think that by the time I had finished the research for this book I would have great sympathy for the Schlafly campaign. Indeed, I could no longer be counted on to vote for the ERA. One unhappy supporter of the ERA hit the nail on the head when she said plaintively "the ERA seemed to be more popular the less people knew about it . . . the longer the fight dragged on the more doubts and fears surfaced about the nature of the amendment."[2] That is exactly what happened to me. The more I understood about this piece of legislation, the less I supported it.

The call for an equal rights amendment was not new in 1971. The amendment had been introduced in every Congress since 1923 and had been given serious consideration on at least three occasions: 1946, 1950, and 1953. In 1970 a group of feminists led by Congresswoman Martha Griffiths of Michigan succeeded in pushing the ERA out of committee onto the floor of Congress. Given the recent passage of the civil rights legislation, everyone thought that the time had come for the ERA. Its backers argued that anyone who believed in simple equality had to support the ERA. All it said was: "1. Equality of rights under the law shall not be denied or abridged by the United States or by any State on account of sex. 2. The Congress shall have the power to enforce, by appropriate legislation, the provisions of this article. 3. This amendment shall take effect two years after the date of ratification."

As Carol Felsenthal recounts in her excellent description of the battle to ratify the ERA,[3] it surprised no one that in October 1971 the U.S. House of Representatives passed the ERA 354 to 23, or that in March 1972 the Senate approved it 84 to 8. ERA opponents were hard to come by. Hubert Humphrey was for it, but so was George Wallace. Bella Abzug rooted for it, but so did Spiro Agnew.

When Congress sent the ERA to the states for ratification, the states fell over themselves to approve it. Hawaii passed it with no opposition within hours of the Senate's approval. Nebraska, eager to be number two, passed it the next day, without a single dissenting vote. Delaware was in such a hurry that it passed the ERA an hour and forty minutes before the U.S. Senate, a fact that later brought a court challenge to Delaware's ratification. Within three months twenty states had ratified the ERA, and within a year thirty states had signed on. At this point only eight more states were needed to produce the two-thirds majority which would make the ERA part of the Constitution, and its supporters had until 1979 to pick up these additional endorsements.

In March 1973—with six years to spare before ERA's time limit expired—leaders of the feminist organizations predicted that within two months they would have the eight additional states. They failed to anticipate one factor: Phyllis Schlafly and her orchestration of a grass-roots STOP ERA movement.

Schlafly was a right-wing political activist who had become nationally known for her successful promotion of Barry Goldwater as the Republican party nominee in 1964. In early 1972 she decided to fight the ERA.[4] As a traditionalist she found the amendment immensely threatening to family life and to the established division of labor between men and women. And as a conservative she found it dangerous. A firm believer in minimal government, Schlafly considered the second section of the ERA, which gives enforcement power to the U.S. Congress, as bad as the first, which decrees a strict equality of rights under the law. According to Schlafly—and to many legal experts in the field—the first section would require states to make extensive changes in the laws in such areas as marriage, divorce, child custody, and adoption, while the second section would give Washington the power to rewrite state laws if they did not measure up.

When the ERA was introduced into Congress in 1970, its sponsors omitted the Hayden modification, which had been part of the pending amendment for twenty years. This rider stated: "The provisions of this article shall not be construed to impair any rights, benefits or exemptions conferred by law upon persons of the female sex."[5] Senator Carl Hayden had been of the opinion that women, in order to be equal, needed more and different rights than men possessed. In 1970, when the ERA was on the floor of the Senate, Senator Sam J. Ervin reintroduced these qualifications by proposing nine amendments that specifically retained preferential laws for wives, mothers, and widows and exempted women from the draft and from combat duty. But Senator Ervin's qualifications were unacceptable to the House of Representatives, and the version that eventually passed Congress in 1971 contained no exceptions.

Schlafly was particularly concerned by the fact that the version of the ERA sent to the states for ratification required absolute equality. She even went so far as to say that she would have supported the ERA had Congress left in the Hayden modification or the Ervin amendments. The omission of these riders meant that once the ERA was passed, the states would have to treat men and women in precisely the same way. To take an example, laws requiring a husband to support a wife would become unconstitutional. In June 1976 Schlafly debated this issue on television with Professor Thomas I. Emerson of Yale Law School. According to Schlafly:

> I asked him what would happen, under ERA, to the New York State support law which now reads tersely: "Husband liable for support of his wife." He replied, "It cannot remain in that form." I asked him how that law would be changed under ERA. He replied that under ERA the law would have to be changed so that the obligation is mutual, or reciprocal, and each spouse would be liable for the support of the other "if he or she were incapacitated."
>
> I looked at him and said, "But I'm a homemaker, and I'm certainly not incapacitated." He replied, "That's right, you're not."
>
> That is the measure of the homemaker's rights wiped out by the ERA: Her legal right to support for all her years as a wife would be cut down to a right to support *only* for the time that she might be considered to be "incapacitated."[6]

In her book *The Power of the Positive Woman* Schlafly wrote passionately about the network of laws that gives a wife "her legal right to be a full time wife and mother in her own home, taking care of her own babies."[7] She cited a Ohio law which states that "the husband must support himself, his wife, and his minor children out of his property or by his labor," and stressed that all these laws would be wiped out by the ERA.[8]

Thus, Schlafly promoted the view that the ERA would weaken the family and make women more vulnerable. Most at risk were middle-aged housewives who had no independent source of income. These women had married in the fifties, when it was taken for granted that the wife would raise the children and look after the home while the husband would earn the family income. It was from this group of homemakers that Schlafly drew most of her support.

An important implication of the ERA to Schlafly was that if it were ratified, the federal law that exempted women from the draft and excluded them from military combat would become unconstitutional. Most experts agreed with her on this issue. According to the House Judiciary Committee, under the ERA "not only would women, including mothers, be subject to the draft, but the military would be compelled to place them in combat units alongside of men."[9] To Schlafly this both flew in the face of the natural differences between the sexes and weakened national defense. She used as ammunition in her argument Pentagon studies which demonstrate that women have, on average, 60 percent of the physical strength of men.

Schlafly stressed other effects of the ERA. She claimed that women's colleges receiving federal aid (and most of them do) would not be able to continue admitting women only because by so doing they discriminated "on account of sex." She also pointed out that protective labor laws for blue-collar women—such as those exempting women from compulsory overtime, allowing women extra rest periods and better rest rooms—would also become unconstitutional. This hit a raw nerve among working-class women, as many pro-ERA campaigners were to find out. My experience was typical:

In 1979 the American Economic Association (AEA) staged its annual meeting in Atlanta, Georgia. Many of us liberal economists were unhappy with the venue. Georgia was a state that still had not ratified the ERA and we were mortified that the AEA was giving its convention business to such a backward state.

To "make up" for such poor judgment on the part of our professional organization, many of us allocated part of our time in Atlanta to canvassing for the ERA. I went with two colleagues to take on the shift workers at a small textile plant on the outskirts of the city. Early Friday morning a cab dropped us off in front of the factory. It was a raw December day with freezing drizzle spitting out of an overcast sky. We huddled together, our fashionable winter coats and high-heeled boots seeming both inadequate and incongruous in this bleak landscape.

At last a siren wailed and a few minutes later workers from the night shift came straggling through the factory gates in twos and threes. I stepped briskly forward holding out my leaflets and reciting my set piece. "Please read about the ERA; it will improve conditions of life for all American women."

The first group of women eyed me suspiciously, then pushed past—roughly. I retreated surprised and intimidated. I was shocked by the appearance of these women: the bulky starch-fed bodies, the careworn faces and bloodshot, exhausted eyes reminded me of the adults who peopled my childhood in South Wales. The minds of these women were clearly on things other than the ERA.

"Can you take little Chrissy today? Ma is laid up; it's her back again, and I've gotta take her in to the clinic," said one to another as she struggled into her plastic raincoat. Her friend sighed. "I guess I can, but drop her off with some milk and food; my old man's drinking again and we don't have much stuff. . . ." Her voice trailed off. These women might have finished work at the factory, but they were about to start another job—dealing with the demands of needy families.

Eventually I engaged the attention of a black woman. Younger than most of the other workers, she accepted some pro-ERA literature and then looked at me antagonistically.

"You know, I've heard of you 'libbers' and your ERA. I've seen that Schlafly person on TV and she says that equal rights for women is a bad deal because we would lose a whole lot. Like us girls get an extra break in the shift, and management can't force us to work overtime the way they force the men."

As she warmed to her theme, her voice rose. "You should try working in this lousy factory week in and week out and I bet you would want all the benefits you could get."

I attempted a comeback. "You know the ERA wouldn't necessarily take job protection away from women; the ones that mean anything would be extended to men. If women need special benefits, so do men."

This factory worker was now really angry. "If you think life's fair, you're crazy," she snapped. "I've got two kids under five and a husband who doesn't lift a finger. What's fair about that? Why shouldn't I get some breaks on the job?" She flung my pamphlets into the gutter and stalked off to the bus stop to wait in the freezing rain for her bus home.

I felt cowed and uncomfortable. It was the last time I canvassed for the ERA.[10]

Schlafly also won support by describing what the ERA *would not do.* She pointed out that it applies only to government action and has no bearing on the decisions of private employers. Paul A. Freund of the Harvard Law School concurs: "Unless equality is denied by a public agency or because of a law the Equal Rights Amendment by its terms has no applications. If we want to see more women in law firms, in the medical profession, in the Cabinet—and I, for one, do—we must turn elsewhere than to the proposed amendment."[11]

Schlafly concluded that "the ERA will add no new employment rights whatsoever, ERA will not add any new rights to those spelled out in the Equal Employment Opportunity (EEO) Act of 1972 which prohibits all sex discrimination in hiring, pay and promotion."[12] Most experts in the field agree with her that the legislation already on the books—Title VII of the Civil Rights Act, the EEO Act—gives women as much employment protection as the ERA. In an interview a prominent labor and civil-rights lawyer told me that "the ERA adds nothing in this area. Indeed, in some respects Title VII is a stronger legal tool."[13]

*   *   *

So Schlafly staked out a position in which she labeled the ERA the "Men's Liberation Amendment," arguing that it would take significant old rights from women and give them to men without giving women any substantial new rights. She made sure to acquire some heavy-duty legal support for her view. At her prompting law professor Philip B. Kurland of the University of Chicago wired the Illinois legislature on June 5, 1972, with the following message: "It [the ERA] is largely misrepresented as a woman's rights amendment when in fact the primary beneficiaries will be men. I am opposed to its approval."[14] Telegrams such as this encouraged the Illinois Assembly to turn down the ERA.

In the fall of 1972 Phyllis Schlafly founded STOP ERA, installing herself as national chairman. Over the course of the next decade she was single-handedly to turn the tide against the ratification of the ERA. How she did this is an amazing story.

Part of it was that Schlafly proved to be an inspired campaigner and strategist with a flair for public relations. When Schlafly called a rally, women came—in the thousands. In Illinois, for example, she could bring together 1,000 women for a routine demonstration by simply notifying her top lieutenants—59 chairmen, one for each of the state's fifty-nine legislative districts. She communicated with them frequently via telephone-chain calls and notices in her *Eagle Forum Newsletter*.

Her "troops"—decorous homemakers in pink, frilly dresses carrying fresh baked bread and other goodies—seemed to come out of the woodwork whenever the ERA was being debated or voted on.[15] Often these troops were spiced up by media events. When Ruth Clusen, president of the League of Women Voters, made a speech in Springfield announcing that the league would give $150,000 to support the Illinois ratification fight, the Reverend John Peck began prancing around the stage in a gorilla suit before presenting to Schlafly a sign which read DON'T MONKEY AROUND WITH THE CONSTITUTION. This was followed by Schlafly's announcing that *Playboy* had just contributed $5,000 to the pro-ERA cause. She then led her troops in a rendering of her composition "Here Comes *Playboy* Cottontail."[16]

But organization and flair were not going to win the fight on their own. Phyllis Schlafly was facing stiff opposition. The entire establishment from Jimmy Carter to Ted Kennedy to Betty Ford to Jane Fonda seemed to be prepared to use their influence and clout lobbying for the ERA.

During his presidency Carter put the enormous prestige of his office behind the ERA. As Bella Abzug points out, Carter wanted to be known as the president who had achieved equal rights for women.[17] In December 1976, just after his election, he personally telephoned wavering Illinois legislators to try to tip the balance in that state—to no avail. Carter used presidential clout in North Carolina, persuading Congressman Lamar Gudger to cast a key vote for the ERA in exchange for $1.6 million in federal funds for the Asheville Airport. Gudger got his airport, but Schlafly organized her troops in a "prayer chain," and the ERA went down to another defeat in this state.[18]

In October 1979 Carter held an ERA Summit at the White House for hundreds of ERA leaders and officials from unratified states. As the *New York Times* put it, at this meeting "Carter pledged the full support of his Administration, including such specific actions as . . . pointedly reminding unratified states of the need for the ERA every time federal grants or loans are made."[19] At approximately the same time, November 1979, thirty-six women's magazines ranging from *Ms.* to *Vogue* ran articles discussing how the ERA would benefit women. The combined circulation of these magazines was 60 million.

This new level of establishment support for the ERA was put to the test in Illinois in 1980. Eleanor Smeal, president of NOW, called the Illinois campaign "the most extensive in the ERA's history."[20] She organized a huge pro-ERA rally, roped in a slew of movie and TV stars and galvanized the politicians. Jimmy Carter invited members of the Illinois legislation to the White House and promised "to do anything that would be helpful," and Mayor Jane Byrne and Governor James Thompson campaigned vigorously for ratification (Thompson is said to have offered jobs, roads, and bridges in exchange for votes).[21] It was a messy campaign. The ERA backers were accused of exerting unwarranted pressure, and at least one of these charges was substantiated.[22]

However, despite all this pressure, that winter Illinois failed to ratify the ERA for the ninth time.

In retrospect it seems clear that as soon as Schlafly started to fight against the ERA, public support for this legislation began to ebb away. In 1974 only three states ratified. In 1975 only one state ratified and sixteen rejected it. In 1977 one more state passed the ERA, but nine states defeated it, and so on until 1979, when the ERA made constitutional history by becoming the first amendment ever to reach its seven-year limit still unratified. Congress then took the unprecedented step of extending the time for ratification from the original seven to ten years, but this extension also expired without ratification. Particularly undermining for those who supported the ERA, five of the ratified states had second thoughts and voted to rescind their affirmative votes.

The question of whether states were allowed to change their minds about a yes vote was eventually settled by Congress when it refused to pass something called the fair-play amendment—which would have allowed states to change their minds from yes to no during the 1979–82 extension period. This meant that Illinois, a state that had voted down the ERA nine times would have until June 1982 to vote yes. But Kansas or Nebraska, states that had voted yes, were not allowed to change their minds from yes to no. As the *Chicago Tribune* said in an editorial titled "Unequal Rights for ERA," if this policy were applied to individual women, "it would surely and properly be denounced as the height of male chauvinistic sexism."[23] But at this stage in the game Congress was a firm ERA backer.

Some ERA supporters explained the success of the STOP ERA campaign by pointing to a right-wing conspiracy of anti-abortionists, John Birchers, and born-again Christians. STOP ERA was even accused of having important links to the Ku Klux Klan and the National States Rights or Nazi Party.[24] Other ERA supporters were content to blame men. As Bella Abzug described the ratification fight, "Time after aggravating time, a hard core of male politicians who controlled the legislatures in those states, most of them in the south, blocked consideration on the passage of the amendment."[25] Feminists were inclined to see Phyllis Schlafly as a mere tool of conservative men; "if it weren't Phyllis it would be some other Barbie Doll of the right."[26]

Undoubtedly the religious and the political right swung behind Schlafly's position on the ERA. From an early point in the battle she had put together a powerful but unlikely coalition of Catholics, fundamentalists, and Orthodox Jews, all of whom feared federal interference in how they conducted their churches. But mainstream political support did not come until late in the game. Remember that until 1980 the Republican party supported the ERA. Indeed, in the late 1970s Betty Ford was a vigorous campaigner for the ERA. It is also true that no one has been able to establish that Schlafly received major financial contributions from any of the obvious right-wing sources. Most ERA supporters concede that "opponents of the ERA spend far less money than proponents."[27] Schlafly's STOP ERA organization was conspicuously lacking the attributes of a well-heeled campaign. The STOP ERA headquarters was her home in Alton, Illinois, and she generally answered the phone herself and was proud of the fact that "I have nothing to offer the people who work for me. . . . I don't have any paid STOP ERA staff, a PR agent, a press secretary or a professional fund raiser." Anyone who works for me "is not going to get any free trips or any nice, paid staff job in Washington like the ERAers have to offer."[28]

The STOP ERA movement was successful not because it was better financed or more powerfully backed than the pro-ERA forces—the opposite seems to have been true—but because ordinary Americans believed that there was real substance behind the Schlafly campaign. Millions of wives and mothers wanted desperately to preserve what was left of the legal props that supported family life. They heard Schlafly loudly and clearly when she told them, "Women's liberation has gone too far. Instead of giving freedom it has relieved men of their responsibilities as head of the family."[29] They were terrified of any further erosion of their rights and privileges as wives and mothers.

When ERA supporters said that the amendment would do away with many old-fashioned laws that limit women's rights during and after marriage, many Middle America housewives suspected that this would be bad news for traditional homemakers. They had a hunch that these old-fashioned laws were more favorable to women than the no-fault-divorce and equitable-distribution laws which had seriously undermined a wife's right to alimony in so many states (see discussion in Chapter Three). Many homemakers did not want to be treated equally; they yearned for the guarantees and protections of the past. Schlafly's appeal was to those "thousands of frightened women who fear ERA will destroy the American family, legalize rape, send mothers into combat . . . and force contented housewives into jobs they don't want."[30]

When you add in the legitimate fears of blue-collar women that they would lose their hard-won protective benefits, you have a powerful constituency ranged against the ERA. There was no need to explain away the STOP ERA campaign as yet another exercise in male oppression. Rational women—homemakers and workers—had some sensible reasons that prompted them to oppose ratification of the ERA.

Schlafly did tap specifically right-wing energies. States' rights, and women in combat weakening national defense, were both issues which appealed to conservatives. Schlafly also tapped some free-floating right-wing paranoia with her talk about "perverts" (i.e., homosexuals) gaining the right to adopt children. But she would not have succeeded had she not spoken for many ordinary Americans—apolitical workers who feared the loss of protection, and those millions of mothers (and fathers) who found their deepest satisfaction in family life and were fearful that it would be undermined even further by the ERA.

In many ways Schlafly's position on these matters was inadequate. She saw the threat posed by the ERA and wanted to derail this piece of legislation, but she failed to complement this with a constructive policy agenda. After all, homemakers were already immensely vulnerable. The 1960s had wrought sweeping changes in American sexual morality and family life. By the late 1970s family life was crumbling, the divorce rate had risen to one in two of all marriages, and alimony and child support provided a woefully inadequate safety net. In short, the network of laws giving a wife a legal right to be a full-time wife and mother that Schlafly vowed to save were, to say the least, inadequate. As Lisa Wohl correctly points out in her 1974 *Ms.* article, "Too often women wake up to find that this right gives them as much effective protection as the emperor's new clothes."[31]

As for women workers, they too were inadequately protected. In the early 1980s, 40 percent had no health coverage and 60 percent had no right to maternity leave.

Ratification might have accelerated the disintegration of traditional family security and wiped out what remained of protective legislation for women workers, but clearly the ERA could not be held responsible for the precarious nature of women's lives. Rejection of the ERA could not reverse larger social trends and magically re-create "the classical family of Western nostalgia" which had reigned supreme in the 1950s.[32]

In short, if Schlafly wanted to make American women secure in their roles as wives and mothers, she needed to do more than stop the ERA (or ban abortion, for that matter). Modern women, traditional or otherwise, need a new set of rights and benefits: tougher divorce laws, child allowances, maternity leave, independent health coverage, and adequate retirement benefits. They also need better jobs and higher pay, and this is the area where Schlafly's nostalgic vision has been damaging to women. For she has failed to grasp the fact that the majority of wives and mothers now work—most of them because they have to. Schlafly has not helped these women in their struggle to earn a decent wage in the labor market. In fact, by coming out against the pay equity or comparable worth concept, she has pitted her considerable forces against them.

Schlafly devoted the entire January 1984 issue of her newsletter *The Phyllis Schlafly Report* to the subject of comparable worth. In it she argues that it's not legitimate to compare women's jobs with those held by "blue collar men (who are generally supporting their families)." She conveniently forgets about those pink-collar women who also support families. In the important area of jobs and earnings Schlafly is not serving women well.

However incomplete and flawed her position is, Schlafly's Middle American supporters rightly see her as holding similar values to theirs. They are convinced that she truly values the family and sincerely wants to preserve a Norman Rockwell vision of the good life.

The liberal establishment never appreciated the substantive base of the STOP ERA movement. It became chic to dismiss Schlafly's troops as dim-witted Barbie dolls who were being manipulated by sinister forces on the lunatic right. They were rarely credited with any point of view, let alone a sensible point of view. Yet Schlafly won in state after state over the course of a decade. Had the ERA backers better understood the concerns of Schlafly's grass-roots constituency, they might have addressed the fears of Middle America and offered a constructive agenda of their own, thus avoiding the colossal waste of time, energy, and resources that the battle to ratify the ERA turned into.

Perhaps if the issues had been better understood, the image of the pro-ERA campaign would have been better crafted. Schlafly, never a woman to mince her words, called feminists "a bunch of anti-family radicals, lesbians and elitists,"[33] and the women's movement seemed to go out of its way to prove her right.

The 1977 International Women's Year (IWY) Conference in Houston is a case in point. Although it was meant to cover the entire range of women's issues from pension rights to child care, this mammoth get-together was dominated by three "hot button" resolutions—those covering the ERA, abortion and lesbian rights. To many these issues became inextricably linked.

Time magazine expressed concern that homosexual rights dominated the conference.[34] Dorris Holmes, Georgia's delegate and state strategist for the ERA, warned, "It will be harder to pass the amendment in conservative states if it is associated with the lesbian cause."[35] Nonetheless, the homosexual-rights plank was approved at Houston by a large majority. The ensuing scene received a great deal of media attention. Lesbians in the galleries roared their approval: "Thank you, sisters!" They sported buttons that read "A Woman Without a Man Is Like a Fish Without a Bicycle,"[36] and released hundreds of pink and yellow balloons with the message WE ARE EVERYWHERE scrawled over them. In response, the Mississippi delegation rose together, turned their backs on the podium and bowed their heads as if in prayer.

The ERA: A Test Case

A *Washington Star* editorial pointed out that the IWY priority list "links many of the emotionally charged issues quite the way an increasing alarmed opposition fears. Yes, publicly financed abortion on demand, equality of everything for homosexuals, full time day care, guaranteed incomes and unilateral disarmament."[37] Nicholas Von Hoffman, newspaper columnist and ERA supporter, commented "the belief persists that the women's movement will celebrate the passage of the amendment by banqueting on roast fetuses."[38]

It is sobering to realize that the ERA was defeated not by Barry Goldwater, Jerry Falwell, or any combination of male chauvinist pigs, but by women who were alienated from a feminist movement the values of which seemed elitist and disconnected from the lives of ordinary people. Worst of all, many women suspected feminists of being contemptuous of their values and aspirations—which centered on family life.

The modern battle over the ERA has a historical parallel. In the 1920s there was a bitter feud between advocates of an equal rights amendment and supporters of protective legislation for women workers. In retrospect, this early fight looks like a dreary rehearsal for the modern struggle. Like the contemporary feud, it centered on opposing visions of what women need to improve their lot in life.

At the beginning of the century many social reformers, including important groups of social feminists at the Labor Department and in the Women's Trade Union League (WTUL), were convinced that woman's maternal and wifely roles, together with her natural weakness, required that the state step in to protect her in the labor force. As Louis Brandeis argued in *Muller* v. *Oregon* in 1908, woman's "special physical organization," particularly her childbearing and maternal functions, required restricting her hours of labor.[39] Alice Paul of the National Woman's party fiercely disagreed. The position of the Women's Party was that "if . . . a law is passed applying to women and not applying to men, it will discriminate against women and handicap them in competing with men in earning their livelihood."[40] Arguments based on physical differences were dismissed categorically: "This is a philosophy that would penalize all women because some women are physically weak."[41] The stage was set for a debilitating struggle.

The body of protective legislation that was in place in the early 1920s was a mixed bag. Some of these protective laws imposed limitations on the kinds of work women could do. Occupations were forbidden to women on a variety of grounds. For example, selling liquor might expose women to lewd men and threaten their innocence; grinding or polishing metal might clog women's lungs with dust; work in underground mines might coarsen women's gentle natures. Operating elevators, reading meters, carrying letters, and driving taxis were all among the occupations denied to women during this period.

Other types of protective legislation attempted to regulate the conditions under which women could work. Most states passed maximum hour laws limiting the number of hours a woman could work in a day. At first it was ten hours, but by the 1920s it was down to eight. In addition, there were provisions for more hygienic working conditions, some attempts to mandate a minimum wage, and legal restrictions against compulsory overtime and nighttime work for women.

The net effect of protective legislation on the well-being of women workers is difficult to assess despite numerous official commissions and a heated contemporary debate. On the whole, it seems that married women with family responsibilities supported the regulations which produced shorter hours and more pleasant working conditions. Interviews carried out by the National Consumers' League and the Women's Bureau of the U.S. Department of Labor reveal a grateful attitude among working mothers who valued the additional time for child care and household chores. As one worker put it, "A woman has work to do at home. It does you all out. When I had small children I have hung out clothes at one o'clock at night."[42] But other working women, particularly single women in badly paying jobs, would have traded in the shorter hours for a higher wage.

One interesting aspect of protective legislation in America was that it restricted and limited paid work for women, but it did little to support working women. In 1916, when the president of the

American Association of Labor Legislation presented a plan to pay hospital expenses and cash benefits to women who withdrew from the work force before and after childbirth, it was shot down.[43] Critics protested that such generosity would give potential mothers an incentive to work, and the proposal was withdrawn.

Contrast this with Europe, where in the early years of this century protective legislation came to encompass maternity leave, the medical costs of childbirth, and certain additional types of health coverage for women and their children. By 1920 Britain, Italy, and Germany all had elaborate support policies in these areas.

One thing protective legislation did manage to do was to split the feminist ranks. Because this legislation produced special treatment for women, it conflicted in a fundamental way with the continuing struggle toward women's equality. It was felt that women could not both be wards of the state entitled to special protection, and achieve equality with men. Starting in the early 1920s, Alice Paul's National Woman's Party led the fight to urge a constitutional amendment guaranteeing equality. The ERA was formally submitted to Congress in December 1923. It was based on the original arguments for women's rights made in 1848 at Seneca Falls: that women were equal to men and therefore were entitled to all human rights. As Paul put it, "If you demand equality, you must accept equality."[44]

Many social feminists were made extremely nervous by the ERA, believing that it jeopardized the gains from decades of struggle to improve conditions for working women. At first the Woman's party was conciliatory and offered to accept changes in the ERA so as not to injure the "8 hour day and other social legislation." But compromise was difficult when the best legal minds in the country, including Felix Frankfurter, were of the opinion that it was impossible to draft a blanket federal constitutional amendment that would not jeopardize the social legislation. In 1921 Frankfurter wrote of his "shock" at learning of the amendment, which "threatens the well-being even the very life of these millions of wage-earning women."[45]

In the event, the Women's Bureau of the Labor Department,

the National Consumers' League, the Women's Trade Union League, and Samuel Gompers himself pulled out all the stops in a fight to defeat the ERA. *Justice,* the newspaper of the International Ladies Garment Workers Union (ILGWU), was typical in its reaction to the amendment: "To destroy industrial laws for women merely because the same laws do not exist for men is . . . the same kind of thing we would have been doing had we sought to deprive men of suffrage because women did not have it."[46] Phyllis Schlafly could not have put the case better.

As time passed, the position of the Woman's party hardened, until the party withdrew its tacit support for protective legislation and became intent on passing an ERA at any cost. Mary Anderson, the director of the Women's Bureau, became increasingly incensed. She had begun her working life as a shoe worker and was deeply committed to protective legislation for women. She accused the "Theoretical Feminists" of the Woman's party of "talking about things and conditions entirely outside their own experience or knowledge." (She would have understood why those women in the leather-tanning factory in Chicago were hostile to the ERA.) She went on to urge that "rights must be interpreted for women workers as something concrete, and we must start with the world where it is today. . . ." Anderson concluded with the statement "I consider myself a good feminist, but I believe I am a practical one."[47]

The constituency of the Woman's party shrank until it was supported only by the National Federation of Business, the Professional Women's Clubs, and other organizations of well-educated career women. Eleanor Roosevelt lined up with Mary Anderson and the social feminists. In 1922 Roosevelt joined the WTUL and worked for the forty-eight-hour week, minimum wages, and the right to organize for women workers. She was profoundly at odds with Alice Paul and the Woman's party. According to Joseph Lash, "she thought the Woman's party opposition to protective legislation for women on the basis of equal rights was downright reactionary."[48]

This schism in the feminist ranks wreaked havoc with the effectiveness of the movement. The ERA was introduced in Congress every year after 1923 but got nowhere, and all factions—

equal rights advocates and social welfare enthusiasts—were discredited and weakened by the conflict.

European feminists seem to have avoided this bloodletting in the early decades of this century. For example, in Britain in the 1920s and 1930s feminists concerned with extending equal rights worked through such organizations as the Fawcett Society, while those interested in welfare measures joined the Women's Cooperative Guild, the Women's Labour League, and other movements for social reform. But there was no sharp conflict between them. One reason was that the welfare current was clearly dominant, and as time passed, the egalitarian goals of the movement were muted in favor of piecemeal social reform. Another reason was that "the new Labour Party acted as an umbrella organization [pulling] together the different groups in the cause of effective action. Politicians were . . . willing to go along with reforms and substantial welfare gains were made."[49] Some of these efforts culminated in the Children's Act of 1948, which helped provide an elaborate safety net for mothers and children.

In contrast, American feminism languished in this period. As historian Alice Kessler-Harris has described it, even during the Second World War the divisions between feminists persisted: "Business and professional women continued to support the ERA and paid little attention to such mundane issues as day care. For them, the important thing, as always, was not resolving the home and family issues that might equalize work force opportunities for all women, but improving their own relative economic positions."[50] When feminism was reborn in the 1960s, the equal rights advocates were dominant and were able to set the agenda for the contemporary movement.

Had the modern backers of the Equal Rights Amendment been more conversant with the history of feminism, they would have had more respect for their opposition. For in the 1920s opposition to the amendment came from within the reform movement, from the trade unions, and from social feminists such as Mary Anderson. It was impossible to dismiss this liberal opposition as so much right-wing hysteria. Had Eleanor Smeal or Gloria Steinem understood that feminists could have a legitimate problem with the

Equal Rights Amendment, the pro-ERA campaign might have been differently crafted.

What is the legacy of nearly 150 years of American feminism? With impressive consistency the best energy of the movement has focused on attaining equal rights for women, rights which were to be won by a separatist strategy uniting sisterhood in mass organizations. In the recent phase of feminism the equal rights issue has been was joined by issues of sexual freedom, but even the modern movement sees the ERA as the bedrock on which all other rights are to be inscribed.

Even in its own terms American feminism has had limited success. By screening out other demands, feminists did enfranchise women in 1920. But it was a limited victory, as they then failed to use the vote for any useful purpose. The separatist organizations of feminism failed to give them any lever on power, and the failure to agree on a substantive agenda after winning the vote meant that the movement fell apart after 1920.

In the modern period the failures of the movement have been more dramatic. The battle to ratify the ERA—the modern centerpiece of feminist demands—was lost in a particularly humiliating way: It was defeated by women. The ERA battle casts the mistakes of the women's movement into stark relief. It points to failures in understanding. The chic, liberal women of NOW have mostly failed to understand that millions of American women like being wives and mothers and want to strengthen, not weaken, the traditional family structure. For them motherhood is not a trap, divorce is not liberating, and many of them find the personal and sexual freedom of modern life immensely threatening. In a profound way feminists have failed to connect with the needs and aspirations of ordinary American women.

But the ERA battle also points to failures in strategy. The separatist feminist organizations chose not to align themselves permanently with political parties, trade unions, or professional organizations and therefore failed to connect with the real centers of political power. Feminists did not heed Eleanor Roosevelt's advice, which was "Get into the game and stay in it. Throwing mud from the outside won't help. Building up from the inside will."[51]

In addition, the umbrella character of the movement meant that the demands of the radicals could not be ruled out of court, and the broad coalition feminists needed to ratify the ERA was needlessly scrambled with extraneous issues of sexual freedom.

If modern American feminists have failed to achieve the goal they themselves define as central to their mission, they have obviously missed out on that other agenda—the support system of concrete benefits and services so important to European social feminism.

This neglect of material realities goes to the heart of the difference between American and European feminism. The American movement has defined the problem of womenkind as that of acquiring a full set of legal, political, and economic rights, and achieving control over one's body. The assumption is that once women possess the same rights as men and can choose not to have children, they achieve true equality of opportunity and are able to attain power, status, and money on the same terms as men.

In Europe social feminists have conceived the problem of the female sex differently. For them, it is not woman's lack of legal rights that constitutes her main handicap or even her lack of "reproductive freedom." Rather, it is her dual burden—in the home and in the work force—that leads to second-class citizenship. The goal of the social feminists has therefore become one of lightening this load by instituting family support systems. The conviction is that because women are wives and mothers as well as workers and citizens, they need special compensatory policies if they are to accomplish as much as men in the world beyond the home. Equal rights are seen as only part of the struggle.

These contrasting visions of the female problem place a very different weight on the issue of motherhood. By stressing equality, American feminists have put aside differences from men, including that of bearing children. This not only has little public appeal, it actually gets in the way of creating the support systems so desperately needed by homemakers and low-income working women. It is hard to imagine that Lillian Garland—the California woman who was fired for taking maternity leave—has much patience with the equal rights arguments of Dianne Feinstein or NOW. Garland desperately needed job protection in the wake of a difficult birth, and feminists lined up against her (and her child) because they did not want to discriminate against men. I cannot think that Garland will be voting for the ERA. But then neither did Eleanor Roosevelt for much the same reasons.

Home and Family, *Norman Rockwell, 1959*

*Tough guys, adoring chicks, role-playing in the fifties:
high-school football game, 1955*

Suburbia—spreading like gangrene through the countryside, Levittown, 1957

The emancipated career woman circa 1940, or 1980?
Joan Crawford in Mildred Pierce, *1945*

Katharine Hepburn as prosecuting attorney in Adam's Rib, *1949*

The submissive woman: Ingrid Bergman in Adam Had
Four Sons, *1946*

Homemaking, fifties-style. Doris Day, Please Don't Eat
the Daisies, *1960*

The fifties sex kitten: Marilyn Monroe in **The Seven Year Itch,** *1953*

PART C

The Aberrant Fifties

Modern mothers—working or traditional—have received little tangible support from the American women's movement. Home-making and motherhood are not valued, and if you want a family as well as a career, the movement is not supportive. Even maternity leave is frowned upon because women are supposed to behave exactly like men in the workplace.

But if working mothers face their double burden alone without support from their "sisters," they also face additional handicaps which grow out of the strange culture that was America in the 1950s.

The years following World War II were a very odd period in the social history of this country. Despite the considerable advances made by women in the first half of this century, in the late 1940s careers went out of fashion and women were expected to devote their prime years and their best energies to home and family. As the country wallowed in an "orgy" of domesticity, the birthrate doubled, and the tasks associated with mothering grew to unprecedented levels.

To be a good mother in the 1920s and 1930s was a role that had finite limits. It involved providing wholesome food, hygienic surroundings, and lots of discipline. To be a good mother in the fifties was a role that knew no bounds, as mothers became personally responsible for the psychological and cognitive development of their children. On the psychic front mothers were burdened with the fearful knowledge that only they stood between their child growing up to be normal or growing up to be a neurotic, screwed-up adult. On the cognitive front the postwar American mother was handed both a challenge and a threat. She was told, "You have the capacity to rear a genius, a masterpiece," but it was also clear that if this child failed to live up to his or her potential, it was very definitely the mother's fault.

This postwar cult of motherhood had profound effects on our society, for it became the standard against which we assess all child-rearing practices. It is the model against which millions of individual women judge their performance as mothers, and it is the norm against which all policy decisions are weighed.

This constitutes a double misfortune. Most mothers in the 1980s have to earn a living in a workplace that is hostile to maternal responsibilities. It is a gratuitous burden to also expect these women to live up to 1950s notions of complete motherhood. All that these wildly inflated notions of motherhood do these days is guarantee a bottomless pit of maternal guilt.

An even more important legacy of the fifties cult of motherhood is the ways in which it colors and distorts our public policies. Presidents from Eisenhower to Nixon to Carter to Reagan have been convinced that there is no substitute for mother in the rearing of children. They have retained a fierce commitment to Mom, apple pie, and the Norman Rockwell vision of American family life. No matter that the 1950s constituted the exception rather than the rule in the broad sweep of American history, no matter that only 6 percent of contemporary American households approximate the ideal family type: breadwinning Dad, homemaking Mom, two-plus kids. Even in contemporary political life it is the fifties family and the fifties mother that constitute both the standard and the norm. This helps explain why as a nation we have failed so miserably in providing public child care and why we have found it impossible to mandate basic maternity leave.

The irony is the postwar cult of motherhood taught us to venerate small children, but this veneration did not translate into policies that would actually help children. Indeed, this ideology—because it was grounded in mother care—actually prevented the emergence of sensible public policies. For like it or not, most modern mothers cannot stay home to look after their children. They have to work, and we make it doubly difficult for them. We load them up with elaborate responsibilities for the emotional and cognitive development of their children, and then fail to provide even the most rudimentary support structures that might help them deal with child rearing in a world in which most parents work. Child-centered America is thus capable of some profoundly irresponsible acts toward its children.

No other country has accumulated such a set of contradictions. In Europe the postwar baby boom was a short-lived pallid affair, and there was no flowering of a cult of motherhood. As a result, European governments had no ideological hang-ups—no commitment to mother care—when it came time to set up nurseries and preschools for children. Conservative countries like France and Italy and socialist countries like Sweden have all been able to make pragmatic adjustments to the modern age and provide family support structures for working parents. America, however, remains handicapped by the fifties and its peculiar vision.

10

ULTRADOMESTICITY: THE RETURN TO HEARTH AND HOME

In May 1983 I interviewed Faith Whittlesey at the White House. At that time she was assistant to the President for public liaison and dealt with policies toward women and children. I told her of my concern for working mothers in this country and explained in vivid detail how very hard it was for them to deal with childbirth and child care in the absence of family support policies. Whittlesey listened carefully and tried to respond. She told me that Ronald Reagan was tremendously concerned about the care and nurturing of children and that he did in fact have a policy in this area. The policy was to lick inflation and encourage the economy to grow so that men could once more earn a family wage. A little puzzled, I asked her how she thought this would help. "Oh," said Whittlesey, smiling, "the rest is easy. Once men earn a family wage, all those women can go home and look after their own children in the way they did when I was growing up."[1] Everything, it seems, would be solved if we returned to the good old days of the fifties, when moms were homemakers and dads were stalwart breadwinners.

The odd thing is Reagan himself grew up in the twenties and had a working mother; she worked in a dress shop for $14 a week in order to help out with the precarious family finances.[2] You might imagine he would relate to the difficulties faced by contemporary working mothers. Instead, he clings to a vision of motherhood fifties-style which did not exist in the 1920s and does not exist today.

The fact is that the 1950s were profoundly aberrant. The trademarks of the period—an extended baby boom, a glorification of domesticity, a turning against careers for women, an impressive elaboration of the maternal role—all run counter to modern values and contradict previously existing trends.

We look back at this period and say to ourselves, "How quaint!" "How bizarre!" almost as though we were describing the customs of some exotic tribe. What we often overlook is the fact that the fifties also look quaint and bizarre from the perspective of the prewar world. In films of the thirties and forties Joan Crawford and Katharine Hepburn played gutsy, intelligent women, women who had nothing in common with the dumb sex kittens of the 1950s. The dialogue in *Some Like it Hot* (starring Marilyn Monroe) is enough to make a modern woman—or a thirties woman—grind her teeth. Monroe spends an indeterminable amount of time insisting to Tony Curtis that she has no brains at all in her pretty little head.

It seems that the fifties were not the olden days. They were different from the years before as well as the years after. But make no mistake, we need to understand this special period because it bred an ideology which conditions many of our private and public responses toward mothers and children.

During the summer and fall of 1949 the American popular press was preoccupied with a scandal surrounding Ingrid Bergman. The beautiful Swedish film star had abandoned her husband and daughter in Hollywood and gone off to Italy, where she was having a torrid affair with film director Roberto Rossellini. Rumor had it that she was pregnant by Rossellini and that her husband was refusing to agree to a divorce. In due course Ingrid Bergman gave birth to a son, Robertino, in Rome on February 2, 1950. Since Bergman was not yet divorced, let alone remarried, Robertino's birth certificate said that he was the son of Rossellini and of some unknown mother.

Ultradomesticity: The Return to Hearth and Home

This illegitimate birth unleashed a storm of public protest in the United States. As film critic John Russell Taylor describes it, "all the self-appointed protectors of public morality in the States were up in arms."[3] The frenzy reached its climax when Senator Edwin C. Johnson of Colorado launched an astonishing attack on Bergman from the floor of the Senate. His tone was unmistakably one of personal betrayal. "She was a sweet and understanding person," he wailed, "with an attractive personality which captivated everyone on and off the screen."[4] Again and again the same tone recurred: How could she do this to us?—as though all the men of America were married to her and all the women of America somehow tarnished by her "moral turpitude."[5]

Although Ingrid Bergman married Roberto Rossellini as soon as she was legally able and went on to have twins by him—in wedlock—the American establishment continued its persecution. The Swedish film star was repeatedly refused a visa by the State Department and was not allowed to reenter the United States until 1957. Her political rehabilitation did not occur until 1972, when Senator Charles Percy put the congressional record straight by making a speech that paid glowing tribute to Bergman. This testimonial effectively blotted out Senator Johnson's denunciation of twenty years before.

When we look back on this furor, it is hard to understand what all the fuss was about. Hollywood, midcentury, was not exactly a bastion of wifely virtue. Film stars such as Mae West and Rita Hayworth had been flouting conventional morality for years. The problem for Bergman was that by the late forties she had come to epitomize the domestic virtues that were aggressively back in style. She played the placid, sweet girl and submissive woman in *Adam Had Four Sons,* the clear-eyed, idealistic heroine in *Casablanca,* and the warmhearted, impulsive nun in *The Bells of St. Mary's.* Postwar American audiences (and politicians!) adored her as the lovely, wholesome girl next door. They would not stand for it when she turned out to be an emancipated woman.

The postwar craving for Mom and apple pie did more than wreck Ingrid Bergman's Hollywood career. It ran full tilt into the career aspirations of less celebrated women. For during this period millions of American women were prodded and pushed until they left the larger world of work and public affairs and became the doll-like creatures so well described by Betty Friedan in *The Feminine Mystique.* They became "feminine women with truly feminine attitudes, admired by men for their miraculous, God-given, sensationally unique ability to wear skirts."[6] They congratulated themselves that "they looked and acted far more feminine than the 'emancipated' girls of the 1920s or even the 30s."[7]

This resurrection of domestic virtues ran counter to historical trends. For at least a century American women had been the proud possessors of a reputation for freedom and independence in the world beyond the home.

In the 1880s the English aristocrat Lord Bryce was mightily impressed by the worldly position of American women. As he put it, "in America it is easier for women to find a career, to obtain work of an intellectual or of a commercial kind than in any part of Europe."[8] And his opinion did seem to reflect real differences in the way the old and the new worlds treated their women. The Swedish feminist Fredrika Bremer in her novel *Hertha,* published in 1856, described America as the "promised land of women."[9] She argued, with considerable force, how Swedish women in the mid-nineteenth century were much more confined to their homes and much less emancipated than their American sisters. Sigmund Freud, on fleeing Vienna in 1938, took himself off to England, rather than the United States, where, in his eyes, "the women were less subservient to men."[10] He felt ill prepared to abandon his European values in this regard.

Throughout the nineteenth century American women were not as protected as their European counterparts. In frontier settings their economic role was too important and they were numerically too scarce to yield much power to husbands, and among the immigrant groups that settled along the eastern seaboard, women were often more employable than their menfolk. During the first third of this century their relative position improved at a rapid clip. American women obtained the vote at an early date (1920, as opposed to 1928 in Britain, 1945 in France, 1946 in Italy, and 1971 in Switzerland); economic growth and a rapidly expanding industrial technology promised to reduce their domestic chores to a minimum; education for women increased at a much faster rate than in Europe; and divorce and contraception became generally available.

The long history of the frontier helps explain this development of greater freedom for American women. In the virgin lands of the westward-moving frontier, life was extremely arduous as families attempted to carve out a living from the wilderness. Because they were equal participants in the family's struggle for survival, women earned the respect of their husbands, their children, and their communities. As historian Joanna Stratton has described it, "the pioneer family existed as a self-sufficient unit that took pride in its ability to provide for itself and persevere in the face of hardship. Men and women worked together as partners, combining their strength and talents to provide food and clothing for themselves and their children. As a result, women found themselves on a far more equal footing."[11]

The importance of the pioneer woman was enhanced by the fact that she was in short supply. During the whole of the colonial period men outnumbered women, and until late in the nineteenth century women remained few and far between in the American West. In 1865 there were three men for every one woman in California, while in Colorado the ratio was as high as twenty to one.[12] The economic importance of women and their scarcity value led to the early emancipation of women in the western states. An Oregon law of 1850 granted land to both single and married women, and several western territories granted suffrage to women at an early date (Wyoming in 1869 and Utah in 1870). In many western townships women were elected to political office; for example, Kansas City had had sixteen women mayors by 1900.[13]

Another important dimension of the American experience was the early extension of education to women. The doors of higher education opened earlier and faster to women in the United States. The breakthrough came during the 1860s, when women's colleges like Vassar and Smith were founded and universities like Michigan and Cornell became coeducational. The process was later and slower for European women. In Britain my alma mater, Girton College, Cambridge University, which opened in 1869 with an enrollment of six students, was the only English institution of higher education available to women until London University accepted women in 1879. On the Continent progress was even slower; e.g., Heidelberg was the first German university to enroll women (in 1900). By this time one-third of college students in the United States were women.

America maintained an impressive lead in higher education for women until the Second World War; indeed, by the mid-1930s women made up 40 percent of students in institutions of higher learning. In Germany just before Hitler took power, no more than 10 percent of university students were female, in Sweden during this time period the figure was 17 percent, and in Britain the figure was 22 percent.[14]

In short, by the 1930s American women had developed a considerable head start over their European counterparts on the slow road to political and economic emancipation. This freedom and independence were to be pushed even further during the Second World War.

In the 1942–45 period, at the peak of the war, 14 million American men were in the armed services. There was a desperate need for women workers—to replace men in the production of essential civilian goods, and to "man" the vastly expanded arms factories. In response to these pressures, almost 5 million additional women workers were drawn into employment during the war years, and the number of wives holding jobs doubled.[15] These women took up traditional female employment in such sectors as food and clothing, but they also took up newly vacant male jobs in chemicals, rubber, petroleum, steel, aircraft, and munitions, where they proved to be indispensable to the war effort. In these male fields women were paid 50 to 100 percent more than in the female sectors of the economy.

"Rosie the Riveter" became a symbol of patriotic endeavor, and a popular song was written about her:

> Rosie's got a boyfriend, Charlie;
> Charlie, he's a marine
> Rosie is protecting Charlie
> Working overtime on the riveting machine.[16]

Ultradomesticity: The Return to Hearth and Home

At the height of the war effort Norman Rockwell painted a picture of Rosie the Riveter for the cover of the *Saturday Evening Post* (May 29, 1943). He depicts her as Junoesque—confident, muscular, yet feminine. With her machine tools and painted fingernails she is clearly the kind of woman you could rely on in any kind of emergency.

Government policy encouraged women in their new work roles. The War Manpower Commission employed the J. Walter Thompson advertising agency to run its recruiting campaign for women workers. In September 1943 the government spent $1.5 million on radio programs designed to drum up women's enthusiasm for war work.[17] And the call to the factories was not clothed in feminine rhetoric. Posters announcing production jobs promised women "man-sized" jobs with "man-sized" wages. War propaganda pictured women operating heavy machinery, while the *Ladies' Home Journal* placed the image of a female combat pilot on its cover. By the end of the war journalists were proclaiming the ability of women to perform all sorts of "male" tasks, while one senior editor congratulated her sex for meeting this test of masculine strength, endurance, and agility. There was even some grudging recognition that since three-quarters of the new workers were married women, problems relating to child care were capable of affecting wartime production. In 1942 the federal government contributed $400,000 to assist local communities in funding child-care centers, and by 1945, 100,000 children were enrolled in federally supported facilities.[18]

In 1945 American women were more powerful than they ever had been before, yet in the years following World War II a strange thing happened. America, that bastion of strong, independent women, became caught up in an orgy of domesticity, and millions of women embraced an existence that was totally centered on home and family. For the first time in history educated women were expected and encouraged to devote their prime years and expend their best energies on housework and motherhood.

These postwar years were marked by a series of retrogressive trends, making the 1950s a strangely aberrant period. To begin with, women got married and had children earlier than ever, cutting short their education and worklife. The average age for women to marry dropped to twenty in 1950, down from twenty-three in the 1920s and 1930s.[19] No other industrial country had such an early average age for marriage in the 1950s. The birthrate rose steadily so that by the end of the 1950s the rate of population growth in the United States was twice that of Europe and close on the heels of Africa and India. In this gigantic baby boom, which lasted until 1960, "the birth rate for third children doubled . . . and that for fourth children tripled."[20] In this era of burgeoning families even the divorce rate fell somewhat.

During this same period women lost ground in educational and career terms. In the early fifties women constituted 35 percent of college graduates, down from 40 percent in the 1930s; women earned 10 percent of doctoral degrees, compared to 17 percent in the 1920s and 30s; and the proportion of law degrees going to women declined from 6 percent in the 1930s to less than 3 percent in 1959.[21]

The clearest sign of retrogression was the decline in the proportion of high-achieving women. Of the people listed in the 1902 edition of *Who's Who in America,* 8 percent were women; in the 1958 edition women constituted a mere 4 percent of the total. As sociologist John Parrish wrote—rather dismally—in 1961, "At this rate of decline there will be no distinguished American woman relative to men, in another generation or so."[22]

Contrast this with Europe, where women were gaining ground in the 1950s. During these years 16 percent of British and French doctors were women, as were 13 percent of Swedish doctors; the figure for the United States was 6 percent. France is a particularly interesting case. Commenting on the French situation in 1954, sociologists Alva Myrdal and Viola Klein said that "it is remarkable to what a small extent professional women are influenced by the size of their families in the pursuit of their careers."[23] At this time 21 percent of all professionals in France were women, and three quarters of French women with college degrees were in the labor force.

In the United States the picture was dramatically different. In the 1950s women with college degrees in the childbearing age-group had a lower rate of employment than any other group of women. As Myrdal and Klein put it, "high-level intellectual activity has suffered under the impact of earlier marriage and larger families."[24] The plain fact was women with college degrees were often married to prosperous men. And in America in the fifties, if the family could afford it, the wife became a homemaker.

In summary, the proportion of American women who went on to have professional careers (as lawyers, doctors, or college professors) was smaller in the fifties than in the prewar period, and American women were increasingly less career-oriented than their European sisters. The ambition of women, even at elite colleges, was to graduate with a diamond engagement ring rather than with high academic honors. Women increasingly held "jobs" before childbearing and after their children entered high school, but they rarely took up "careers."[25] Women of the fifties vested their best energies in their homes and in their children.

The paradox is that as they entered the postwar era, American women were the best-educated and the most equal in the world. Why did they give up their independent ambitions and go home?

The postwar orgy of domesticity owed much to public policies put in place by a government attempting to cope with the aftermath of the Great Depression and World War II. These policies provided a variety of incentives that greatly encouraged traditional roles for women.

In 1945 not only were Americans recovering from the dangers and dislocations of a major war, but they still had deep and painful memories of the Great Depression, which lasted much longer in America than in Europe. We have largely forgotten the agony of the 1930s, and it is hard for us now to appreciate that the depression was a very close call not just for the economy but for the coherence of our liberal capitalist society. The suffering and deprivation of the 1930–39 period were phenomenal. As William Manchester describes it, "Millions stayed alive by living like animals. In the Pennsylvania countryside they were eating wild weed-roots and dandelions. . . . City mothers hung around docks, waiting for the spoiled produce to be discarded and then fighting homeless dogs for possession of it. . . . Whole families were seen plunging into refuse dumps, gnawing at bones and watermelon rinds."[26] In New York Thomas Wolfe observed the homeless men who prowled in the vicinity of restaurants, "lifting the lids of garbage cans and searching inside for morsels of rotten food."[27]

In particular, the depression wreaked great psychological havoc on American men, who found themselves out of work for many consecutive years, unable to perform their role as breadwinner and generally powerless to control their destinies. Joseph Pleck in his book *The Myth of Masculinity* argues that the Great Depression was the historical event that caused "the single greatest crisis in the traditional and institutional basis of the male role, that of family economic provider."[28]

Ten years of deep depression were followed by a bloody and destructive world war. Four hundred thousand U. S. servicemen lost their lives, and tens of thousands more were seriously injured. Come 1945 there was enormous pent-up demand for a normal life—for a family, a house, and a decent job. This became the stuff of the postwar American Dream.

But the men guiding U.S. policy in 1945 were not sure that they could conjure up the jobs that were so desperately needed if the expectations of the returning soldiers were to be realized. There was a great fear that with the return of peace, the economic gains of the war years would vanish and the country would plunge once more into deep depression and massive unemployment. Economist Alvin Hansen, who was president of the American Economic Association in the mid-1940s, saw the provision of jobs as the greatest postwar challenge but feared that stagnation and unemployment were the most likely economic scenario.[29] One strategy was clear to the economic planners: Encourage women to leave wartime employment and return to their homes. Jobs were going to become scarce, and they would be needed by the returning soldiers. As one commentator put it, "The nation has a powerful responsibility to the returning soldier. The veteran has been promised his old job. He will get it."[30]

In the event, the postwar scene was one of great prosperity. By the late forties the economy was growing at an impressive clip, and between 1945 and 1955 the American GNP more than doubled. During the early fifties, the years of the Korean War, the expansion was particularly breathtaking.[31] But policy makers had not expected this postwar boom. According to historian Richard

Hofstadter, "we were surprised by the fact that instead of having a tremendous depression after the war which those of us who were mature in the 1930s thought surely was coming, we entered upon one of the greatest boom periods in history."[32] Contemporary policy action was predicated on a gloomy view of the postwar period, and top priority was given to sending women workers home. In February 1946 a *New York Times* article declared that "the courtship of women workers has ended."[33] By the end of that year 4 million fewer women were working than had worked at the peak of wartime production. The decline in women's employment was particularly pronounced in well-paid heavy industry, where returning veterans were particularly anxious to take back their jobs. Few women retained skilled craft jobs after the war. A document released by the Women's Bureau concluded sadly that "only a few women have been allowed to continue in the newer fields of employment, and thus to continue to use the skills learned during the war."[34]

Both persuasion and coercion were used to lure women away from their jobs. Traditionalists had a field day resurrecting a feminine vision of womankind that was directly at odds with the capable powerful image projected by Rosie the Riveter just a few years earlier. In 1946 Margaret Pickel, dean of Barnard College, declared solemnly in an article for the *New York Times Magazine* that women workers were decidedly inferior to men. Not only did they have less physical strength than men but "by middle age, when men are at their best, a devoted woman worker is apt to degenerate into fussiness or worse."[35] Meanwhile, a stream of vituperation was being directed at those mothers who still wanted to work. Mothers, argued Agnes Meyer in the *Atlantic Monthly,* were needed at home to restore a sense of security to our insecure world. She called on middle-class women to resist pressure to enter the labor market and to renounce any job except that of housewife and mother. "What ails these women," she asked, "who consciously or unconsciously reject their children? . . . The poor child whose mother has to work has some inner security because he knows that his mother is sacrificing herself for his well-being. But the neglected child from a well-to-do home, who realizes instinctively that his mother prefers her job to him, often hates her with a passionate intensity."[36] In rather more measured tones Ashley Montagu proclaimed in the *Saturday Review,* "Being a good wife, a good mother, in short a good homemaker is the most important of all the occupations in the world. . . . I put it down as an axiom that no woman with husband and small children can hold a full-time job and be a good homemaker at one and the same time."[37]

Some women were happy to be told that they should go home at the end of the war. One female union leader announced her retirement plans with girlish enthusiasm: "When the war is over I'll get a manicure, put on the frilliest dress I can find, pour a whole bottle of perfume over my head and then I will be glad to give up my union chair . . . to some boy who comes marching home deserving it."[38] But when persuasion failed to work, coercion was used. Many women didn't graciously resign from their jobs at the end of the war; they were fired. In the two-month period immediately following V-J Day, women were laid off at a rate of 175 per 1,000 workers, double the male rate, and layoffs were particularly drastic in the heavy industrial sector, where women did not quit at the end of the war because they very much wanted to hang on to their well-paid jobs.[39]

A less-than-subtle form of official coercion was the closing down of government-sponsored child-care programs which had made it possible for mothers with young children to work. Women protested the dismantling of these programs but to no avail. In New York State, when Governor Thomas Dewey discontinued state support for child care, angry women organized public demonstrations and formed picket lines—one around the governor's home in Pawling.[40] But such action proved to be fruitless. Federal support for child-care facilities ceased in March 1946, and by the beginning of 1948 all state support had ended. Public child care was terminated as part of a national movement to return children to their mothers and working mothers to their homes. "The women, so lately the darlings of the nation's factories, were summarily sent home to stay."[41]

Government policy did not rest only on sticks to drive women out of the labor force. It also employed carrots to lure women back to hearth and home. Among the juiciest carrots were the GI Bill and the Highway Act.[42]

Ultradomesticity: The Return to Hearth and Home

At first glance the GI Bill and the Highway Act said nothing about women. The GI Bill, which was officially called the Serviceman's Readjustment Act of 1944, provided 14 million returning veterans with free college tuition, subsistence allowances (which were increased by 50 percent if one had dependents), and extremely low-cost mortgages (guaranteed loans for thirty years at 3 to 4 percent interest); while the Highway Act of 1944 pumped $1.3 billion of public money into a road network around and between cities. But the effect of these pieces of legislation was to subsidize, to the tune of several thousands of dollars a year per household, a particular kind of family—one that comprised a breadwinning husband, a homemaking wife, and one or more children. How precisely did this happen?

In the first place, through the GI Bill men received free education and training. They acquired a head start in the job market and were able to become good providers. It made little sense for couples to invest in the skills of a wife since she couldn't compete with all this free training. Secondly, since dependents were at least partially supported through the provisions of the GI Bill, this legislation encouraged early marriage and procreation. Why not avail yourself of free income? Finally, the roads provided by the Highway Act and the cheap financing provided by the low-cost mortgages of the GI Bill extended the possibility of living in a house in the suburbs to millions of young American couples. In just five years (1950–54) the suburban rings around the cities increased their population by 35 percent.[43] This trek to the suburbs, which was to become the largest internal migration in American history, removed wives to distant locations far from most job opportunities. All these factors helped domesticate the American women.

If the returning soldiers, frustrated by years of depression and war, yearned for home and hearth, wife and children, the GI Bill and Highway Act permitted gratification of these fantasies. A cute house in the suburbs, a doll-like wife with all the homemaking skills, a brood of high-achieving children were magically conjured up and became the ingredients of the postwar dream. The "classical family of Western nostalgia" was born.[44] But the dream was nourished by something more substantial than hope and fantasy. It was grounded in some special postwar policies: It was fu-

243

eled by massive government subsidies, and it was sustained by unprecedented economic growth. For if the American economy had not grown so fast in the 1945–60 period, those well-educated GIs would not have earned enough to support the large families of the period, no matter how generous the government subsidies. The sticks and carrots of these public policies could only work well in a context of growth and prosperity.

The ideal of family life that pervaded the American consciousness during this period is perhaps best exemplified by the work of the artist Norman Rockwell, who for many years had been depicting scenes from American life on the covers of the *Saturday Evening Post*.[45] In the late forties and in the fifties Rockwell was to achieve his greatest fame. His sentimental glorification of joyous domesticity and his unabashed delight in the suburban life-styles of Middle America exactly matched the contemporary mood.

Public policies designed to get women out of the work force and into the home were buttressed by some powerful new ideologies. One grew out of the grim politics of the thirties and forties and saw state-supported child care as part of totalitarianism. Another was Freudian theory, which saw women as inferior and childish, with no prospect of happiness unless they relinquished independent work and adjusted to being wives and mothers.

Once World War II was over, firm discipline, rigid schedules, and group care for children became thoroughly unfashionable.[46] These practices now smacked uncomfortably of the Third Reich and Stalin's Russia. The mood of the day was to allow the children of the free world more freedom (under proper maternal supervision, of course) than children ever had before. The cold war, which started up in the late 1940s, was, after all, a war about ways of life as much as markets and territory, and in these postwar years much political capital was made out of contrasting stereotypes of domestic life.

Child-rearing models on both the fascist right and the Communist left were seen as threatening. Ever since the 1917 Bolshevik victory in the Soviet Union, American leaders had been suspicious of Communist baby-raising techniques. In the early 1920s Henry Ford accused American women who were demanding maternity benefits of "taking orders from Alexandra Kollontai" (Kollontai was a leading Bolshevik feminist).[47] In a similar spirit and during the same period, Senator Reed of Kansas described a "noxious plan [that] had reached its highest degree in Russia, there every child was looked upon as a ward of the state, motherhood and birth control were established by law and children were taken from their mother's arms and turned over to public officers."[48]

After the Second World War this type of hysterical reaction from the right was put to more systematic use and bent to the purposes of the cold war. Anti-Communist sentiment was used as yet another reason for why women should go home and rear their children themselves, and it constituted an additional nail in the coffin of public day care. In 1947 the *New York World-Telegram* charged that state-supported child care was conceived by leftists operating out of Communist "social work cells." The campaign for day-care centers, the *Telegram* said, had "all the trappings of a Red drive, including leaflets, letters, telegrams, petitions, protest demonstrations, mass meetings and hat passing."[49] Much to the *Telegram*'s approval, New York's Governor Dewey refused to yield to pressure from women's groups. Instead, he called working women Communists, accused them of contaminating our free society, and, in early 1948, discontinued state support for child care.

These sentiments have pursued us into more recent times. When President Nixon vetoed the Comprehensive Child Development Bill in 1971, he declared that the federal government should not plunge headlong into supporting child development because this would "commit the vast moral authority of the national government to the side of communal approaches to child rearing over against the family-centered approach."[50] He was applauded by conservatives who saw the Bill as "the boldest and most far-reaching scheme ever advanced for the Sovietization of American youth." According to columnist James J. Kilpatrick, if Richard Nixon had signed that Bill he would "have forfeited his last frail claim on Middle America's support."[51]

Freudian theory, which swept through American middle-class life during this period, provided additional energy for the return to hearth and home. Many of Freud's disciples, who were in the main German and Austrian Jews, fled Europe in the 1930s and early 1940s and settled in the United States. Helene Deutsch, Paul Federn, Edward Hitschmann, and Hanns Sachs were among the refugees from Hitler's Europe who became part of the rapidly growing psychoanalytical community in the States.[52] "By 1952 64 percent of the members of the International Psychoanalytical Association were in America."[53] In the postwar period serious scholarship and pop psychology became replete with Freudian ideology.

Modern Women: The Lost Sex, a 1947 best seller by Ferdinand Lundberg and Marynia Farnham, is a case in point. This book declared: "Careers produce the masculinization of women and with it enormously dangerous consequences to the home, to the children who depend on it, and to the ability of the woman as well as the man to obtain sexual gratification."[54] Lundberg and Farnham were of the opinion that "Women would do well to recapture those functions in which they have demonstrated superior capacity. Those are, in general, the nurturing functions around the home." To women who chose to enter "fields belonging to the male area of exploit or authority—law, mathematics, physics, business, industry and technology—government should make it clear that such pursuits are not generally desirable for women." If women, despite their natural bent, insisted on entering such fields, Lundberg and Farnham held that they deserved to be discriminated against. The psychic maladjustment that had led them to leave their homes made them intrinsically poor risks at the office. They were described as emotionally unstable, quarrelsome, and apt to foment feuds on the job. In particular, they lacked "the gift for teamwork that makes for coordinated research."[55] As professionals they were indecisive; as union members they were disloyal. Worst of all, their interest in work distracted attention from what should have been a primary concern with the home and with their children.

A curious aspect of this inveighing against careers for women was that the inveigher was nearly always a career woman. Thus, when in 1944 Helene Deutsch published her two-volume *The Psychology of Woman: A Psychoanalytic Interpretation,* she attributed a woman's discontent with her feminine role to a "masculinity complex." According to Deutsch, women who "had achieved eminence by activity of their own in various fields had done so at the expense of their feminine fulfillment." The remedy: to relinquish any goals of her own and "to identify and fulfill herself through the activities and goals of husband and son." If she had to work, she was advised to do such things as "the basic research for her male superior's discoveries. The daughter who devotes her life to her father is also making a satisfactory feminine sublimation."[56]

Of course, Deutsch was not about to publish any of *her* scholarship under any name but her own, and she took care to hire a nurse for her own child so that he did not interfere with the development of her career. "Immediately after her son's birth, Dr. Deutsch hired a nurse, Paula, and installed her and infant Martin in a vacant room next to her office."[57] Finding breast-feeding rather an exhausting business—despite its importance in Freudian theory—Helene Deutsch acquired two goats to provide little Martin with milk. These goats proceeded to graze and fight in the courtyard of the clinic where Deutsch worked, providing an endless source of amusement for visitors.

The contradiction between what Deutsch advocated as proper feminine behavior and what she herself chose to do did not seem to strike anyone as peculiar. Postwar America was focused wholeheartedly on the necessity and desirability of women's fulfilling their "natural" domestic role, and Deutsch's book was just that much more ammunition in a worthy cause.

Today it is hard to appreciate how thoroughly domestic American women became in the 1950s.

In 1957 Betty Friedan as part of her research for *The Feminine Mystique* surveyed her class at Smith—the class of '42—to find out what her classmates were doing with their adult lives. She found that these well-educated women were thoroughly immersed in being wives and mothers. Of the 189 women who returned Friedan's questionnaire, 179 were married, 6 were single, 1 was widowed, and 3 were divorced. Only 11 did not have children. Indeed, on average these women had 2.9 children, and 52 had 4 children or more. The great majority of these Smith graduates were full-time homemakers. Even those whose children were in school had few ambitions outside the home; they had absorbed the conventional wisdom of the 1950s and did not think it was possible to have both a family and a career. As one thirty-seven-year-old housewife wrote in her questionnaire, "the highly educated career-trained woman who is in mental competition with men must fight frustration in marriage and emotional chaos."[58]

Only 12 out of these 189 women held full-time jobs, and only 1 had embarked on a serious professional career. A further handful worked part time "directing the choir," "teaching piano," or "typing for husband."

Magazines of the era were full of bright and smiling housewife-mothers, who cherished their "unique femininity" and the "receptivity and passivity implicit in their sexual nature."[59] A 1956 article in *Look* magazine celebrated the new domesticity:

> The American woman is winning the battle of the sexes. Like a teenager, she is growing up and confounding her critics. . . . She works, rather casually, less towards a "big career" than as a way of filling a hope chest or buying a home freezer. She gracefully concedes the top jobs to men. This wondrous creature also marries younger than ever, bears more babies and looks and acts far more feminine than the "emancipated" girl of the 1920s or even 30s. Steel worker's wife and Junior Leaguer alike do their own housework. . . . Today, if she makes an old-fashioned choice and lovingly tends a garden and a bumper crop of children, she rates louder hosannas than ever before.[60]

Time magazine called the suburban housewife

> "the keeper of the American Dream. In the absence of her commuting, city-working husband, she is first of all the manager of home and brood, and beyond that a sort of aproned activist. . . . With children on her mind and under her foot, she is breakfast-getter, laundress, house cleaner, dishwasher, shopper, gardener, encyclopedia, arbitrator of children's disputes [and] policeman. If she is not pregnant, she wonders if she is. She takes

her peanut-butter sandwich lunch while standing, thinks she looks a fright, watches her weight (periodically) and jabbers over the short-distance telephone with the next-door neighbor."[61]

In the fifties the media heaped scorn on feminists, the emancipated "career girls" of yesteryear. The antifeminist backlash extended to conceptions of women's education. High schools and colleges began to teach courses on such topics as mate selection, adjustment to marriage, and education for family living. The president of Stephens College touted programs on interior decorating, home economics, cosmetics, and grooming, declaring that for women "the college years must be rehearsal periods for the major performance"—which was, of course, marriage. At another college "The Theory and Preparation of a Well-Marinated Shish Kebab" replaced "Kantian Philosophy" in the curriculum.[62]

This approach to education was self-fulfilling. As education for women became increasingly watered down, the adult destiny of the female sex became even more predictable. Women became homemakers and mothers, at least partially because they were ill-equipped to do anything else. No wonder there were fewer women lawyers, engineers, and college professors in the fifties than in the thirties!

It is almost shocking to modern sensibilities to realize that when Adlai Stevenson made a commencement address at Smith College in 1955, he graciously conceded that "women, especially educated women, have an unique opportunity to influence us, man and boy."[63] The founders of Smith College would have been infuriated by this remark, and so would today's students. In the mid-1950s it was taken as meant—a supreme compliment.

Freudian theorists did not stop at exterior phenomena; they redefined the very nature of women's sexuality as part of this retreat to the home.

The sex act itself came to constitute a model for female happiness. During intercourse woman's role was passive, receptive, and accepting, based on the notion that sexual pleasure could come

249

only from vaginal orgasm and from the phallus. The one prerequisite for sexual fulfillment was that the woman "accept with deep inwardness and readiness . . . the final goal of intercourse— impregnation."[64] The desire to be a mother constituted the core of sexual pleasure, and the climax of the sex act really occurred when the mother nursed the child who had been conceived. For the fifties mother breast-feeding became a complement to the act of creation. It gave her a heightened sense of fulfillment and allowed her "to participate in a relationship as close to perfection as any that a woman can hope to achieve."[65] (So began the glorification of breast-feeding that caused me such pain and grief in the late seventies.)

Thus the conventional view of the psychology of women in these postwar years came to be an extension of Freudian theory. The woman who wanted complete fulfillment had only to extend the attributes displayed during intercourse to the rest of her life. Passivity, dependence, and the desire to raise children constituted the formula for female contentment. Feminism was seen as a serious illness caused by—guess what—penis envy! "The shadow of the phallus lay darkly" over those masculinized females who still wanted careers.[66]

Even the movie industry reflected the changing cultural mores. As film critic Molly Haskell has pointed out, the 1930s featured "whole genres of working-women films" which supplied "details about working women and jobs, salaries, what goes on in offices."[67] During these years "women careerists enjoyed great popularity with such actresses as Katharine Hepburn, Rosalind Russell, Bette Davis, and Joan Crawford playing commercial artists, writers, reporters, lawyers and businesswomen."[68] In *Mildred Pierce* Joan Crawford played a bored middle-class housewife who "opted out of her socially well-defined milieu to become a free agent and successful businesswoman."[69] In those years Bette Davis fought a court battle with Warner Brothers for meatier roles, reinforcing her movie heroine message that "one's identity, regardless of gender, comes from work not from one's spouse [or] children."[70]

The film stars of the fifties were very different. Marilyn Monroe, with her moist, candy-colored mouth, voluptuous pop-up breasts, and cooing helplessness, catered shamelessly to "a false, regressive, childish idea of sexuality . . . and was never permitted to mature into a warm, vibrant woman."[71] In *All About Eve* she was a sex object and nincompoop. In *Bus Stop* she played an ingenuous earth mother, and in *Gentlemen Prefer Blondes* she played a floozy who is most comfortable with older men. Debbie Reynolds as "professional virgin" and Doris Day as "happy housewife" round out the fifties conception of womankind.

The favorite plot in Doris Day movies went something like this. A glamorous, sexy woman gives her man a thoroughly hard time threatening his masculinity. In the last reel she discovers true love and undergoes a Pygmalionesque transformation into a submissive housewife. For the millions who sat through *April in Paris* (1952), *Calamity Jane* (1953), *The Pajama Game* (1957), and *Teacher's Pet* (1958) the message was loud and clear: A woman might be as free and as clever as a man, but her real destiny and happiness lay in being a wife and a mother. Popular TV series reinforced this image of joyous domesticity. *I Love Lucy* (1951–57), which was the first television program to be seen in 10 million homes, and *Ozzie and Harriet* (1952–66), which became television's longest-running sitcom, depicted a world where women were silly, lovable homemakers. Debbie Reynolds summed it all up in *The Tender Trap* (1955): "Don't you think a man is the most important thing in the world? A woman isn't a woman until she has been married and had children."[72]

Thus the social history of the postwar years is very curious. In the late forties and fifties the most educated and most independent women in the world became ultradomestic creatures who centered their lives on family and home. This revolutionary shift was due to the interaction of government policy with some powerful intellectual currents.

In the mid-1940s American policy makers urgently desired women to leave their wartime jobs and go home. The returning soldiers deserved to get their jobs back. Besides, economists were convinced that stagnation and unemployment were just around the corner, and women should not be allowed to compete with men for a finite (or even declining) pool of jobs. Complementing this push to get women out of the work force were the GI Bill and the Highway Act. These pieces of legislation provided free education for men (which enhanced their breadwinning capabilities), offered allowances for dependent wives and children, and subsidized homes in suburban locations far removed from most job opportunities. In short, government policy provided the carrots and sticks that encouraged a full time homemaking role for women.

In such an economic context the Freudian view of womankind—as passive wife and wholehearted homemaker—became immensely popular because it helped justify what was going on. The gutsy, emancipated women of the 1930s and war years had to be redefined if they were to become the keepers of the postwar American Dream.

This transforming of independent women into domestic dolls was not easy, and it would not have succeeded without one more ingredient: the emergence of a veritable cult of motherhood which was tremendously effective in convincing everyone that child rearing was woman's authentic calling. It is important to bear in mind that housekeeping and wifely duties had finite limits in the 1950s. Given the laborsaving equipment in suburban homes and the long hours worked by breadwinning husbands, homemaking was not capable of filling the lives of educated, energetic postwar women. So child rearing was recast and reformulated until motherhood became loaded with heavy responsibilities. As we shall see in the next chapter, it became a role capable of infinite expansion.

As droves of postwar women became full-time homemakers, they read the child-rearing manuals written by Benjamin Spock, Selma Fraiberg, and Berry Brazelton. Who among them "did not worry that their child's bedwetting, thumbsucking, over-eating, refusal to eat, withdrawal, lack of friends, inability to be alone, aggressiveness, timidity, slow reading, too much reading, lack of discipline, rigidity, inhibition, exhibitionism, sexual preciousness, or sexual lack of interest was a sign of incipient neurosis."[73] Motherhood, under the spotlight of the modern experts, became a full-time career, even a cult. As the *Saturday Evening Post* put it in 1962, to make a woman completely content, "it takes a man, but the chief purpose of her life is motherhood."[74]

11

THE RISE OF A CULT
OF MOTHERHOOD

It was late on Friday afternoon in February, and my weekly "play group" was meeting at Sarah's* apartment on West Eighty-first Street, in Manhattan. For the last two years seven women, who were both friends and neighbors, had brought their toddlers to play together for a few hours at the end of the week.

The play group was particularly important for those of us who had jobs. It substituted for the park bench (which none of us had time for) and provided a comforting support network. In emergencies we didn't hesitate to call on one another—to pick a sick child up from school or to take in a child or two when a baby-sitter failed to turn up. For all of us it had grown into an invaluable forum where we could share the indignities of toilet training or the anxieties induced by Charlie's most recent attack of croup or strep throat. By 1984 all such topics were taboo in smart society. To talk about one's three-year-old at a party or in the office was a social faux pas of the first order; it might lead someone to suspect you of being "just a housewife"—the contemporary nonperson.

*Pseudonym.

A Lesser Life

This particular Friday the women settled themselves around Sarah's dining-room table, which was laid with teacups and a big pot of Earl Grey tea. The children drifted off to Philip's room (Philip was Sarah's three-and-a-half-year-old) and were largely forgotten as the women launched hungrily into conversation.

Beth* had had something on her mind for two days. "Hey," she said eagerly, "did anyone read that article in the Living Section on Wednesday where all those experts discussed how to teach your toddler to read?[1] Has anyone tried any of the new techniques they were talking about?"

Linda* had read the article in the *New York Times* and jumped in immediately with "Don't talk to me about that article. It made me so angry I practically tore it up."

Beth was surprised at the intensity of Linda's reaction and prodded her with a mild "What do you mean?"

"Well, you see, I dislike that whole approach—the notion that mothers should try to get their kids on some cognitive fast track. It offends me. Imagine putting a three-year-old under that kind of pressure!" She paused and then added, "Besides, who has time to fool around with multimedia techniques designed to teach simple skills that all children eventually pick up in school?" Linda subsided. Her outburst was obviously related to the fact that she was the most career-oriented woman in the play group and spent a limited portion of the week with her children. A senior editor in the textbook division of a large publishing house, Linda still worked full time despite two toddlers. She had a stake in not taking these particular experts seriously.

Beth attempted a comeback. "But, Linda, some of these techniques don't take up much time, and they really work!" Warming to her subject, she went on to say, "When Eric was two, I bought him a set of flash cards and those Fisher-Price magnetic letters. At that stage he was too young, and although I worked with him every afternoon, he didn't seem interested in learning. But last month I had a breakthrough. He finally asked for 'those word games,' and now we spend an hour or so every day learning the

*Pseudonym.

254

letters and sounds of the alphabet. You see it is just a question of persevering."

Linda still looked unconvinced, so Beth had one last stab at converting her friend. "Don't you think it will be wonderful if our kids can read before they hit kindergarten? You know, if I can give Eric that kind of advantage, I will really feel good about taking these years out of my career."

I opened my mouth, intending to give Linda some support, but decided to close it again. I realized that this conversation was getting a little heavy. If Beth (one of the two nonworking women in the group) was having trouble with her decision to stay at home and found teaching Eric to read an effective way of bolstering that decision, who was I to interfere? Besides, Beth's speech had served to trigger my own ever-sensitive store of maternal guilt. My children had never even owned a flash card, and it was also true that neither Lisa nor David could read. Their teachers assured me that both children were doing just fine, that when the time came, they would learn easily, but in my heart of hearts I suspected that it was one of those areas where I was failing my children. They probably spent too much time with baby-sitters and not enough time with me.

Marcia* took over for me and stepped in with some evidence that supported Linda's policy of nonintervention. "You know, Beth, I once heard a talk given by a child psychologist on precisely this subject. He said that it was wrong to encourage your child to read too early because the child might then focus exclusively on deciphering letters and words and lose the ability to concentrate on pictures, colors, and shapes. I pushed Emily to read when she was four years old, and she did it beautifully, but as soon as she could read, her artwork became much more restrained and rigid. It was as though all that struggling with words stifled her imagination, and she didn't have energy left over for anything else." Marcia giggled. "But I must admit that it's very convenient for me to revise my theories with Thomas [her second child]. Now I am working, there is no way I could find the time to teach him to read." She stopped for a while and then said more

*Pseudonym.

reflectively, "I wish those child-rearing experts would let mothers off the hook. On the surface I can be very rational about the decisions I make as a working mother, but in my gut I feel tremendously guilty about not sacrificing myself for Thomas the way I did for Emily." She paused and, searching for words, said, "It is as if I thought that women have no right to both have children and fulfill their own ambitions."

Marcia's remarks seemed to touch a chord in Linda. Her face clouded, and she said in a subdued voice. "I for one am always comparing myself to my mother. She had four kids—imagine that!—and yet was always so patient, so serene. . . . I guess she was really proud to be a mother and homemaker."

A pall had been cast over our small meeting. Several women looked pensive; others sighed and stirred restlessly. All of us were lost in thought. The conversation had exposed a collective raw nerve—maternal guilt. No matter what our individual choices, we all recognized that there are no easy ways of dumping society's extravagant expectations of how we should bear and rear our children. But why were all of us so passionately vested in being all-providing and all-encompassing mothers to our children? And why did we take direct personal responsibility for molding perfect human beings? We were, after all, modern liberated women with other urgent goals to fill our lives. The explanation lies in our heritage. Not only do we carry the normal load of mothers—we love our children, unreasonably and irrationally—but in addition, we have inherited (many of us unknowingly) the most powerful cult of motherhood this world has ever seen.[2]

The ultradomesticity of the postwar period begat the ideal of complete motherhood. It is an ideal that haunts our consciousness to this day. Like Linda, many of us grew up during this era and tend to see motherhood fifties-style as the yardstick against which we judge our performance as mothers. It is also the standard against which our public policies are weighed. For this cult of motherhood convinced most politicians that children should be raised solely by their mothers, that there is no adequate substitute for mother love and mother care. For a generation, child-rearing experts declared that "the worst natural mother is better in the long run than the best [day-care] mother."[3] No wonder day care came to be seen as a third-rate alternative, suitable for the disadvantaged but not for "normal" American families.

The odd thing is complete motherhood was a new idea in the late 1940s. The idea of devoting the better part of one's day to child care had seldom occurred to anyone. In every other culture throughout history, including our own, mothers had always occupied themselves with other tasks and raised their children as a kind of parallel activity. In the 1930s mothers were even warned to stay away from their children and told to use day camps and preschools to foster independence. The conventional wisdom of the prewar period was that "mother love is a dangerous instrument" liable to impede self-reliance in children.[4]

But fashions change, and with the new psychoanalytical perspective of the postwar period, child rearing became enshrined as the special responsibility of mothers. It was something only mothers could do and was more important than anything else they might do. Inspired by Sigmund Freud and Jean Piaget, a new postwar generation of child-rearing experts encouraged mothers to take responsibility for the psychological and cognitive development of the child and mold its total character and future potential. Any shortcoming in adult life was now seen as rooted in the failure of mothering during childhood. This was a remarkable view of child rearing, and it was to have serious repercussions on public policy. How it became entrenched in postwar America is a fascinating tale.

Before the nineteenth century child-rearing practices were dominated by the question of survival. Parents were much less involved in the lives of their children than today largely because so few of these children survived infancy.

Three centuries ago, of every two babies born alive, only one was likely to be living on its first birthday. Evidence of the dreadful toll of death in childhood can be found in any seventeenth- or eighteenth-century churchyard. Take the colonial family of Cotton Mather. Cotton Mather had fourteen children. Seven Mather babies died soon after birth, one died at age two, and of the six who survived to adult life, five died in their twenties. In one epidemic of measles Cotton Mather lost his wife, a maid, and two daughters with resignation, but the death of a third daughter, little Jerusha, was almost too much for even this eighteenth-century Puritan to bear. "Betwixt 9h and 10h at Night, my lovely Jerusha Expired. She was two years and about seven months old. . . . I begg'd, I begg'd, that such a bitter cup, as the Death of that lovely child, might pass from me. . . . Just before she died, she asked me to pray with her; which I did with distressed, but resigning Soul; and I gave her up unto the Lord. The Minute she died, she said, that she would go to Jesus Christ. . . . Lord I am oppressed."[5]

Although parents did grieve, often quite bitterly, losing one's children by death was so common that it fostered a resigned, even a detached attitude among parents, especially with regard to their younger children. In eighteenth-century France, Philippe Ariès reminds us, an infant who died was buried as casually as a pet cat or dog, for "he was such an unimportant little thing . . . inadequately involved in life."[6]

In England during this period similar attitudes held sway. In 1770 Hester Thrale, close friend of Dr. Johnson and devoted mother of thirteen children, was extremely upset when one of her older children died but showed no grief over the deaths of her infants. Indeed, she took an instant dislike to one baby, saying that "she is so very poor a creature I can scarce bear to look on her." Later, when another newborn baby died, she commented, "One cannot grieve after her much, and I have just now other things to think of."[7] It is difficult to imagine a modern mother voicing such a sentiment.

If high rates of infant mortality engendered a detached attitude among parents in the premodern age, such detachment was further encouraged by the social and economic arrangements of the times. For example, up to the eighteenth century most children of wealthy parents were sent away to wet nurses until they were two or three years old. They then returned home to the care of servants and, at age seven, were often sent away again, either to serve apprenticeships or to attend school. Wet nurses ceased to be used in the early part of last century, but servants and boarding schools severely limited contact between parents and children in middle- and upper-class circles until well into the twentieth century. It was not unusual for a professional middle-class household to have both a nanny and a nurserymaid. A conscientious nine-teenth-century mother would supervise the care of her children, making sure that they ate wholesome food, dressed warmly in winter, behaved politely, and said their prayers, but contact between mother and children was often restricted to an hour or less a day. Scrubbed and fed by Nanny and her helpers, a child would be allowed to sit in the parlor with Mother (and perhaps Father) for a short period at the end of his day. Occasionally an upper-class parent, fiercely determined to produce a genius, would devote innumerable hours trying to teach a small child to read Greek or to play Bach fugues on the piano, but these were rare and eccentric cases. Most affluent nineteenth-century mothers were content with a hands-off approach to child rearing.

Winston Churchill remembered his mother in the following terms: "My mother always seemed to me a fairy princess: a radiant being possessed of limitless riches and power. . . . She shone for me like the evening star. I loved her dearly—but at a distance. My nurse was my confidante."[8] Churchill's mother was a beautiful upper-class socialite and, as was the custom in her circle at the end of the nineteenth century, saw very little of her son.

Servants were hardly peculiar to the Old World. Walter Lippmann, growing up in New York in the early years of this century, remembered his childhood as a time largely spent with servants and where contact with his mother was extremely limited.[9] And Sloan Wilson (author of the fifties best seller *The Man in the Gray Flannel Suit*), describing his upbringing in a professional upper-middle-class family in the 1920s, says, "I was brought up mostly by a Scottish nursemaid named Annie. Most of my time was spent in the kitchen with Annie and a variety of Irish servants who came and went. In those early years I rarely saw my mother."[10]

For working-class people of the eighteenth and nineteenth centuries, looking after children had to be a part-time activity because mothers were engaged, perforce, in arduous productive activity and expected their children to pitch in or, at the very least, not get in the way.

In pioneer families of the American frontier, "for children of all ages, the daily work load was both physically demanding and time-consuming. For the younger ones [three to six years of age], there were the daily chores of carrying water buckets, gathering the buffalo chips and picking wild fruits. In later years they joined in the heavier work of plowing and planting, building fences and cabins, trapping small animals and helping about the house."[11] In the tenements of the eastern cities a mother would park her small children in the corner of a crowded room while she stitched shirts for sale. Any child age five or more would be expected to help out, either with household chores or in simple commercial tasks, e.g., making matches on a piecework basis was often done at home by small children. Many children were sent to work in factories. As late as 1900 it is estimated that 2 million children were in the industrial labor force, where their small, dextrous fingers were prized. Unfortunately children tended to get sleepy in the afternoons and often "mangled themselves in the machines."[12]

As we enter the modern age, attitudes toward children change dramatically. The enormous medical advances of the late nineteenth and early twentieth centuries began to free parents from many of the health-related anxieties of the previous era. It was time to become more self-conscious about child rearing. The first modern school of thought on child-rearing practices emerged in the latter half of the nineteenth century and is associated with the names Luther Holt, Truby King, and John Watson. These experts were to dominate the field of child rearing until the late 1930s. They were the authorities who helped determine how our parents and grandparents were brought up. It comes as a shock to realize that their views of childhood and their recommendations to parents on how best to bring up children are as foreign to Dr. Spock and the contemporary conventional wisdom as the thoughts of Dr. Johnson's friend Mrs. Thrale.

Luther Emmett Holt, a New York pediatrician, published his influential book *The Care and Feeding of Children* in 1894. Holt was obsessed with cleanliness—a sensible preoccupation in an age when childhood diseases could still end in death. Much of the book was concerned with the details of dealing with nipples and bottles and getting rid of germs. Breast-feeding was frowned upon as unscientific. Holt carried his concern for hygiene to the extreme of advising against mothers kissing their babies because of the dangers of transmitting tuberculosis, diphtheria, syphilis, and other disease. Mothers were also discouraged from handling their babies in case they injured their spines or brains. Instead, they were to put them in playpens. "A nursery fence two feet high, made to surround a mattress," wrote Holt, "makes an excellent box stall for the young animal."[13]

The English equivalent of Holt was Truby King. He also believed passionately in proper hygiene and thought that raising babies in an environment as free from germs as possible was the most important aspect of caring for them. King paid little attention to mother love. To him a loving mother was no good to her infant if she infected him with lethal diseases.

Truby King worked out a scheme of rigidly regular four-hour feedings which became popular on both sides of the Atlantic. No baby was to be fed until the clock struck, no matter how much he cried. Most particularly babies were not to be fed at night. They had to learn to sleep at the proper times and not be allowed to manipulate and dominate their mothers by their demands. Regularity of bowel movements was seen as very important, and King advocated toilet training from the age of two months, aided by enemas if the baby did not perform. He advised against much physical contact between mother and child, particularly at bedtime.[14]

John B. Watson, who succeeded Holt as the most influential child-rearing expert of this period, was even more severe in his attitude toward maternal attachment. His major book, *Psychological Care of Infant and Child,* published in 1928, was dedicated to the first mother who brings up a happy child. He warned that doting mothers could retard the development of children, encumbering them with archaic values and constricting ties to the home. He maintained that excessive maternal affection rendered children incapable of assuming self-reliant positions in the adult world. ". . . remember, when you are tempted to pet your child that mother love is a dangerous instrument! An instrument which may inflict a never healing wound, a wound which may make infancy unhappy, adolescence a nightmare."[15] Demonstrations of affection were therefore limited. "If you must, kiss them once on the forehead when they say goodnight. Shake hands with them in the morning."[16]

Watson's great complaint was that mothers were not sufficiently disciplined to keep away from their children for a large part of the day. "I sometimes wish that we could live in a community of homes where each home is supplied with a well trained nurse so that we could have the babies fed and bathed each week by a different nurse. . . . Somehow I can't help wishing that it were possible to rotate the mothers occasionally too."[17] Most modern experts would disagree violently with such advice.

In more mundane matters Watson followed Holt and King in recommending feeding on a rigid schedule (and by bottle, not breast), early toilet training, and such hardening techniques as moderate exposure to heat, cold, and pain. The objective of these strict regimens was to foster the child's independence, which was then to be reinforced by the use of preschools and summer camps so that children could be emotionally weaned from their mothers.

It is easy to understand why this first modern school of child-rearing experts emphasized the dangers posed by germs and the importance of hygiene. By the turn of the century infant mortality was dramatically down but still significant enough to pose a real threat. Until the advent of antibiotics in the 1940s parents would have to devote some of their best energies to warding off infections and ensuring the physical health of their offspring. It is much harder to relate to the rigid schedules, firm discipline, and emotional distance advocated by this school of thought. These tenets are hard to empathize with because they flout the spirit and purpose of all that modern mothers have been taught to believe in.

In the postwar world child-rearing theories underwent a revolutionary change. For mothers the pendulum swung from one extreme to another. In the thirties they were told to keep their distance and avoid harming the child with that dangerous instrument mother love. In the late forties the advice of the experts was the exact opposite. Now they were supposed to root the child in an all-encompassing maternal passion. As Erich Fromm put it in 1948, "The child in these decisive first years of life [should have] the experience of his mother as the fountain of life, as an all-enveloping protective, nourishing power. Mother is food; she is love; she is warmth; she is earth. To be loved by her means to be alive, to be rooted, to be at home."[18] Fromm clearly disagreed profoundly with Watson, Holt, and King.

In the thirties, before Freudian enlightenment, mothers thought that they had done a good job if their children were healthy and well behaved. If a child also turned out to be dull and unimaginative, that was generally blamed on genes or temperament, elements over which the mother happily claimed no control and for which she took no responsibility. In the postwar period child rearing became a much more demanding occupation, for "Spock orientated mothers believed, deep in their hearts, that if they did their job well enough all of their children would be creative, intelligent, kind, generous, happy, brave, spontaneous, and good—each, of course, in his or her own special way."[19]

Freud's contribution to the changing fashions in child rearing was his great emphasis on the importance of the maternal tie and of early childhood experience (particularly any traumatic childhood experience) on the development of the adult personality.[20] Freud's preoccupation with the oral, anal, and phallic phases of psychological growth in the very first years of life and with such specific problems as anal retentiveness, penis envy, castration anxiety, and oedipal conflict were seized upon by the postwar generation of child-rearing experts and translated into an impressive concern for mother-child separation, nursing, toilet training, sex-role identification, and sibling rivalry. The fear was that if the early years were mishandled in any way, "the child would be irretrievably fixated at that stage of abandonment and the child's character would carry with it a tiny spot of vulnerability for the rest of its life."[21]

Spock, Fraiberg, and others called upon mothers to expend a limitless amount of energy in protecting the child against a host of fears and anxieties which could, it was believed, produce deviant emotional growth and neurotic behavior in the future. A single false step, a traumatic experience, might cause a child to develop insomnia, impotence, or homosexuality later in life. The fact that between the trauma and the consequent neurosis could lie a seemingly normal childhood made the situation all the more un-nerving. Like those long-incubating viruses that produce minor symptoms when they first enter the body and twenty years later result in multiple sclerosis, so parental miscalculations, missteps, misunderstandings, and mistakes might lead, after a long hiatus, to the most untoward consequences.

I have one extremely vivid memory of imagining the beginnings of neurotic behavior in my then three-year-old daughter, Lisa.

The fall and winter of 1981–82 had been hard, the family had moved to a new apartment, and I had changed jobs. I liked my new position quite a lot, but the hours were more rigid, and the children had had to adjust to seeing less of me in the late after-noon and early evening than they had been used to.

In November Lisa started to twitch. The child did not seem to be aware of what she was doing, but every sixty seconds (I timed her) the left side of her face went into an involuntary slight spasm. Not wanting to give her a "complex," I kept my mouth shut, hoping the twitching would just go away.

In December Lisa started to sniff. She didn't seem to have a cold; she just sniffed, about every sixty seconds in between the twitches. I began to worry that these symptoms were the first signs of some deep neurosis. Something had gone wrong in Lisa's emo-tional development, and the problem was leaking out in these twitching and sniffing symptoms. Perhaps the baby-sitter had been too authoritarian on the toilet-training front? Or maybe Lisa had failed to "bond" with me and therefore was now having problems separating? I was certain that whatever the specific cause of these problems, it had something to do with my decision to continue in my career and not become a "complete mother." Aside from these large issues, there were also appearances to con-sider. Lisa had some important nursery school tests and interviews in January, and I very much wanted her to stop this behavior by then. Besides, what would all the other mothers think? (Though I hated to admit it, I felt disapproved of by the nonworking moth-ers of Lisa's friends and felt sure that this twitching and sniffing syndrome would be used as ammunition in the cause of putting down working moms.)

I plucked up my courage and tried talking to Lisa about her

twitching and sniffing. Lisa did not appear to know what I was talking about, but she generally twitched and sniffed more rapidly after these conversations. Richard refused to take this family emergency at all seriously. Sometimes he said, "Come off it, Sylvia; don't let this thing get to you. Lisa's probably trying to get a little more attention, and if you stop attaching importance to it, she will give up. Just leave the kid alone." Other times, when he found me stalking my twitching and sniffing daughter around the apartment trying to pick up the scent of a neurosis or two, he would laugh uproariously—much to my chagrin. But then he had great trouble taking Freudian child development theorists seriously, and since he didn't take Lisa to school that year, he had never faced all those nonworking mothers smirking at one's twitching and sniffing child.

By Christmas my more subtle energies were exhausted, and I found that I had to clamp my mouth shut and sit on my hands in order to prevent myself yelling at or slapping Lisa as she twitched and sniffed her way through yet another family meal.

Lo and behold, the twitching and sniffing syndrome did go away later that winter (just after the nursery school tests!). One day Lisa just stopped. In retrospect, the family pediatrician blamed the symptoms on a low-grade upper-respiratory condition, Richard stuck to his attention-getting theory, and I secretly blamed it on myself. In my heart of hearts I suspected that those other mothers were right. It was a direct result of my new job. If I had not been working during those critical late-afternoon hours, if I had not taken this glamorous new job and "put my career before my children," Lisa would never have developed such distressing symptoms. Of course, only I had thought Lisa's condition at all serious, but maternal guilt is such an extremely pervasive phenomenon that it is hard to avoid it, no matter what you do or don't do.

Three years and two children later I look back at this episode and have to concede that Richard had a point, it was pretty funny. But at the time I really believed that Lisa might have some major emotional problem. I had read enough Spock and Fraiberg to be nervous about any unusual behavior and had a large enough store of job-related maternal guilt to be easy prey on the anxiety front.

* * *

Piaget did for cognitive skills what Freud had done for the emotional side of a child's life. In the 1920s and 1930s Piaget developed a theory of cognitive growth which divided childhood into distinct developmental stages. The first two years of the infant's life, the period when language had not yet emerged, was described as the sensory motor period. From two to six years the child went through a preoperational period, and from six to twelve years, a concrete operational period when he or she could begin to think logically and manipulate symbolically. Finally there was the formal operational period when all the characteristics of adult reasoning were potentially available to the adolescent.[22]

The concept of developmental stages lent itself to use—and considerable abuse—by postwar child-rearing experts. Authorities such as Burton White developed elaborate new tasks for mothers. There were ways of playing with, talking to, and encouraging baby so as to speed up the growth of cognitive skills and push him or her to the next stage of development. For example, a five-year-old who could be persuaded to perform concrete operations was said to have a mental age of six or seven. Mothers fueled by the lure of turning their children into high-achieving adults never questioned the benefit to the child of being ahead of his normal "age-appropriate" stage of development. Never mind the conspicuous lack of evidence that child prodigies grow up into adult geniuses. (In fact, what evidence there is points the other way, the great majority of precocious children do not fulfill their early promise.) As Glenn Doman, chairman of the Institutes for the Achievement of Human Potential, rightly surmised, thousands of mothers were willing to turn their best energies to the task of getting their child on the cognitive fast track. In 1975 he started intensive residential courses at his Better Baby Institute in Philadelphia. Lois Reed* was one of his students.

In the fall of 1982, when her daughter, Julia, was nine months old, Lois Reed attended a seven-day course entitled "How to Multiply Your Baby's Intelligence" at the Better Baby Institute

*Pseudonym.

in Philadelphia. She wanted to learn how to maximize her child's potential. Lois paid $500 tuition, plus the cost of her food and lodging.

During the morning sessions the chairman of the institute, Dr. Glenn Doman, a kindly-looking man with a white beard and glasses, lectured the eighty assembled mothers on the philosophy of the school. According to Doman, tiny children have limitless potential to learn. "They can grow up speaking many tongues, fluently reading the most complex of languages, doing instant mathematics, swimming, riding horseback, painting in oils, playing the violin." All of this by age two or three, but *only if the mother provides enough love, joy, respect, and training.* Doman impressed on the mothers that if their babies did not get onto the fast track, it was their fault.

Other staff members then elaborated on the process of producing a "Better Baby." The mind of the young child was like the memory of a computer waiting to be programmed. It needed to be fed with data, and the earlier the input, the easier it was to enter. "The ability to take in raw facts is an inverse function of age." Stimulation should begin immediately after birth, by the mother's shining bright lights on and off into a baby's eyes, clapping wooden blocks behind his head, and perhaps even putting a little mustard on his tongue. Once the baby has mastered this input—presumably by reacting—the next stage was to program him to recognize shapes by holding huge black cards cut into triangles, circles, etc. between the light and his eyes. This training ensured that by the time he was a few months old he would be ready to learn the beginnings of reading. Although Lois had missed out on these two stages, it wasn't too late to save her baby's potential. By working especially hard and doing some makeup exercises with Julia, she could move right into the third stage—reading.

Teaching a baby to read involved the intensive use of flash cards with letters and simple words on them. If mothers conscientiously flashed cards in front of their child six times a day, it actually seemed possible to get most normal babies to read simple words (or at least go through the motions of reading them) by the time they were two years old. The afternoon sessions at the institute were devoted to technique and demonstration. To prove the efficacy of the institute's methods, properly trained one- and two-year-olds were brought into the auditorium to demonstrate their accomplishments.

Lois was dismayed by the sheer amount of time it seemed to take to produce a "Better Baby." If training a baby to read took six intensive sessions a day, and reading was but one of the several skills the institute deemed necessary to prepare your child for life, was a mother supposed to do nothing else with her life except devote herself to maximizing her child's potential? And what of her daughter, Julia? Was it right and proper to bring her up to fulfill her potential if she was expected to turn around at age twenty-five or so and devote her best adult energies to *her* children? When Lois raised this question in class, Dr. Doman quickly ruled it out of order and relegated her to the back row of the auditorium for the rest of the course. Only boys apparently are supposed to grow up to use their maximized potential in the outside world.

Thousands of mothers have attended the courses or bought the books and teaching kits of the Better Baby Institute and have religiously tried to improve their babies by sneaking up on them with scarlet flash cards bedecked with letters, dots, and other "pieces of information." Some mothers attend these courses "even before their child is conceived . . . so they'll be prepared to teach their infants math, reading, music and foreign languages with flashcards from birth."[23] While it is not clear that these techniques have increased America's output of geniuses, they do seem to have added to American mothers' impressive load of maternal guilt and frustration.

Lois still feels that she let Julia down since she failed to teach her to read or do algebra by the age of two—or even five, for that matter. "All those exercises made both of us irritable and anxious. I guess I couldn't put together enough joyful enthusiasm, and gradually I just gave the whole thing up." Her inability to give her daughter that "special edge of excellence" promised by the Better Baby Institute made her feel that she had failed in her maternal duties.[24]

Thus the theories of Freud and Piaget filtered down through Benjamin Spock, Burton White, and the other postwar experts to leave the modern mother with some weighty and time-consuming responsibilities. In his influential book *The First Three Years of Life* White even inserts a graph purporting to show (scientifically) by what age mothers' arduous efforts at optimum child rearing would begin to show results. The typical onset of developmental divergence begins at nine months, and the well-developing child, spurred on by Mother, takes off on a special curve where he or she consistently outperforms his or her age group.[25] There is only one problem: There is no firm scientific evidence to support White's view that precocious nine-month-old babies will maintain their advantage throughout childhood and into adult life. According to Harvard psychologist Jerome Kagan, small differences in child-rearing techniques "will have little predictive consequences for differences amongst [children] five or ten years hence."[26] Factors such as a family's education, vocation, and income are much more powerful predictors of adult success. Despite this lack of evidence, any mother reading Burton White (as I did when Lisa was born) is left with an urgent sense that she has to work fast and hard.

Spock is perhaps the most disarming of the postwar experts. His advice is so down-to-earth, so practical, and he seems to be such a kindly man! All of which is true, but Spock trained as a psychiatrist before becoming a pediatrician, and underlying the 666 pages of *Baby and Child Care* (in all three editions) are some rigorous Freudian assumptions about the role of the mother in child rearing. A mother is supposed to monitor her own behavior so as to provide the proper environment for a child's "self-realization" through "self-discovery" and "self-motivated behavior." In fact, all the developmental tasks are now defined as mother work, for it is she who must preside over the teaching of bathroom protocol, restraint of aggression, and adjustment to peers. In toilet-training the child, Dr. Spock instructs a mother to watch her toddler—if necessary for eighteen months—to see what stage of readiness he or she is in. Watching, considering whether or not to intervene, and determining the magnitude of insistence to use in guiding the child's potty behavior are time-consuming and fraught with risk. For, as Spock points out:

> [Toilet training is] actually the foundation for a lifelong preference for unsticky hands, for clean clothes, for a

neat home, for an orderly way of doing business. It's from their toilet training that children get some of their feeling that one way of doing things is right and another way is not; this helps them to develop a sense of obligation, to become systematic people. So toilet training plays a part in the formation of a child's character and in building the basic trust between them and their parents.[27]

Selma Fraiberg in *The Magic Years* gives this classic Freudian theme even greater weight. She spends fifteen pages describing how a mother can go wrong potty-training her child. Elimination is vested with almost mystical significance. Fraiberg describes the child as regarding "this act in the same way that an older child regards a gift to a loved person."[28] To insensitively flush the feces down the toilet is "a strange way to accept an offering of such value."[29] Moreover, the toilet itself has created quite new twentieth-century problems: "This vitreous monster with its yawning jaws does not quite invite friendship or confidence at this age. The most superficial observation will reveal that it swallows up objects with a mighty roar, causes them to disappear in its secret depths, then rises thirstily for its next victim which might be—just anyone."[30] Dealing with such a loaded scene is obviously a complex task, difficult to delegate to a baby-sitter. It is almost enough to make a working mother yearn for the simple discipline of Watson, who dealt with toilet training by recommending that at eight months a baby should be strapped into a special toilet seat and left alone in the bathroom with the door closed for half an hour or so, however long it took before he or she performed.

The conventional wisdom of the early decades of this century was altogether easier on the mother. The advice of experts such as Holt and Watson trickled down to the general population via the Children's Bureau, which began publishing a pamphlet called *Infant Care* in 1914. The early editions of *Infant Care* provoked thousands of letters from mothers requesting additional advice, and contrary to the traditions of the Washington bureaucracy, these letters were answered personally by the author of the original pamphlet, Mary West, and other staff members of the Children's Bureau. The tenor of the early editions of *Infant Care* as well as the responses to letters demonstrates that the convenience and needs of the mother were often put center stage.

Infant Care, following the fashion of the day, touted strict scheduling, ignoring crying, and early toilet training and advised against rocking, tickling, or playing with infants. But *Infant Care* saw these rules as primarily protective of the mother: "The care of a baby is readily reduced to a system. . . . Such a system is not only one of the greatest factors in keeping the baby well and in training him in a way which will be of value to him through life, but it also reduces the work of the mother to a minimum and provides for her certain assured periods of rest and recreation."[31] For example, the use of a playpen was seen from the point of view not of the child but of the mother: thus "an older child should be taught to sit on the floor or in his pen or crib during part of his waking hours, or he will be very likely to make too great demands upon his mother's strength."[32] Mrs. West comments sympathetically in one of her letters, "No one who has not tried it realizes how much nervous energy can be consumed in 'minding' a baby who can creep or walk about, and who must be continually watched and diverted, and the mother who is taking the baby through this period of his life will need to conserve all her strength and not waste it in useless activity."[33]

Contrast this with Burton White, who strongly urges mothers to do without playpens because "there is no way of keeping most children from being bored."[34] White sees everything from the child's point of view and has very strong feelings on the subject of playpens. "To bore a child on a daily basis by the regular use of a playpen is a very poor child-rearing practice in terms of the child's educational needs."[35] What is more, he extends the same principle to the use of cribs, jump seats, high chairs, and play and feed tables. These prohibitions tend to guarantee that a mother has to creep around after her baby for the majority of the day.

Mrs. West in *Infant Care* advocated a 6:00 P.M. bedtime. Again the main rationale is the convenience of the mother, for "if you have not tried putting away your children at six o'clock, you have no idea what a relief it will be to you. It can be done, I have done it myself with three boys, and no mother who knows the satisfaction of having the care of her children cease before her evening meal, and the quiet comfort of a still household in the evening, would fail to immediately begin the training to make it possible."[36] What mother would not respond to such advice! (When I discovered this passage in my research, I stopped and read it several times; it sounded like music to my modern ears. We are all so used to reading the child-centered contemporary advice which can make us feel either guilty or angry—depending on our level of confidence—but rarely soothes.)

Spock tells us contemporary mothers that the central problem we should worry about at bedtime is making sure that it is "agreeable and happy" for the child. "Try not to rush going to bed no matter how much of a hurry you are in." Don't "turn it into an unpleasant duty," and above all, "trust an infant to take what rest he needs."[37] Not a word about how frayed a mother might be after a day of crawling around after her infant (or toiling away at her job).

Considering the developmental tasks given to the mother by postwar child-rearing experts, it is hardly surprising that these experts have heavily backed the notion that she stay out of the labor force the better to perform her maternal duties.

For thirty years Spock (who is still the most widely read expert; *Baby and Child Care* has sold 30 million copies) told us that the children of working mothers may grow up neglected and maladjusted. Unless a mother absolutely must work, it makes no sense for her to "pay other people to do a poorer job of bringing up [her] children."[38] In the 1976 edition of *Baby and Child Care* Spock tries to adjust to modern times and to the fact that many mothers are now in the work force. He calls his babies she instead of he and inserts some language about women's liberation. But his heart is not in it. His preference is still that "there will always be men and women who feel that the care of children and home is at least as important and soul satisfying as any other activity, and neither men nor women will feel the need to apologize for deciding to make that their main career."[39] The very conditions he sets up for substitute care—continuity in the person of the caretaker for the first three years of life—would rule out a job for most women.

Pediatrician Berry Brazelton continues to express negative views on nonmaternal care, putting forward the untestable argument that separation from the mother affects the child in ways "that cannot be measured in observable behavior."[40] Psychologist Lee Salk tells us that "of course no one can replace the mother if she must work,"[41] and Selma Fraiberg stresses the dire consequences of maternal deprivation before a child is eighteen months old.[42] Burton White is even more emphatic. In 1981 he brought all his credentials to bear—as director of the Harvard Preschool Project—in a heavy-handed piece of advice to mothers: "For more than 20 years I've specialized in the study of successful child-raising. . . . I've had the privilege of being able to compare the everyday experience of many children getting off to a fine start in life with those not so fortunate. . . . I firmly believe that most children will get off to a better start in life when they spend the majority of their waking hours being cared for by their parents." White goes further: "Government . . . should resist the cries for free full time substitute care for babies for all who want it."[43]

Interestingly enough, Burton White is so caught up in hostility toward working mothers that he does not devote any attention to maternity leave. Given his conviction that the first six months of life are absolutely critical and that the child "has to be responded to intensely in this period,"[44] you would think that he would urge government to guarantee a maternity leave for working women that lasted at least this long. Not so. White concentrates on advising mothers to stay out of the labor force. As he told me in March 1983, "I am not too interested in advocating maternity leave as this might encourage the mothers of young children to stay in the work force."[45] Unfortunately, in the mid-1980s, 48 percent of mothers with children under twelve months old are already in the labor force, and most of them work out of economic necessity. What these women need is decent maternity leave and high-quality child care, not another guilt trip.

The cult of motherhood may have made some kind of sense in the 1950s, but the American economy and society have changed dramatically since that time. Today 56 percent of mothers with pre-school children work—as opposed to 12 percent in 1950—and divorce rates have quadrupled over the last thirty years. The Norman Rockwell family, the classical family of Western nostalgia, is a thing of the past. Only 22 percent of families can now boast an at-home wife (compared with 61 percent in 1950), and families comprising a breadwinning husband, a dependent wife, and two or more children now represent a mere 6 percent of American families.[46] In 1985 it is easier to find a "classical" family on a cereal box than in real life.

Despite these changed circumstances, the popular child-rearing manuals are still hopelessly grounded in the assumptions and prescriptions of the postwar world. Psychologist Claire Etaugh finds that only seven out of the twenty most influential child-care books published in the 1970s approved, even grudgingly, of women working while they have young children. In her opinion, the popular child-care books tend "to perpetuate the belief that non-maternal care is harmful to young children."[47] A survey in the medical journal *Pediatrics* comes to a similar conclusion: "[T]he popular literature still regards the working mother as deviant."[48]

The early 1980s have seen a further flood of books on child rearing, but once again working mothers are either ignored, or segregated in a section on "special problems." For example, in 1984 the second most popular book on child rearing (after Spock) was *Babyhood* by Penelope Leach. In a thoughtful chapter on mother-infant attachment Leach makes absolutely no mention of the working mother.[49]

But despite all this hostility toward the working mother on the part of the child-rearing "experts," the serious scholarship in the field casts doubt on the notion that working mothers raise less happy or less successful children. In a highly respected study Jerome Kagan, Richard B. Kearsley, and Philip R. Zelazo find that "attachment to the mother and rate of cognitive development, the two critical concerns of American parents, did not appear to be altered by day care.... The assessments of language, memory, and perceptual analysis failed to reveal any obvious advantages or disadvantages to the day care experience ... all the children preferred the mother to any other adult by a factor of 7."[50] In an exhaustive review of the evidence, Etaugh finds that "high quality nonmaternal care does not seem to have adverse effects on the young child's maternal attachment, intellectual development or social-emotional behavior."[51]

It seems that young children can form as strong an attachment to a working parent as to a nonworking one if the parent interacts frequently with the child during the times they are together and provided that the substitute care arrangements are stable and stimulating. A major conclusion of the research in the field is that "satisfied mothers—working or not—have the best adjusted children."[52] Another finding in the maternal employment literature is that the children of working mothers perceive women as being more competent than do the children of nonworking mothers. In a similar vein, the daughters of working women have higher aspirations for themselves than do the daughters of nonworking women.[53] All of which makes intuitive sense; once one stops focusing on the first three years of life and takes a longer view and considers those other influences in later life, the role model a woman presents to her children becomes centrally important.

Policy makers need not be inhibited by Benjamin Spock (or Burton White for that matter); day care need not harm children. There are, of course, some things to avoid. Young children develop badly if they are physically neglected, if they have no continuity in people entrusted with their care, and if they are put in care situations with such low adult-child ratios that they have no individual attention. But "attendance at a day care center should not in itself affect the child's development in serious ways, as long as the parents hold a positive attitude toward their children and the surrogate caretakers are nurturant, attentive and conscientious."[54] There is no evidence that begins to suggest that "the worst natural mother is better in the long run than the best [day-care] mother."[55]

The irony is that so little attention and so few resources have been devoted to day care in this country that much of what exists is substandard. This tends to reinforce our ideological bias against out-of-home care. "A lot of what we have today in commercial day care [in the United States today] is kennels," says Dr. Irving Lazar of Cornell University, "and in a kennel there is no opportunity for learning."[56] Dr. Lazar is right. We do not want kennels for our children. Unfortunately, until our government decides to subsidize child care on a substantial scale, millions of American children will be forced to spend their days in kennels. It is not that we don't know how to run high-quality day-care centers, for the United States has done more research on early-childhood development than any other country. It's just that we have decided not to allocate public resources to small children.

Did other Western industrial countries develop a similar cult of motherhood in the postwar period? Not to nearly the same extent as the United States. In many European countries one can detect a similar swing in child-rearing fashions from the discipline and rigid schedules of the 1920s and 1930s to the psychological and developmental preoccupations of the postwar era. In Europe as well as in America this led to greater maternal involvement in child rearing (especially since this swing coincided with a decline in the availability of nannies and other household servants). However, there were significant countervailing trends in Europe which precluded the development of a cult of motherhood.

To begin with, in contrast with the American experience, most European nations did not undergo an extended baby boom in the postwar period. In 1955, for example, the U.S. birthrate was running at 25 per 1,000 of the population, while in France the figure was 18.5; in Britain, 15.4; and in Germany, 15.7.[57] The lower European birthrate was accompanied by a steady rise in female employment. In 1950 only 37 percent of American women were in the labor force, compared with 44 percent in Germany and 50 percent in France.[58] This difference in labor force participation meant that European countries were forced to grapple much earlier with issues of maternity leave and substitute care, and mothers did not pick up so many responsibilities.

Secondly, America has always been more child-centered than Europe and therefore likely to provide the most fertile ground for a cult of motherhood. Children were scarce and therefore prized in this long-underpopulated country, and there has also been a firmly entrenched regard for the importance of the individual. Indeed, "Europeans have always felt that American parents paid far too much regard to their children's needs and far too little to the demands of adult social occasions."[59]

Thirdly, there is a pronounced tendency for American parents to consider the child at least as important as themselves—perhaps potentially more important than they. An English anthropologist once said that whereas in other countries children were taught to look up to their parents as rather distinguished superior people whatever their objective place in the society, the remarkable thing about the United States is that parents will say to their child, "If you don't do better than I've done, I won't think much of you."[60]

This expectation of upward mobility goes along with two other distinctively American traits: geographic displacement and the lack of a firm class structure. In many European countries parents absorb the goals and methods of child rearing from family traditions and from having grandparents nearby to advise and help them. These props are often lacking in America. Massive immigration and frequent moves (between cities and between regions in search of better economic opportunities) mean that American parents are often bringing up their children hundreds of miles away from relatives and in a socioeconomic context that may be quite different from that of their own parents. So they are much more likely to turn to professional advisers, books, and new fashionable theories for the help they need. This obviously increases the impact of any new style in child rearing. In Italy I was impressed by the fact that bookstores in major cities carried very few manuals on child rearing. Italian mothers I interviewed relied mainly on family tradition.

Claudia* grew up in northern Italy, came to this country as a student, and married a New York businessman. She is now bringing up her children "American style" and has an extremely clear sense of the difference between the cultures.

"In Italy young marrieds are supposed to have a good time, and it is perfectly OK to hand the baby over to relatives for large chunks of time. Some friends of mine, who live in Genoa, seem to

*Pseudonym.

go skiing or sailing most weekends. A grandmother and a spinster aunt live just around the corner and are delighted to take the children." Claudia paused for a moment and then said disapprovingly, "It is all very convenient for the parents, but it does mean that child-rearing practices remain dreadfully old-fashioned. You know I bought Sonia [the wife of the couple that lives in Genoa] a copy of Dr. Spock's book when her second child was born, and I am sure that she hasn't even opened it. She says she doesn't like modern ideas, and I suppose that since the family are doing all the child care, she cannot turn around and tell them how to do it."

I asked Claudia what she thought about traditional Italian methods of bringing up children. She confessed to a great deal of ambivalence. "I suppose it has its good points. Children get a lot of affection from their relatives, they are allowed to stay up late, and in many ways childhood is very enjoyable in Italy; but really, attitudes about how to develop emotional maturity and cognitive skills are very primitive." I asked Claudia to give me an example. After a little thought she said, "A woman friend of mine runs a small business in Milan. She hired a nanny for her baby when he was three months old. When I saw her last summer, her child was about a year old, and she boasted to me that he was no trouble at all, that her nanny was able to leave him in his playpen all day long, and that he didn't bother anyone. Imagine," said Claudia with a smile, "an American middle-class mother boasting about such a thing. Why, here in America everyone knows that a child needs constant stimulation, and the last thing one should do is confine a child in a playpen all day long!" Claudia had read all the well-known American child-rearing manuals and had found Selma Fraiberg and Burton White particularly illuminating. As she put it, "Fraiberg's book *Every Child's Birthright* convinced me that I should give up my career when Jonathon was born. It made me realize that no one could take my place." Claudia paused and then added hesitantly, "The odd thing is I would never had read those books had I stayed in Italy, and as a result, I wouldn't have given up my profession for my children."[61]

All these distinctions contributed to a very different policy climate in Europe from that present in America in the postwar years. For example, in the late forties France developed a whole range of benefits and services to support the family. A family allowance system was instituted, infant nurseries (crèches) were publicly subsidized for the first time, and the network of public preschools (*écoles maternelles*) was greatly expanded. By the 1950s most French three- to five-year-olds were enrolled in these *écoles maternelles*.[62] An explicit goal of these family support policies was that mothers be free to choose between homemaking or working outside the home.

Contrast this with America, where the belief that mothers should stay at home and look after their own children reverberates through postwar policy. In 1960, at the beginning of the Kennedy administration, a conference was convened at the White House to consider services to working mothers and children. The main recommendations of this conference were:

> —that to maintain the important relationship of infant and mother, children under 3 should remain in their own homes unless there are pressing social or economic reasons for care away from home.
> —that social casework and other counseling services be available both before and during employment of the mother, to help parents decide wisely whether her employment will contribute more to family welfare than her presence in the home.[63]

These recommendations could have been taken directly from Spock. In *Baby and Child Care* he says, "If a mother realizes clearly how vital this kind of care is to a small child it may make it easier to decide that the extra money she may earn . . . is not so important after all."[64] Needless to say, this conference did not spur much action on the public child-care front. There was a small federal appropriation for day care in 1962 ($4 million), the first such appropriation since World War II, but it was cut out of the budget in 1965.[65] The Vietnam War was beginning to produce fiscal pressure, and child care was one of the easiest items to cut.

By 1971 a third of all preschool children had mothers in the labor force, and Congress did pass the Comprehensive Child Development Bill (sponsored by Senator Walter Mondale and Representative John Brademas) in December of that year. It was promptly vetoed by Nixon. Nixon took a strong ideological stance. He talked emotionally about his desire to "cement the family in its rightful position as the keystone of our civilization"[66] and stated categorically that "good public policy requires that we enhance rather than diminish both parental authority and parental involvement with children—particularly in those early years when social attitudes and a conscience are formed."[67]

According to Nixon, it was OK to have day care "for the children of the poor so that their parents can leave the welfare rolls," but it was "unacceptable to encourage or support middle-class mothers who leave the home."[68] Nixon seemed not to know—or to care—that a third of these mothers had already left home for the workplace, and most of these women were propelled by economic pressures. His veto did not resurrect motherhood "fifties-style." It merely left "thousands of children with no care and hundreds of thousands of others in inadequate and sometimes even destructive care."[69]

Nixon couched his 1971 veto in such strong ideological language that the Comprehensive Child Development Bill could not be revived; he had succeeded in reestablishing day care as an un-American activity. A scaled-down version of the bill was introduced—again by Mondale and Brademas—in 1975, but no action was taken by either the Senate or the House.

In 1983, at the time of my interview with Faith Whittlesey at the White House, half of all preschool children had mothers in the work force, yet despite this trend line, Whittlesey assured me that Ronald Reagan was confident that once the economy picked up, "all those women can go home and look after their own children in the way they did when I was growing up."[70] As if to encourage this return to complete motherhood, the Reagan administration has been careful to cut back even further this nation's very modest commitment to public child care: Title XX funds which provide child-care subsidies to poor families have been cut 21 percent since 1980.

In some of its aspects the culture of the 1950s seems strange but distant. A rerun of *I Love Lucy* is not threatening because most of us recognize the styles and values of the show as a relic from another age. Not so when we come to fifties attitudes toward motherhood and child rearing. The cult of motherhood is alive and well; our standards are still set by the "smother love" of the 1950s. Images of the complete, all-providing mother remain powerful enough to furnish working women with a bottomless pit of maternal guilt. It was this guilt that reverberated around the Eighty-first Street play group on innumerable Friday afternoons.

My children were born in 1977, 1980, and 1984, and I have been an active consumer of child-rearing manuals for the better part of the last decade. Every few years I make the dreary round and discover that the most recent edition of Spock, Brazelton, and White, and the new best sellers by Leach and Salk, continue to pretend either that mothers don't work (Leach), or that mothers can deal with their work commitments during a baby's naptime (White). The overwhelming message remains: Mothers should devote themselves to their children for the first three years of life, mothers are responsible for developing a child's total potential, and full-time work is incompatible with good mothering. The fifties lure is held out to the eighties mother: "that with attentiveness, emotional vigilance and her uninterrupted presence she can provide an environment from which a superior individual will emerge."[71] As Nancy Weiss has so aptly put it, "child rearing manuals might [well] be renamed mother rearing tracts."[72]

The advice of the child-rearing "experts" is irresponsible and counterproductive in the modern world. It is irresponsible because there is no evidence that supports the notion that mother-intensive child-rearing techniques constitute the only good way of bringing up children. And it is counterproductive because it impedes the development of sensible child-care policies in this country. The majority of mothers work, and the misguided notion that governments cannot and should not help provide a substitute for mother love and mother care has prevented us from creating high-quality day-care facilities. As a result, millions of children spend their waking hours in "kennels," and their mothers (and fathers) are subjected to high levels of strain and stress. The glorification of the fifties mom and the fifties approach to mothering helps explain why child-centered America can be so neglectful toward children.

One more question needs to be answered. If we can put Doris Day and Lucille Ball in perspective and have no problem recognizing that being a dizzy blonde or a nincompoop is not going to get us very far in the 1980s, why can't we do the same with Benjamin Spock and Burton White? After all, their values and methods are also at cross-purposes with the needs of our age.

When Adam was born in the spring of 1984, I picked up Burton White's *The First Three Years of Life* and felt my anxiety level rise as I read, once again, of all the tasks I should be engaged in to give my son a head start in life. I had a little perspective but clearly not enough. (Adam was, after all, my third child, and I had done all this research on child rearing and knew that my grandparents had followed the advice of Truby King. Consequently, my parents had gotten lots of discipline but little maternal attention. They had turned out OK; why shouldn't my kids?) But somehow I couldn't put the cult of motherhood into the same distant, unthreatening perspective as Doris Day and fifties ideas of femininity.

This is because the modern women's movement has helped us change our image of women—particularly of women as workers—but has failed to deal with motherhood. As we saw in Chapter Eight, the women's movement has alternatively ignored or reviled mothers, which has not put feminists in a good position to either understand or come to grips with the cult of motherhood. True, the movement has been concerned with issues such as regaining control over the birth process and raising children in a nonsexist way. But this feminist agenda has served to add to the long list of maternal responsibilities rather than lighten the load.

This failure of the women's movement to connect with motherhood and family has had some extremely serious repercussions. It has made modern mothers vulnerable to the expectations of Spock and White because we are not equipped with an alternative vision of how to mother. Feminism has given us alternatives to Doris Day. Whether one's tastes run to Geraldine Ferraro or Jane Fonda, most of us understand that nowadays it is good to be an accomplished, independent woman. But on the mothering front we have merely added to the burdens of the fifties. As one eminent New York obstetrician put it, "modern superwomen take it for granted that they can hold down a job as vice-president of Chase Manhattan Bank, give birth naturally, and breast-feed. Few realize before the fact that this is an impossible set of demands."[73]

Had coming to terms with motherhood been a central task of feminism, we might have cut the overblown fifties vision of mothering down to size. We might also have acquired some concrete help in discharging maternal responsibilities. For the failure of the women's movement to deal with motherhood left a vacuum in public policy which was filled by traditionalists. These men (and women) are all too comfortable with the fifties notion of complete motherhood and find it easy to stick their heads in the sand and pretend that we don't need maternity leave or child care. Like Nixon, they glorify Mom and apple pie and believe that it is "unacceptable to encourage or support middle-class mothers who leave the home."[74] For we should not underestimate the powerful hold the decade of the fifties has on the American imagination. Many mainstream Americans—not just Jesse Helms and Phyllis Schlafly—would like nothing better than to return to that golden age. Their vision is, of course, a nostalgic vision and has little to do with modern America, yet it has informed our policies on the child-care front. The women's movement, which should have been the countervailing force, producing policies which more nearly fitted the needs of contemporary families, was busy on other fronts. And because feminists abdicated their rights to this important territory, family policy has become the preserve of nostalgic traditionalists.

Of course, the real victims of our lack of public child care and job-protected maternity leave are working-class women and their children. A vice-president of Chase Manhattan Bank might have a rough time of it when she attempts to breast-feed without missing a beat on the work front, but Chase Manhattan has a decent maternity policy (decent, that is, by American standards), and the odds are she can afford to pay the market rate for a full-time baby-sitter. For fast-food waitresses and retail clerks, the consequences of our lack of support policies are more severe. Most of them have no rights to maternity leave, and they can't afford adequate child care. Tell them that America is a nation that venerates mothers and children, and they will tell you a different tale.

PART D

---·◆◆◆◆·---

Revolt and Reaction

Precisely because ultradomesticity fifties-style was aberrant and artificial, it provoked fierce waves of reaction. By the early 1960s a steady diet of breadwinning to support wife and kiddies in the suburbs had begun to pall for many men, and at least some of them decided that they had been taken for a ride. The male revolt was slow and cumulative, but during the next two decades millions of stalwart breadwinners took off into the sunset, leaving their family responsibilities behind them.

Joining the revolt in the late sixties and seventies, a new wave of feminists lashed out at everything the fifties stood for. They wrote books called *Marriage Is Hell* and *The Baby Trap* and declared that the tyranny of the biological family should be broken. Ex-housewives were most incensed by the fifties cult of motherhood because they knew through direct experience that the responsibilities inherent in this cult were inimical to any form of equality between the sexes. In their rage they were often driven to deny the relevance of children to the lives of liberated women and, in so doing, alienated many.

Finally, in the 1970s, the traditional women spawned by the fifties and its cult of motherhood found themselves isolated and vulnerable. They, in their turn, lashed out, and their targets were liberated women, whom they blamed for undermining marriage and family.

Thus the 1950s with its glorification of hearth and home, far from representing a golden age, emerges as so profoundly aberrant both historically and culturally that we are still living with the backlash.

12

THE UNRAVELING
OF THE FIFTIES

In the spring of 1968, while I was a graduate student at Harvard, I attended a two-day conference in San Francisco. On my way back to Cambridge, Massachusetts, I met Nancy Barrett.* Her life story throws into sharp relief the painful undoing of the fifties.

I had left the conference a few hours later than expected and, as a result, missed my flight to Boston. The next direct flight was full, so eager to get back before the weekend, I booked myself onto a plane to Chicago which had a connecting flight to Boston. Once aboard, I had settled down with a pile of conference papers, intending to do a little serious reading, when I realized that the woman sitting next to me was quietly crying. She was a pretty blond woman of about forty. In her fresh spring suit and matching accessories she looked well groomed enough to have stepped straight out of the pages of *Good Housekeeping*. At first I thought that she was merely shedding a tear or two on account of saying good-bye to her husband or children at the airport. But as time went on, the discreet, ladylike sobs became more desperate, and small moans of misery began to escape the damp wads of Kleenex

*Pseudonym.

287

she had hidden behind. I offered her a handkerchief and made sympathetic noises. In return she began to confide in me. To begin with, she talked mostly to let out some of her pain, but after a while she came to see me as a potential ally, a sympathetic member of a generation that she found alien and hurtful.

Nancy Barrett was returning from a week in San Francisco, where she had been visiting her three children, all of whom had dropped out of school and were living in the countercultural mecca of Haight-Ashbury. Her eldest child, Franny, had dropped out of college when she was nineteen; her two sons, Mark and Robert, aged sixteen and seventeen respectively, had recently dropped out of high school. All were into drugs and chic revolutionary movements. Nancy was particularly worried about Franny, who she thought was being exploited by the "hip" man she was living with. As Nancy put it rather bitterly, "In the last year Franny has had two illegal abortions, at least one of them dangerously late. She had to come to her parents for the money to pay for them because her groovy man wasn't into responsibility." These thoughts occasioned a fresh outburst of weeping, and it soon transpired that Nancy's problems went beyond the countercultural rebellion staged by her children.

As Nancy saw it, her entire world—the safe, predictable world of the 1950s—was coming down about her ears. Way back in her teens Nancy had been a superior student and a talented violinist, but as was the fashion in the postwar period, she had gotten married as a sophomore in college. She had then left college to take a clerical job in order to put her husband, John, through medical school.

The years when the children were little had been tough. John's residency had been followed by military service and a series of jobs in teaching hospitals up and down the eastern seaboard. They had little money and moved, on average, once every eighteen months. Since John worked long, hard hours on the job, Nancy had pretty much managed the domestic scene and brought up the children on her own. Eight years ago they finally were able to reap the rewards of their hardworking partnership. John obtained a prestigious appointment at Northwestern University and started a lucrative private practice, while Nancy settled into a gracious home in suburban Evanston. She took up tennis, became active in the PTA, and even started playing the violin in local amateur groups.

But the suburban idyll was soon shattered. First came the rebellion of the children. Somehow, somewhere, all three kids had learned to despise their parents. They acquired weird friends, wore their hair long and dirty, were abusive to adults, smoked pot, played truant from school, allowed their grades to slip out of sight, and finally absconded to Haight-Ashbury. John's reaction had been one of disgust and disillusionment. "Why have I striven all these years to be a good provider if all I get is ingratitude!" was his oft-repeated refrain. According to Nancy, John was now thoroughly alienated from the children. He had refused recent requests for money from both Franny and the boys and did not want to see any of them until they "shaped up."

Nancy, on the other hand, was still trying to bridge the gulf between the generations. She started to cry again. "When I see how vulnerable, how bewildered my kids are, and when I read about teenagers dying from drug overdoses, I feel such anguish I have to try to help them." It turned out that Nancy had not been visiting her children in Haight-Ashbury but had gone, uninvited, to try to bring them home. She had pretended to her husband that she was visiting her sister and her brother-in-law, who live in Marin County. John would have prevented her from going had he known that she was going to try to see the "ingrates" (he could easily do that since she didn't have any money of her own).

Nancy had succeeded in tracking down Franny and Mark and had talked to them—to no avail. Fran had told her that she had no intention of becoming a plastic, sanitized suburbanite like her mother, and Mark had been too stoned to say anything coherent at all. As for Robert, she had not even been able to find him, and she was incredibly anxious because one of his friends had told her that he was in Mexico dealing drugs. "My poor baby, for all I know he might be dead or in some Mexican jail."

If Nancy's problems had started with the defection of her children, the current crisis centered on her husband. His disillusionment with family life ran so deep that in recent months he had had at least three affairs, all with much younger women. Two were graduate students; the other was a secretary at the university. John had recently bought himself an Alfa Romeo sports car and had taken to reading *Playboy* and wearing bell-bottomed jeans. Nancy was terrified that he was going to ask her for a divorce. That prospect truly frightened her. As she put it, "The thing is, I have no skills. All I can do is give violin lessons to little kids, and what kind of income does that bring in? Maybe a thousand dollars a year!"

By the time the plane landed at O'Hare Airport Nancy and I were enthralled with each other. I was fascinated by her story. She was tremendously excited at having found a member of the sixties generation who was willing to listen and even to sympathize with her side of the story. Nancy impulsively invited me to spend the weekend at her home, and instead of getting my connecting flight to Boston, I found myself shaking hands with a rather startled John Barrett and being driven in a large, luxurious automobile to Evanston. Conversation was strained. Nancy had put on fresh makeup just before we landed, and with her husband she was perky and bright, full of tales of her sister's new house and her brother-in-law's new job. John was courteous enough but quite distant. As soon as he had unloaded the luggage and fixed the drinks, he disappeared to his study "to catch up on some work."

My weekend in Evanston was full of strange and oddly moving experiences. I still remember some of the scenes. I had cocktails with Nancy on the fortieth floor of some new skyscraper in the Chicago Loop and saw the streets below us fill with smoke and angry lurching shadows as blacks reacted with violence to the news of Martin Luther King's assassination. That particular evening the rioting became so ugly that the National Guard was called out and a curfew was imposed in the downtown area. Somehow these scenes of violence and frustration seemed a fitting backdrop to our talk, which centered on the clash between values and between generations.

That night Nancy, talked out and exhausted, went to bed early. I, on the other hand, was far from sleepy; my imagination had been working overtime. About midnight I went down to the Barretts' kitchen and was making myself some tea when I was startled out of my wits by a hand on my shoulder. It was John Barrett. He now wanted to talk, to pour out to me his side of the story. No one had ever understood how hard it was to make it in his profession and how little psychic support he had ever gotten from his wife or children. All they had ever understood was "how to spend my money." I can remember wanting to listen and understand better where this troubled and isolated man was coming from. But he touched me again and muttered something about the sexual revolution, and I knew the time had come to beat a hasty retreat. Clutching a teacup in my hand, I muttered good night and backed up the stairs to my room.

That next week, when I got back to Cambridge, I sent Nancy Barrett some flowers—a token of my appreciation for her hospitality and her trust. She called me to say thank you and to tell me that she had decided to enroll for a master's degree in education. She was preparing herself for a belated teaching career and a lonely middle age. She made one bitter comment: "Given my age, I guess teaching is the best thing I can do, but I will never earn even a quarter of John's salary."

Nancy Barrett's story contains many of the ingredients of postwar social history. It conjures up the extremely differentiated world of the 1950s, when men and women led such separate lives. Nancy kept house and reared the children while John clambered up the slippery pole of career success. Nancy's life story also runs full tilt into the countercultural explosion of the mid-sixties. It was a time when many young people rejected the life-styles of their parents and dropped out of the system. By moving to Haight-Ashbury and taking up drugs and chic radical causes, Franny, Mark, and Robert were merely doing the same as hundreds of thousands of their contemporaries.

By the time I met Nancy in the late sixties, she and her husband were themselves poised on the edge of major life changes. Her husband was ready to kick over the traces. He had had his fill of life in the work harness, bringing home the bacon for a bunch of ungrateful children. He was ready to spend money on himself and experiment with (sexually liberated) younger women. After all, his kids were reaping the rewards of the sexual revolution.

Why shouldn't he? Nancy herself was beginning to face a very different future from that which she either wanted or expected. She did go ahead with her plans for graduate study, and in the fall of 1968 John left her, taking off into the sunset with one of his graduate students. Nancy's experience was not unusual. The American divorce rate doubled between 1965 and 1975, and millions of "displaced homemakers" became downwardly mobile as they struggled to earn some kind of a living in their middle years. I was last in touch with Nancy in 1970. I called her from O'Hare Airport; I was changing planes again and had thirty minutes to spare. The news was not good. She had not seen her children recently. Franny and Robert had joined a commune in New Mexico, and Mark was in India, where he had linked up with some religious sect. John had ceased to pay alimony, and the lawyers could not track him down. Nancy was deeply in debt, and although she had qualified as a teacher, she had not yet found a job. The only bright spot on the horizon was that she had just joined a consciousness-raising group and was feeling good about having found some supportive women.

Why has postwar America been so marked by fierce clashes between the generations and violent battles between the sexes? We all know at least one Nancy Barrett because our contemporary society is littered with the survivors of these wars. Most of us over twenty-five are ourselves veterans of several battles.

A large part of the explanation lies in the cozy and oppressive postwar world. For the fifties succeeded in defining men and women in an exceedingly narrow way, and both sexes have expended a great deal of energy in a struggle to break loose and better fulfill their individual identities. It is often not fully understood how aberrant our society was during those formulative postwar years. In the late forties and fifties Americans developed a type of exaggerated role playing that was deeply at odds with history. As described in earlier chapters of this book, our traditions are grounded in independence and equality, and both men and women have cherished a reputation for strength. But during this postwar period relationships between the sexes became deeply distorted, and we are still suffering the consequences of this distortion, for many of the subsequent clashes and battles can be explained as waves of reaction to what was a profoundly artificial social scene.

America in the fifties was also out of step with other advanced democracies. The courtship rituals, the homemaking role, and the breadwinning role all seem to have been more intricately wrought—and more onerous—than in other nations. As David Bouchier has put it, "the baroque elaboration of the full-blown American suburban life" was outside the experience of Europeans.[1]

When I was growing up in a backward corner of Britain in the fifties, tales and images of the strangely elaborate and exotic roles played by American men and women drifted across the Atlantic—via television, films, and novels. The courtship rituals seemed to start early. The thought of dating at age twelve ("mere children," our parents would mutter) and pink tulle gowns and tuxedos to high school dances (just like royalty!) made us British teenagers very discontent as we struggled into our short white socks and bottle green uniforms and dragged off to our single-sex schools.

As an undergraduate at Cambridge University in the mid-1960s I knew a few American men. I remember thinking that they seemed to spend a lot of time running around cars opening doors for able-bodied young women, and most were distressingly eager to spend lots of money on girls they hardly knew. But then I told myself that only ultra-polite and super-rich American men ever strayed into British universities.

In the late sixties, when I arrived in Cambridge, Massachusetts, as a graduate student at Harvard, I confronted the natives on their own territory and discovered that many of these exaggerated impressions held true at close quarters. American men and women were engaged in elaborate and antagonistic courtship rituals. They ranged up in opposing camps, and social life consisted of carefully orchestrated forays into enemy territory, where you were supposed to win points and become "popular." As an outsider I caused great confusion by unintentionally breaking the rules. Simple gestures like inviting a man to share some concert tickets, or offering to meet a date at a restaurant instead of being picked up, were capable of triggering panic in a well-brought up member of the opposite sex. It took me a long time to realize that dating was not primarily about romantic love and need not entail friendship. Contrary to conventional wisdom, the spirit of court-ship "American-style" was that of an adversarial business rela-tionship, and it was imperative for the more hungry player (the woman) to "know the score" and "cut the best deal."

Barbara Levine,* a college professor who went to college in the late fifties, sums up the spirit of the age: "The boy was your enemy; you 'negotiated' all the time. Even if you didn't want him, you couldn't afford to antagonize him; he might say bad things about you that (true or not) might lower your status in the mar-riage market. But even if you did like him, you had to watch your step and make sure you didn't give him anything physically be-fore it was 'proper' to do so, because that would downgrade your status not only with him but with other men. While he might not be able to ruin your chances for marriage totally, by gossiping he could considerably narrow your pool of 'availables'—i.e., the nice, bright, *serious* boys (the ones who went to medical school and so on) who would earn good salaries and be able to support you in style. These boys wouldn't want you if you had a tarnished repu-tation.

"Virginity was the *big thing*. If you didn't have that to offer a potential marriage partner, you didn't have any marbles to play with. I remember this girl who had slept with a boy and then married him. We all were shocked. We thought it was great but couldn't understand why he would marry her once he had slept with her. After all, he'd gotten *it*—her virginity—without having to 'pay' for it.

"Even when the two of you were going steady, you were still in an adversary relationship. He was supposed to spend money on you, and you were supposed to respond physically in certain ritu-alistic ways. The first signal that you found him acceptable was when you let him hold your hand. On the first date, no kiss ever. But if you didn't let him kiss you on the third date, that was usually a signal for him to give up, though a really popular girl

*Pseudonym.

could make the guy come back for four or even five dates without even kissing him. It was as if you got points for holding out and making him come back again and again. You were supposed to try to make him desire you like crazy, but you yourself weren't supposed to be affected by all this because after all, you were 'innocent.' You were merely displaying the wares that would be available to Mr. Right for the 'best offer' marriage.

"How could you tell who was where physically in the sexual sweepstakes? Fraternity pins were one clue. Most of those pins were in two parts, with one part dangling from the other, and the girl would always wear the pin on the tip of one breast, so the dangling part really jiggled all the time. If you were sporting an engagement ring, slightly heavier petting was allowed—i.e., below the belt. But no bride-to-be was supposed to 'go all the way.'

"To maintain your status in the marriage market, you *had* to be busy Saturday night; it was proof of your desirability. If you weren't, you hid out in your room at the dorm. One girl I knew even put out her light and just listened to the radio in the dark all evening so that no one would know she didn't have a date. If you stayed at home by choice, you were considered a *freak*. It didn't matter that you would have preferred to settle down with a good book that night, or you just weren't in the mood or didn't like the guy who asked you out. You went.

"When I was a senior in college and still unattached, my parents absolutely panicked. I was obviously going to be an old maid if I didn't get married by the time I graduated. I had an incredible rash of blind dates that year; even the rabbi fixed me up once. One Saturday night, when I was still living at home, I had this blind date who came all the way out to Queens. He had a car. We drove back to New York and had dinner and went to the theater. Then he drove me all the way out to Queens. Naturally I refused to kiss him good night. My brother had exercised his male prerogative and spent the entire evening at home reading. When I came inside, the two of us sat down and, for a laugh, started to figure out exactly how much this poor guy had spent on me: the cost of theater tickets, the dinner at an expensive restaurant, the tolls and the parking. It came to quite an impressive sum.

"Naturally, once you did manage to marry someone, you were

supposed to be as devoted to his welfare as you previously had been to 'landing' him. After all, he was your breadwinner."[2]

The elaborate role playing of the fifties was fundamentally at odds with the egalitarian roots of American culture. Precisely because of this, it provoked fierce waves of reaction as both men and women sought to escape the confines of this rigid and artificial era.

The hands-off approach to mothering

Getting a head start in life: an infant being introduced to Glenn Doman's methods at the Better Baby Institute, 1983

GROWING PAINS

"My God! Ethel, he's shrunk!"

"I'm worried about him, Paul. He doesn't listen to his cereal any more."

"There's nothing in Dr. Spock about it."

"Don't call me, I'll call you."

The British make fun of Dr. Spock, Punch, August 1960

The trials of breadwinning, The New Yorker, *May 1963*

"*By God, you young people today have all my admiration! You cut right through our sham and hypocrisy, our myths of achievement and meaningless success. Here, let me give you some money.*"

The rebel, sixties-style, The New Yorker, *May 1969*

*The flower children confront the military police, the
Pentagon, Washington, D.C., October 1967*

*Women protest the war in Vietnam, the Pentagon,
Washington, D.C., October 1967*

*Hundreds of thousands celebrate love and peace,
Woodstock, 1969*

13

THE MALE REBELLION

Fifties men came to feel oppressed by their role as breadwinner, and at least some of them tried to escape the narrow confines of a life dominated by the need to earn the money to buy the goodies to support wife and children. Like Peter Pan, they decided that the life of a grown man contained precious little fun:

> PETER: "Would you send me to school?"
> MRS. DARLING: "Yes."
> PETER: "And then to an office?"
> MRS. DARLING: "I suppose so."
> PETER: "Soon I should be a man."
> MRS. DARLING: "Very soon."
> PETER: "I don't want to go to school and learn solemn things;" he told her passionately. "I don't want to be a man. O Wendy's Mother, if I was to wake up and feel there was a beard!"
>
> "Peter," said Wendy the comforter, "I should love you in a beard"; and Mrs. Darling stretched out her arms to him, but he repulsed her.

A Lesser Life

> PETER: "Keep back, lady, no one is going to catch me and make me a man. I want always to be a little boy and have fun."[1]

American literature is full of tarnished images of male success. Titles such as *The Hucksters, The Gilded Hearse,* and *Death of a Salesman* speak for themselves. As C. Wright Mills saw it, in plays and novels men are often portrayed as external success stories but underneath they are "ulcerated people of uneasy conscience, miserably at war with their tormented self."[2] Part of the problem lies in the stifling nature of most jobs. Biff in *Death of a Salesman* (1949) gives vent to this typically male complaint: "... it's a measly manner of existence. To get on that subway on the hot mornings in summer. To devote your whole life to keeping stock or making phone calls, or selling or buying. To suffer fifty weeks of the year for the sake of a two-week vacation, when all you really desire is to be outdoors with your shirt off."[3]

Twentieth-century literature also tells of a double standard. Men slave away, often under great pressure, while their wives and children enjoy the "good life." In Herman Wouk's novel *Marjorie Morningstar,* published in 1955, the father stays at his job in Manhattan during August while his wife and daughter leave to stay at the Prado, a luxurious resort hotel on Long Island:

> Mr. Morgenstern was remaining in the city; the summer was his busiest season. They [his wife and daughter] had stopped briefly in his office in the garment district to pick up some cash and Marjorie had all but fainted in the windowless little office smelling so strongly of ink, stale coffee and the peculiar dust of the feathers and straws lying baled in the shop. Mr. Morgenstern, in a gray tie and coat despite the killing heat, with a face almost as gray wished them a pleasant time.[4]

They drove out to the Prado, which "had smooth green lawns, a white crushed-stone driveway, broad terraces, red clay tennis courts crisscrossed with new whitewash, and a huge blue swimming pool full of bronzed young people diving, splashing and laughing."[5]

If breadwinning had its downside, the male role had other attributes which were equally limiting. Warren Farrell in *The Liberated Man* describes the emotional and sexual straitjacket of his fifties generation. Men were supposed to be invulnerable and to have great psychological strength; they suppressed their fears and controlled their emotions. They were expected to know all the answers; they never sought help and were tough and independent. They had ambition and were physically and sexually aggressive. Above all, they were in control, in sexual relations and in all relations. They initiated sex and got what they wanted when they wanted it. Farrell remembers in graphic detail his own initiation into male sexual values: "The circle jerk—that's one of my first memories. We all stood around in a circle and told stories about girls or rubbed our penises until we got hard-ons. Then we ejaculated. The purpose was to see who could ejaculate the farthest. The guy whose sperm went the farthest was 'the biggest man.' He was the one who could really 'give it to some chick.' The guy who couldn't produce or who had a dinky little ejaculation—well, we sort of laughed at him."[6]

These pressures—to succeed, to perform, to control—in the financial and sexual arenas have conditioned men's lives for centuries. Why did these pressures become particularly acute in the postwar years? Part of the answer lies in the fact that men of the fifties were under special strain and faced a unique set of disappointments.

By the early fifties the consumer society was in full swing, creating a treadmill of relentless earnings pressure. As Sloan Wilson, author of *The Man in the Gray Flannel Suit,* puts it, "For almost all of us the scramble for the buck, if not morally uplifting, was pressingly necessary, for there were never enough dollars to raise a family, to build the kind of house which filled our dreams—or at least those of our wives."[7]

The men and women of the fifties had looked forward to material abundance for so long. The extended agony of the Great Depression and the Second World War had been made somewhat bearable by visions of the good life that was to follow. And in

America the postwar years did bring incredible prosperity. The economy grew at an unprecedentedly high rate; between 1945 and 1955 the GNP more than doubled. But an abundance of well-paid jobs, the house of one's dreams, a late-model car, and an elaborate set of household appliances failed to fill the souls of men with satisfaction and contentment. This array of goods merely whetted the appetite for a bigger and better life-style. The whole population moved "endlessly and breathlessly up one long, unbroken, incline of acquisition . . . from every point on the unbroken incline one can see others with more than one has oneself."[8]

Many men felt they had been "had." The long-heralded era of widespread and considerable affluence failed to produce fulfillment. For two decades men had yearned for material abundance, had looked forward to being "good providers" and to proving their manhood in the marketplace. But the dream was not what it had been cracked up to be. The rapidly expanding economy of the fifties and sixties used up men, and uninhibited consumerism created an exhausting treadmill. As Charles A. Reich describes it in *The Greening of America,* the end result was "a hollow man."[9] The goals of the era—status, promotion, institutional approval, and a correct image for the outside world—were hollow in terms of personal satisfaction. Men worked under terrible stress, which prevented them from finding more genuine meaning and drove them to ulcers, heart attacks, and the psychiatrist's couch. In the fifties ". . . freedom came to mean consumer freedom . . . freedom to buy anything and go anywhere. For work, on the other hand, there was no longer any concept of freedom at all."[10]

In frustration and anger, disillusioned men began to lash out. One target was the suburbs, for the massive postwar migration to suburbia had produced the daily commute and increased the price men had to pay for career success. As one commuter of the period put it, "I soon came to detest a way of life which required me to travel almost a hundred miles a day."[11] The magazine titles of the period point to serious male discontent with suburban life-styles: "Life and Love in the Split Level Slums," "The Crab Grass Roots of Suburbia," and "On the 5:19 to Ulcerville."[12]

In *The Crack in the Picture Window,* a national best seller, John Keats invents an imaginary couple who move first to Rolling

Knolls and then to Maryland Dell. Keats describes these communities as comprising "row on row of identical boxes spreading like gangrene" through the countryside.[13] The family featured in his novel contracts money ills, is weakened by Dad's long commute to the city, and finally collapses into a permissive child-centered matriarchy.

But although suburban living came in for some harsh criticism, it was generally thought to be a symptom rather than a cause of the problem. The prime cause of male discontent was seen as the parasitic woman of the "feminine mystique" and her ever-increasing brood of children. After all, most men sought out the spacious houses and good schools of the suburbs not for themselves but for their wives and children.

The family responsibilities of fifties men were heavy. The most common age of marriage for men was twenty-three—an all-time low. And men had, on average 2.8 children—a twentieth-century record. For the first time in history these children needed to be supported through to their early twenties as college became an expected component of middle-class education.

The ethos of the day demanded, in no uncertain terms, that men grow up, marry, and support their families. The individual who deviated was a social outcast. As Philip Roth points out in *My Life as a Man,* for those "young men who reached maturity in the fifties ... there was considerable moral prestige in taking a wife."[14] Not only that, men could not afford to scoff at marriage because if they did, they laid themselves open to the charge of "immaturity," if not "latent" or blatant "homosexuality."[15] During this period nothing was more frightening to an establishment man.

Fifties men lived by onerous rules. According to Morris Dickstein, they belonged to "a generation that willed itself from childhood directly into adulthood."[16] They spent their late teens and early twenties getting on the slippery rungs of the career ladder. They then quickly found a wife, bought a house, and started a family. The next forty years were spent trying to fill a bottomless pit of demands emanating from wife and kids. It wasn't just a question of food, clothing, and shelter; a second car, elaborate dental work, ski vacations, and country-club membership—all became standard features of middle-class family life in this afflu-ent decade. The male workhorse died in harness in his sixties, a good seven or eight years before his idle wife. Practicing home-maintenance skills in the basement, or cooking frankfurters in the backyard on Saturday night, hardly seemed compensation enough for a life of unremitting toil.

Some dissidents in the fifties dreamed of becoming great art-ists or writers, of chucking it all and absconding to Paris. Frank Wheeler, the protagonist in Richard Yates's novel *Revolutionary Road,* "was among the few who bucked the current."[17] Despite the fact that he was a low-echelon bureaucrat at Knox Business Ma-chines, he persisted in dreaming of a lifework somewhere in the humanities that would involve his early and permanent with-drawal to Europe, which Wheeler saw as the only part of the world worth living in. To his chagrin this self-styled "intense, nic-otine-stained, Jean-Paul-Sartre sort of man"[18] ended up like ev-eryone else in the suburbs, where he had moved to produce a better life for his wife and children.

The happy housewives of the 1950s may have been bored out of their skulls and popping Valium, but disgruntled men of the period often saw these same wives as leeches sucking the lifeblood of their hardworking husbands. Men were developing a growing aversion to "the feminine millstones hanging around their necks."[19] Consider the Texas housewife described in a magazine of the period:

> Janice Crabtree lives in a handsome pink, brick ranch house on the best and newest street in Grapevine, Texas. She is a comely young woman of 34 with wavy blue black hair and very even white teeth. Even at this hour in the morning—it is barely 9 o'clock—she is wearing rouge, powder and lipstick, and her summer dress is immaculately fresh. The somber chords of Beethoven's Fifth Symphony crash majestically from the phonograph as she sits serenely enjoying a fourth cup of coffee.
>
> "Friends seem continually amazed at me," says Janice. "By 8:30 am, when my youngest goes to school,

my whole house is clean and neat and I am dressed for the day. I am free to play bridge, attend club meetings or stay home and read, listen to Beethoven and just plain loaf."

How does she do it? According to husband Billie, every morning at 7:00 am she hits the housework like "greased lightning."

Hurrying through the house in her pajamas and robe, she makes four beds in quick, stepsaving motions and hangs up night clothes. She wipes the bathtubs and washbowls and straightens the towels. Then she may run a dustcloth over the grand piano or pick up some crumbs with the vacuum. By 8:00 am she is done.

Mornings she is having bridge at her house are the busiest, for then Janice must get out the tables, cards, tallies, put up fresh coffee and prepare lunch. During the winter months she may play as often as four days a week from 9:30 am to 3 pm. Janice is careful always to be home, before her sons return from school in the late afternoon.

"Sometimes I feel I'm too passive, too content," remarks Janice, fondly regarding the bracelet of large family diamonds she wears. "But I'm grateful for my blessings . . . for my good health and faith in God and such material possessions as two cars, two TV's and two fireplaces."

Her favorite possession is her four-poster spool bed with a pink taffeta canopy. "I feel just like Queen Elizabeth sleeping in that bed," she says happily. Since her husband snores he sleeps in an adjoining room.[20]

If you were a breadwinner sick of the relentless pressures of corporate life or fed up with the dreary monotony of the assembly line, such a portrait might make your blood boil. After all, you were footing the bill for this leisured existence, for the pink-brick ranch house, the four-poster spool bed, and the two fireplaces, and you were the one relegated to the spare bed.

A male revolt against the breadwinning role began to gather

momentum in the fifties. Magazines such as *Look* and *Playboy* ran bitter articles about how the male sex was being held ransom by predatory women. Bob Norman's attack on alimony captures the "we've all been had" spirit of the period:

A young couple gets married. They're in love, or think they are, but for one reason or another marriage doesn't work. Maybe it's the guy's fault; maybe it's the girl's. Could be neither one is to blame—just two nice people who aren't really suited for one another.

You might assume that having discovered their mistake, a couple could successfully call it quits, no strings attached, and try to find happiness elsewhere. 'Tain't so.

When the time comes for going their separate ways, the young lady may, if she is so inclined, stick her ex-spouse for a healthy chunk of his earnings from that day forward, for the rest of his unnatural life. . . . The marriage has ended. The unhappy stag is entitled to none of the privileges of a husband, but he's expected to pay for them as if he were.

It doesn't matter who is to blame for the marriage going on the rocks. The wife may be a trollop with the disconcerting habit of crawling in and out of bed with the husband's friends. She may be a spendthrift whose expensive tastes he cannot afford. No matter. When the judge grants the divorce, he will also grant the little missus a healthy stipend for future escapades and extravagances.

Nor is modern alimony merely a matter of principle. For many men it is a serious question of economic survival.

A young TV director was overpowered by a 37″ 25″ 37″ brunette early in his career and happily exchanged the vows that were to guarantee a lifetime of marital bliss. Five years later his 37″ 30″ 37″ wife sued for divorce. In claiming her severance pay, she explained that she had inspired her husband, contributing nightly to whatever success he now enjoyed.

The judge listened to this tender American love story and ordered the defendant to fork over 50 percent of his present salary—plus 50 percent of whatever he earned in the future. The man was professionally whipped.[21]

A small group of men did more than complain about their domestic burdens. Toward the end of the decade, the beats and their imitators, the beatniks, staged a more thoroughgoing revolt. Led by such colorful personalities as Jack Kerouac and Allen Ginsberg, these movements flourished in a twilight world of poetry, jazz, drugs, and violence. The beats spurned steady work as well as family responsibilities, but because they remained a minuscule minority, mainstream society was shocked rather than threatened by their antics.

A much bigger wave of rebellion hit in the mid-sixties as the countercultural revolution swept through the country. In mid-decade hundreds of thousands of young people rejected the values and life-styles of their parents. Some dropped out of school, grew their hair, donned flowing, funky costumes, and moved to Haight-Ashbury or the East Village, where they shared crash pads and dealt drugs. By 1967 as many as 75,000 young people were living in the Haight-Ashbury psychedelic community.[22] Others, more idealistic, went on freedom marches in the South, protested American involvement in the Vietnam War, or joined the Peace Corps. Most were middle-class kids who professed to despise the conformist, constrained, and sanitized lives of their suburban parents. Like Nancy Barrett's three children, they wanted to be free—from the panoply of consumer goods and from family commitments.

A major reason the countercultural rebellion came to involve so many people was the Vietnam War. Close to 3 million American men fought in the debilitating failure that was Vietnam and 100 million more watched the war on television. Every evening, before dinner, one was treated, in full color, to the spectacle of malnourished peasants being pounded by the technological might of an ugly and impotent America. One way of coping with the gratuitous brutality and the impending military defeat—not to mention the danger of being drafted to fight this war—was to reject the whole set of establishment values that had created the war in the first place. Cold war militarism, the capitalist system, aggressive masculinity, marriage, monogamy, the nuclear family, and suburban existence—all got lumped together by the angry young men of the sixties as being part of a value system that had failed them. The rebellion deepened and spread in 1967, when President Lyndon Johnson extended the draft to students. Privileged youths were particularly loath to fight in this vain and inglorious war. Who needed to die in the jungles of Southeast Asia? Even your countrymen would not consider you a hero. In October 1967 several hundred thousand young rebels marched on the Pentagon in a mammoth antiwar demonstration. Norman Mailer called them the Armies of the Night. In a haze of marijuana and tear gas they attached flowers to the bayonets of the military police and vowed to make love, not war.

The issues that galvanized the hippies of the counterculture—consumerism, commitment, the draft—were predominantly male issues. The tensions of climbing the career ladder, the pressures of being the family breadwinner, the dangers of fighting the war in Vietnam were, in the main, male problems, and men had a lot to gain by denying their legitimacy. Sure, there were women around and about the counterculture, but they were treated as camp followers, not as equals. "Liberated men needed groovy chicks who could swing with their new life style,"[23] but God forbid that the chick got it into her head to demand an equal role in the rebellion or some old-fashioned return commitment. If she did, she was "uptight," "screwed-up," or, worse yet, a "real bringdown." A chick was expected to stuff envelopes and operate the mimeograph machine for the movement, and to take birth control pills and go for VD checkups so that she didn't become a drag on her old man.

The youthful male rebels of the sixties seemed to reject the "straight" values of the previous decade in a highly selective way. They ruled out conventional fifties expectations of career success, marriage, and family but retained the equally conventional notion that women should be subservient to men. Stokely Carmichael accurately reflected the spirit of the sixties rebellion in his famous remark "The only position for women in SNCC [Student Nonviolent Coordinating Committee] is—prone."[24] Even the songs of the period were "full of sardonic put downs of women."[25] A Mick Jagger song, "Under My Thumb," is a case in point: "Under my thumb the girl who once had me down / Under my thumb the girl who once pushed me around."[26]

As the chicks became older and wiser, they realized that they had been had. As Marge Piercy described in her 1969 exposé of sex and politics in the counterculture: "A man can bring a woman into an organization by sleeping with her and remove her by ceasing to do so. A man can purge a woman for no other reason than he has tired of her, knocked her up, or is after someone else: and that purge is accepted without a ripple."[27] Robin Morgan wrote in 1970, "We have met the enemy and he's our friend. . . . It hurts to understand that at Woodstock or Altamount a woman could be declared uptight or a poor sport if she didn't want to be raped."[28] She described a young male revolutionary "supposedly dedicated to building a new, free social order . . . turn around and absent-mindedly order his 'chick' to shut up and make supper or wash his socks."[29]

The sexual revolution of the counterculture was decidedly lopsided: It boasted a single standard, but the burdens of free sex were very unequally distributed. The women of the sixties increasingly found themselves "traded, gang-banged, collected, collectivized, objectified, and turned into the hot stuff of pornography."[30] One embittered feminist described it as a sexual revolution that did not free women. Its purpose was "to free men to use women without bourgeois constraints."[31] Needless to say, the easiest way for a woman to become a victim of this new sexual code was—to become pregnant. In the mid- and late sixties abortion was still illegal, and the flower girls found that they "did not want to claw out their own insides or pay someone else to do it."[32] But the alternative—to bear and raise a child without a husband or a home—did not look very appealing either.

Women were both the idealists and the victims of the counterculture. They promoted noble causes and laid to one side their

315

own self-interest. They opposed the Vietnam War, although their own lives, unlike the men's, were not at stake. They learned to despise the consumer culture, the rat race, and the traditional family, yet this rebellion imperiled their own security and that of their children. And they joined in a sexual revolution which left them dangerously vulnerable. For a while the free-floating idealism and the soft, androgenous imagery that characterized this period obscured the fact that the counterculture had an exclusively male agenda. But by the late sixties women had had their fill of noble male causes and left the men in droves to form their own autonomous women's movement.

The women's movement sped up the male rebellion. New antagonism between the sexes was triggered by the fact that radical feminists saw men as enemy number one. As the Redstocking Manifesto puts it, "*All men* receive economic, sexual and psychological benefits from male supremacy. *All men* have oppressed women."[33] Men did not like being described as oppressors—or male chauvinistic pigs, for that matter. Most were still hard at work breadwinning and resented the attacks of feminists. Herb Goldberg in his book *The Hazards of Being Male* records the bitter comments of a fifty-seven-year-old college professor: "The famous male chauvinistic pigs who neglect their wives, underpay their women employees and rule the world—are literally slaves. They're out there picking the cotton, sweating, swearing, taking lashes from the boss, working 50 hours a week to support themselves and the plantation, only then to come home to do another 20 hours a week rinsing dishes, toting trash bags, writing checks and acting as butlers at the parties."[34]

If the rhetoric of the women's movement increased male disaffection, the practical effect of the movement was to facilitate the escape of the disaffected male. For women's liberation supported women in their attempts to work and become self-sufficient; it also encouraged wives to leave unhappy marriages. Both of these trends increased male freedom. In his book *The Liberated Man* Warren Farrell lists a multitude of reasons why men should welcome the women's movement. Many of his reasons hinge on the increased economic and emotional independence of liberated women.[35] He sees this independence as allowing men greater freedom to pursue their own goals. Karen De Crow, a former president of NOW, could not have been more supportive. "Men are not money machines put on this earth to fight wars and support women and children,"[36] she declared flatly.

The net result of these waves of rebellion is a generation that contains a significant proportion of men who successfully avoid the heavy family responsibilities of the 1950s. In the contemporary world many men marry late and believe in the "family of limited liability." That is to say, if a marriage fails to fulfill their needs, these men feel quite free to move on to another (younger) woman and a new set of children. A 1979 survey of the values and goals of American males tells us about these new men. For starters, a large and increasing proportion are narcissistic—that is, they are "individualistic, self-centered and pleasure orientated in their approach to life." Twenty-five percent of all men and 35 percent of younger men in this survey display these narcissistic characteristics. The study finds that one of the main distinguishing characteristics of this "new" man is that he believes in the family of limited liability. In concrete terms, this means that he seeks out an independent mate who is capable of supporting herself, that he prefers a small family, and that he would contemplate divorce if the quality of a marriage deteriorated. Specifically he "would not remain in an unsuccessful marriage for the sake of the children." These men are not deviant in other aspects of life; they hold jobs, earn and spend money, and are "effective participants in the system."[37]

Psychiatrists confirm the advent of the narcissistic man. Dan Kiley, psychiatrist and author of *The Peter Pan Syndrome: Men Who Have Never Grown Up,* reports that his private practice is increasingly peopled with young men who cannot make commitments, who refuse to come of age. "Narcissism locks them inside themselves . . . [and] temper tantrums are disguised as manly assertion. They take love for granted, never learning how to give it in return. They pretend to be grown up but actually behave like spoiled children."[38] In other words, they behave just like Peter Pan.

* * *

Paul Johnson* is a thirty-four-year-old musician who lives and works in Boston. He teaches in a private school, gives private piano lessons, and has a modest career as a concert pianist. All this adds up to a sixty- to eighty-hour week. Paul is a good-looking, gregarious man who enjoys being single. He says reflectively, "I am very glad I got away from the whole concept of commitment. Ten years ago I almost married a college classmate. Luckily the engagement fell through. Now I am not sure that I will ever choose to tie myself to one person." In his free time Paul practices the piano, collects rare books, and takes sailing lessons. His savings are earmarked for a boat he plans to buy this coming summer. I asked Paul how children fitted into his life. He thought about the question for a few minutes and then said, "I like children, and I know I am good with them; but you know, I work with kids all day long, and I am not at all sure I want to come home to them in the evening. I don't think that I will be having children." Paul hesitated and then added, "A lot of single women I know in their mid-thirties desperately want a baby, and without wanting to sound callous"—Paul smiled charmingly—"I have little patience with the problems that revolve around women's biological clock. Quite frankly I prefer to go out with women in their twenties. They aren't so uptight about having kids."[39]

These new men are impressively different from the commuting family men of the fifties. Over the course of the last thirty years societal values have changed so as to permit men more freedom. The sexual revolution snapped the link between sex and marriage. Amendments to the divorce laws (no fault and equitable distribution) paved the way for simpler, less cumbersome legal procedures and weakened the rationale for alimony—all of which made divorce a much less expensive proposition. Feminists encouraged men to get off the hook. As Betty Friedan pointed out, "perhaps men may live longer in America when women carry more of the burden of the battle with the world, instead of being a burden themselves."[40] And finally, millions of women entered the labor market and took up (badly) paid work, which lessened fe-

*Pseudonym.

male dependence and facilitated divorce. All these changes permitted the new men of the eighties to realize the family of limited liability.

The fact that men have managed to dump at least some of their family commitments is borne out by the statistics. The easiest way to dump a wife is, of course, to divorce her. In the eighties this is a relatively simple and inexpensive process—for men! In Chapter Three we described some of the contemporary consequences of divorce. In the wake of divorce men increase their standard of living by 42 percent, while women take a 73 percent cut in their incomes. Alimony is regularly paid in a mere 5 to 10 percent of divorces, and even in these rare cases it is paid for an average of only 4 to 5 years. Bob Norman's attack on alimony is both exaggerated and out of date.

Dumping children should be harder because society still disapproves. But the facts speak for themselves: Forty-nine percent of the children of divorce never see their father,[41] fewer men are seeking custody of their children than did ten years ago,[42] and only a third of custodial mothers receive child support. As we saw in Chapter Three, divorced men are more likely to come through with their car payments than on the child-support front.

In short, many men have achieved the family of limited liability. The vast majority of divorced women are expected to support themselves, *and* they are increasingly left with complete financial and physical responsibility for the children of divorce.

But all this evidence does not mean that men are without their grievances. If mothers get custody of the children in 90 percent of all divorces, it still means that thousands of children end up with their fathers. If alimony is only paid in 5 to 10 percent of divorces, it still means that thousands of men feel ripped off. In short, America is a big enough country for 5 or 10 percent to be a large number of people capable of making a lot of noise.

Listen to Harold Varrick, forty-three, who is the assistant superintendent of a school district in Massachusetts. He tells how he felt when his wife left him after fourteen years of marriage:

> ... Even though it's a joint custody situation and she initiated and filed for divorce, I'm still winding up stuck with the tab. I have to pay her as though she had

sole custody. . . . The victimization of the male is such that even though it's a no-fault divorce I still legally wind up with the responsibility of spousal support.

Men are stuck with the responsibility that everyone else finds so repressive and fascist and they have to sit there and take it. They're dying earlier and earlier, and they're rushing around like crazy trying to keep it all together, to keep going, trying hard to make it, to achieve, to be successful, and it just turns to ashes in their hands.[43]

Divorce is a miserable business, and there is usually more than enough pain and hardship to go around. But most often it is women and children—not men—who become downwardly mobile and suffer the largest cuts in income.

"New" men look least good on the fathering front, and once again it is a conspicuous minority that distorts the overall picture. A few modern fathers have gotten into nurturing.[44] Like Dustin Hoffman in *Kramer Vs. Kramer,* they deal with nightmares, meet the kids from school, cook dinner, and sometimes even put parenting ahead of career. I am married to such a man, so I know that they exist. However, for many new men fathering is largely a verbal accomplishment. They take natural childbirth classes; talk with great eloquence at dinner parties about bonding, separation anxiety, and role models; and quite convince themselves that they are great fathers. When push comes to shove, they are often missing. Only a third will come through with child support in the event of divorce, and on a daily basis the division of labor remains the traditional one. It is Mom who gets to make the school lunches, buy the gift for the birthday party, wipe up the vomit, and stay home with the sick kid. Parenting mostly involves hard, relentless work and the willingness to be there when needed. Most upscale new men do not arrange their priorities that way. As Donald Bell puts it in *Being a Man,* "for many adult males there persists a gnawing sense that we have more important things to accomplish than to be stuck changing diapers, feeding a drooling infant, or arranging for playmates or babysitters . . . childcare tends to turn the adult mind to mush [and] since contemporary middle-class men work mainly with their minds, we can ill afford to allow our minds to become mushy."[45] What of women? I guess it's all right if their minds turn to mush!

In June 1984 my stepdaughter, Shira, graduated from sixth grade. It was a simple ceremony, and her class was allowed to choose one song. It chose "Cat's in the Cradle" by Harry Chapin:

> My child arrived just the other day;
> he came to the world in the usual way.
> But there were planes to catch and bills to pay;
> he learnt to walk while I was away.
> And he was talkin' 'fore I knew it,
> and as he grew he'd say,
> "I'm gonna be like you, Dad,
> you know I'm gonna be like you."
>
> Chorus
> And the cat's in the cradle and the silver spoon,
> little boy blue and the man in the moon.
> "When you comin' home Dad?"
> "I don't know when,
> but we'll get together then;
> you know we'll have a good time then."
>
> My son turned ten just the other day;
> he said, "Thanks for the ball, Dad, now come on let's play.
> "Can you teach me to throw?" I said, "Not today,
> I got a lot to do." He said, "That's okay."
> And he walked away, but his smile never dimmed, it said,
> "I'm gonna be like him, yeah,
> you know I'm gonna be like him."
>
> Chorus
> And the cat's in the cradle and the silver spoon,
> little boy blue and the man in the moon.
> "When you coming home Dad?"

"I don't know when,
but we'll get together then;
you know we'll have a good time then."

He came home from college just the other day;
so much like a man I just had to say,
"Son, I'm proud of you, can you sit for a while?"
He shook his head and he said with a smile,
"What I'd really like, Dad, is to borrow the car keys;
see you later, can I have them please?"

Chorus
And the cat's in the cradle and the silver spoon,
little boy blue and the man in the moon.
"When you coming home, son?"
"I don't know when,
but we'll get together then, Dad,
you know we'll have a good time then."

I've long since retired, my son's moved away;
I called him up just the other day.
I said, "I'd like to see you if you don't mind."
He said, "I'd love to, Dad, if I can find the time.
You see, my new job's a hassle and the kids have the flu,
But it's sure nice talkin' to you, Dad,
it's been sure nice talkin' to you."
And as I hung up the phone, it occurred to me,
he'd grown up just like me;
my boy was just like me.

Chorus
And the cat's in the cradle and the silver spoon,
little boy blue and the man in the moon.
"When you comin' home, son?"
"I don't know when,
but we'll get together then, Dad,
we're gonna have a good time then."[46]

It seems that today's twelve-year-olds are not convinced that much fathering is going on in our society.

14

CONTEMPORARY WOMEN: TWO HOSTILE CAMPS

The feminist revival of the late sixties drew its energy from two sources. It was a rebellion against the ultradomestic, stultifying world of the 1950s, and it was a revolt against the male-centered counterculture. The women who had been radical in countercultural terms now became radical in feminist terms. They were through being menial servants and unpaid prostitutes to left-wing men and through with chic male causes. From now on they sought succor and support from their own sex. As we saw in Chapter Eight, by the early 1970s this radical segment of the women's movement was deeply man-hating.

But the ex-housewives didn't feel too sympathetically disposed toward men either. Marilyn French in *The Women's Room* describes her reaction: "My feelings about men are the result of my experience. I have little sympathy for them. Like a Jew just released from Dachau, I watch the handsome young Nazi soldier fall writhing to the ground with a bullet in his stomach and I look briefly and walk on. I don't even need to shrug. I simply don't care. What he was, as a person, I mean, what his shames and yearnings were, simply don't matter. It is too late for me to care."[1]

Disillusioned housewives felt justified in ignoring men because of an urgent need to deal with their own problems. They felt that they had been ripped off and put down. It was hard to feel good about what had been their main activity—homemaking. Despite all that heartwarming rhetoric about Mom and apple pie, it was by now an open secret that large segments of American society thoroughly despised homemakers. These women believed that they had vested their best energies and their prime years in a socially devalued role. In one Labor Department ranking of jobs according to complexity of skills required, homemaking got the same ranking as parking lot attendant and was ranked below marine mammal handler.[2] How could these women derive much self-esteem from a role that society thought so little of?

Many of these women looked back at the years of homemaking and were bitter. It had been so arduous and so little understood, let alone appreciated, by husband and children. In retrospect they resented all that household drudgery, they regretted that they had sunk quantities of precious energy into "his" career, and they were horrified to discover that even their sexuality had been distorted to serve male needs. These grievances were to become potent sources of feminist anger.

Take housework. Janice Crabtree, with her four-poster spool bed and two fireplaces, seems to have been the exception rather than the rule. In 1953 sociologist Mirra Komarovsky found that a day in the life of a "typical" housewife was something like this:

> I get up at 6 A.M. and put up coffee and cereal for breakfast and go down to the basement to put clothes into the washing machine. When I come up I dress Teddy (1½) and put him in his chair. Then I dress Jim (3½) and serve breakfast to him and to my husband and feed Teddy.
>
> While my husband looks after the children I go down to get the clothes out of the machine and hang them on the line. Then I come up and have my own breakfast after my husband leaves. From then on the day is as follows: breakfast dishes, clean up kitchen. Make beds, clean the apartment. Wipe up bathroom and kitchen floor. Get lunch vegetables ready and put potatoes on to bake for lunch. Dress both children in

outdoor clothes. Do my food shopping and stay out with children until 12. Return and undress children, wash them up for lunch, feed Teddy and put him to nap. Make own lunch, wash dishes, straighten up kitchen. Put Jim to rest. Between 1 and 2:30 depending on the day of the week, ironing, thorough cleaning of one room, weekend cooking and baking etc.; 3 P.M. give children juice or milk, put outdoor clothes on. Out to park; 4:30 back. Give children their baths. Prepare their supper and help put them to bed. Make dinner for husband and myself. After dinner, dishes and cleaning up. After 8 P.M. often more ironing, especially on the days when I cleaned in the afternoon. There is mending to be done; 9 P.M. fall asleep in the living room over a newspaper or listening to the sound of the radio; 10 P.M. have a snack of something with my husband and go to bed.

I read this account to my husband and he said that it sounded too peaceful, that the children seem to keep out of the way too much. I haven't conveyed to you all the strain of being constantly with the children for twelve hours a day, day in day out.

I wouldn't call myself a contented housewife. I find it hard to be so tied down. . . . I have sometimes the feeling of being imprisoned.

Besides, I find my life dull. I described my day to you. It isn't just one day—it is every day. Believe me there is not enough stimulation in the incessant dishwashing, picking up, ironing, folding diapers, dressing and undressing the kids, making beds day in and day out. My social life with the other mothers on the park benches is depressing. I cannot get them away from the same old talk. They have nothing fresh to give me because they, too, are up to their necks in the same routine. . . . I think there must be something wrong with this setup.[3]

But this wasn't the whole picture. Fifties women pumped an extraordinary amount of energy into the emotional and cognitive development of their children and into supporting their husbands' careers, efforts which went well beyond the physical care of home and family.

It was the era not of the dual-career family but of the two-person career. The competitive pressures of the male work world created great tensions, which the wife was supposed to offset by providing elaborate emotional support. William H. Whyte, Jr., describes how a wife was meant to liberate her husband's total energy for the job. She must maintain their home as an island of tranquillity, and herself act as "sounding board," "refueling station," and "wailing wall."[4] Philip Slater writes of the "opiate role" played by wives. Men are daily buffeted by the economic structures they have created, and they tend "to use their wives as opiates to soften the impact of the forces they have set into motion against themselves."[5] In 1956 Sloan Wilson in an article for the *New York Times Magazine* describes the male executive as being totally dependent on his spouse: "Without a capable wife to screen his speaking and social engagements, keep track of his personal finances, run his house and take care of his children, he would have been 'lost.' Modern man needs an old-fashioned woman around the house."[6]

One of the most draining of the support roles was that of moving. The expectation was that if a husband's career could be enhanced by relocating, the whole family pulled up stakes and moved, no matter what this meant in terms of loss and disruption—and studies show that moving produces almost as much strain as the death of a spouse.

Wives were often expected to settle into new homes, build new friendships, and launch their children into new schools every few months. In the late fifties one out of every five American families was changing homes at the rate of once a year. As *McCall's* put it, "Each year a quarter of a million corporate families crisscross the country in a frantic relocation tango."[7] This rate of change was not to slow down until the mid-seventies, when working wives began to resist repeated moves, and their husbands began to balk at corporate policies that produced this relocation tango. Women seem to have borne the brunt of all this shifting around. After all, the husbands generally stayed within the same corporate culture, while their wives were forced to start from scratch in strange communities. One study reported that "some women in their 30s have lived in 16 different communities since they married; a few have even moved four times in a single year. . . . Often they become defeated people . . . chronically depressed, addicted to alcohol."[8]

It is interesting to note that European societies have not experienced this frantic mobility. A recent study shows that 70 percent of West Germans live within five miles of their birthplaces.[9] Similar statistics could be found for most other European countries. Only in America has geographic mobility played such a disruptive role in the lives of women and their families.

On the sexual front disillusioned housewives felt that they had been taken for a ride. In retrospect, the pop psychology that flourished in the fifties and early sixties seemed guaranteed to stunt women's lives. As we saw in earlier chapters, many of the attitudes of this period rested on Freudian theory. Freud was convinced that all females suffered from penis envy. As a result, little girls came to perceive themselves as mutilated boys, a trauma the resolution of which could take the neurotic form of seeking for the lost penis through an imitation of masculine activity (to wit, pursuing a career) or take the proper form of translating the wish for a penis into the wish for a child. This notion had all sorts of ramifications for the relations between women and men. For example, Freudian theorists decreed that true sexuality for a woman resided in her capacity for a vaginal orgasm as the vagina was seen as the only authentic female organ of erotic sensation and release. The clitoris, on the other hand, was seen as a hidden vestige of (or shrunken surrogate for) the penis. In short, it was the instrument of arrested childish narcissism.

The end result was that in the 1950s orgasm was presented to women in a hierarchy of virtue and achievement. A clitoral orgasm was a "bad" unwomanly experience, while the vaginal orgasm was not only "good," but constituted the only full testament to womanhood. One need hardly point out that the good orgasm was dependent on an erect penis, and a woman could achieve sexual satisfaction only as a concomitant of a man's seeking his. A clitoral orgasm was judged to be of no account because it was "unfunctional, gratuitous, masturbatory, required no penis and led to no possibility of conception."[10] The superiority of the vaginal over the clitoral orgasm was proclaimed in novels, Broadway plays, and popular magazines as well as by psychologists and marriage counselors. Clitoral women were deemed immature, neurotic, bitchy, and masculine; women who had vaginal orgasms were maternal, feminine, mature, and normal. Although frigidity should technically be defined as total inability to achieve orgasm, the Freudian experts of this era preferred to define it as an inability to achieve vaginal orgasm—a definition which proclaimed three-quarters of all adult women frigid failures.

In 1966 Dr. William H. Masters and Mrs. Virginia E. Johnson published *Human Sexual Response,* a massive clinical study of the physiology of sex. Their main conclusion was that the dichotomy between vaginal and clitoral orgasms is entirely false. Anatomically, all orgasms are centered in the clitoris, whether they result from direct manual pressure applied to the clitoris, indirect pressure resulting from the thrusting of the penis during intercourse, or generalized sexual stimulation of other erogenous zones like the breasts."[11]

So much for Freud. Scientists had discovered (rather belatedly) that the noble womanly vagina was inert and nerveless, while the subversive clitoris was the true site of female erotic pleasure. But this discovery was a little late for fifties women who had wasted years trying to achieve authentic vaginal orgasms. Many were enraged. They saw that even their sexuality had been "defined by men to benefit men."[12] They realized that they had been conned into making the vaginal orgasm a status symbol in a male-dictated system of values. For women had persuaded themselves that a preference for clitoral orgasm was ignominious, a source of secret shame. This internalization is amply demonstrated in the novels of the period. Mary McCarthy and Doris Lessing wrote about orgasm in much the same way as D. H. Lawrence and Ernest Hemingway, and even Simone de Beauvoir is an unreconstructed Freudian in this matter. In *The Second Sex* she refers to vaginal orgasm as the only "normal satisfaction."[13]

Thus the decade of the 1960s saw the emergence of two types of bruised and bitter women. A group of young women, burned by their experiences in the counterculture, "and without firm roots in family or career, gave vent to their rage in the rhetoric of sexual politics."[14] They became radical feminists. Older women of the fifties generation had a different grievance. Many of them were disillusioned wives or ex-wives, and at least some of them were "displaced homemakers." Their prime had coincided with the fifties, and they had used up their youth on home and family—some with precious little to show for it. As Nancy Barrett found out, your children could just drop out of sight and you could lose your husband to a younger playmate. Most of these ex-housewives headed off into the job market, where they had indifferent luck, and some of them joined NOW and became mainstream feminists.

In view of this history, it comes as no surprise that some of the best energies of modern feminism have gone into avoiding the whole family trip. Radical feminists became passionate in their pursuit of self-sufficiency, and many tried to build a life without men. Mainstream feminists, on the other hand, have concentrated on cloning the male competitive model in the marketplace, which they see as more reliable than family life as a source of long-term satisfaction. Both factions have ignored children.

But a large group of American women see all feminists (radical or mainstream) as destructive elements in our society. These are the traditional women of Middle America, who by the early seventies were hanging on by their fingernails to the American Dream. In the main they had a simple ambition: They wanted to be able to continue their lives as mothers and homemakers.

These women knew that they were living in treacherous times. The divorce rate, which had been inching upward, suddenly doubled in the decade between 1965 and 1975. Breadwinners were rapidly becoming an endangered species, at least over the long haul. Traditionalists blamed the breakdown of the family on a variety of factors: no-fault divorce laws, legal abortion, gay rights, and permissive child-rearing practices. But mostly they blamed those "women libbers": "Women's liberation wants to liberate us from the very institution that is most indispensable to overcoming our present social crisis: the family. They want to make marriage more open, more flexible, revocable at a time when it is already opening up all over the country and spewing forth swarms of delinquents and neurotics."[15] Women's liberation was seen as "relieving men of their responsibility as head of the family. That makes it easier for a man to walk out" on his wife and children.[16]

Traditional women were and are deeply suspicious of the package we call the sexual revolution. They know that in the past women were valued for sex and reproduction, and they believe that wives should hang on to their monopoly on legitimate sex for the very simple reason that it enhances their value. Their abhorrence of abortion stems from religion, but it also stems from crude self-interest.[17] They see the fear of pregnancy as a powerful brake on sexual freedom and pregnancy itself as the ultimate sanction—the only consequence of sex that makes men accountable to women for what men do to women. In Andrea Dworkin's words, "they use sex and babies to stay valuable because they need a home, food, clothing."[18]

Traditional women are thus convinced that sexual freedom and legal abortion bring with them an increase in female vulnerability. The 1960s did not pass them by. They learned from what they saw, and what they mainly saw was the sexual exploitation of woman. To them the new morality is a cheat and a thief. As Phyllis Schlafly points out, "It robs the woman of her virtue, her youth, her beauty and her love—for nothing, just nothing."[19] At least under the traditional rules a woman would get a husband in exchange for sex and homemaking, a breadwinning husband who would support her "until death us do part."

These women have an agenda. In the political sphere their goal is to turn the clock back, to return to the simple social order of yesteryear, in which women were guaranteed the basic protections of shelter, support, and love. They wage campaigns against legal abortion, no-fault divorce, and gay rights; they attempt to prevent passage of the ERA; and they advocate school prayers. All this political activity is meant to bolster the old-fashioned, familial props of women's lives.

In the personal sphere these traditional women devote a great deal of effort to techniques that will make them better loved and more secure. Marabel Morgan in her book *The Total Woman* promises that it is possible "for almost any wife to have her husband absolutely adore her in just a few weeks' time."[20] The trick is to cater to a man's special quirks, whether "it be in salads, sex or sports"[21] and to improve her "curb appeal." Morgan goes to some lengths to explain the relevance of curb appeal—the term real estate people apply to the outer shell of a house. She feels that all wives should ask themselves the tough question "Is your curb appeal this week what it was five years ago?"[22] She reminds them, "Before a man can care about who a woman is, he must first get past the visual barrier of how a woman looks."[23]

Much of Morgan's advice on how to improve one's curb appeal is exceedingly concrete. When hubby comes home, "waltz to the door in a cloud of powder and cologne."[24] She tells how "for an experiment I put on pink baby doll pajamas and white boots after my bubble bath. . . . When I opened the door that night to greet Charlie, I was unprepared for his reaction. My quiet, reserved, nonexcitable husband took one look, dropped his briefcase on the doorstep, and chased me around the dining room table."[25]

The reward for developing one's curb appeal is not just love and kisses. Total women also get loaded up with presents from their appreciative husbands. Said one graduate of Morgan's "Total Woman" course, "He began to bring me gifts. One afternoon he called to find out if I'd be home at 3 o'clock. I couldn't imagine what was coming and I was stunned to see a truck pull up with a new refrigerator and freezer. I had nagged for a new one for years and for years he had refused."[26]

If the man in your life fails to come through, traditionalists offer women the love of Jesus, who is portrayed as the beautiful brother, the compassionate friend, and the perfect healer of sorrow and resentment—in short, the man who will never fail you.

In *The Gift of Inner Healing* Ruth Carter Stapleton advises a young woman who is in a desperately unhappy marriage, "Try to spend a little time each day visualizing Jesus coming in the door from work. Then see yourself walking up to Him, embracing Him. Say to Jesus, "It's good to have you home Nick."[27] Stapleton used this technique herself with great success. Her own marriage at age nineteen (to Nick) had been desperately unhappy. After the birth of her fourth child she attempted suicide by jumping from a moving car. Shortly afterward she found peace by surrendering to Jesus.

Anita Bryant appears to have spent a good part of her life on her knees begging Jesus to help her love her husband, Bob Green. She writes candidly of her near-constant struggle. Green's demands—which ranged from enshrining her as the spokeswoman of antihomosexual bigotry to doing all the child care for four children—were endurable only because Bryant took Jesus as her real husband. As Bryant describes in *Bless This House,* "Only as I practice yielding to Jesus can I learn to submit, as the Bible instructs me, to the loving leadership of my husband. Only the power of Christ can enable a woman like me to become submissive in the Lord."[28]

This right-wing school of thought displays a type of bleak realism. Traditional women are not dumb Barbie dolls. They are essentially correct when they say that they are worth more in the house than outside it. A wife is still "given" more money by her husband than she herself could earn at a job. All women need do is look around them to realize that work for wages outside the home does not effectively free women because of the undervaluation of their work. As we saw in Chapter Four, many women cannot earn enough money (while working full time) to lift themselves out of poverty. Many housewives "do not buy the argument that work outside the home makes women sexually and economically independent of men. They see that the streets are cold, and that the women on them are tired, sick and bruised."[29] Women are paid too little in the labor force. And many traditional American women are clear-sighted enough to know it.

At bottom traditional women see feminists as traitors and fools. They are traitors because they undermine the traditional family-support systems for other women and their children. And they are fools because they do not seem to understand that there is no point in alienating men. Most women want children, and most women have no alternative to marriage if they want decent lives for themselves and their children. Traditionalists see feminists as out of touch with reality. Only elite East Coast "libbers" would be foolish enough to imagine that independence can be found in the labor market, a truth that Nora Ephron discovered in *Heartburn.* "Wives went out into the world free at last, single again and discovered the horrible truth: that they were sellers in a buyer's market and that the major concrete achievement of the women's movement in the 1970s was the Dutch Treat."[30]

The other day I received through the mail a document prepared by some of these right-wing women. They called themselves the Concerned Women for America, and their pamphlet was entitled *To Manipulate a Housewife*.[31] It comprised a collection of quotes from prominent feminists:

Dr. Mary Jo Bane: "It [divorce] makes for better family life. . . . Divorce improves the quality of marriage."

Gloria Steinem: "By the year 2000 we will, I hope, raise our children to believe in human potential, not God. . . ."

Betty Friedan: "The ERA has become both a symbol and substance for the whole of the modern women's movement for equality. . . . I am convinced if we lose this struggle we will have little hope in our own lifetime of saving our right to abortion. . . ."

And from a publication of the movement entitled *Women's Liberation, Notes from the Second Year:* "We must destroy love. . . . Love promotes vulnerability, dependence, possessiveness, susceptibility to pain, and prevents the full development of woman's human potential by directing all her energies outward in the interest of others."

The Concerned Women for America felt so threatened and betrayed by feminists that they printed a selection of quotes from the movement in order to warn other women of the powerful destructive force of feminism. They obviously believe that nothing explains their anti-ERA case better than a few statements from the pro-ERA feminist camp. In her brief introduction to the quotes which constitute *To Manipulate a Housewife,* Beverly Lahaye (described as author, lecturer, mother, and pastor's wife) writes, "Before you and I decide about ERA let us consider from what motivation it was born."[32]

Thus in the mid-1980s two opposing movements seek to represent women in a hostile and insecure world: the feminist movement (pro-ERA) and the antifeminist movement (STOP ERA). As a woman you must either go out and compete as a male clone in an unequal labor market, or you must attempt to bind men more tightly to you in an era when familial bonds have become increasingly thin and fragile. For we must recognize the limits of the right-wing program. Fighting the ERA or banning abortion may slow the pace of change, but there is no effective way of putting the clock back and re-creating the values and life-styles of the fifties. It's a little like trying to unscramble an egg. The attitudes and beliefs of people—toward sex, toward the family—have permanently shifted. Men, and at least some women, have grown to depend on their new freedoms and are unlikely to give them up. In short, there is a depressing futility to much of right-wing strategy.

One thing seems sure: Neither the feminist movement nor the antifeminist movement has yet had much success in improving women's economic security.

The war between the sexes has waged particularly fiercely in postwar America. Most of us know the truth of this; we have had firsthand experience of battle and carry with us partially healed wounds. The breeding ground for the conflict was the fifties, that strangely aberrant period in American history when men and women played such exaggerated roles. The best-educated women in the world were asked to find fulfillment in the "search for the missing matching mitten," while men cultivated coronaries in their quest for "diamonds in the jungle."[33] It was a recipe for disaster. Men learned to see women as parasites and fools; women learned to fear men because they could not survive without them. In many ways "the fifties were the seedbed of our present cultural situation and the ground against which the upheavals of the sixties sought to define themselves . . . [and] we are still living with the consequences."[34]

Starting in the late fifties men rebelled against the breadwinning role. They began to reject the notion that it was up to them to finance, single-handedly, the American Dream. Some of the rebels were hardworking establishment types who merely wanted to discard wife and family or trade them in for newer models. They had no quarrel with steady work or the consumer culture. Others wanted to drop out of the system altogether. Antiestablishments rebels such as the beats and the hippies wanted to throw overboard the whole can of worms—career, ambition, material success, as well as marriage, children, and other sundry family commitments.

Contemporary Women: Two Hostile Camps

In the late sixties women began their own more self-conscious liberation movement. Disillusioned housewives struggled to free themselves from the suffocating trap that was the "feminine mystique" and began a search for dignity in the labor market.

In *The Women's Room* Marilyn French describes how Mira became a slave to housecleaning: The house got hard to handle so Mira

> bought herself a small file box and some packages of 2×3 cards. On each card she wrote one task that had to be performed and filed them in sections. The section headed WINDOW WASHING would contain cards for each room of the house. Whenever she washed the windows in one room, she would mark the date down on the card, and place it at the end of the section. The same was true for FURNITURE POLISHING, RUG SHAMPOOING, and CHINA. Regularly she removed all the dishes from the dining room closet, washed them by hand—they were good china, not to be entrusted to the dishwasher—and returned them to their freshly washed shelves. She did the same in the kitchen; she did the same thing with the books, removing them, dusting them carefully, and returning them to clean, wiped and waxed shelves. She did not make cards for ordinary, daily cleaning, only for the large special tasks. So each day, after the small chores of cleaning kitchen, making beds and cleaning the two main bathrooms, she would also perform a thorough cleaning of one room, washing mirrors and windows, waxing any visible wooden floors, cleaning the small ornaments, dusting ceilings and walls and furniture surfaces and vacuuming. She would then mark on the appropriate card the large task accomplished. That way, she reasoned, she would always keep it up. It took her two weeks to go through the whole house—ten working days.
>
> Mira would feel tremendously satisfied when she finished her mornings' work. . . . She would walk through the house, dressed to go out, relishing the silence, the order, the shine of polished wood in the sun.[35]

When her husband walked out on her after fifteen years of marriage, Mira felt that it all was a colossal waste of time—her time. She went back to school and started a belated teaching career.

At about the same time radical women were fleeing from the exploitative chic men of the counterculture. The "chicks" who had fought on the streets against the Vietnam War and in the South for civil rights felt betrayed. Their male comrades of the counterculture had failed them. From now on they were to seek freedom and inspiration in the company of other women.

By the mid-1970s these new male and female liberation movements had prompted a right-wing backlash. Traditionalists—men, but mostly women—undermined and frightened by the new freedoms, fought a rear-guard action, attacking legal abortion, no-fault divorce, the ERA, gay rights, and anything else they thought contributed to the breakdown of the family. Women have dominated the backlash movement because they have been most threatened by liberation. After all, those first-round rebellions had asymmetric results. Both men and women achieved a greater degree of personal freedom, but while men attained a certain right to discard their families and dispose of their incomes as they saw fit, women failed to achieve significant economic independence, which they now needed because they were more frequently on their own. In the modern age the family still comprises the most important female life-support system, and wives are still "given" by their husbands a higher standard of living than they can earn in the labor market.

Thus in the postwar period several waves of reaction have swept over the American social landscape, waves that found their original energy in the cozy but oppressive world of the "feminine mystique." For the fifties succeeded in defining men and women in an exceedingly narrow way and in so doing laid the groundwork for intense antagonism between the sexes. Remember Barbara Levine, the college professor? She was brought up in the fifties to believe that the boy was your enemy, but a special kind of enemy, one whom you were supposed to entice into your net and then hook, for he could serve as a meal ticket for the rest of your life. These predatory and oppressive attitudes did not sit well with the free and equal roots of our American culture.

All this helps explain why, over the course of the next twenty-five years, both sexes expended such a lot of energy in painful struggle. They have needed to break loose and better fulfill their individual identities. Perhaps the greatest casualties of the liberation movements have been middle-aged women who still want and need to be homemakers. They have been made immensely vulnerable by the cold winds of change that have swept through our society, and they are generally misunderstood by younger, elite women who are in the vanguard of change. In many cases these "liberated" women identify so completely with men that they too have learned to regard homemakers as parasites and fools. One of the challenges for the future is to bring these two groups of women together so that they can make a common cause. For they both suffer tremendous economic insecurity.

PART E

Political Possibilities

As originally conceived, this book was meant to end on a rousing note of optimism. I would turn to my think tank—the Economic Policy Council—and persuade a slice of the establishment to come up with a policy agenda for the United States. This exercise seemed to be full of promise: It would produce realistic solutions, not pie in the sky; and because it would engage the attention of big shots—people close to the centers of power—it might even prod the nation into action. If people like Gerald Ford and Katharine Graham can't make things happen, I thought, no one can.

I look back at these aspirations and think, How could I have been so naïve? After all, in doing the research for this study, I had uncovered profound reasons for why our government doesn't subsidize child care and for why most American women have no rights to maternity leave. How could I think that it would be easy to change these deeply held beliefs, these entrenched positions, especially in an era when social policy is ruled by conservatism and nostalgia?

But despite the frustrations and disappointments of my policy panel, I am glad that my idealism lasted long enough to trigger this project. It served to expose what the establishment really thinks about women, children, and families, and it confirmed the main thrust of this book.

My exercise in policy making had one other legacy. Because my policy panel could offer little hope that government was going to move quickly or effectively to solve the problems of women, it pushed me to explore the potential of labor unions. Could ordinary women derive significant support from those traditional allies of working people—trade unions? In this endeavor I uncovered a ray of hope.

15

WHAT CAN TRADE UNIONS DO FOR WOMEN?

Jane Brenner* lives in Oakland, California. She is a flight attendant with Pan American Airlines, a job she has held—with one interruption—for seventeen years. Her base pay is $22,000 a year, but with overtime she can sometimes earn as much as $29,000. Jane is divorced and has a fourteen-year-old daughter.

Jane and I had breakfast together in the spring of 1985. We talked about her life, her job, and—surprisingly—her union. As she put it, "The union has really come through for me. It has given me a much better deal on the job, and it has provided real security. Since my divorce [six years ago] this has been particularly important to me. You see, I wasn't entitled to any alimony, and my ex-husband pays only a hundred dollars a month in child support—despite the fact I was awarded two hundred and twenty-five dollars. All this means I am pretty much on my own financially." Jane hesitated and added rather defiantly, "I know it sounds kind of crazy, but my union has watched out for me and protected me. It has been like a father."

I hastened to assure Jane that her point of view did not strike

*Pseudonym.

me as odd. In Europe most people, even highly educated people, looked to their unions for a basic set of rights and benefits. It was only in America that unions were seen as an irrelevancy to modern life. On hearing this, Jane relaxed and said with a small smile, "I am so used to getting these hostile looks when I say that my union is important to me, it's as though I had confessed to some subversive activity."

Jane's history is the following. She joined Pan Am as a flight attendant in 1968. At that time the Transport Workers Union (TWU) represented most of the Pan Am employees. Jane does not remember the TWU as being particularly supportive. For example, when she became pregnant in 1971, she was immediately fired (airline policy in the early 1970s). A group of flight attendants brought a class action suit against the airline industry, but although they eventually won the suit and established their right to keep their jobs through pregnancy, the TWU was not particularly interested in this fight and did not get too involved. Jane was reinstated in her job in 1973, and several years later a new union was formed by the flight attendants at Pan Am. According to Jane, this new union—the Independent Union of Flight Attendants—has done a terrific job.

"They get us big pay increases, but that isn't all. They understand that the conditions of work are at least as important as the rate of pay. I guess it's because the new union leaders are mostly women, and they have faced the problems involved in holding down a job and looking after a family. For example, if you have kids, it's important to be able to plan ahead so that you can arrange child care. Before this new union the airline could break your line whenever they wanted to—that is, they could tell you in London that you had an extra flight to Frankfurt and wouldn't be going home for another forty-eight hours. They can't do that any longer without paying a big penalty, and as a result, I now know my schedule ahead of time. The union has also won other rights. For instance, on long trips flight attendants are now entitled to rest seats or bunk beds, and if the aircraft is understaffed, they are entitled to overtime. All this makes for a much better job. The TWU never clued into these issues. The leadership of that union was composed of older men, and they couldn't get inside our skins and figure out what was important to us."

What Can Trade Unions Do for Women?

I asked Jane what kinds of benefits were now in place for pregnancy and childbirth. Her eyes lit up, and she said enthusiastically, "You're not going to believe this, but most women I know get at least nine months, and they can arrange it so that about half that time is paid." I looked at Jane in disbelief. I was simply not used to interviewing women with good news on the maternity leave front. So I asked Jane to explain how these generous policies came into being.

"Pan Am employees get six to eight weeks' paid disability leave for childbirth. On top of this our union contract gives us the right to accrue sick leave at the rate of two and a half days per month and use it as supplemental maternity leave. Most women who have been in the job awhile can accumulate several extra months of paid leave this way. And what is more," said Jane, taking a deep breath, "if you can get a doctor's note saying that you need more time to recover from the birth or to breast-feed, the union will stand up for you and get you a job-protected leave of absence for another three to six months." Jane paused and then said more reflectively, "You see, the union can bargain for things an individual would never get on his or her own. Imagine marching into the personnel office at the end of a four-month leave and asking for another few months off! You would most likely be fired. No matter how many doctor's notes you had, it wouldn't do you any good."

Jane had one last thought: "No one expects flight attendants to join a union. Most of us are college-educated, and many of us are nurturing, feminine women; we just don't fit the union stereotype of militant blue-collar workers. But despite our glamorous image, we don't work for pin money. These days we work for the same reason men work—we need to support ourselves and our children—and earning a good wage and getting decent working conditions have to be top priorities. If the union helps us achieve these things, of course, we will become loyal members of the union."[1]

It seems an obvious alliance—the one between trade unions and working women. To put it baldly, they need each other. Women need better pay and better working conditions, and unions can help them fight for these things; unions need more members, and women are potential candidates because they comprise the fastest-growing segement of the labor force.

Women continue to confront major obstacles in the workplace. They bear the burden of a double work load, at home and on the job; they are segregated in low-wage jobs (which carry meager benefits); and have earned less than two-thirds of the male wage—regardless of occupation—since time immemorial. In short, they are at the end of the line when goodies are handed out. Today 51 percent of female workers earn less than $15,000 a year (compared to 28 percent of men), and only 6 percent of women workers earn over $30,000 a year (compared to 25 percent of men).[2]

As individual workers most women are powerless because they have few skills and little market power. A waitress, an office cleaner, or a flight attendant is dispensable and easily replaced. It therefore makes sense that women workers should band together and use their collective strength to raise wages and improve working conditions. Threatening to shut down a plant or to paralyze a bureaucracy by striking is one of the few ways unskilled workers can produce leverage over management and win a better deal on the job. The fact that unionized women workers earn, on average, 30 percent more than nonunionized women workers speaks for itself.[3] Collectively women workers do better.

For more than a century this is what trade unionism has been about. Workers who are individually weak and disadvantaged join forces to improve their earning power and conditions of work. It is a practice which has been successfully followed by male workers in every industrial country, but curiously not one which women have used to nearly the same degree—especially in America. For Jane Brenner is the exception rather than the rule. Only 14 percent of working women in the United States belong to unions.[4]

Dana Stark's* experience is typical of the other 86 percent. Dana is in her early thirties and is married to a postal worker. She has two sons, aged six years and twelve months, and she works as a

*Pseudonym.

kindergarten teacher in a private school in Boston. She does not belong to a union. Ever since her first child was born, Dana has found it a continuous struggle to both hold down a job and raise her children. In the fall of 1982, when her second child was born, she ran into some particularly severe problems. It all started when Dana took a three-month leave of absence in the wake of the birth. She had verbal assurances that her job would be kept open for her, and she had also been told that six to eight weeks of this period would be covered by disability insurance. Both things turned out not to be true. When she reported back for work in January 1983, she discovered that all the school would offer her was a part-time job at half her former salary. Her old job had been filled. Dana said, "It was a real shock to be treated so badly. I thought I had such a good relationship with the head of the school that I had neglected to obtain anything in writing." As for the disability insurance, it just failed to come through. When I interviewed her in the fall of 1983, Dana had yet to be paid for the weeks she had been out of work. She had filed her claim five or six times, but nothing happened. As she put it, "I think the insurance company is just waiting for me to give up."

Reflecting on her recent experiences, Dana told me, "It's very hard fighting big bureaucracies on your own, especially if you have just had a child and are up to your eyeballs in sleepless nights and dirty diapers. I really needed some protection this last year, someone to help me deal with the insurance company, someone to help me get my full-time job back at the school." Dana could have used a union.[5]

If women need unions, unions need new members. Over the past decade organized labor has suffered massive membership losses in the industrial sector of the economy, its traditional power base. Fierce foreign competition has spurred many corporations to shift production to low-wage countries. Coupled with a severe recession, the result has been exceptionally high levels of unemployment, especially in manufacturing industry. The AFL-CIO lost 2.7 million members between 1980 and 1984, even though employment in the United States rose by 3.8 million during this period.[6] If organized labor wants to avoid becoming just a part of our folklore, it must move into nontraditional areas and recruit workers in the fast-growing financial and service sectors. Since more than two-thirds of new jobs in these sectors are going to women, this means that unions need to make women a central part of their constituency. As Murray Seeger, director of the department of information for the AFL-CIO, puts it, "the future of labor is women and minorities."[7]

Some unions are seizing this opportunity. For example, the American Federation of State, County and Municipal Employees (AFSCME) now sees itself as "a leading advocate for the rights of women workers,"[8] and declares in its promotional literature that "the battleground for women's rights is the workplace."[9] AFSCME has 600,000 women members (out of a total membership of 1.1 million). It makes excellent sense for this union to take up women's issues; it helps recruitment.

AFSCME has been concerned with work and family issues for a decade. For example, AFSCME's District Council 37 in New York has negotiated child-care leaves for both mothers and fathers in many of its contracts. The leave, at the time of birth or adoption of a child, is unpaid but fully job-protected for a period of four years for a first child and three years for each subsequent child. The union has also actively pursued flextime. The exact form of the arrangement—whether it features alternate starting times or a compressed workweek—depends on the agency the employee works for, but approximately 25 percent of DC 37's workers are now on some kind of flextime schedule.

But AFSCME has been most active on the issue of comparable worth. AFSCME President Gerald W. McEntee has called it the most critical issue of the 1980s because "it is one of the few good ways of raising salaries at the lower end of the scale."[10]

Many of AFSCME's women members are segregated in low-paying women's fields; indeed, half of them work in clerical jobs. And to help these workers improve their earning power, AFSCME has become a vigorous proponent of the principle of equal pay for jobs of comparable value. As we saw in Chapter Four, the argument is that women have been segregated into jobs on the basis of sex and as a result are paid less than employees in male jobs which require an equivalent amount of skill, effort, and responsibility. The strategy is to conduct job evaluations, measure the intrinsic value of different jobs, and come up with a numerical rating for each. If a secretary is rated the same as a janitor, then a secretary should be paid the same as a janitor.

In July 1981 AFSCME Local 101, representing city workers in San Jose, California, went on strike for nine days over the issue of pay equity for its women workers. This strike was the culmination of a four-year effort. The union first bargained for and obtained an agreement by the city to pay for a study to investigate whether there was internal equity in the city's pay system. The city and the union also agreed to negotiate the implementation of the study.

The study showed that the San Jose work force was heavily sex-segregated—that is, in most occupational classifications 70 percent or more of the incumbents were of the same sex—and that the female-dominated jobs paid on average 18 percent less than male-dominated jobs of comparable value. For example, clerk-typist 1, a "female" job, received the same number of job evaluation points as custodian, a "male" job. The salary for custodian, however, was $90 per month more than the salary for clerk-typist 1. Similarly, the female-dominated job of principal clerk received 201 job evaluation points but was paid $290 per month less than the male-dominated job of painter, which was valued at only 178 points.

Despite the fact that San Jose had a woman mayor and a female majority on the City Council, the city refused to do anything about its pay scales. So AFSCME filed sex discrimination charges with the Equal Employment Opportunity Commission (EEOC) for failure to correct the discrimination shown in the study. To speed up the process, the union also called a strike.

The nine-day strike was settled when the city agreed to provide $1.5 million for pay equity adjustments of 5 to 15 percent over two years for more than sixty female-dominated job classifications. These increases were in addition to the 15 percent pay raise negotiated for all union members over the two-year contract.[11]

Over the last few years AFSCME has taken such a leading role in fighting for pay equity for women that some observers refer to this union as the shadow EEOC.[12] Its most conspicuous success story was in Washington State (see description in Chapter Four), but AFSCME has also been successful in negotiating pay equity raises for its members in Minnesota; San Jose, California; New York State; New York City; Green Bay, Wisconsin; Los Angeles; San Mateo County, California; Belmont, California; San Carlos, California; Illinois; Portland, Oregon; and Spokane, Washington. Most of the more than 260 charges alleging sex-based wage discrimination that are currently backlogged at the EEOC have been filed by this union.[13]

Unions are a natural vehicle for combating discrimination through occupational segregation. Attempting to prove that secretaries, nurses, or social caseworkers are systematically underpaid is an arduous and expensive process. It often involves underwriting the costs of job evaluation studies, negotiating collective bargaining agreements that include equitable wage increases, filing litigation against employers, and educating employees through meetings and publications. Few individuals could begin to underwrite this process.

Despite the enthusiasm displayed by Jane Brenner and AFSCME President Gerald McEntee, there are some powerful obstacles in the way of organized labor's forging an across-the-board alliance with women workers.

First there is the historical legacy. Unions in America have a history of either ignoring or being hostile to women workers. From the beginning of the labor movement in the mid-nineteenth century the focus was on the white male breadwinner; women were regarded as second-class workers. They were excluded from all but two of the thirty national unions formed during the 1863–73 period, and discrimination worsened under the influence of the American Federation of Labor (AFL), founded in 1886 by Samuel Gompers. Gompers created the AFL as a vehicle to organize skilled workers on the basis of craft. This automatically kept out women, who were clustered in unskilled and less prestigious work. But the AFL's antagonism to women ran deeper than this.

According to historian William Chafe, the AFL was hostile to women workers on pragmatic grounds.[14] The transient, impermanent, and unskilled nature of most women's work made organizing women workers a difficult and time-consuming process, and in the end the gains would be small. The AFL thought that its energies were better invested in male workers, who, if the efforts of the union were successful, would earn enough to support entire families. The goal of achieving a "family wage" for the working man was touted loudly and continuously by the AFL, despite the fact that many women also needed a decent wage (more than 90 percent of working women at the turn of the century were single, and many of them belonged to families that were in no fit state to support them).

Trade union pragmatism on the subject of working women was embedded in an overall conservative philosophy. The AFL believed in a bread-and-butter labor movement, the goal of which was to protect the wages, skills, and status of the native-born craftsmen who formed the elite of the American working class. This philosophy stood in sharp contrast with the radical socialism espoused by less influential workers' organizations such as the Industrial Workers of the World (IWW). The conservatism of the AFL spilled over into its stance on women workers. In 1887 Gompers spelled out the consequences of organizing women: "We know to our regret that too often wives, sisters and children are brought into the factories and workshops only to reduce the wages and displace the labor of men—as heads of families."[15] In Gompers's eyes, once the family wage was won, no proper woman would need to enter the labor force. "We stand for the principle that it is wrong to permit any member of the female sex of our country to be forced to work, as we believe that the man should be provided with a fair wage in order to keep his female relatives from going to work. The man is the provider and should receive enough for his labor to give his family a respectable living."[16] The AFL's hostility toward organizing women had predictable results: In 1908 women represented a mere 2.9 percent of union members.[17]

In response to this exclusion from the male unions women formed their own organizations. The WTUL (the Women's Trade Union League) was founded in 1903 at an AFL convention in Boston by Mary Kenney O'Sullivan and William English Walling.[18] During its first twelve years it concentrated on organizing. Led by a national policy-making unit and supported by local leagues in cities such as New York, Boston, Chicago, and St. Louis, the WTUL provided money, publicity, tactical advice, and political support for women attempting to unionize around workplace issues. The league demonstrated its success in the 1909–10 strike of women in the New York garment industry, which resulted in better working conditions for women in this sector of the economy.

Despite this encouraging beginning, the WTUL soon became mired in tensions with the AFL. O'Sullivan quit the league in the wake of the American Woolen Company strike when she failed to get AFL backing, and by 1915 the WTUL had turned away from the direct organization of workers. From then on it sought to solve the problems of women at work by involving government in regulatory activities. By the 1920s the WTUL was almost exclusively oriented toward protective legislation. As we saw in Chapter Nine, its sponsorship of protective legislation put it at odds with the dominant feminist groups of the day. Organizations such as the National Woman's party were interested in equal rights, not in special treatment.

The late 1920s and early 1930s were a difficult time for organized labor, and in these chaotic years unions increasingly concentrated their energies on protecting their unionized male workers. With the expansion of the CIO (Congress of Industrial Organizations) in the mid-1930s things started to look up. It proved easier to organize women workers along industry rather than along craft lines, and in the mass CIO-sponsored organizing drives of the 1936–39 period, significant numbers of women were recruited into the labor movement. For the first time large numbers of women workers won the right to adequate pay, vacations, seniority, and fringe benefits. But even the CIO did not treat women equally. In male-dominated industries union contracts featured unequal pay scales for men and women and separate women's seniority lists. During the Second World War some unions did fight for equal pay for women, but generally only for women who took over men's jobs. The main goal was to preserve high pay rates for the men who would be reclaiming their jobs after the war.

In the postwar era the CIO continued to have some success in organizing women. But in general, modern American unions have failed to become a primary vehicle for solving the problems of women workers. In the 1980s only 14 percent of women workers belong to unions (compared with 23 percent of male workers), and women constitute only 28 percent of union membership despite the fact that they now make up 45 percent of the total work force.[19]

The historical antagonism to women workers and the orientation toward the male breadwinner spills over into the modern labor movement.

Lisa Gorden* is twenty-seven years old and has worked for the phone company since she was sixteen. She started out as an operator but about four years ago was promoted and is now a communications technician. She earns approximately $35,000 a year, and as Lisa says, "That's not bad for a working woman." Ever since she started work, she has been a member of the Communications Workers of America (CWA). Indeed, for a couple of years in her early twenties she was a shop steward in this union.

Lisa was married in 1982 and gave birth to a daughter in May 1984. Before her baby was born, Lisa knew she would return to work. Her husband works nights as a security guard and is not well paid; Lisa's salary represents 65 percent of total family income. They could not make ends meet on her husband's salary alone. Besides, she feels she has put in a lot of time at the phone company and doesn't want to leave all that accumulated seniority. She would never be able to find another job as well paid.

Before her daughter was born, she did not anticipate any difficulty. She would take the six-month maternity leave she was guaranteed in her union contract (six weeks at full pay, the rest unpaid but with a job guarantee) and then leave her daughter with a baby-sitter while she went back to work.

The first week back at work Lisa realized that the baby-sitter she had lined up (an unemployed teenager) was not going to work

*Pseudonym.

out. The sitter couldn't handle the baby and kept calling Lisa at work. Lisa didn't know what to do. She couldn't just go home and get her baby; she was afraid of losing her job. As it turned out, she spent a good part of that week crumpled up in the ladies' room crying. But at least she punched the time clock, and no one could say she wasn't putting in the hours.

Lisa finally found a family member (her husband's cousin) to look after her daughter. But the cousin lives far away, and Lisa has to get up at 5:30 A.M. and take her daughter there by bus before taking the train to work. Often either the bus or the train is late, and by the time Lisa gets to her office "I'm all wound up and in a foul mood."

Lisa knows what she needs: on-site child care. Failing that, she would settle for part-time work or a job-sharing arrangement.

Despite her previous union involvement (or perhaps because of it!), Lisa has not taken her problems to the union. "I know that they are totally uninterested in providing child care. The official CWA position is that child care should be a government responsibility. Fat lot of good that does me. As for part-time work and job sharing, they are not strong advocates of either one. You see, the union is still oriented toward men with stay-at-home wives, and these men don't want job sharing. In fact, they find the whole concept threatening." Lisa paused and then said thoughtfully, "I guess that by catering to the male head of household, the union did become pretty good at negotiating high wages, but this same orientation gets in the way of helping women workers deal with family demands." (One fact seems to support Lisa in her contention that the CWA continues to orient itself toward the male breadwinner: The union is still led by men. As of early 1985 only one out of a twenty-three-member executive board was a woman.)

I asked Lisa one last question. Did she think that the women's movement had helped people like her? Lisa hesitated before answering. "That's a hard question," she said. "You see, the goals of the feminists are great, we all want to be equal, but I can't think of anything concrete they have accomplished for working women like me. I wish they had spent less time on ERA and more on child care. Access to high-quality day care—now that is something that would really make a difference." She paused and then added, "I guess those women libbers can mostly afford private baby-sitters and don't realize how hard it is for regular families."[20]

If unions are handicapped by their historical orientation toward the male breadwinner, they are also inhibited by their declining strength and by their political unpopularity.

In 1945, 35 percent of employed wage and salary workers in America belonged to unions. By the mid-1980s this figure had dropped to 19 percent.[21] The decline in union strength has been particularly pronounced over the last five years. Union members as a proportion of all employees fell from 23 percent in 1980 to 19.1 percent in 1984. An important contributing factor in the recent decline was the 1981–82 recession because "unemployment hit hardest in industries where unions were strong, but, to date, the recovery has been most vigorous in industries and occupations that typically have low levels of unionization."[22]

For union membership in the United States is concentrated in declining sectors of the economy. In mining, construction, and manufacturing more than 30 percent of all workers are unionized.[23] However, because of fierce foreign competition, this so-called sunset segment of the economy suffered a net employment loss of 800,000 jobs between 1980 and 1984.[24] Most unions in this sector—and they include the UAW (the United Auto Workers), the United Steel Workers of America, and the ACTWU (the Amalgamated Clothing and Textile Workers Union)—have their backs to the wall and spend their best energies keeping as many of their members as possible in work. The UAW has started to organize office workers, and the ACTWU has attempted to recruit workers in the plastics industry, but by and large, industrial unions have failed to move aggressively into growth areas of the economy.

In addition to the problems posed by its declining industrial base, labor is currently operating in a hostile political environment. This was signaled early in the Reagan administration when 12,000 striking air traffic controllers were fired and their union was decertified. Recent political appointees at the Department of Labor and the National Labor Relations Board have been openly antagonistic toward the labor movement.

As the political influence of organized labor reaches a new low, so, too, does the appeal of the movement to the average American worker. Unions currently win fewer than 43 percent of representation elections, compared with winning 55 percent of these elections in 1970 and 94 percent in 1937. Union decertification drives are successful 75 percent of the time, and in 1982, 682 union locals were decertified.[25] These trends are due to stepped-up anti-union activity on the part of employers. But they are also due to disillusionment with the goals and strategies of the labor movement. For example, the givebacks conceded by unions during the 1981–83 recession were seen by many rank-and-file members as the leadership "selling out." As one UAW member put it, "the unions don't work for our interest. They are just another power structure. Uncle Sam takes our taxes, and the union takes our dues. Neither does anything for us."[26]

All these factors argue for a change in focus. If unions are to recoup their strength, they have to shift gears. They have to move away from their historical identification with the male breadwinner and the industrial sector and become relevant to women workers in service-sector employment. For the American labor market is undergoing massive change. In the 1980–84 period, when 800,000 jobs were lost in the industrial sector of the economy, employment in services grew by 5 million as health care, business services, finance, insurance, and real estate expanded rapidly. More than 3 million of these jobs went to women.[27] These new recruits to the labor force have a long list of unmet needs. If unions were to put the needs of working women center stage, they would have a rapidly expanding new constituency.

Trade unions in Europe have done more for working women. For starters, they have organized a much larger proportion of the female labor force and provided them with a standard set of benefits and protections—a better wage, job security, seniority rights, health and retirement benefits. They have also been successful in fighting for items that are of particular concern to women workers: subsidized day care, generous maternity and parental leave, better conditions for part-time work, and pay equity (narrowing the gap between male and female earnings). Sometimes unions have included these items in their contract negotiations; sometimes they have prevailed on government to provide these benefits to the population at large.

Marie Norstrom is thirty-six years old. She is a blue-collar assembly-line worker at an aerodynamics plant in Stockholm, Sweden. Altogether she has worked there for fifteen years. Her husband and her ex-husband both work in the same plant.

She has two sons, a ten-year-old from her first marriage and a three-year-old from her present marriage. She works part time (seven hours a day instead of eight) and will be allowed to keep this part-time schedule until her youngest child is eight. This is important because otherwise, she would have to leave for work too early to drop off the youngest at the day-care mother on her way to work. She brings him to the day-care mother at 7:30 A.M. and starts work at 8:00 A.M. Her husband, who is a foreman at the plant, starts work at 7:00 A.M., as would she if she worked full time. The older boy goes to school by himself. In the afternoons he goes to the same day-care mother as the younger child. This day-care mother also looks after three other children. Marie and her husband pay an income-adjusted fee for family day care; it amounts to 10 percent of Marie's salary. They pay the city government, and the city pays the care provider directly. The day-care mother has a good income from her job and runs a comfortable home with lots of special equipment for the children. Marie is very satisfied with the care her children receive.

When her first child was born, maternity leave was not an issue because Marie was not working. When her younger son was born, she took nine months off at full pay and one additional month at reduced pay. After the tenth month she went back to work and the baby was placed in the care of the same day-care mother who cares for him now. Marie is also entitled to leave from work to care for her children if they are sick. Over the past year she has taken twenty-three days for this purpose.

Marie feels very satisfied with her life. She says that even if she didn't need to work, she would work. Because of her divorce, she is aware of how important it is for women to be economically independent. Her one wish would be for a larger apartment, but they are hard to find and very expensive. Her apartment is clean and modestly furnished, but small. There are three rooms plus a kitchen and bathroom. Each boy has his own room, and Marie and her husband sleep in the living room.

I asked Marie if she belonged to a union. She looked at me in surprise. "Of course," she said. "In Sweden almost everyone belongs to a union." I then asked her if the union provided important benefits. Marie thought for a moment and then said, "Fifteen years ago workers—particularly women—had to fight hard to get decent wages and decent conditions of work. They mostly fought for these things through the LO. I remember the women in my union fighting very hard to get union support for day care. I guess most of these battles were won, and eventually the government passed laws that gave working people a whole range of benefits and services. These days we don't need the union to fight for parental leave because now it is available to everyone." Marie paused and then added, "Most of us take these benefits for granted."[28]

Sweden is an example of a country where organized labor has done much to improve the economic conditions of women's lives. The labor force participation rate and the union membership rate for women are among the highest in the world. Of working-age women, 65 percent are in the labor force, and women constitute 45 percent of the labor force. Of these women workers, 70 percent are unionized, a figure that rises to 90 percent among manual workers.[29]

The early history of labor organizations in Sweden is similar to that of other Western countries. Trade unions grew up in the late nineteenth century, and the early days of the movement were marked by sex-segregated unions and separate and lower pay scales for women workers.

In the 1940s the LO (the federation of workers) and the SAF (the employers federation) began to work together. In 1948 a joint LO-SAF committee was formed to investigate women's pay, and in 1951 a joint LO-SAF Women's Labor Council was formed. The council supported ways to get women into the labor force and advocated higher wages, part-time work, and subsidized child care. But not too much happened until the labor shortages that accompanied the economic expansion of the early 1960s. Other European countries solved the labor shortage through guest worker programs, but the LO strongly opposed this option, stating that it would "slow down the trend towards greater equality for women in the labor market . . . which is taking place too slowly in any case."[30] To encourage women to join the work force, the LO supported policies designed to reduce women's double burden in the home and in the workplace. Subsidized day care, extensive maternity leave, and the right to part-time work for mothers with young children were part of this initiative.

The single most important initiative for women workers was the solidarity wage strategy adopted in agreements between the LO and the SAF in the mid-1960s. The first step in this plan was the phasing out of separate pay scales for women, and further steps included raising the wages of low-paid workers and of workers within low-wage industries. Women benefitted disproportionately from the solidarity wage strategy since they were concentrated in low-paid jobs and industries. The wage gap between women and men in manual occupations narrowed from 30 percent in 1959 to 7 percent in 1981.[31]

In the late 1960s Swedish attitudes underwent a further change, and a concern for women's rights was replaced by a concern for gender equality. The trade unions and the Social Democratic party began to realize that true equality would require changes in the social role played by men. In keeping with this new thinking, the unions abolished their women's councils toward the end of the decade and replaced them with family councils. Meanwhile, the Social Democratic party launched a program to achieve equal status for men and women in work and family life. It included legislation to enforce nondiscrimination in hiring, promotion, and wage determination; parental leave at the time of childbirth (for women and men); separate taxation for married couples; and training programs for men and women entering nontraditional fields. The LO remains skeptical of the effectiveness of legislation and has insisted on keeping wages, hiring, and promotion practices within the sphere of collective bargaining.

Italy is another example of a country where unions have helped upgrade the economic position of women.

The modern Italian labor movement emerged after World War II with the formation of three major union confederations: the CGIL (dominated by the Communists), the CSIL (dominated by the Catholics), and the UIL (dominated by the Social Democrats). All three union confederations and their affiliated unions had women's commissions. It was through these commissions that union policies toward women workers were formulated.[32] In 1946 the CGIL and the employers' federation signed an agreement on maternity leave. The provisions of the leave were improved upon four years later, when national legislation, proposed by the CGIL, was passed. This legislation provided for a compulsory leave from work at 80 percent of normal wages for three months prior to, and two months following, childbirth. It also required employers to allow work breaks for breast-feeding for the first year of a child's life, and made it the employer's responsibility to provide special nursery space for this purpose. In addition, it became illegal to fire a woman while she was pregnant or for a full year following childbirth. In 1971 this legislation was expanded to include health care benefits and a six-month additional, partially paid maternity leave. Over the last ten years the unions have been involved in the successful effort to establish subsidized day care, and they have been strong advocates of the Family Charter described in Chapter Seven.

On the wage front Italian unions, like Swedish unions, have been concerned with upgrading the weakest elements in the labor force. They supported the 1960 legislation on equal pay for women, but they have also fought to raise the wages of the lowest-paid workers by pushing for flat-rate wage increases. Since women predominate in low-paid work, this has had the effect of narrowing differentials between men and women. Between 1962 and 1980 women's wages in the industrial sector rose from 70 percent of men's earnings to 84 percent.[33]

Article 37 of the Italian Constitution endorses equality between men and women in regard to work and wages as long as the conditions of work do not endanger "women's essential family and maternal roles."[34] This wording was the result of a compromise among the political parties, the labor unions, and the Catholic Church. The modern Italian state tries to promote both equality of opportunity and a strong family life. It sees the need for equal rights in the sphere of work and social benefits to ease the family responsibilities of working women.

Sweden and Italy are examples of countries where trade unions have significantly improved the lot of women workers. In other Western European countries organized labor has been less aggressive in its pursuit of women's economic rights.

Cathy Holdern is thirty-two years old, teaches in a primary school in Oxford, England, and is an active member of a union—the National Union of Teachers (NUT). She is also the mother of a ten-month-old daughter. When she gave birth, she was entitled to a six-month, job-protected maternity leave—the first month at full pay, the next two weeks at nine-tenths pay, the following three months at half pay, and one and a half months at no pay. Cathy and her husband could not manage without her salary, so after four and a half months she returned to work, leaving her daughter with a child minder, a neighborhood woman who was licensed to look after several children in her home. This day-care arrangement is not subsidized and costs about half of Cathy's salary.

Cathy has mixed feelings about how much her union has helped her cope with her new responsibilities. "The union did negotiate a better maternity leave than I would have been entitled to under the Employment Protection Act, but progress on other fronts has been minimal." For example, Cathy would prefer to put her child in an on-site nursery, but when she tried to drum up support for this idea within the union, she failed to get any response from her male colleagues. "Given the glut of teachers, most union members are afraid of losing their jobs and won't stick their necks out on any issue," said Cathy in a resigned tone of voice. She finds that the problem of stirring up interest in child care is compounded by the difficulties she now faces in attending union meetings—a problem that most working mothers have to contend with. "Local meetings are held at four-fifteen, and since babies and young children are allowed to come along, I can attend these, but regional and national meetings are another story. These are invariably held in the evenings or at weekends, and there are no arrangements for baby-sitting, so there is no way I can go." Partly as a result of this, the leadership of Cathy's union remains predominantly male—despite the fact that 70 percent of the members are women.

Cathy sees herself as a feminist and has been active in a wide array of feminist causes and organizations. Her considered judgment is that the lack of affordable, high-quality child care is the major obstacle preventing women from achieving equality in the British labor market. She told me rather bitterly, "It's the old story: Women get penalized for having children, and men get promoted for having children to support. Child care is society's responsibility, but this will come about only if individual women band together and fight for it. The labor movement is a good place to start, although not much has happened yet."[35]

Cathy Holdern is right: British unions have made little headway on the child-care front. They have failed to persuade the government to provide day care and preschools for the children of working parents, and unions have done little to subsidize child care directly. But in other areas their performance has been better. First and foremost, British unions have been aggressive in their recruitment of women workers—no mean accomplishment in view of the stagnant economy and high rates of unemployment. Between 1971 and 1981 there was a 50 percent increase in the number of women in trade unions; indeed, fully 40 percent of women workers are now organized.[36]

The trade union movement has been active in the campaign to close the earnings gap between male and female workers. The TUC (Trades Union Congress, the equivalent of the AFL-CIO) was instrumental in helping pass the Equal Pay Act of 1970, which was partly responsible for the narrowing of the wage gap in the mid-1970s.[37] And in the recent period British unions have pushed employers and the government to move toward equal pay for work of equal value. For example, in early 1985 the Society of Graphical and Allied Trades, a 214,000-member union, used the threat of what the British call equal value lawsuits to close the wage gap between jobs held mostly by women and those held mostly by men.[38]

The TUC has also been involved in the campaign for a statutory maternity leave and was instrumental in passing the 1975 Employment Protection Act, which gave women additional paid leave and protection against job loss at the time of childbirth. The benefits granted were lower than the provisions the TUC had lobbied for, and many unions pushed for better protection in contract negotiations. However, despite these actions, the TUC does not see itself as doing as much as it should for women: "There have been obvious improvements in the attitude of unions to women members. . . . However, although improvements can be seen there is certainly no room for complacency."[39]

Like Britain, trade unions in France have a mixed track record when it comes to women workers, but there are some early examples of constructive action. The *Accords Matignon* negotiated in 1936 was an agreement between the government and the unions to establish a code of work regulations for the treatment of pregnant women and the equalization of women's wages with men's. The laws established maternity leave for women workers and guaranteed benefits and job security. They reflected the unions' and the government's shared belief that motherhood was "a social function, similar to military service for men, that had to be financially supported by the whole community."[40] The *Accords* guaranteed maternity benefits to housewives as well as workers, thus gaining the support of conservatives and Catholics. The 1936 union-government agreement had a significant effect on women's wages. Up until 1935 women had earned one-half of men's wages; after the agreement the gap narrowed by 15 percent.[41]

There are some obvious differences between the labor movement in the United States and in Europe. In many Western European countries trade unions hold a legitimate and powerful position in the overall structure of society. Today 53 percent of all workers are unionized in Britain; 60 percent, in Italy; 25 percent, in

France; 70 percent, in Sweden; and 42 percent, in West Germany.[42] Contrast this with the United States, where only 19 percent of the labor force belongs to labor unions.[43] Cathy Holdern might be critical of her union, but one should not lose sight of the fact that some protection is better than none. At least 40 percent of British working women have better maternity leave and better job protection because they belong to unions, while only 14 percent of American working women have these advantages.

The greater strength of the labor movement in Europe is a result of the deeply ingrained class structure of most European countries, the socialist tradition that runs through their histories, and the strong alliances most labor unions have with the established political parties. Unions in Europe exert their power differently—through strikes in Britain and Italy and through codetermination and cooperation in Germany, France, and Sweden. However, in all these countries trade unions do have tremendous power to exert. Their power may be modified in times of recession, but it is not fundamentally questioned.

The greater strength and legitimacy of trade unions in Europe have enabled them to do more for working women. They have supported "protective" or gender-specific social legislation that has led to extensive rights and benefits for working women at the time of pregnancy and childbirth. And they have successfully narrowed the gap between male and female earnings by working to raise the wages of the lowest-paid workers in the labor force.

But it is not just that European labor unions have greater power than their American counterparts; the specifics of their political agendas owe much to the goals and strategy of social feminism. As we saw in Chapter Eight, European social feminists, unlike American feminists, chose not to form their own separatist organizations. Instead, they decided to work through political parties and trade unions to obtain concrete benefits for women. Relatively less concerned with formal equality, they openly pressed for special support structures that would help women bear their double burden in the home and on the job. When Marie Norstrom talked about Swedish women's successfully pressuring the union to support day care, she was describing social feminism in action.

What Can Trade Unions Do for Women?

Contrast this with the United States, where protective or special legislation for women workers has always attracted the vehement opposition of feminists. This is a result of the American preoccupation with equal rights, but it also flows from the elitism of the feminist organizations. In the 1920s it was difficult for the upper-middle-class supporters of Alice Paul's National Woman's party to grasp that ordinary working women might need protection and support. And in the 1980s it is hard for Yuppies on the fast track—the constituency of NOW—to figure out that bank tellers or nursery-school teachers need maternity leave even though such leave discriminates against men. Lisa Gorden is right when she accuses the women's movement of being out of touch with the reality of working-class life.

The American labor movement is at a crossroads. Most labor leaders have come to understand that they will have to make a run for it. The question is, in what direction? Will they follow their traditional path, only more aggressively, and continue to cater to the needs of male breadwinners in the sunset industries? Or will they follow a new path and respond to the massive increase of women workers in the sunrise service sector of the economy?

Women are also facing a turning point. More than half of all adult women now work outside the home, and the context of their lives is very different from that of thirty years ago. Concerns like earning a livable wage, time off from work to bear children, and quality care for their children while they are working are now critical issues. Will organized labor, partially for self-serving reasons, be the force that pushes for change and helps produce higher wages and family support structures for working women?

Some union leaders voice great optimism; they do see trade unions forging a valuable alliance with working women. Joyce Miller, a vice-president with the Amalgamated Clothing and Textile Workers Union, says with quiet confidence, "We in the labor movement know the fastest way for women to gain economic equality is to join a union,"[44] while a senior officer at the Communication Workers of America told me that "pushing for women and women's issues would definitely be a way of getting us [labor] out of a hole."[45] And it is clear that some unions—especially those, like AFSCME, that are based in the expanding service section—have begun to address these issues. However, it must be said that most unions and most union leaders have not shifted gears. One fact speaks for itself: Between 1980 and 1984, years when service-sector jobs increased by 5 million, the number of service-sector employees belonging to unions fell by 700,000.[46] Despite valiant attempts by AFSCME and other unions spearheading change, the labor movement has actually lost ground in the most dynamic segment of the economy. It seems that most unions are too busy fighting rearguard actions in declining industries to see even their own self-interest. For make no mistake about it, the labor movement is fighting for its life and can no longer afford the luxury of concentrating on male industrial workers. Industry is a declining segment of the American economy, and men are a declining proportion of the labor force. In 1984 for the first time white men did not represent a majority of the work force.[47]

One thing seems sure: Trade unions are much more likely to take up the cause of women workers if feminist leaders encourage them to do so. Feminists can help unions broaden their appeal because they can help reach out to women in offices, banks, and stores. These women tend to associate unions with factories and like to identify themselves as middle-class. But as Jane Brenner found out, even college-educated women can learn to value the protections and benefits conferred by trade union membership.

To date in America union leaders and feminist leaders have had different agendas. While feminists have been separatist and elitist in orientation, unions have been dominated by men and male concerns. Moreover, the feminist focus on legal equality has been inconsistent with bargaining for special benefits to meet the needs of working women.

But the time has come for concerted action and the catalyst could well be pay equity or comparable worth. We have already discussed how this has become a major focus for AFSCME and other public employee unions. The mainstream feminist organizations have also committed themselves to this cause. The National Organization for Women (NOW), the Women's Equity Action League (WEAL), and the Women's Legal Defense Fund have all actively campaigned for adoption of pay equity-comparable worth as a goal of the women's movement. Judy Goldsmith, president of NOW from 1983 to 1985, even promised that "women's groups will join unions in litigation to force an end to discriminatory wage structures."[48] Feminists are capable of giving visibility and legitimacy to the campaign to end low pay in the pink-collar ghetto, and if they attach a high enough priority to this campaign, they can also provide the resources needed to fund the job evaluation studies and the organizing drives necessary before these campaigns can get off the ground.

If feminists and trade unions pool their resources and energies and succeed in upgrading the wages of low-paid working women, the benefits could be enormous. This achievement would make a critical difference to the lives of millions of needy women. But trade unionism and feminism would also benefit because these movements would take on a new relevance and a new vitality.

A final note. Shortly after interviewing Jane Brenner, I came across a newspaper account of a new agreement between Pan Am and its flight attendants. The *New York Times* announced: "The Independent Union of Flight Attendants . . . agreed to major concessions to Pan Am, including more flexible work rules and starting pay for new attendants that is 37 percent lower than the pay at which current attendants started."[49] My heart sank. Jane's confidence in her union had been contagious; I did not want to know that this confidence had been misplaced. I read the rest of the article and was somewhat cheered to learn that flight attendants currently employed by the airline would receive a wage increase of 21.5 percent over a three-year period, and at least some of their protective work rules would be maintained.

I guess the moral of this story is that when the going gets rough—and since deregulation the going has been very rough in the airline industry—workers need union protection more than ever. I talked to Jane about the new agreement, and she is convinced that without her union she would have lost her job. As she put it, "why not get rid of expensive older workers and bring in twenty-one-year-olds at a much cheaper rate? After all, there are no skills in this business. A twenty-one-year-old can serve drinks as well as I can. . . . The only reason I am still around is that the union fought for our jobs real hard . . . and they even got us a raise."[50]

16

THE ESTABLISHMENT
GROPES FOR AN ANSWER

Many of us have opinions on what policies our government (or our private sector) ought to put in place to help women. I, in particular, have well-developed opinions, given the fact that I have thought about this topic a great deal over the last three to four years.

But strong opinions or even well-informed opinions do not, on their own, produce policy changes. I decided that if I were to come up with a policy agenda that carried any conviction, if I were to avoid building castles in the sky, I would have to engage the energies of people close to the centers of power. So during the course of 1983 I obtained permission from my chairman and steering committee to set up a family policy panel at the Economic Policy Council.[1]

To begin with, the project went very smoothly. My chairman, Robert O. Anderson (chairman of the Atlantic Richfield Company), gave his enthusiastic endorsement to the panel; John Sweeney (president of SEIU, the Service Employees International Union) and Alice Ilchman (president, Sarah Lawrence College) came on board to chair the panel; I was able to enlist the special support of two in-house economists, Ray Marshall and Carolyn

Shaw Bell, to help frame an agenda for the panel; and both the Ford and the Rockefeller foundations contributed generous grants to fund our work.

We decided to call the panel Parents and Work: Family Policy in Comparative Perspective. Its goals and objectives were carefully crafted by myself; the chairpersons; a core group of EPC members, including Marshall and Bell; and program officers from the Ford and Rockefeller foundations. The language of the panel's mission paper was cautious and convincing:

> The purpose of this study is to analyze current trends in the U.S. labor market, specifically the relationship between the changing composition of the work force and the changing structure of the family.... If current changes are not to have adverse effects on individuals and on the productive capacity of our society as a whole, we believe that . . . the concerns of parents-workers must be addressed and family support structures must be developed.
>
> The need for support systems will continue to grow in importance, especially in the 1990s when it is predicted that the U.S. will be experiencing a period of labor shortage. By 1990 60% of American women will be employed and women will account for the majority of new entrants into the labor force between now and then. Employers will find that family support structures are in their immediate self-interest as they reduce absenteeism and turnover rates, and increase productivity and growth.

I was pleased with the final statement of the goals and objectives of the panel. I believed that the issues had been presented so as to appeal to constructive energies within the EPC and, I hoped, in the nation at large, and I looked forward with considerable enthusiasm to starting our work. I was totally unprepared for the problems I would encounter.

Trouble started when I began to invite EPC members to join the panel—absolutely standard procedure once the chairpersons and funding are in place. I had always known that it would be important to include a large contingent of prominent men in this work. All too often issues such as child care and parental leave are treated as women's problems, and most committees and panels on these subjects feature women sitting around talking to the converted. If I was interested in the view of the establishment, or if I was interested in raising the consciousness of the power structure, my panel had to speak for and to male leaders.

To begin with, I did not envision a problem in getting my male membership involved. In 1983 the Economic Policy Council had approximately 100 members, and since these members were from the topmost ranks of business, academe, and organized labor, very few of them were women. I had struggled to bring more women on board and had managed to increase the female membership from two to ten, but since most panels comprised twenty-five or more council members, it seemed clear that more than half this new panel would be male.

Quite aside from counting on the numerical dominance of men within the Economic Policy Council, we all had done careful groundwork for this panel and thought that we had set the stage for enthusiastic male participation. The project was developed in such a way so that it stressed: the importance of bolstering the family; the parenting burdens faced by fathers as well as by mothers; the price paid by children for our lack of family support systems; and the desirability of investing in the next generation. The hidden agenda was, of course, the need to convince mainstream establishment men that these problems go way beyond women's rights and the politics of liberation. Conservatives have an interest in keeping the family healthy and strong, and most businessmen can see the point in investing in human resources.

But when I attempted to convene my panel in the spring and summer of 1983, I got a rude awakening. Most of my distinguished male members were simply not interested; they either yawned or raised their eyebrows when I insisted on explaining to them why they should get involved. After listening to my pitch, one eminent banker looked embarrassed and told me rather lamely that he was not "up to speed" in this policy area, and couldn't he join one of our other panels? I should point out that these men were not, in general, shrinking violets and had no problem in speaking out on Japanese defense policy or third world debt even when they had no fine-grained expertise in the area. Somehow issues like maternity leave and child care made them very nervous. But it was not just nerves; I could have overcome an attack of nerves. When pushed, they revealed another reason behind their reluctance to get involved: Family policy had no standing in their world. Being involved in this project would get them no brownie points in boardrooms or at cocktail parties. It seemed clear that while they might sacrifice precious time getting up to speed on Japanese defense policy, they were not prepared to do so for "women's stuff"—as one member called it.

If the male reaction was bad, the female reaction was even more difficult to take. I discovered that most of my distinguished women members weren't interested either. I remember feeling almost numb when one woman, a senior vice-president at a major manufacturing corporation, excused herself on the ground that she could not afford to become identified with this panel. She explained, "It has taken me fifteen years to get a hard-nosed reputation, and I just daren't risk it. If I were to get involved in these messy women's issues, it could do me a lot of harm in the company." She was a kind woman and followed this up with a piece of personal advice: "You know, if I were you, I would drop this whole project. You are an economist who has had enough sense to build a career in serious fields such as development economics. Why risk all that by getting everyone's back up?" The most depressing thing about her response was that I knew enough about her personal history to understand that she herself had encountered difficulties in bearing children mid-career. If she wouldn't take these issues seriously, who would?

Another corporate woman did allow herself to be persuaded to join the panel but halfway through the project threatened to resign because I would not take child care off the agenda. Needless to say, we had always planned to spend at least two panel sessions on the critical problem of child care. Imagine, then, my surprise when this top-ranking woman executive called, just before the first child-care meeting, and tried to derail it. "I don't know what child care has to do with the employment problems of women," she said militantly. "If a woman chooses to have children, then she should deal with the consequences." I opened my mouth, intending to explain how children were a societal as well as an individual responsibility. But then I closed it again. I didn't know how to combat such entrenched hostility toward working mothers. This particular corporate woman was in her fifties and childless. I suspected that she had mixed in with her policy perspective a great deal of bitterness and resentment.

A word on feminist participation in my family policy panel. I never thought it appropriate to involve a large contingent from the women's movement. The EPC was, after all, a labor-management group and our task was to work with business and labor leaders. Despite this constraint, I did try to involve two influential feminists. I thought they could help us by bringing information and experience to our deliberations, and we could help them by providing a policy agenda for working women that stood a chance of being supported by the establishment. I was wrong in supposing I could produce this kind of collaboration. One of my two hand-picked feminists (chosen because she claimed to care about the economic plight of women and children) did not participate at all. After accepting the invitation to join the group she failed to turn up at any meeting, and subsequently declined to comment on a draft of the report. My other feminist came to the first meeting, left a little early, and quite soon after resigned from the panel. She told a staff member that the issues we were discussing lay outside her field of interest. All of which confirmed me in my view that family policy hardly figures on the feminist agenda.

Disillusioned but determined, I went to work recruiting new members to strengthen the panel. Slowly and painfully I was able to find concerned individuals. I wrote innumerable letters: to senior executives of corporations that have innovative policies in this area; to labor leaders who are beginning to think of these issues. Over the course of the next two months I talked myself hoarse over countless breakfasts and lunches trying to convince busy executives to devote their precious time to this project. Finally, by the winter of 1983, I was able to put together an eminent group of individuals, and we officially launched the panel in January 1984. At this point it included, in addition to the chairpersons: Gerald Ford (former president), Katharine Graham (chairman, the Washington Post Company), Steven Ross (chairman, Warner Communications), Sheila Kamerman (professor of social work, Columbia University), Betty Friedan, Ray Marshall (economist and former secretary of labor), Gerald McEntree (president, AFSCME), and Carolyn Shaw Bell (professor of economics, Wellesley College). I did not abandon my goal that more than 50 percent of the panel be male.

The hardest part was accomplished, but the panel had recurrent difficulties in hanging on to the loyalties of its members. A disappointing number of panelists failed to show up at sessions, and some resigned when they discovered (with the appropriate expressions of surprise) that their calendars did not allow them to honor this particular commitment. Every few sessions it seemed necessary to recruit new members so as to fill gaps and keep the panel up to strength. Sometimes Alice Ilchman, an extremely responsible participant herself, started a meeting by scanning the room to see if she recognized anyone. She often quipped that I was so good at getting new bodies on board that this panel had a good shot at rotating through the entire corporate community! But despite a certain amount of gallows humor, we all got tired of working with a revolving door.

Even those panel members who stayed with us found that their attention easily strayed into more "serious" fields. For example, in September 1984 the panel met in Washington, D.C., during the annual plenary session of the EPC. At this event all three policy panels of the Economic Policy Council held special meetings.[2] Alice Ilchman chaired a session of the family policy panel, Henry Kaufman (executive director, Solomon Brothers, Inc.) chaired a session of the financial panel, and Douglas Fraser (president emeritus, United Auto Workers) chaired a session of the jobs panel. These sessions were held concurrently on the morning of September 17, before the EPC convened for a lunch with some congressional leaders. Several of the family policy panel members—perhaps a third of the total number—decided to abandon their own meeting in order to sit in on one of the others. One woman member just walked out after sitting through five minutes of a presentation on parental leave. She crossed the hall to join Henry Kaufman and his group.

Things reached a new low in October 1984, when John Sweeney offered to resign as co-chair of the panel. As he told me over the phone, he continued to believe in the importance of the subject matter, and he wanted to commend me on how well I had run the panel to date, but since he had missed one or two meetings, he felt that he should not continue in a leadership role. Knowing that the project would totally disintegrate if a chairperson resigned, I put all my persuasive skills to work, and eventually Sweeney agreed to stay on. To his credit he then shouldered more responsibility for the remaining life-span of the project. But it was a depressing episode and pointed to the real difficulties even enlightened labor leaders have in taking these issues seriously. Sweeney is, after all, the head of a union that is 70 percent female, and his union, the Service Employees International Union, is aggressively trying to organize women in the fast-expanding service area of the economy. If he cannot see the logic of developing policies that speak to the concerns of working parents, what labor leader will?

The entire staff of the EPC worked very hard at keeping things going. We pumped all our panel members—new and old—full of working papers, fact sheets, transcripts, and clippings. We brought in powerful speakers from Europe—cabinet ministers and famous scholars (Europeans, it seemed, had no trouble in taking these issues seriously). We even scheduled special briefing sessions for panel members who couldn't make regular meetings but showed some interest in what had gone on. The EPC staff was committed to the project, as was a tiny core group within the panel; Alice Ilchman and Sheila Kamerman stand out as being particularly loyal and hardworking. We would not allow it to die, so the panel did, in fact, limp along.

Despite all these problems, over the course of the eighteen months or so of the panel's existence some new light was shed on family policy.

Of all the foreign case studies that were explored by the panel, the one that members found most appealing was that of France. They liked the conservatism of French family policy, the fact that it is designed to strengthen traditional family ties (e.g., by providing preschool for the children of at-home mothers) as well as dealing with the casualties of the modern age (e.g., by providing benefits for single parents). They were impressed by the national consensus that the French have managed to build around family policy and by the fact that the Catholic Church and right-wing political groups join with labor unions and the Socialist party to support such measures as child allowances and generous maternity benefits. Finally, they liked the French mind set, which regards motherhood as "a social function similar to military service for men, that had to be financially supported by the whole community." One panel member remembered that twenty years ago, when he did National Guard duty, he had no trouble getting a six-month paid leave from his job as a junior executive with a Madison Avenue advertising firm. He told the panel that giving a child a good start in life was probably just as important to the nation as a tour of military duty.

Visiting French experts, in their turn, were somewhat stunned by the almost total lack of family support systems in the United States. Olga Baudelot, a well-known French scholar, came to talk to the panel about French policies toward children. At the end of her session she asked as many questions as she answered. "If only 40 percent of working women have any right to maternity leave, how on earth do the others manage?" she asked in shocked tones. A little later she asked, "But why don't you women just scream and shout until the politicians produce maternity leave and child care?" To illustrate her point, Baudelot told the story of how in 1982, Jacques Chirac, the conservative mayor of Paris, was browbeaten by militant groups of working women into expanding the crèche system so as to provide many more places for infants and toddlers. In her words, "Chirac would have been voted out of office if he hadn't caved into these demands."

I didn't have any good answers for Baudelot, but her questions did make me realize how backward—and barbaric—these areas of American social policy must seem to most Europeans. One of Baudelot's more telling questions was: "Why have issues such as child care become so politicized in the United States?

Why, in France presidents as far apart in their political philosophy as Charles de Gaulle and François Mitterrand have had no trouble in providing support systems for children. How can prenatal care, family allowances, or nursery school be issues that belong to either the right or the left?"

Baudelot is, of course, right. America has succeeded in politicizing these issues so thoroughly that it takes a brave candidate for public office to even mention the words *child care* for fear of running into vast quantities of negative political energy.

Another distinguished visitor, Anna-Greta Leijon, the Swedish minister of labor, also asked a lot of questions. "What really puzzles me is that the far right seems to be the only group that even talks about family policy in the United States. Why is this so?" was one of her queries. To illustrate her point, she gave the example of Senator Jesse Helms's 1981 family protection bill, which sought to get rid of sex education, eliminate birth control information, and repeal federal wife and child abuse laws in the name of supporting the family. Leijon had a great deal of trouble in seeing this right-wing agenda as answering the desperate need of American families for concrete benefits and services. One reason she agreed to come and speak to the EPC's family policy panel was that she was hopeful that a mainstream group was beginning to think sensibly about these issues.

There were, and are, no easy answers to Baudelot's or Leijon's questions. Comprehending the politicization of child care in the United States entails coming to terms with the 1950s, a decade which was so different in Europe and America. In France the 1950s were a time when free public preschool came to be regarded as a given; while in Sweden these years featured a joint LO-SAF Women's Labor Council that supported higher wages for women, part-time work, and child care. In America, on the other hand, it was the decade of complete motherhood, when putting your child in group care was seen as a subversive act.

Another by-product of the family policy panel was that I came to understand anew the irrelevancy of the ERA. I did not expect the ERA to be a useful policy tool in obtaining maternity leave or child care for working women. As we have seen, equal rights are often a stumbling block in the way of special benefits and services for women. However, I did think that the ERA might be an important item on the agenda when we talked about pay equity. But although the panel deliberated long and hard over how to close the gap between male and female wages, the ERA never came up. We had a session on pay equity with our corporate members center stage, and we had a session on pay equity with our union members center stage. We argued the issue of comparable worth *ad nauseam* with our pro-market corporate members, and we invited economists from both the left and the right of the discipline to advise us on this topic. But over the course of the months we debated this critically important issue *no one mentioned the ERA.* It is not as though we had ruled the ERA out of bounds because it was too contentious; most people on the panel had political positions that supported the ERA. Rather, it just didn't come up as a policy measure relevant to obtaining a better economic deal for women.

At one of our fall 1984 sessions we invited a prominent lawyer to speak about the legal aspects of the comparable worth cases. Knowing him to be a longtime supporter of feminists' causes, I asked him after the meeting why the ERA had never surfaced in the work of the family policy panel. He thought for a moment and then said, "Well, in the area of employment and earnings the ERA doesn't provide any additional safeguards for women. The legislation we have on the books, particularly Title VII of the Civil Rights Act, is actually stronger than the ERA would be." I then asked him why the women's movement had stressed the ERA so heavily if it didn't have any teeth in an area as important as work and wages. My prominent feminist lawyer hesitated for a minute or so and then decided to spill the beans. He leaned toward me, and, glancing around to make sure no one was listening, said in a quiet voice, "You know, just after Judy Goldsmith took over as president of NOW, she tried to dump the ERA. She called it an albatross and said she wanted NOW to move on to more useful and more winnable issues. Frankly I encouraged her to do this as I have never thought the ERA was of much practical use to women. But the odd thing was the ERA would not go away. A lot of people were just too identified with this issue. It had acquired a momentum of its own. So it's back there on the NOW agenda and still has the number one slot."[3]

By the summer of 1985 the EPC's family policy panel had a tentative list of recommendations. They were:

1. *Pay Equity:* The panel recognizes the existence of widespread wage discrimination and supports movement towards greater parity between men's and women's earnings. While the appropriate method for achieving greater pay equity is dependent upon the specific setting, the panel endorses the use of collective bargaining, stricter enforcement of existing legislation and job evaluations as potentially effective solutions. Strengthening women's earning power will enable many dual-paycheck and female-headed households to pull themselves out of poverty and to become self-sustaining. As a result, the opportunities offered to the 20% of American children currently living in poverty will be greatly expanded. This will lead to a more productive use of human and capital resources, and to an increase in our country's economic strength.

2. *Maternity and Parental Leave:* The panel supports: A) Federal legislation mandating temporary disability insurance in the 45 states that currently do not require such coverage. B) An expansion of the definition of disability to give women the right to 10 to 12 weeks leave at the time of birth with some wage replacement during this time and a job guarantee at the end of the period. C) A partially paid parenting leave for either parent for up to 6 months after birth. D) Employers should also be encouraged to provide a gradual phased-in return to work for mothers, and the opportunity for parents of small children to choose part time work without losing job related benefits.

3. *Maternal and Child Health:* The federal government must give priority to health coverage for pregnant

women and children. Not only are these two groups disproportionately impoverished and disproportionately uninsured, but there is extensive evidence that increases in preventative maternal and child health care reaps substantial long range savings in catastrophic care programs.

4. *Flexible Work Schedules:* Working parents of small children need, more than anything else, time. Employers should be encouraged to make more work-sharing and part-time employment available at all occupational levels including management, without curtailing the promotional opportunities of the employees. Flextime, or flexible work hours, should be implemented on a larger scale to allow employees to better integrate their work and family responsibilities. Special leave time for parents to care for sick children should be permitted by all employers. Traditional career paths should be reassessed in relation to the family responsibilities of working parents, since more and more men and women in traditional career trajectories find that the most critical phases of their work and family lives coincide.

5. *Preschool and Early Childhood Education:* In the US today there are approximately 8.5 million children under 6 years of age with working parents. Preschool can play a much needed and valuable role in boosting the quality of early childhood education and in meeting childcare needs. By making preschool available on a voluntary basis to 3, 4 and 5 year olds, and by extending the school day, the public school system could serve important educational and childcare objectives. In addition, school facilities should be used for before- and after-school programs. Such policies would reduce the need for, and therefore the cost of, remedial education programs.

6. *Childcare—Public Sector Initiatives:* The variety of programs through which the US government currently

subsidizes childcare is very limited. Still, it seems unlikely at this time, when government is reducing spending on all social programs, that there will be any
significant increase in direct funding for childcare.
However, funding for programs such as Title XX of the
Social Security Act should be restored and even expanded. In addition the Childcare Tax Credit—which
is the largest single expenditure on childcare—should
be broadened and made refundable so that low income
families can also benefit from it.

7. *Childcare—Private Sector Initiatives:* A growing number
of companies are interested in organizing or in subsi-
dizing childcare programs, and the private sector could
become an important source of childcare in this country. Labor unions, community groups and corporations
should be encouraged to develop childcare services in-
dependently, jointly and in consortiums.

These recommendations constitute, in my view, a realistic list
of what might be done in contemporary America. But given the
rocky history of the EPC's family policy panel it is hard to get too
excited about these recommendations. I now think that figuring
out what should be done is not the problem. Any group of intelligent people is capable of doing this. Family policy is not an obscure area. It does not need fine-grained technical analysis, for the
facts are clear and they speak for themselves. What is conspicuously lacking is any sense that this is an important policy area
worthy of serious attention. Until the establishment makes this
commitment, there will be no action.

I found the experience of directing the family policy panel
profoundly disturbing, even radicalizing. The panel was the
eighth I had directed at the Economic Policy Council, and before
I took on this project, I saw myself as an old hand at running policy panels. But none of my previous experience had prepared me
for the difficulties I encountered with this one. And it isn't because the EPC generally took on straightforward topics or made a
habit of working only with easy personalities.

In 1981 the Economic Policy Council ran a panel on immigration policy, an extraordinarily difficult project given the fact that the EPC comprised a labor-management group and labor and management had very different political positions on this issue.[4] But we nevertheless debated this problem for a year and came to a tough set of policy recommendations that had some effect in Congress. The following year we tackled the question of what to do about the International Monetary Fund, another sticky topic considering that we had commercial bankers, industrialists, and labor leaders in our group. But once again we were able to reach a consensus and write a hard-hitting report. I was proud of the fact that the EPC, under my stewardship, had built up a reputation for commitment among its members. Up until the ill-fated family policy panel, no one had resigned mid-panel, and on average, 85 percent of our panelists turned up at each meeting. In view of the standing of our members, I felt extremely proud of this figure; such a high attendance rate is almost unheard of in policy panels of this sort.

Yet the family policy panel failed to generate loyalty from most of its members despite all the energy I pumped into it. It is true, we have recommendations and we will publish a report, but on the important level of involvement of panel members the project failed.

I have often tried to explain why this happened and find it tough going. You see, my panel members are not just powerful people; they are concerned citizens who often devote time, energy, and resources to worthy causes. The very fact that they are members of the EPC speaks for itself. These men and women are willing to spend time on public policy questions; they cannot be accused of having narrow, selfish attitudes. Yet they could not work up any real enthusiasm for this topic, which touched them in more important ways than any other. What business leader should not be concerned about how to hang on to his or her best female managers and avoid the risk of losing them when they are forced—by an unyielding workplace—to choose between a career and a family? What labor leader should not be addressing the concerns of women workers as the labor movement struggles for survival in an age when most new jobs are going to women? But the case is stronger than this. Business executives and labor leaders are also husbands and fathers, wives and mothers and have firsthand experience of the need for better policies. It is truly hard to explain why these powerful people were much less interested in family policy than in immigration reform or the International Monetary Fund.

I reluctantly came to the conclusion that my panel members did not warm to these issues for all the reasons explained in this book. Many men on the panel had been molded by the fifties and at some level believed that children should be looked after by their mothers and that child care is not an appropriate sphere for government action. The career women on the panel were resistant to the idea that working women might need special benefits in the workplace; they had absorbed the feminist message of the 1970s, which was that if women wanted equal opportunities, they should behave exactly like men. And the trade unionists had risen to power fighting for a family wage for family men; they had not yet adjusted to the labor market realities of the 1980s. For one reason or another these enlightened men and women maintained a residual hostility toward working mothers. When forced to confront the facts, they did sign off on a rather obvious program of reform. But their hearts were not in it.

It is, of course, infuriating to think through the consequences of continuing to neglect these issues. Over the last few years women and children have fallen below the poverty line at a frighteningly rapid rate. During the Reagan years 3 million more children and 4 million more women have slithered into poverty. This is not a record we should be proud of. We are, after all, a nation that prides itself on being child-centered, and we are a people that venerates mothers.

But national pride is not the only thing at stake. We pay a double price for our failure to provide support structures for today's families. We sacrifice efficiency. For money spent on day care and preschool is not money down the drain. Investment in our human resources actually saves money in the long run. As Albert Shanker said in his testimony before Congress, "The nation goes on year after year spending excessive time, money and effort on the problems of juvenile delinquency and crime. We are looking in the wrong place for solutions to problems resulting from a generation of children growing up without proper supervision."[5]

We also sacrifice our humanity. Millions of women workers have no right to job-protected maternity leave and many of these women can't just chuck their jobs in when they have children; they need to continue working. They end up in the position of Gail Tobias, who, as described in Chapter Four, went back to work two and a half weeks after giving birth by cesarean section. As Gail told me in an interview, "I don't know how I lived through those first weeks back at work. I was exhausted and in pain from the surgery. I could hardly drag myself around. The worst thing was the lack of sleep. Annie woke to be fed at least three times a night, and by midday I was ready to kill for sleep. But somehow I had to work—and to smile and pretend to my boss that I didn't have a family care in the world." Gail Tobias is not a masochist. The only reason she did these things to herself and to her child was to keep her job. No other civilized nation makes it so difficult for women to bear children while working.

— *17* —

EPILOGUE: VOICES FROM THE POST-FEMINIST GENERATION

In the fall of 1984, as I approached the end of my labors on this book, I decided to test my ideas against the sensibilities of today's young women. By this time I had directed a policy panel, analyzed large quantities of data, and interviewed hundreds of workers, mothers, and government officials. But I wanted to know the reactions of a group that I knew and thoroughly understood. So I turned to my ex-students.

How had the young women I had taught at Barnard College come out of the pressure caldron of the 1970s? How are they coping with the expectations of the 1980s? Do they see themselves as being "squeezed between the devil and the deep blue sea"? Or do they feel that they can have it all—career success, marriage, and children? I also wanted to probe on other fronts. What do these women think of motherhood? Where do they look for role models? How do they relate to the men in their lives? And what do they think of the women's movement? In other words, I wanted to share the thoughts and feelings of a group that includes some of the best-educated and privileged women of this post-feminist generation.

In September 1984 I staged a reunion for the women I had

383

taught at Barnard College during the years 1974–81. I invited all those whom I had known well, women who had majored in economics and written their senior essays under my direction—some fifty students in all. I was able to track down thirty-five of this group of fifty. Seventeen came to a reunion at my home, eight met me for lunch or talked to me long distance, and ten filled out questionnaires. With the exception of five students who had come to me for career advice shortly after graduating, I had not seen or heard of these women since they left Barnard College.

At 8:00 P.M. on September 21, 1984, my apartment filled with excited young women greeting long-lost classmates. They ranged in age from twenty-three to thirty-three, and half were married. Some were self-consciously businesslike in skirted suits, little string ties, and cropped hair. But even the more feminine members of the group, in elegant dresses and clever makeup, carried bulging briefcases. Most of them had come straight from work, two brought spouses, and one woman was conspicuously pregnant. After an hour of eating, drinking, gossiping, and cuddling my children (my third child, Adam, was just five months old and particularly popular, despite a tendency to dribble down silk blouses) the serious business of the evening began. We sat around in a big circle, and after some encouragement (I, after all, was an old hand at conducting seminars) everyone started to talk. The first topic these women gravitated toward was how to combine careers with children (a rather surprising choice, for although one of these women was pregnant, *none* had yet had children).

Marion,* age twenty-four, class of '81, one of the most able students of her year, now holds an entry-level position at an investment banking firm, a job she took after completing a master's degree in economics. Marion likes her work and looks forward to building a career in international finance. Marion is getting married in the spring, and her one great worry is: "Can I make room in this career for children?" She recognizes that she has chosen a very time-intensive profession: "Ten to twelve hours a day plus a lot of travel. Not only does my job require me to travel abroad ten

*Pseudonym.

days of each month, but I have a ninety-minute commute, which means that I never get home until eight in the evening." Marion particularly regrets that there are no role models in her field. "In my firm there are a hundred partners, only three of them are women, and none of these are in my department, so I don't know them." In the larger financial world Marion has found some women, "but if they are married, they tend to be childless."

Marion does not see herself attempting to have children for at least five years, yet, as she freely admits, "it is a question I think about a lot." Her great hope is that by then "I will be in control of my career and have much more ability to dictate my terms to it."

At this point Marion was interrupted by Laura,* age twenty-nine, class of '77, who said quietly but with conviction, "It's not as easy as that. Things don't resolve themselves. In some ways the choices get harder.

"My situation is typical. I'll be thirty in July and am beginning to feel enormous pressure to have a child. I read somewhere that infertility problems begin to mount in your early thirties, and I would very much like to avoid that kind of trouble. Besides, I've been married for seven years, and both of us want a child quite badly. The other day Michael told me that he 'needed' a child. Yet I cannot decide how to reconcile a family with my work. The basic problem is that my career cannot be put on hold for a few years. If I were to take time out, there would be no way of picking up the threads two or three years down the line."

Everyone in the room was listening very closely to Laura. She was seen by her classmates as an immensely efficient woman thoroughly in control of her life. If she was encountering problems, they were surely significant ones. Marion pushed Laura to be more explicit. "I don't understand. I thought it was OK to slow down once your career was established."

Laura decided to tell of her experience in some detail, and as she talked, her voice rose and became filled with emotion. Clearly her dilemma was causing considerable pain.

"Professional careers do not become easier or plateau out in your late twenties or early thirties. At these critical early stages

*Pseudonym.

there is always *the next step.* I work in a commercial bank. When I started seven years ago, my first goal was to become an officer. Then I wanted to become a higher-level officer, then assistant vice-president. And now I am waiting for my vice-presidency.

"I put in twelve- to fourteen-hour days. I have taken only four sick days in seven years, and I have earned my medals; but that does not mean that I can relax a whole lot now. There just isn't much flexibility in my career. Citibank thinks it has a decent maternity policy—three months' leave—but the kid is not even sleeping through the night by then. The bank will not tolerate part-time work or flextime and has no child-care facilities. Besides, as soon as you get pregnant, people at work start viewing you differently. They assume your priorities have changed and you will have less energy for your job.

"We bought a house in the suburbs a year and a half ago, and since my husband wants to be a neurosurgeon and has four years of specialized training in front of him, there is no way we could keep the house if I stopped work.

"So you see, despite the fact that I have launched my career, delayed childbearing, and done all the things I was supposed to do, I face some very tough choices.

"When we have a child, I can do one of three things. I can continue my career by hiring enough help for full-time coverage at home. I have priced it out; it would cost twenty thousand dollars a year. The snag is I would have to resign myself to seeing my baby only an hour or two a day. Or I can opt out of my banking career and work part time for my father (who has a small business). This way I can make enough money to pay the mortgage and still have time to see my child and manage the house. Or, finally, we could sell the house, move into an apartment, and I can take time out of the work force and become a traditional homemaker.

"All three options entail huge costs for me. I can already visualize the massive guilt I would feel if I took option number one. I had a very traditional upbringing, and an important part of me believes that mothers should be with their children. I have nightmares about my child forgetting that I am its mother, preferring the baby-sitter to me. I can deal with hard work and crazy hours,

I would even get up at five A.M. to spend some quality time with my child, but can I cope with the guilt? I don't think so.

"Option number two would kill my career—at least any ambitious version of my career. If I took even a few years out of banking, there is no way I could get back on the fast track in my mid or late thirties. In other words, if I opted to work part time for my father, I would have to permanently lower my expectations of money, status, and power.

"Option number three is the least attractive to me. I would not like losing the house; I have worked hard for my creature comforts and value them. But more than that, if I were to stay at home all day, I would more than likely go crazy. I thrive on stimulus and love my work. I am now a formed person and cannot change my personality or temperament because it's convenient to do so."

Laura's painful choices seem not to be shared by her husband. When asked, Laura stressed that Michael very much wanted children and could maybe pick up 30 percent of the child-care and 10 percent of the household responsibilities if she continued in her high-pressure career, "but his schedule is worse than mine, so he could not do more." Obviously Michael's decision to take on four years' extra training in order to become a neurosurgeon had not been influenced by child-raising considerations. Laura had not even considered that he might modify his career aspirations in order to help raise a child, and this was despite the fact that she earned considerably more than he did.

By the time Laura finished her story a rather somber mood had gathered in the room. Laura tried to lighten things up by saying rather jokingly to the pregnant woman sitting next to her, "All my views are in the realm of speculation. Debbie is really facing these problems and probably has come up with all kinds of solutions."

Debbie,* class of '80 and an associate editor at a top women's magazine, was six months pregnant. She tried to rise to the challenge that had been thrown her and said with some irony, "I wish I did have some solutions, but in many ways my options are

*Pseudonym.

387

more limited than Laura's. You see we face a Catch-twenty-two situation. Both John and I work in low-paying fields, so I need to earn money for us to survive. And I mean, survive. We rent a small apartment in Brooklyn, we don't own a car, yet we barely get by on our two salaries. Despite this need to earn money, which will become more acute when we have a child, it will be impossible for me to keep my job. My maternity benefits are far from good—four weeks of partially paid leave before the birth and four weeks afterward. But even if I could cope with so little time off, full-time high-quality child care would consume all my salary. So my solution (if you can call it that) is to leave my job after the birth of my child and become a free-lance writer. This way I can do a large part of the child care myself and continue to earn at least some money.

"But it's scary. I'm afraid of becoming isolated and unproductive—at home all day with a tiny child. And I'm afraid that John and I will lose the equality we have so carefully built up. If he begins to earn much more than I, it will obviously be difficult to maintain an equal division of household tasks, and I think I will become resentful if I end up with all the cooking and cleaning."

Debbie paused and then added reflectively, "You know, there are a lot of women on the creative, editorial side of the company [the Hearst organization, which owns several magazines including the one Debbie works for], but in management, upper management, I don't think there is one woman, and it is in management that the high salaries are. Even Helen Gurley Brown has no clout; she is not even on the board. All these women's magazines are supposedly setting up role models for women, but good role models don't exist at the source."

Debbie had one final comment: "This past summer I have been troubled by the fact that I could not work up much enthusiasm for Geraldine Ferraro. Somehow I felt guilty about not giving her more support. I think the problem is that her life has been so unreal. She took thirteen years off to have her children and then was able to jump back into the work force and get back on track as a lawyer and a politician. I guess I don't believe that you can do that unless you are married to a wealthy man and have great political connections. Most of us need to earn money in order to survive, and many of us are in competitive professions, where it just isn't possible to take a few years off to have a family, let alone thirteen years off. Ferraro talks a lot about her hard life, but she really hasn't faced the toughest issue—rearing children and building a career at one and the same time. I suppose that makes it hard for me to see her as a role model." Debbie stopped and said with a small smile, "But that won't stop me voting for the Mondale-Ferraro ticket. Reagan has been a disaster for women."

Role models—whether these women perceived them to be there, how appropriate they are—was another important theme of the evening. Kathryn,* twenty-five, class of '81, currently in her second year of law school, described the two most important role models in her life: "My mother is a typical fifties woman. She was well educated and worked before she was married yet chose to take eighteen years out of the labor force to rear three children. She is a practical, personable woman and has tremendous energy. During her years as a homemaker she was always involved in volunteer work in the community, frequently holding positions of considerable influence such as being president of the school board. As a child I remember her writing proposals, reports, and budgets, but I also remember that she was a regular mom. She was always there when I came home from school, and she baked bread, sewed Halloween costumes, took me to ballet lessons, and showed up at school events like all the other suburban mothers.

"In addition to bringing up us kids and doing all this community work, my mother was a corporation wife. She devoted huge amounts of energy to holding dinner parties, traveling to conferences, remembering people from the past, and in general keeping up the personal contacts so important to my father's business life.

"But in her middle years my mother has encountered difficulties. She went out and got a teaching job when my youngest sister left for college, but two years ago she was 'excessed' when the enrollment in our school district fell. She says that volunteer work no longer satisfies her, that she is now old enough to appreciate an

*Pseudonym.

income of her own and some professional status. She feels this especially acutely since we kids are gone and my father is at the peak of his career, with all kinds of invitations to be the guest of honor here and the featured speaker there.

"When I look at my mother's life and contemplate my own future, I am torn between contempt (did I say contempt? I am not sure I should use such a strong word!) for her lack of a career that transcended family life and admiration for her ability to do so many things well. I know that if I want to be a person with an exciting and challenging career, I can't be the person my mother was—someone who was always there for her children, who devoted much of her life to helping other people, who did not measure her time and energy in terms of paid work. But seeing her frustrated attempts to build a working life in her fifties, I think I will try not to sacrifice career for family in the extreme way she did."

Kathryn's alternative role model is Lauren Siegel*—a successful woman lawyer in her late thirties. Lauren is a friend of Kathryn's family and is also a former employer; Kathryn worked for her two summers ago. Kathryn sees Lauren Siegel as "a typical product of the 1970s. Just fifteen years older than me, she is a high-powered lawyer, a partner in a prestigious firm, and well respected by her colleagues. But her personal life is a shambles. She works tremendously long hours and is always traveling. She is divorced with a twelve-year-old son, who recently chose to move from her house to his father's. She clearly has had problems being a parent. Oftentimes she would call on my mother to help out; if her son were sick or alone in the afternoons, he would come to our house, where my mother would look after him. She also felt the pressure of raising a child alone—for example, creating appropriate after-school activities when she was hardly ever there. It seems to me she always expressed considerable relief when her son went off to camp for the summer.

"She has recently been seeing a divorced man who also has children, and their life together is almost a caricature of the modern dilemma. He has joint custody, and until recently she had full custody. They are continually balancing children's schedules with

*Pseudonym.

busy work schedules and never seem to have time alone. In any case, she always seems very wired up, somewhat tense, and often looks to my parents for advice and support. I can't say that I find her life-style very appealing; the money, status, and responsibility of her job don't seem worth the screwed-up family life she has, although I am well aware that one didn't necessarily cause the other.

"I would like to choose what I like from my mother's life and from Lauren's life and combine them. But I fear that these two goals—a high-powered career and a rich family life—conflict with each other. I worry a good deal about how to make these goals merge and become less of a fantasy and more of a reality."

When Kathryn finished, the room was full of glum faces. No one jumped in to reassure her or to say, "My mother has achieved both goals." One woman did mutter something to the effect that her mother had recently gone through a divorce at age fifty-five and was a really sad example of being ditched in middle age. However, she did not want to talk about her mother; perhaps it was too painful! She was eager to get back to discussing her life.

The topic I pushed hardest to talk about was the women's movement. It did not come up spontaneously, it seemed peripheral to these women's lives, yet I was interested in whether it had influenced these women, and if so, how.

Jackie,* age thirty-three, class of '75, was at Barnard during the time when a fairly militant brand of feminism was sweeping the campus. She tried to remember how it affected her.

"You know, back then I had a steady boyfriend and liked clothes and dances. I just didn't have anything in common with the women in the movement. All I saw was the dirty jeans, the hairy legs, and the lavender T-shirts, and all they saw was a young lady who shopped at Bonwit Teller's. I guess we just couldn't communicate. It's odd to think that despite appearances, we probably shared certain values. I have always felt as able and as capable as a man, and that's the kind of thing the movement has tried to promote.

"The thing that really turned me off was the tremendous hos-

*Pseudonym.

tility toward men, family, and children, as though you couldn't be a feminist unless you gave up all the good parts of being female. Remember all those weird groups like WITCH and SCUM and the time one of them tried to castrate Andy Warhol? I never did work out where all that anti-men sentiment came from."

Jane,* twenty-four, class of '82, jumped in eagerly, "It's a great pity the radicals have dominated the movement to the extent they have because it has alienated a lot of mainstream support. Just before I graduated from Barnard in May 1982, there was this huge uproar because the Women's Center had published a diary of sexual options open to women which featured some very graphic pictures of naked women. The diary was published just before Barnard's annual "The Scholar and the Feminist" conference, and the Helena Rubinstein Foundation withdrew its funding for this conference because of the controversy surrounding the diary. I remember being very fed up that the radical feminists had undermined the conference, which is a first-class event with national standing.

"Barnard tries to prepare women for being successful in the world, and I feel that the college really strengthened me in terms of skills and self-confidence. But somehow the women's movement on campus never seemed to address the concerns of us mainstream types; it was always off into some fringe issue. Why, in my senior year the Women's Center was more likely to run a talk on matriarchy in Finland than on parenting and careers." There were assenting smiles all around the room. Jane had obviously hit a nerve.

Laura offered this comment on the movement: "You know, when I was at Barnard, the activists at the Women's Center were mainly into sexual freedom and abortion rights. I remember that if you were having trouble deciding whether or not to have an abortion, or if you were trying to figure out which was the best place to have one, there was this hot line you could call for advice. I am sure that kind of help was very much needed. But now here I am facing the problems involved in trying to have a child and the movement couldn't be less interested; there is no feminist support

*Pseudonym.

network for women like me. It's time the movement concentrated on helping women have children." Laura paused for a moment and then said rather self-consciously, "I'm prochoice and all that, but now I'm approaching thirty. For me the right to have a child is more important than the right not to have one." Laura paused and then laughed ruefully. "One thing I will say for the movement: It helped raise the ambitions of women like me. Without this burning desire to have a career, to do something with our lives, none of us would be facing these crummy choices."

Kathryn volunteered one last thought on the movement: "One thing I often resent is the way women's liberation has increased the expectations of men. Last summer I worked for this big Washington law firm, and in August the firm threw a big party—an elaborate dinner dance at the Hay-Adams. I remember thinking that twenty years ago it would have been *de rigueur* for every young male lawyer in the firm to arrive with a drop-dead blonde on his arm. But last summer there was even greater cachet in turning up with a high-achieving woman. All those young male lawyers tried to adorn themselves with a doctor or, at the very least, another lawyer. The only catch was that these yuppie women had to look every bit as glamorous as the drop-dead blondes of the past. I found it depressing. It's as though men now expect women to be beautiful traditional women and hard-bitten professionals. I can't see how anyone does it over the long haul."

An important theme of the evening was the angst associated with being single and childless in your thirties (the condition of a quarter of the women in the room). Elizabeth,* class of '75, at thirty-two was one of the older women at the reunion. With her long blond hair and aristocratic good looks she has always reminded me of Meryl Streep. For the last several years Elizabeth has worked as a fund raiser for a large nonprofit organization. She lives in a house she owns in Old Greenwich, Connecticut.

"I have a pleasant life. I earn a good salary without having to work crazy hours. I have a five-minute commute to my office, and my work hours are eight-thirty A.M. to four-thirty P.M. In the

*Pseudonym.

393

summertime I get out of the office at three-fifteen P.M. on Fridays and can be on the tennis court at four. But my personal life is drying up. There are dozens of us single women in the suburbs, but most of the good men I know are married. The few who are divorced seem to be exclusively interested in twenty-year-old kids." Elizabeth paused and said with humor, "Some weekends the most I have to look forward to is working on my cellulite at the club!

"Last night I woke up in the middle of the night to go to the bathroom. As I padded around my empty house at two A.M. and thought about today's reunion, I wondered what I will do if I am alone and childless when I am forty-five. It gave me the shivers, imagining myself dealing with having missed out on children, knowing that I would never have a child. It would seem like such a chasm, such an unfillable gap in my life. I don't know how much of this need is social conditioning and how much is individual desire, but I do know that I will never see my life as being complete unless I have a child." Elizabeth thought for a while and then said pensively, "So many of my career choices have been conditioned by my wish to create good conditions for a family. You see, an important reason I took this job was that it had great hours and meant I could live in a house with a yard. I know it sounds a little weird, considering I am not even married."

Elizabeth looked over at Laura and Debbie and said rather apologetically, "Listening to you both describing your problems in reconciling career and children, I felt this great ground swell of jealousy. I would give anything to be dealing with that particular dilemma. I guess I will give myself another three years, and if I haven't found Mr. Right by then, I will consider having a child on my own."

The whole room was still as Elizabeth said these words. Her anguish was palpable, yet she was only thirty-two. Theoretically she had another ten years before this sense of loss need seem real. But the single women in the room could clearly relate to Elizabeth's feelings. Sonia* broke the silence. She is a contemporary of Elizabeth's, newly divorced and childless; she has recently been promoted to vice-president at a high-tech firm in Boston.

*Pseudonym.

"It's so sad that we feel such time pressure. It's as if women have to succeed on three fronts by the time they are thirty-five or else resign themselves to huge holes in their lives. If your career is not well developed by this point, you might as well give up since in most professions you have to be halfway up the ladder by your mid-thirties. But somehow or other you have to find the time and energy to pick up a husband and a child while you are in the throes of establishing a career, for both these projects become increasingly difficult as you move through your thirties. Men have much more flexibility, for time is on their side. If he wants to, a man can devote his twenties and thirties to his career and defer family until his forties, when he can still pick and choose from a whole selection of younger women. And a man in his fifties can still have children." Sonia paused and then said hesitantly, "In today's world men and women have roughly the same goals, but a woman has less time to put together what she needs and, I guess, runs a bigger chance of failure."

Sonia offered one last bleak comment. "You know I had an abortion four years ago, when I was twenty-eight. Jim and I had just gotten married, and I was in the middle of a very tough career change. It just wasn't a convenient time to have a child. You can't imagine how much I regret that decision."

Elizabeth looked as though she were on the brink of tears; she clearly could imagine how Sonia felt. She reached over and put her hand on Sonia's shoulder, offering some silent comfort.

Several of the women I contacted and interviewed could not attend the reunion because of geographical distance; they now lived in Atlanta, Los Angeles, Chicago, or Dallas. Many of them had moved to follow husbands or boyfriends. The special trials of relocation dominated the telephone calls, lunches, and dinners I had with my far-flung ex-students.

Paula,* class of '79, is now an editor in the publications department of a museum in Los Angeles. She earns $19,000 a year, which is less than what she earned two years ago, when she was the managing editor of a New York journal. She left this job in 1982 to follow her husband (then fiancé) when he joined a private

*Pseudonym.

law firm in Los Angeles. When Paula arrived on the West Coast she did not find a job for eight months, and her memories of this period are painful.

"I followed every lead there was in the West Coast publishing industry, but despite the fact that I had skills and experience, all anyone ever asked me was 'How is your typing?' It had a bad effect on my self-esteem, and even my relationship with Bob changed as I felt so much less attractive as a person. Some days it took an incredible amount of energy to get dressed and make myself beat on some more doors. Finally I got this job at the museum. It's low-level work—mostly copy editing—and I do not have nearly as much responsibility as I did in my last job, but I am thankful to be working." Paula thought for a while and then added, "You know I used to be ambitious, but the move and that period of unemployment have really shaken my confidence.

"The thing that really worries me is that there is now this huge economic gap between Bob and myself. In New York he was a law student with much less money to spend than I did. Now he earns four times as much as I do. I can see that over the last two years there have been all kinds of changes in who does what around the house. It used to be that he would do the laundry and shopping while I would cook and clean. Now we have a fairly conventional division of labor since his work takes up more of his time and is more 'important' than mine. And we don't even have children! Imagine how skewed things will become once there is a baby. Sometimes I wonder how a liberated seventies woman like myself ever got into such a traditional scene."

The loss of career opportunities and the loss of earning power were recurring themes in the conversations I had with ex-students who had followed their men to distant cities.

Dana,* class of '78, now lives in Chapel Hill, North Carolina. She moved there in 1981, when her husband accepted a tenured appointment at the University of North Carolina. Dana is a well-qualified woman. She obtained a master's degree from Northwestern University in 1980 and had just started a policy job at a prestigious private foundation in Chicago when she and her hus-

*Pseudonym.

band pulled up stakes and moved to Chapel Hill. As Dana put it, "There is nothing to do in Chapel Hill except teach, and I can't compete for the regular teaching jobs because I don't have a Ph.D. The chair of the political science department has promised me that I can teach one course next academic year. But do you know what that means? It means a few weeks of work and about three thousand dollars in pay. To think that I was earning thirty-two thousand dollars a year in Chicago!"

What did I learn from my Barnard reunion?

Most of the facts I uncovered are quite predictable. With the exception of Dana in North Carolina, all the women are either working or finishing graduate school. This is to be expected given the fact that none has a child and only half of them are married. The average salary for the working women in the group is $28,000. At first glance this seems low considering the qualifications and experience of these accomplished women. But women don't earn nearly as much as men in our economy, and $28,000 easily places them within the top 10 percent of all women workers.

Most of my other findings are also unsurprising. Remember Kathryn, the law student? Her failure to integrate the two role models in her life is commonplace since most women her age have inherited from the fifties and the seventies two contradictory models of what women should do. And it is also predictable that most of these women found little support in the women's movement for their family ambitions.

I was even prepared for the degree to which these women were obsessed with the problems of reconciling career and family life (a particularly striking fact since none of them has yet had a child). There is a lot of evidence in this book that supports the perception of these Barnard women that figuring out how to deal with their double burden might be the central problem of their adult life.

A recent study by the *Wall Street Journal* dramatizes the constraints imposed by the double burden and confirms the findings of my small and informal survey.[1] This study took a close look at 722 female executives, each of whom had the title of vice-president or higher and found:

As women move into corporate management they're finding it difficult to balance the competing demands of their private and professional lives. Married women, including many who earn more than their husbands, still find themselves doing most of the chores at home. [When there are children] only very few of the husbands—5 percent or less—assume chief responsibility for any duty involving children.

Single women worry that they're focusing on their jobs to the exclusion of all outside interests. One way or another, women executives feel that they have made substantial [personal] sacrifices to further their careers.

But perhaps the most significant finding of the *Wall Street Journal* survey was that 52 percent of these women executives are childless, compared with only 7 percent of their male contemporaries.[2]

Several recent studies have come up with the same result: Half or more of today's high-achieving women do not find it possible to have children. A 1983 survey by *Fortune* magazine of the women graduates of the Harvard Business School class of 1973 found that 54 percent had no children.[3] A 1982 report by the *Wall Street Journal* of 300 senior women executives found that 61 percent of these women were childless.[4] And a 1985 survey of executive women by Basia Hellwig of *Working Women* found that 61 percent of the women in the sample had no children.[5] In these studies the average age of the women ranges from late thirties on to mid-forties, indicating that most are nearing the end of their childbearing years.

It's a sad commentary on life in the fast track for today's women that so few of them find it possible to have children, or be married for that matter. Many fewer female than male executives are married. In its 1982 study the *Wall Street Journal* found that 48 percent of the women executives were married, compared with 96 percent of the men, while in the 1985 *Working Women* study 59 percent of the women executives were married, compared with 96 percent of their male colleagues.

Thus many high-achieving women do not have children because they are single or because they genuinely cannot figure out a way of combining child care with home management and high-pressure careers. Only 5 percent of the husbands surveyed by the *Wall Street Journal* pick up any significant responsibility for their children, and things are just as bad on the housework front. As Philip Blumstein and Pepper Schwartz find in *American Couples,* "married men's aversion to housework is so intense it can sour their relationship. The more housework they do, for whatever reason, the more they fight about it."[6] Despite all the talk about men being into nurturing and homemaking, modern men are failing most tests in these spheres. When a career woman has children, she most surely takes on a double burden.

Many career women end up alone and childless, but it is not because they want it this way. Like Elizabeth and Sonia, they are desperately anxious to find mates and to have children. Some are even prepared to have children on their own. In 1983, thousands of women underwent artificial insemination at private clinics in New York City.[7] In the same year hundreds of single women adopted children on their own. Most of these women were professionals in their late thirties who had given up on finding Mr. Right but could not reconcile themselves to childlessness. Like Elizabeth, they were fearful of the great chasm it would produce in their lives.

In her 1984 book *Sex and Destiny* Germaine Greer accuses modern society of being profoundly hostile to children.[8] She describes motherhood as being "virtually meaningless in our society"[9] and states categorically that "there are practically no good reasons left for exercising one's fertility."[10] She is partially right. Our work ethic and our public policies fail to support women in their struggle to bear and to rear children. It also seems to be true that most men do not give children a very high priority in their lives. But in one respect Greer is way off base. She accuses individual women of not wanting and of not liking children.[11] She is dead wrong. At the September 21 reunion at my house, if there was one note that rang loudly and clearly through the room, it was that modern women—no matter how ambitious—yearn to have children. They tie themselves into knots, trying to figure out how to do this, but despite desperate effort, the odds are that a high proportion of them will fail. Still, it will not be through lack of trying. Modern society in general and America in particular has put all kinds of barriers in the way of these women having children. Laura, the assistant vice-president at Citibank, was well ahead of the game. At age twenty-nine she had made significant progress in her career and had a solid marriage, yet as she contemplated having children, she was preparing herself for some major sacrifice. Like the women surveyed by the *Wall Street Journal* and *Fortune* magazine, the women at my reunion mostly look forward to a future of compromise.

Despite my knowledge that the experience of these Barnard women was a long way from being exceptional, it did not prevent me from being disappointed in what I found. Perhaps it's because I had shared the youthful aspirations of these women. I had been their confidante when they were eighteen and twenty, when they truly felt the world was at their feet. I remember Laura as a junior blithely telling me that of course, she would marry a man who would share housework fifty-fifty, otherwise, how could she realize her ambitions? I remember Elizabeth telling me on her commencement day that she was going to have three children and be a vice-president by the time she was thirty. Somehow I had harbored the thought that at least some of these hardworking, accomplished women would have been able to beat the system. But they were clearly not turning into superwomen, the sort featured in *Business Week and Forbes* magazine who handle with ease rich, multidimensional lives. Instead, these Barnard women were running into all the problems that have dominated my adult life and which permeate the pages of this book.

The mood of anxiety that possesses these young women is impressive. They feel they have so little time to negotiate the central tasks of their lives, and despite their youth, they feel close to failure. Psychologist Willard Gaylin put it very well when he wrote that "women approaching their mid-thirties feel enormous pressure converging on them from every quarter. They have so much to put together but not much time left to do it, it all must happen *now*."[12] They worry about their careers, staying in that fast lane; they worry about their biological clocks, bearing children before infertility problems mount up; and they worry about their mating clocks, for with each passing year the pool of available men shrinks. The truth is that their anxiety is well founded. We have not yet created a context that allows a woman to reasonably expect that she can have both a career and a family.

I am reminded of the writings of Charlotte Perkins Gilman, the nineteenth-century feminist. In 1897 she wrote, "We have so arranged life that a man may have a house, a family, love, companionship, domesticity and fatherhood, yet remain an active citizen of age and country. We have so arranged life, on the other hand, that a woman must 'choose'; she must either live alone, unloved, uncompanied, uncared for, homeless, childless, with her work in the world for sole consolation; or give up world service for the joys of love, motherhood and domestic service."[13]

Things have not changed very much. A century later women have more choices, but to use Laura's words, they are often "crummy choices."

My Barnard reunion serves to underline a major argument of this book: that women need more than equal treatment if they are to find fulfillment in both love and work. They need equal opportunities—in education and in the job market—but they also need a plethora of family support structures that range from job-protected maternity leave to subsidized day care and flextime. For whether they are in fact mothers or simply have the potential to be mothers, the lives of women are conditioned by and constrained by child-related responsibilities. As the rock star Madonna reminds us in so many of her songs: "Women aren't like men / They can do things that men can't do."[14] These differences produce burdens as well as opportunities.

In the 1970s it was thought that all you had to do was to break down the barriers so that women could fully participate in the mainstream of society. The spirit of the decade was to pretend that there were no differences between men and women. Well, the results are in. More women than ever before are working outside the home, and at least some of them have broken into the previously closed ranks of executives and professionals. But despite all of this "progressive" change, most women are in worse economic shape than their mothers were. They have lost the protections and guarantees of traditional marriage without improving their earning power in the marketplace.

The crux of the problem lies in the fact that *there have been no cultural or institutional changes in the way children are supposed to be raised*. Sooner or later almost every working mother in America has to face the hard truth: that she is either shortchanging her child or her career. In fact, many of us manage to do both, for the standards are hard to live up to. We are expected to raise our children according to the example set by the complete mothers of the 1950s, and we are also expected to clone the male competitive model in the workplace.

Author Elizabeth Janeway hit the nail on the head when she told a 1985 gathering of Barnard College alumnae: "Recently we've been hearing a lot about women 'having it all.' Myself, I think that is not really an accurate description of female lives today. It seems to me that what we have been up to is—DOING it all."[15] Doing it all does not turn most women into superheroes; it merely produces strain, stress—and low pay. For swimming in the mainstream and taking your chances don't produce equality if you are picking up 75 to 85 percent of all family responsibilities. Formal equality has to be supplemented by special support systems if women are to become equal participants in the world of work.

The Europeans got it right when they decided to push not only for equal rights in the sphere of work but also for social benefits to ease the family responsibilities of working women. Both are needed. As Warren Farrell pointed out in *The Liberated Man*, "Liberation will mean little for men or women if women enter men's world on men's terms."[16]

The problems of contemporary American women are not the result of some massive or inevitable conflict between work and family life. Rather, they result because the United States does less than any other advanced country to make life easier for working mothers. We have less maternity leave, less subsidized child care, less job flexibility. And partly due to this deficit in our public policies, women in America earn less, proportionately, than their counterparts in other nations.

This is not to argue that supportive social policies would solve the problems of all women. Better benefits and services for working mothers would still not resolve the deeper issue of how anyone—man or woman—with family responsibilities can compete in the most competitive fields, "where workaholics with virtually no private lives often set the pace."[17] If you want to be a chief executive officer you should probably think twice about having children. But this issue should not be confused with the concrete, practical problems most working women face. Most careers are not in the fast lane. Only 7 out of every 100 employed women work in the elite professions, and even within this small group, most do not need to put in a sixty-hour week in order to fulfill their responsibilities. The great majority of all jobs could be combined quite satisfactorily with child rearing if more supportive policies were adopted in the workplace and in the country at large. If Debbie had access to generous maternity leave, subsidized child care, and flextime, her problems would be greatly eased.

Which brings me back full circle. The impetus to write this book came from my own experience, prompted by the difficulties and frustrations I encountered when attempting to bear two children mid-career. Why should it be so hard? I wondered. Now I know. It shouldn't.

Afterword

A Lesser Life was published in hardcover in March 1986. It received massive attention from both the elite and the popular media and provoked a series of fierce debates. One of the first reactions came from the women's movement. In the main, feminists were feisty, riled up and hopping mad.

Robin Morgan opened the offensive in a March issue of *Ms.* magazine. In it she described my book as an exercise in "tediously familiar right-wing anti-feminism" and accused me of "blaming the victim" because I point out the feminist organizations have neglected to support motherhood.[1] Eleanor Smeal (president of NOW, the National Organization for Women) dismissed my analysis as being "very uniformed" and full of "cheap shots at the movement,"[2] while Betty Friedan joined the bandwagon in a March issue of *Time* magazine and dubbed *A Lesser Life* a "deceptive backlash book."[3] Surprisingly enough, the leaderhip of NOW felt so threatened by *A Lesser Life* that in April 1986, Kathy Bonk—NOW's media director—attempted to organize a boycott of the public relations firm that handled publicity for my book.

I did have some feminist defenders. Erica Jong in *Vanity Fair* wrote that my book was the kind of work that "could start a revolution. It could stoke up the still-smoldering coals of a women's movement that has gone cold in the last few years for lack of young leadership and new focus." In her eyes "it could serve as blueprint for a new era of feminist activism."[4]

Elinor Guggenheimer (president of the Child Care Action Campaign), in a letter published by the *New York Times,* supported one of my basic contentions: that none of the feminist organizations has ever given meaningful support to children: "The women's movement has given short shrift to child care. To date I know of no conference held by a woman's advocacy group where a major address on child care has been given, nor of any feminist publication whose major focus has been on child care."[5]

In the heat and energy of this debate no one contested my central finding—that modern American women are in poor economic shape. The data are dramatic:

• Two out of every three adults in poverty in America are women.

• One quarter of all women earn less than the poverty level when working full-time.

• In 1985 American women earned 64 percent of the male wage, up only one cent since 1939.

And, a real shocker:

• Women in the U.S. are worse off than their West European sisters.

Despite hostility from the elite ranks of the women's movement, the reaction to *A Lesser Life* from the heartland of America was overwhelmingly positive. Ordinary women in the mainstream of society connected strongly and passionately with the themes and voices of my book.

Over the course of three months in the spring of 1986 I was part of a snowballing media tour. On TV and radio talk shows (all 110 of them!), in book-signing sessions in shopping malls, in hundreds of letters written in response to my book, I heard directly from the women of this vast country. They know what the score is.

For a lucky few the 1970s did bring new freedoms in the marketplace. Barriers fell and young liberated women beat a noisy path into the male worlds of medicine, law and corporate management. But most women were left behind to cope with a deteriorating economic and social reality. The economic reality is that women still earn very little on their own, and the social reality is that contemporary women are more likely to be on their own. Too many married women are just a man away from poverty.

The women who called in on the talk shows, who sat in the TV audiences, and who read articles about my book in *Family Circle* and *People* magazine understood these facts. All over the country—in Cleveland, Phoenix and Oakland—working moms, divorcees and widows told the same tale. It is almost impossible to raise a family and earn a decent living in liberated America. Despite all the new opportunities, in their gut, these women feel immensely vulnerable.

Mothers of young children responded with particular passion to the themes of *A Lesser Life*. Anne Eggebroten of Newport Beach, California, shared her reaction in a letter:

> I cry as I read Chapter Two of *A Lesser Life*. I cry for your anguish and my own. You see I never thought I would fail in my ambitions. In eighth grade I wanted to become a geologist. In high school I dreamt of being a writer. I spent the next nine years in pursuit of degrees in medieval English and in 1979 I began my first college teaching job. It only lasted a year as a full-time position. My first child was born and I couldn't find affordable child care so I cut back to spend time with Ros. Once Ellen was born I took a whole semester off. It was risky, but there was no maternity leave policy where I worked and I knew there was no way I could return to teaching immediately after birth with a newborn and a toddler to look after. As it turned out, postpartum exhaustion plus germs from nursery school triggered a long bout of illness. I asked for another semester of unpaid leave and was fired. I am now an unemployed Ph.D. frankly too tired to hit the job market again until my children are much older. Will there be a job slot for me when I am forty years old? I doubt it. In this profession it is almost impossible to get back on the train once you have gotten off.
>
> Carrying a heavy, sick baby up and down the room to put her back to sleep, trying to avoid the clutter of unsorted laundry and leftover food, I understand the trapped feeling that so many homemakers have had—even as they enjoy those baby smiles. I cannot even type this letter but have to

write it out in longhand because my sleepy infant wakes at the sound of my typewriter.

Although I grew up assuming that I would not waste my time on such a menial occupation as child care, I now have new respect for women who devote their time to raising children. I see both the difficulty and the value of surrounding small people with stimulation, safety, patience and support. It is a pity that mothering has been so devalued in our society.

Cynthia Wall of Salt Lake City spoke to me on a morning talk show; like Annie, Cynthia felt strung between motherhood and marketplace.

For years I ruminated over the same issues you have raised in your book and yet I never found another soul who understood the conflict I felt between work and family.

I am a mother of two boys, ages three and six. I have a B.A. in journalism, but have not used it well—I chose to squeeze working in between having children, as opposed to the other way around. Boy have I taken it in the shorts career-wise! Last year my earnings from my "writing career" totalled $620. I operate out of my bedroom and can only work seriously when Tommy naps. If my husband were ever to walk out I couldn't begin to support my kids; it worries me a lot.

Some of the most poignant letters came from women suffering the economic fallout of divorce.

Jacquelyn Porter of Owensboro, Kansas, has a typical story:

I am living *A Lesser Life* and thousands of other women can echo my plight. Until recently my family was living the great American dream: Dad, Mom, three kids, nice house, two cars, even a dog. Then, as of January 13, 1986, I became a statistic—a white, middle-aged, divorced female with a job earning

$10,750 a year (which as you know is below the poverty line). I was one of those foolish women who put all her faith and trust in the man of her dreams. He has already remarried.

The court awarded me $100 a week maintenance for five years and $50 a week child support. A paltry reward for nineteen years of being a loving wife and homemaker! I was totally unprepared for these economic difficulties; they make the emotional trauma pale in comparison.

Donna Andersen of New York City has also gone through a divorce and knows the scene—too well:

I am part of the middle-aged or midlife generation of women. Most of my friends are divorced and have raised children quite alone. Many of us are former wives of professional men who pleaded poverty when it came time to support us in our struggles to get back on our feet; oftentimes they even refused to contribute to the education of their children. Somehow we made it. Many of us held down two jobs while the children were young trying to make ends meet. We even found time to go back to school part-time, to continue that education we gave up in the 1950s and 1960s to put our husbands through college.

Between education (it took me a mere eighteen years to get a B.A. degree!), cooking, cleaning, child care, work at menial jobs that led nowhere and the like, we scraped through, kept up the house payments, the insurance, the Cub Scouts, the dance lessons, etc. It wasn't easy but we did it.

Now with our children educated and grown, many of us have our B.A. degrees but to what avail? Our strange work histories do not fit us for on-track positions in the real world. "Such an interesting work background" mumbles a prospective employer, and then proceeds to fill the position with a raw twenty-three-year-old with tight smooth skin and perky breasts. Most agencies see us as "over-the-hill" and "difficult-to-place."

So we take temporary work, pay our own health insurance (or, more often, have none), and generally do something else on the side, hoping that we don't have to make the choice about whether this month we eat or pay the rent!

These poignant stories from California, Utah, Kansas and New York City share one critical characteristic. One way or another these women have been derailed by motherhood.

In *A Lesser Life* I show that the most urgent problem facing modern American women is reconciling the demands of childbirth and childrearing with those of earning a living. For modern mothers conditions are onerous and getting worse. Consider the following facts:

• 60 percent of working women have no right to job-protected maternity leave. And yet these days women do not work for pin money; they need to hang on to their jobs to buy the groceries and pay the rent.

• half of babies under one year of age have mothers in the workplace, but perversely, Federal funds for day care assistance have been cut by a quarter since 1980.

• half of all divorced men neither see nor support their children in the wake of divorce.

The plain fact is American mothers run huge economic risk. In the labor market, pregnant workers are routinely fired; others are defined as "new hires" when they come back to work after childbirth and lose seniority rights; and large numbers of new mothers fail to find affordable child care and are forced to take a third-rate job with short hours close to home. Overall, working women lose a fifth of their earning power in the two years following childbirth.

In the home, mothers also face significant risks as women who choose to stay at home with their children are faced with a 50 percent divorce rate and the prospect of picking up the physical and financial load of single motherhood in a world without alimony or significant child support.

To date the American women's movement has given little attention to issues of motherhood and children—which is why so many feminists were defensive in their reaction to my book. For the early leaders of the movement "family" was part of the problem, not part of the solution. In the late 1960s and early 1970s feminists were trying to escape the boundaries of traditional domestic roles which had become particularly confining in Norman Rockwell "fifties" America. The focus of the struggle was to win formal equality of rights between the sexes—to get out there and clone the male competitive model.

Many of the battles fought in the 1970s were important. American feminists did manage to open up the labor market and women gained new access to jobs, education and credit. But when we were out there in the trenches dressing for success in our business suits and little string ties, we tended to forget that 90 percent of women choose to have children, and that women would remain seriously handicapped in the workplace unless we established a new system of family supports.

In her *Vanity Fair* review article Erica Jong describes her own brush with feminist reactions to motherhood:

> One of my own bitterest memories of being an American-style superwoman feminist trying to have it all goes back to the fall of 1978, when my daughter was just four months old...I had been invited to read my poems at a women's poetry festival at the Palace of Fine Arts in San Francisco, and though I had not done any public speaking since Molly was born, I felt that this was the perfect time to come out into the world again.
>
> During my pregnancy I had composed a sequence of poems about the experience and I thought the poetry festival would be an appropriate place to share them....

Imagine my dismay when I was virtually booed off the stage by a feminist audience of the lesbian-separatist variety for reading a series of poems that celebrated pregnancy and birth while affirming a woman's strength and power. The poems in no way idealized pregnancy, but you couldn't prove it by an audience of women in rebellion against fifties notions of happy motherhood. To say anything positive about motherhood was to push every one of their emotional buttons. I left the stage devastated and confused. Clearly, I had been expected to toe the feminist party line, which in that atmosphere was feverishly anti-male and anti-nuclear-family, and I had dared to celebrate motherhood instead.

This experience plunged me into one of the deepest depressions of my life.... Never had I felt so betrayed by my own sex, or so fervently wished I had stayed home with the baby. It is unpleasant but predictable to be put down by male chauvinists, but when feminists attack at such a vulnerable time as new motherhood, the experience is devastating.[6]

There is no doubt in my mind that American feminism has had a strongly anti-child bias. True, there have been babies on the cover of *Ms.* magazine, and such feminists as Letty Pogrebin and Phyllis Chesler have written passionately about mothers and children. But the overall thrust of the movement in America has been to stress equal rights for both sexes and to pretend that men and women are identical.

Women can function successfully as male clones in the marketplace only if they never have children, and to demand this of most women is to thwart their deepest biological need. (This attitude also ensures that if women do have children, many of them will be doomed to poverty and exhaustion.) A movement that looks away from the central fact of most women's lives—motherhood—will never win widespread support.

A second, and in many ways more important, round of reaction to *A Lesser Life* came from the Democratic Party.

By the beginning of 1986 it was obvious to party leaders that the whole territory of family policy had been taken over by conservative Republicans. During the 1980s even the phrase "pro-family" had become a right-wing slogan. It was time the liberal establishment laid claim to this critical policy arena.

I have been involved in this effort. Since my book came out eight months ago Senator Moynihan, Governor Cuomo and representative Oakar have sought my counsel. How can Democrats best address the needs of families? Governor Bruce Babbitt (Arizona) asked me to serve on a fourteen-member national "Project on the Welfare of Families"; representative Pat Schroeder (Colorado) invited me to testify in Congress on the Parental and Medical Leave Bill of 1986; and I have given a keynote address at the Woman's National Democratic Club in Washington.

Modern-day liberals find my analysis convincing and my policy agenda useful because they are grounded in economic reality. As the *Washington Post* described the family policy package contained in *A Lesser Life:* This is "not a wish list from working mothers. Far from it. It is a hard-nosed analysis of what is needed to improve the productivity and economic well-being of the current work force and what steps can be taken now to ensure the stability of the future work force." The *Post* wrote that I put forth the most convincing argument for my recommendations: "in the long and the short run they are cost effective."[7] In an era of budget cutting and limited social conscience this is the best kind of rationale for any new policy initiative.

In September 1986 the Democratic National Committee under the chairmanship of Paul Kirk released a statement of Democratic Party principles entitled "New Choices for a Changing America." This document is designed to create a new image for the party in preparation for the 1988 presidential campaign. The first two principles could have been taken directly from *A Lesser Life.* No. 1 priority "Stronger families" features tax exemptions for children and expanded child-care credits. No. 2 priority "Flexible work places" includes parenting leave, expanded child-care choices and the creation of greater flexibility for working parents.[8]

I am proud to be part of this effort by the Democratic Party to make American family life stronger and more secure. Nothing is more important for the well-being of women and children in our society.

In some ways, family support policy is a natural for Democrats. Liberals are able to design programs that address the needs of working parents, children in poverty and displaced homemakers in a way that is impossible for conservatives committed to minimal government and free markets. The fact is there has been a lot of conservative pro-family rhetoric coming down the pike in recent years but very little has actually been done to make American family life more viable. The Reagan administration may be pro-life but it certainly isn't pro-child. Since 1980 an additional 3 million children have slithered into poverty and by mid-1986 a quarter of all American children were growing up below the poverty line. Barney Frank (Democrat, Massachusetts) summed up administration attitudes when he said Ronald Reagan seems to believe that "life begins at conception and ends at birth."[9]

Quite aside from powerful substantive reasons, Democrats should pay more attention to family policy because it will win them votes. Family problems are no longer the prerogative of the ghetto but reach deep into the mainstream of our society. Dealing with the economic fallout of divorce, insuring a better start in life for the children of working parents—these are among the central problems of our age because for the first time they involve the majority of Americans. More than half of all families are now "dual paycheck" families, and millions of working parents are hanging on by their fingernails barely coping as the demands of small children and paid employment clash and collide.

In June I was on a radio talk show in Phoenix and a young father called in. Jim Kasten wanted to share a painful problem:

> I have a three-week-old baby daughter who is in a day care center nine hours a day because neither myself nor my wife has the right to job-protected

maternity or paternity leave. The strain and stress of this situation is unbearable. We both feel so badly for Jennifer and are scared that she will fail to bond with us properly and have big emotional problems later on in life. But we also feel badly for us. Julie— my wife—is dog-tired and aches to be with the baby. I feel frustrated and bitter that I am missing out on the beginnings of Jennifer's life.

Jim's voice rose in anger:

But what kind of choice did we have? I was out of work for a while last year and my present job is much too insecure to allow Julie to risk losing hers. Parents in this country sure get a bum rap. We don't even have the right to spend a few weeks with a new baby.

On my book tour a third of the call-ins on the radio shows were from men, many of them fathers with working wives desperately in need of the kinds of family supports I describe in *A Lesser Life*. My book prompted working parents of both sexes to come out of the closet with a sigh of relief. Finally somebody was recognizing their problems and telling them that the demands of family should have more legitimacy in our workplaces and in our government. One thing seems sure, if the Democratic Party chooses to design a thoroughgoing package of family supports they will be applauded by the hard-pressed families of America.

Some of the most heart-rending of the letters I received in response to *A Lesser Life* demonstrate the extreme fragility of our family structures. Kathleen Swaney of Whittier, California, has dealt with some of the standard problems:

I am thirty-five years old, the oldest of eleven children in a working class family. In the late sixties I went to UC Berkeley and earned a B.S. in Mineral

Engineering. I was the only woman in my major at that time and after graduating obtained a good job in Houston, Texas. During my first year on the job I unexpectedly got pregnant, and had a daughter as a single mother. This triggered major trauma and expense. I got another job shortly after the baby was born, this time in Southern California. I even took the baby to the job interview.

On my second job I met my husband. We got married a year after we met, and soon after decided to have a baby together. When the new baby was a few weeks old I was let go; the company was cutting back and since my pregnancy leave was not job protected I was one of the first to be fired.

I couldn't find another job. The mining industry was so depressed and I was tied down with family. The awful thing was that I was our family's sole breadwinner. My husband had gone back to college after our marriage in order to get his B.S. degree, so that he could get a decent job.

Things got real rough. My husband stayed in school because after a three-month search he couldn't find a regular-paying job. The children and I moved into my mother's house for seven months. I was pregnant again expecting my third child. My husband was 400 miles away living with his parents.

A couple of months before the baby was due we moved into my in-laws' house with my husband. We were real crowded but happy to be together again.

After the birth my husband found a part-time job which paid $400 a month. We applied for student financial aid from the state and the Federal government. We applied for Medicaid and food stamps. We spent so many hours on the paperwork and in the end were turned down for all these benefits. My husband couldn't get student aid because we were living with his parents and they had some savings for retirement. The welfare people turned us down because my husband was a student.

So, we've been limping along. Hopefully, by this time next year my husband will have a full-time job, and we will be able to rent a place of our own. Meanwhile we are very poor. I have to go twice a week to stand in the breadline to get a little free food to supplement our inadequate food budget. I spend hours and hours taking the children to Los Angeles County medical clinics for their checkups.

Since we can't afford nursery school, I have the three children at home all the time. I have no social life. My career is ruined. I'm down in the dumps most of the time, which means I overeat and am fifty pounds heavier than I was when I got married.

In the future I hope to work and to develop new friends—but it's going to be a tough struggle, real tough. My days of dreaming big are over. I'm hoping we can make some progress as a society, though, so things won't be so tough for my daughters. I'm still a little optimistic.

Such a brave letter. The thought occurs to me that Kathleen's story, despite its pathos, is not one of the worst cases. Kathleen is, after all, white, educated and married and yet hers is surely *A Lesser Life*. The problems of out-of-wedlock birth, the absence of job-protected parenting leave and the lack of affordable day care and nursery schools penetrate deep into the mainstream of our society. We simply have to do much more to make American family life stronger and more secure.

—Sylvia Ann Hewlett
November 1986

Notes

1: Introduction

1. Alexis de Tocqueville, *Democracy in America* (New York: Vintage Books, 1945), vol. II, 224.

2. *UN Demographic Yearbook 1981* (New York: UN Department of International and Social Affairs, Statistical Office, 1983), 461–63. See discussion in Chapter Three.

3. Lenore J. Weitzman, "The Economics of Divorce: Social and Economic Consequences of Property, Alimony and Child Support Awards," *UCLA Law Review* 28 (August 1981), 1181–1268. Much of Weitzman's research quoted in this book is collected together in Lenore J. Weitzman, *The Divorce Revolution: The Unexpected Social and Economic Consequences for Women and Children in America* (New York: The Free Press, 1985).

4. Joyce Everett, "Patterns and Implications of Child Support and Enforcement Practices for Children's Well-Being," Wellesley College Center for Research on Women, Working Paper No. 128 (1984), 2. See also Weitzman, op. cit., 1253.

5. Figure obtained in interview with Maria Morales, Bureau of the Census, Department of Commerce, Washington, D.C., January 4, 1985.

6. *Money, Income and Poverty Status of Families and Persons in the US: 1984,* Current Population Reports, Series P-60 (Washington, D.C.: Bureau of the Census, August 1985), 17.

7. *UN Demographic Yearbook 1981,* op. cit., 461–63.

8. *Eurostat,* "Hourly Earnings—Hours of Work," various issues (Luxembourg: Statistical Office of the European Community). See discussion in Chapter Four.

9. For example, in Europe the minimum paid maternity leave is fourteen weeks; the most common paid leave granted is five months. In addition, most European countries provide at least one year of unpaid but job-protected leave, and all European countries have some form of national health insurance to cover the costs of prenatal and postnatal care. See Sheila B. Kamerman and Alfred J. Kahn, "Company Maternity-Leave Policies: The Big Picture," *Working Women* (February 1984), 80.

10. The main source of maternity leave and benefits in the United States is disability insurance. The Federal Pregnancy Discrimination Amendment of 1978 requires that all employers who have disability

plans must treat pregnancy as they would any other disability. However, since only five states (New York, New Jersey, Hawaii, California, and Rhode Island) require private employers to provide disability coverage, the majority of pregnant working women in the United States are not covered by disability. See Sheila B. Kamerman, Alfred J. Kahn, and Paul Kingston, *Maternity Policies and Working Women* (New York: Columbia University Press, 1983), 97.

11. The great majority of American women are mothers by the end of their childbearing years. In 1980 only 6 percent of ever-married women (94 percent of all women) aged forty to forty-four remained childless. Of the 6 percent of women who never married, at least some had children out of wedlock. Thus the Bureau of the Census estimates that 90 percent of the generation of women who were forty to forty-four years of age in 1980 bore at least one child. See *American Women: Three Decades of Change* (Washington, D.C.: Bureau of the Census, August 1983), 4–5.

12. *Wall Street Journal*, September 7, 1983.

13. Ibid.

2: A Personal View

1. Burton L. White, *The First Three Years of Life* (New York: Avon Books, 1975), 134.

2. Dr. Benjamin Spock, *Baby and Child Care*, 2d ed. (New York: Simon & Schuster, 1967), 570. This was the edition of Spock I used when Lisa was a baby. A subsequent edition of the book was kinder to working mothers, but even in the later edition Spock still argues that the best caretakers in the first three years of life are the parents. Group care is not considered a good alternative until the child is at least three years old. See Dr. Benjamin Spock, *Baby and Child Care*, 3d ed. (New York: Pocket Books, 1976).

3. T. Berry Brazelton, *Infants and Mothers: Differences in Development* (New York: Delacorte Press, 1969), 164.

4. White, op. cit., 148.

5. Ibid., 70.

6. Ibid., 71.

7. Ibid., 73.

8. Rudolph Schaffer, *Mothering* (Cambridge, Mass.: Harvard University Press, 1974), 69.

9. Ibid.

Notes

10. See (1) a *Fortune* magazine survey of women in the Harvard Business School class of 1973: In 1983, 60 percent of these women were married and 46 percent had children; the average age of these women was thirty-seven (*Fortune* [July 11, 1983], 58). See (2) the *Wall Street Journal* report on a survey of 300 senior women executives in the 1,000 largest U.S. industrial companies: "52% of women surveyed are single, compared with only 4% of the men. In addition, 61% of the women are childless, while 97% of the men were parents"; the average age of the women in this survey was forty-six, and most of them were vice-presidents (*Wall Street Journal*, February 11, 1982). See (3) *Male/Female Careers: MBAs a Decade into Their Careers*, by Mary Anne Devanna, which comprises a sample of several hundred M.B.A.'s who received their degrees from Columbia University in the period 1969–72: "73% of men in the sample are married as opposed to 58% of women.... Less than 10% of the married men have no children, 22% of the married women are childless." In short, close to 70 percent of the female executives in this sample are childless. See also (4) Basia Hellwig, "The Breakthrough Generation: 73 Women Ready to Run Corporate America," *Working Women* (April 1985), 98–146. Hellwig finds that 61 percent of the women in this sample have no children.

11. Interview, January 6, 1984.

12. Infertility is normally defined as the inability to conceive after a year of intercourse without contraception. Under this definition 14 percent of married couples aged fifteen to forty-four are infertile. The rate for older couples, aged thirty to forty-four, is more than twice that for younger couples fifteen to twenty-nine. See William F. Pratt, William D. Mosher, Christine A. Bachrach, and Marjorie C. Horn, "Understanding U.S. Fertility," *Population Bulletin*, 39 (December 1984), 28.

13. *Children's Defense Budget* (Washington, D.C.: Children's Defense Fund, 1985), 40.

14. At Columbia University the situation in the fall of 1984 was the following: Of the nontenured faculty 28.1 percent were women while only 8.7 percent of the tenured faculty were women (interview, Caroline Sperberg, Columbia University, September 28, 1984).

15. At one point in our negotiations the lawyer acting for the Barnard administration suggested that the 1978 Pregnancy Disability Amendment solved the problem since pregnant women were eligible for the same benefits as persons with other physical disabilities. Our committee did not agree. For starters, no one was taking disability for childbirth (the senior faculty and the administration discouraged it). And even if disability was to become a reality, it covered only a few weeks of

partially paid leave around childbirth. We felt strongly that we needed to have lighter work loads for the first year of a child's life and the possibility of stopping the tenure clock for this period. Only then would mothers (or parents for that matter) have a reasonable shot at promotion. See discussion of the Pregnancy Disability Amendment in Chapter Four.

16. Betty Friedan, *The Feminine Mystique* (New York: Dell, 1963), 237.

17. The classic books on the subject are Fernand Lamaze, *Painless Childbirth* (New York: Pocket Books, 1965); Frederick Leboyer, *Birth Without Violence* (New York: Alfred A. Knopf, 1975); and Grantly Dick Read, *Childbirth Without Fear* (New York: Harper, 1953). It is interesting to note that all the founders of this movement were men and therefore couldn't possibly have known whether childbirth hurt or not.

18. Barbara Grizzuti Harrison, "Men Don't Know Nuthin 'Bout Birthin Babies," *Esquire* (July 1972), 109.

19. Robert A. Bradley, *Husband-Coached Childbirth* (New York: Harper & Row, 1965), 168.

20. Ibid.

21. Ibid., 18.

22. Ibid., 19.

23. Ibid., 20.

24. Genesis 3:16.

25. Edward Shorter, *A History of Women's Bodies* (New York: Basic Books, 1982), chap. 5 and 9.

26. Ibid., 59.

27. Franz Boas, *Kwakiutl Ethnography* (Chicago: University of Chicago Press, 1966), 361.

28. Margaret Mead, *Growing Up in New Guinea* (New York: Blue Ribbon Books, 1930), 322. In some other primitive societies—e.g., among the Mundagumor—women are abused for becoming pregnant (see Margaret Mead, *Sex and Temperament in Three Primitive Societies* [New York: William Morrow, 1935], 189). In others they are forced to practice infanticide (see Yolanda Murphy and Robert F. Murphy, *Women of the Forest* [New York: Columbia University Press, 1974], 165–66).

29. Karen Pryor, *Nursing Your Baby* (New York: Harper & Row, 1973), 8.

30. Ibid., 9.

31. Ibid., 233–34.

32. Interview with Sheila Kamerman, March 27, 1985.

33. Sheila B. Kamerman, Alfred J. Kahn, and Paul Kingston, *Ma-*

ternity Policies and Working Women (New York: Columbia University Press, 1983), 75.

34. It is instructive to note that most women either fail to breast-feed or choose not to breast-feed for any length of time. One survey found that while 51 percent of infants were breast-fed immediately after birth, numbers dropped dramatically after they were taken home from hospital; at six weeks only 4 percent of babies were being exclusively breast-fed (See Penelope Leach, *Babyhood* [New York: Alfred A. Knopf, 1983], 22–23.)

35. Interview, November 10, 1983.

36. Marvin S. Eiger and Sally Wendkos Olds, *The Complete Book of Breastfeeding* (New York: Workman Publishing Co., 1972), 174–75.

37. Ibid., 112.

38. "Report of the Dean of Barnard College," *Columbia University Bulletin of Information,* 33d series, no. 1 (October 1, 1932), 6.

39. Ibid., 7.

40. Ibid.

41. Interview, senior member of Barnard faculty, September 28, 1984.

42. See discussion in *Columbia Spectator* (November 13, 1984), 1.

43. Reported in the *New York Times,* February 6, 1984.

44. Interview with Betty Vetter, executive director, Scientific Manpower Commission, Washington, D.C., February 8, 1985.

45. This approximates the gap in salaries in the country at large. In 1983–84 female full professors earned, on average, $33,730 a year while male full professors earned $37,860 a year (*Academe* [July–August 1984], 12).

3: The Economic Fallout of Divorce

1. *Monthly Labor Review* (December 1983), 18. This increase in the rate of divorce was across the board, affecting long-standing as well as new marriages. For example, by the late 1970s, 25 percent of marriages fifteen years or more in duration ended in divorce; the rate in the 1950s was 4 percent.

2. *New York Times,* October 4, 1984.

3. Interview, December 3, 1983.

4. In the mid-seventies, as the divorce rate rose steeply, the number of displaced homemakers increased to such an extent that their predicament finally began to penetrate the public consciousness. National mag-

azines (*McCall's, New York,* and *Time*) ran poignant articles, and several centers to help displaced homemakers appeared around the country. Most of these centers were started and staffed by displaced homemakers themselves. "Don't agonize, organize" was their motto. They concentrated on career counseling and training, and had considerable success in preparing women for modest jobs in the labor market. However, the centers were able to reach only a tiny fraction of the women who needed help. In the late seventies the federal government finally stepped in with funding for an umbrella organization, the Displaced Homemakers Network, which for a short time provided assistance to centers around the country. Unfortunately the network was a casualty of the Reagan budget cuts and in 1983 was drastically reduced in its scope. Although there are more displaced homemakers than ever, less is being done for them.

5. Erica Abeel, "School for Ex-Wives," *New York* (October 16, 1978), 97.

6. *What Happens When Homemakers Lose Their Jobs* (Washington, D.C.: Displaced Homemakers Network, Inc., November 15, 1983).

7. Quoted in Lenore J. Weitzman and Ruth B. Dixon, "The Alimony Myth: Does No Fault Divorce Make a Difference?," *Family Law Quarterly* XIV (Fall 1980), 143.

8. G. B. Trudeau, *San Francisco Chronicle,* January 18, 1976.

9. Weitzman and Dixon, op. cit., 143. On the national level only 14 percent of the divorced wives in a 1975 national poll said they were awarded alimony.

10. Ibid., 144 (1977 figures).

11. Ibid., 161–62.

12. Ibid., 158.

13. Quoted in the *Wall Street Journal,* January 21, 1985.

14. Weitzman and Dixon, op. cit., 154–55. The percentage of women awarded monthly payments dropped from 19 to 13 percent between 1968 and 1972.

15. Ibid., 163.

16. Quoted in the *Wall Street Journal,* January 21, 1985.

17. Ibid., 18.

18. Katherine Bouton, "Women and Divorce," *New York* (October 8, 1984), 36. This magazine exposé of the effects of the equitable-distribution law on women provoked a flurry of letters to the editor. That written by Ronna Brock Youdelman of Northport, New York, was typical: "Thank you Katherine Bouton. 'Women and Divorce' touched me most painfully. My attempts to be free of a 23-year marriage were portrayed poignantly in each of your vignettes. The good *intentions* of the 1980 di-

vorce law need to be replaced by good *laws.*" *New York* (October 29, 1984), 6. More recently, the bar associations have decided that the equitable distribution laws are unfair to women and should be substantially revised. *New York Times,* August 5, 1985.

19. Bouton, op. cit. 35.

20. Interview, October 10, 1984.

21. Forty-two percent of divorcing women are awarded some property, but the 1979 mean value of such property was only $4,650 (see the First-Year Report of the New Jersey Supreme Court Task Force on *Women in the Courts* [June 1984], 80).

22. Interview, September 25, 1984.

23. New Jersey Task Force, op. cit., 80.

24. Ibid., 99.

25. Ibid., 99.

26. Lenore J. Weitzman, "The Economics of Divorce: Social and Economic Consequences of Property, Alimony and Child Support Awards," *UCLA Law Review* 28 (August 1981), 1254.

27. Weitzman and Dixon, op. cit., 143.

28. Ibid.

29. Interview, September 25, 1984.

30. Weitzman and Dixon, op. cit., 182.

31. *Globe* (May 29, 1984).

32. Interview, November 29, 1983.

33. *Reducing Poverty Among Children* (Washington, D.C.: Congressional Budget Office, May 1985), 6.

34. Joyce Everett, "Patterns and Implications of Child Support and Enforcement Practices for Children's Well-Being," Wellesley College Center for Research on Women, Working Paper No. 128 (1984), 2. Weitzman reports similar data: "only half of the women who were awarded child support received it as ordered, about a quarter received less than the full amount, while another quarter never received a single payment" (Weitzman, "The Economics of Divorce," loc. cit., 1253). Weitzman warns that these data which are for one year after divorce overestimate the degree of long-run compliance.

35. Linda Bird Francke, *Growing Up Divorced* (New York: Linden Press/Simon & Schuster, 1983), 28.

36. Thomas J. Espenshade, "The Economic Consequences of Divorce," *Journal of Marriage and the Family* 41 (August 1979), 622.

37. Weitzman, op. cit., 1256. Weitzman finds that when the father's yearly income is in the $10,000 to $20,000 range, 27 percent do not comply with child-support orders. When a father's yearly income is in the

Notes

$30,000 to $50,000 range, 29 percent do not comply with child-support orders. Her figures are based on a weighted sample of interviews with divorced people, Los Angeles County, 1978.

38. Lucy Marsh Yee, "What Really Happens in Child Support Cases: An Empirical Study of the Establishment and Enforcement of Child Support Orders in the Denver District Court," *Law Journal Denver* 57 (1980), 21–36. The average father for whom data were available paid $136.97 per month for his car and $113.59 per month for his 1.6 children.

39. Information supplied by the Office of Representative Barbara Kennelly (Democrat, Connecticut), March 9, 1985.

40. New Jersey Task Force, op. cit., 100.

41. Between 1978 and 1981 the average child-support payment decreased by 16 percent in real terms (ibid., 62).

42. The cost of raising a child to age eighteen in 1980 ranged from $71,712 (when family income is less than $10,000) to $159,430 (when family income is in the $20,000 to $40,000 range); these estimates *do not include child care or college education* (New Jersey Task Force, op. cit., 76).

43. Interview, December 5, 1983.

44. Term coined by Marcia Guttentag and Paul F. Secord, *Too Many Women: The Sex Ratio Question* (Beverly Hills, Calif.: Sage Publications, 1983), 18.

45. Noreen Goldman, Charles F. Westoff, and Charles Hammerslough, "Demography of the Marriage Market in the United States," *Population Index* 50 (Spring 1984), 16.

46. Ibid., 20.

47. Ibid., 16.

48. *American Women: Three Decades of Change* (Washington, D.C.: Bureau of the Census, August 1983), 4–5.

49. Beverly Stephen, "In Pursuit of Justice for Women in the Courts," *Daily News,* August 11, 1984, 10.

50. Weitzman and Dixon, op. cit., 185.

51. Weitzman, op. cit., 1266.

52. Ibid., 1252.

53. New Jersey Task Force, op. cit., 80.

54. Ibid.

55. In the United States the divorce rate in 1981 was 5.3 divorce decrees granted for every 1,000 persons, while in Sweden the rate was 2.4 per 1,000; in Britain, 3.0; in Canada, 2.6; in France, 1.6; and in Italy, .2. *UN Demographic Yearbook 1981* (New York: UN Department of Interna-

tional and Social Affairs, Statistical Office, 1983), 461–63. See also discussion in Robert Chester, *Divorce in Europe* (Leiden: Martinus Nijhoff Social Science Division, 1977), 302–06.

56. Quoted in Lenore J. Weitzman, *The Marriage Contract* (New York: The Free Press, 1981), 152.

57. Interview with Olga Baudelot, Institut National de Recherche Pédagogique, Paris, February 2, 1985.

58. Interviews with Swedish journalist Karl Ahlenius, May 30, 1984, and West German sociologist Greta Tullmann, June 5, 1984.

59. Frank F. Furstenberg, Jr., and Christine Winquist Nord, "Parenting Apart: Patterns of Childrearing After Marital Disruption," *Journal of Marriage and the Family* (November 1985), 874.

60. Study by Dr. E. Mavis Hetherington of the University of Virginia at Charlottesville, reported in the *New York Times,* December 13, 1983.

4: The Wage Gap

1. Roy Rowan, "How Harvard's Women MBA's Are Managing," *Fortune* (July 11, 1983), 64.

2. Jill Bettner and Christine Donahue, "Now They're Not Laughing," *Forbes* (November 21, 1983), 117.

3. A 1984 study talks about "the puzzle of the essentially constant male-female incomes ratios over the last 50 years," James P. Smith and Michael P. Ward, "Women's Wages and Work in the Twentieth Century" (Santa Monica: Rand Corporation, October 1984), 26.

4. 7.4 percent of women hold high-level managerial or administrative positions. See testimony of Dr. Lenora Cole Alexander, director of the Women's Bureau, U.S. Department of Labor, before the Joint Economic Committee of the U.S. Congress, April 3, 1984, 3. See also opening statement by Congresswoman Mary Rose Oakar, chair, Subcommittee on Compensation and Employee Benefits, Hearings HR 4599 and HR 5092, April 3, 1984, House of Representatives, 2. As of the beginning of 1984, 48.5 million women were in the labor force.

5. *Money, Income and Poverty Status of Families and Persons in the US: 1984,* Current Population Reports, Series P-60 (Washington, D.C.: Bureau of the Census, August 1985), 21.

6. For 1939 figure see: Dorothy S. Brody, "Equal Pay for Women Workers," *Annals of the American Academy of Political and Social Science* 217 (May 1947), 54. For the 1984 figure see: Bureau of the Census, op. cit., 17. The wage gap seems to go back a long way. In biblical times, says

Leviticus 27:3–4, women of working age were valued at thirty silver shekels, while men were valued at fifty.

7. Hourly Wages of Women

Year	All Women	White Women	Black Women
1956	64.3	62.9	35.3
1960	60.7	60.6	41.1
1964	59.1	59.4	41.2
1968	58.5	58.2	43.4
1972	57.4	56.5	48.9
1976	60.0	58.7	55.2
1980	60.5	59.3	55.6
1983	64.3	62.3	56.6
1984	63.6	n.a.	n.a.

Source: *Money, Income and Poverty Status of Families and Persons in the US,* Current Population Reports, Series P-60, various issues (Washington, D.C.: Bureau of the Census). The ratios here are median earnings of year-round full-time workers. The "All Women" column represents the wages of all women to all men. The reference group for the first column is all men; for the second and third columns it is white men.

According to Ray Marshall, in the 1981–83 recession the relative position of women improved slightly because of the worsening economic conditions for men, who were heavily concentrated in the declining industrial sector, not because women were improving their absolute positions (interview, April 3, 1985).

8. Bureau of the Census, 1985, op. cit., 17.

9. *Philadelphia Inquirer,* July 15, 1984.

10. *Money and Income of Households and Families in the U.S.* (Washington, D.C.: Bureau of the Census, 1982).

11. Older Women's League, "Older Women's League Protests Change in Poverty Definition" testimony before the Joint Economic Committee, June 6, 1984, 3.

12. *New York Times,* May 22, 1984.

13. Peter J. Sloane, "The Trend of Women's Wages Relative to Men's in the Postwar Period in Great Britain," paper presented to the Economic Policy Council's panel "Parents and Work: Family Policy in Comparative Perspective," Washington, D.C., June 12, 1984, 23–29.

14. Annual earnings of all full-time year-round workers. These figures are comparable to the U.S. figures. See annual report of the Central Bureau of Statistics and various issues of *Allman Manadsstatistik,* Stockholm, Sweden.

Notes

15. In Britain earnings figures are generally presented as average gross hourly earnings. Under this measure working women earned 74 percent of the male wage in 1982, up from 60 percent in 1968 (the figures include manual and nonmanual workers and are for both the public and the private sectors). The British data are also available in the form of full-time gross weekly earnings. Under this measure women earned 66 percent of the male wage in 1982, up from 54 percent in 1970. The lower figures are due to the fact that weekly earnings take into consideration the effects of overtime and the shorter workweeks typically worked by women workers. These weekly earnings figures can be compared with the U.S. data. See *New Earnings Survey 1970–1982,* part A, tables 10 and 11. See also analysis in Sloane, op. cit., 1–43.

16. The Italian, West German, French, and Danish figures refer to manual workers in industry.

Hourly Earnings Differentials in Various Countries of the European Community
Manual Workers in Manufacturing Industry
Female Earnings as a Percentage of Male

	1968	1977	1982
Belgium	67%	70%	72%
Denmark	74%	85%	86% (1981)
France	n.a.	76%	78%
West Germany	69%	72%	73%
Italy	74%	84%	86%
Netherlands	55%	75%	75%
Sweden	78%	87%	90%
Switzerland	64%	68%	n.a.
U.K.	60%	72%	74%

Source: *Eurostat,* "Hourly Earnings—Hours of Work," various issues (Luxembourg: Statistical Office of the European Community).

Within the EEC there is no systematic collection of nonmanual earnings figures. However, the patchy data that do exist suggest that nonmanual earnings follow a similar trend, though at a lower level. For example, in France women in nonmanual occupations earned 62 percent of the male wage in the mid-1970s. In Italy the figure was 68 percent, and in West Germany it was 65 percent. See United Nations, *The Economic Role of Women in the EEC Region* (New York: 1980).

Australia is another country where the wage gap has narrowed considerably in recent years. Female earnings as a percentage of male earnings rose from 70 percent in 1968 to 82 percent in 1977. See discussion in the testimony of Robert C. Gregory before the Equal Employment Opportunity Commission Hearings on job segregation and discrimination, April 28 and 30, 1980, 611.

17. Smith and Ward, op. cit., 35. Figures are for the birth cohort 1951–54. See also *Employment in Perspective: Working Women,* Report 650 (Washington, D.C.: Bureau of Labor Statistics, 1981); this shows that younger women have a considerable educational advantage over younger men.

18. *Hansard,* vol. 13, November 17, 1981; *UNESCO Statistical Yearbook,* 1982, table 3.10.

19. *The Wage Gap: Myths and Facts* (Washington, D.C.: National Committee on Pay Equity, 1982), 5.

20. Bureau of the Census figures, quoted in the *Wall Street Journal,* November 10, 1983.

21. *Business Week* (October 1, 1984), 126.

22. *New York Times,* January 16, 1984. Green's analysis is of all workers who entered the labor force in 1970 and 1980. He documents the educational gains of women: In 1970, 19 percent of white women entering the job market had four or more years of college; by 1980 this figure was 27 percent. For white men the figure stayed constant at 27 percent.

23. See discussion in Barbara R. Bergmann, "Feminism and Economics," *Academe* (September–October 1983), 22–25. It should be pointed out that much of the disagreement in the economics profession over how to explain the wage gap is over differences in emphasis, not over facts. As Ray Marshall has put it, "I don't know of a liberal who believes all of the pay gap is due to discrimination or a conservative who believes it is all due to human capital factors. There is a sizable unexplained residual in most econometric studies." (Interview, April 3, 1985)

24. Bureau of the Census figures, quoted in the *New York Times,* November 25, 1984.

25. National Committee on Pay Equity, op. cit., 5.

26. 1983 figures from the Bureau of Labor Statistics, quoted in the *New York Times,* November 25, 1984, 32.

27. Preamble from a suit filed against the state of California by the California State Employees Association, quoted in the *New York Times,* December 9, 1984.

28. Before the Civil Rights Act was passed, Westinghouse had a completely sex-segregated work force. Jobs were explicitly designated as "men's jobs" or "women's jobs." The company evaluated all jobs and

specifically instructed its officials to pay less for female jobs than for male jobs rated equally in the job evaluation study.

After the Civil Rights Act was passed, making it clearly illegal to have jobs designated male and female, the company removed the designations, but the sex segregation continued. The company combined the male and female wage schedules, with the result that all the women's jobs were placed in the lower pay grades and all the men's jobs were placed in the higher pay grades.

The IUE sued under Title VII, claiming sex-based wage discrimination. After a legal battle the Supreme Court let stand an appeals court decision finding Westinghouse guilty of Title VII violations. The Court held that the Westinghouse system perpetuated past discrimination, and the fact that the jobs were different did not matter.

29. See reports of the Washington State case in the *New York Times,* January 1, 1984, and April 9, 1984. It should be pointed out that this decision was overturned by a federal appeals court in September 1985. The case will now go to the Supreme Court.

Comparison of Worth and Salary of Selected Jobs from a Job Evaluation Study, Washington State

Job Title	Monthly Salary	Number of Points
Registered nurse (F)	$1368	348
Highway engineer (M)	$1980	345
Laundry worker (F)	$ 884	105
Truck driver (M)	$1493	97
Secretary (F)	$1122	197
Maintenance carpenter (M)	$1707	197

Source: "State of Washington Study," *Public Personnel Management Journal* (Winter 1981–82).

30. *New York Times,* April 9, 1984. For a discussion of the conservative viewpoint see Michael Levin, "Comparable Worth: The Feminist Road to Socialism," *Commentary* (September 1984), 13–19.

31. *Washington Post,* November 17, 1984.

32. Interview with Ray Marshall, April 3, 1985.

33. Approximately 15 percent of the wage gap is due to occupational discrimination. Polachek explains between 12 and 21 percent of the wage gap using this methodology (see Solomon William Polachek, "Women in the Economy: Perspectives on Gender Inequality," paper presented at the U.S. Commission on Civil Rights Conference on Com-

Notes

parable Worth, June 6–7, 1984). Treiman and Hartmann explain between 11 and 19 percent of the wage gap this way, and Fuchs explains 6 percent (see Donald J. Treiman and Heidi I. Hartmann eds., *Women, Work, and Wages: Equal Pay for Jobs of Equal Value* [Washington, D.C.: National Academy Press, 1981], and Victor Fuchs, "Differentials in Hourly Earnings Between Men and Women," *Monthly Labor Review* 94 [May 1971], 9–15). The explanatory power of this approach depends on how many occupational groups are considered. The larger the number, the higher the proportion of the wage gap explained. However, even with 479 occupations (a degree of disaggregation many economists think is unwarranted) less than half of the wage gap (between 35 and 39 percent) can be attributed to occupational segregation (see discussion in Earl F. Mellor, "Investigating the Differences in Weekly Earnings of Women and Men," *Monthly Labor Review* [June 1984], 26, 17–19).

34. Interview, October 10, 1984.

35. See discussion in Cynthia B. Lloyd and Beth Niemi, *The Economics of Sex Differentials* (New York: Columbia University Press, 1979).

36. Polachek, op. cit., 24.

37. Ibid., 22.

38. Smith and Ward, op. cit., 12. See also: Mark B. Stewart and Christine A. Greenhaigh, "Work History Patterns and the Occupational Attainment of Women," *Economic Journal* (September 1984).

39. Polachek, op. cit., 13–14.

40. Corcoran and Duncan explain 44 percent of the wage gap by analyzing tenure in job, on-the-job training, and number of years of work life at full-time jobs (Mary Corcoran and Greg J. Duncan, "Work History, Labor Force Attachment and Earnings Differentials Between Races and Sexes," *Journal of Human Resources* [Winter 1979], 3–20). Rytina finds that work history and labor force attachment account for 25 percent of the wage difference between the sexes (Nancy F. Rytina, "Tenure as a Factor in the Male-Female Earnings Gap," *Monthly Labor Review* [April 1982], 32–34).

41. Bureau of the Census data reported in the *New York Times,* April 14, 1984, and August 3, 1984. For a more detailed analysis see Gus W. Haggstrom, Linda J. Waite, David E. Kanouse, and Thomas J. Blaschke, "Changes in the Life Styles of New Parents" (Santa Monica, Calif.: Rand Corporation, December 1984), 61.

42. Interview, April 13, 1985.

43. National Committee on Pay Equity, op. cit., 3.

44. Lester C. Thurow, "62 Cents To The Dollar; The Earnings Gap Doesn't Go Away," *Working Mother,* October 1984, 42.

45. Lester C. Thurow, *The Zero Sum Society* (New York: Basic Books, 1980), 19.

46. Quoted in Barbara A. Brown, Thomas I. Emerson, Gail Falk, and Ann E. Freedman, "The Equal Rights Amendment: A Constitutional Basis for Equal Rights for Women," *Yale Law Journal* 80, 5 (April 1971), 973.

47. Kathleen Sylvester, "Women Gaining, Blacks Fall Back," *National Law Review* (May 21, 1984), 41, and Kathleen Sylvester, "Minorities in Firms," *National Law Journal* (May 21, 1984), 3.

48. Jill Abramson and Barbara Franklin, "Are Women Catching Up?" *American Lawyer* (May 1983), 79.

49. Ibid., 84.

50. Much the same pattern is emerging in investment banking. "It's been a good decade since large numbers of women began emerging from top business schools and embarking in earnest on careers in finance. Yet, with rare exceptions, women have so far failed to achieve that most hallowed of Wall Street goals: being named partner, or in public firms, managing director." Women now comprise something like a quarter of all professionals in investment banking, but the proportion of female partners and managing directors is a miniscule 1 percent. Beth McGoldnick and Gregory Miller, "Wall Street Women: You've Come a Short Way, Baby," *Institutional Investor,* June 1985, 239.

51. Polachek, op. cit., p. 17.

52. Heidi I. Hartmann, "The Family as the Locus of Gender, Class and Political Struggle," *Signs* (Spring 1981), 366–94. See discussion in Dolores Hayden, *Redesigning the American Dream: The Future of Housing, Work and Family Life* (New York: Norton, 1984), 64.

53. Hayden, op. cit., 65.

54. Joseph H. Pleck, "Husband's Paid Work and Family Roles: Current Research Issues," in Helena Z. Lopata and Joseph H. Pleck, eds., *Research in the Interweave of Social Roles,* Vol. 3. (Greenwich, Conn.: JAI Press, 1982), 251–333. See also discussion in Joseph H. Pleck, "Husbands' and Wives' Family Work, Paid Work and Adjustment," Working Paper No. 95 (Wellesley, Mass.: Wellesley College, Center for Research on Women, 1982).

55. Hartmann, op. cit., 380.

56. Hartmann, op. cit., 383.

57. Philip Blumstein and Pepper Schwartz, *American Couples: Money, Work and Sex* (New York: William Morrow, 1983), 145.

58. Lopata and Pleck, op. cit., 253.

59. Nora Ephron, *Heartburn* (New York: Pocket Books, 1983), 104.

Notes

60. Simone de Beauvoir, *The Second Sex* (New York: Alfred A. Knopf, 1952), 536.

61. Blumstein and Schwartz, op. cit., 53.

62. See A. Beller, "The Impact of Equal Opportunity Policy on Sex Differentials in Earnings and Occupations," *American Economic Review (Proceedings)* (May 1982), 171–75.

63. Sheila B. Kamerman, Alfred J. Kahn, and Paul Kingston, *Maternity Policies and Working Women* (New York: Columbia University Press, 1983), 66. Much of the discussion of maternity leave is based on the work of Sheila B. Kamerman.

64. Caroline Little, "Mother Load or Overload: The Need for a National Maternity Policy," *Journal of International Law and Politics* 17 (1985), 3.

65. Testimony of Dr. Lenora Cole Alexander, op. cit., 9.

66. Naomi Barko, "Maternity Leave—American Style," *Working Mother* (November 1983), 45–46.

67. Kamerman, Kahn, and Kingston, op. cit., 56.

68. "When the Mother-to-Be Is an Executive," *Business Week* (April 11, 1983), 128.

69. Interview, January 10, 1983.

70. Interview, November 18, 1984.

71. Interview, March 1, 1983.

72. Interview, March 6, 1983.

73. Sheila B. Kamerman and Alfred J. Kahn, "Company Maternity-Leave Policies: The Big Picture," *Working Women* (February 1984), 80. In Europe the minimum paid maternity leave is fourteen weeks, and the most common leave granted is five months. In addition, most European countries provide at least one year of unpaid but job-protected leave, and all European countries have some form of national health insurance to cover the costs of prenatal and postnatal care. For more details see Sheila Kamerman *Maternity and Parental Benefits and Leaves* (New York: Columbia University, Center for the Social Sciences, Monograph No 1, 1980).

74. *Equality Between Men and Women in Sweden* (Stockholm: The Swedish Institute, May 1983).

75. "Parental Leave: A New Proposal for a Directive," *Social Europe* (May 1984) No. 1, Brussels Commission of the European Community, 24.

76. "Maternity Rights and Benefits: The Current Situation" (London: Equal Opportunities Commission, 1983), 7.

77. Interview, November 20, 1983.

78. Interview, November 30, 1983.

79. *OECD Employment Outlook* (Paris: OECD Labor Force Statistics, September 1985), 40. The figures are for working women ages 16–64 as a percentage of the working-age female population.

80. Marvin Harris, *America Now: The Anthropology of a Changing Culture* (New York: Simon & Schuster, 1981), 92.

5: Children: The Other Victims

1. The statistics in this paragraph are from the Select Committee on Children, Youth and Families, *U.S. Children and their Families: Current Conditions and Recent Trends* (Washington, D.C.: U.S. Government Printing Office, May 1983), 6; and the National Citizen's Board of Inquiry into Health in America, *Health Care USA* (October 1984), vol. 1, p. 1.

2. Mayor's Task Force on Child Abuse and Neglect, "Report on the Preliminary Study of Child Fatalities in New York City," November 1983. See also *New York Times,* October 23, 1983.

3. *American Children in Poverty* (Washington, D.C.: Children's Defense Fund, 1984), 14. See also *New York Times,* September 2, 1983.

4. *Money Income and Poverty Status of Persons and Families in the U.S. 1983,* Current Population Reports, Series P-60 (Washington, D.C.: Bureau of the Census, 1984).

5. Quoted in Letty Cottin Pogrebin, *Family Politics: Love and Power on an Intimate Frontier* (New York: McGraw-Hill, 1983), 60.

6. *New York Times,* September 2, 1983.

7. Interview with Michelle Seligson, Center for Research on Women, Wellesley College, July 24, 1985. See also: "What Price Day Care?," *Newsweek* (September 10, 1984), 14.

8. Interview with Sheila Kamerman, March 27, 1985.

9. Interview, October 3, 1983.

10. Ann C. Crouter, Jay Belsky, and Graham B. Spanier, "The Family Context of Child Development: Divorce and Maternal Employment," *Annals of Child Development* 1 (1984), 207. See also Select Committee on Children, Youth and Families, op. cit., 14.

11. Interview, January 14, 1984.

12. Barbara Ehrenreich and Karin Stallard, "The Nouveau Poor," *Ms.* (August 1982), 222.

13. Michael Rutter, "Protective Factors in Children's Response to Stress and Disadvantage," in *Primary Prevention of Psychopathology,* vol. 3; *Promoting Social Competence and Coping with Children,* eds., M. W. Kent and

Notes

J. E. Rolf (Hanover, N.H.: University Press of New England, 1978). See also E. M. Hetherington, "Divorce: A Child's Perspective," *American Psychologist* 34 (1979).

14. Interview, February 12, 1984. See Linda Bird Francke, *Growing Up Divorced* (New York: Linden Press/Simon & Schuster 1983). This book contains vivid portraits of the children of divorce.

15. Joyce Everett, "Patterns and Implications of Child Support Practices for Children's Well-Being," Wellesley College Center for Research on Women, Working Paper No. 128 (1984), 2.

16. *Money, Income and Poverty Status of Families and Persons in the US: 1984,* Current Population Reports, Series P-60 (Washington, D.C.: Bureau of the Census, 1985).

17. Bishop's Pastoral, "Catholic Social Teaching and the U.S. Economy," *Origins* 14 (November 15, 1984), 363.

18. Mayor's Task Force, op. cit.

19. Interview, March 2, 1984.

20. *New York Times,* July 20, 1983.

21. Interview with Michelle Seligson, July 24, 1985.

22. *Child Care Arrangements of Working Mothers,* Current Population Reports, Series P-23 (Washington, D.C.: U.S. Bureau of the Census, 1983), 22.

23. *New York Times,* September 3, 1984.

24. Interview, January 10, 1983.

25. *Child Care: The States' Response* (Washington, D.C.: Children's Defense Fund, 1983–84), 1.

26. *New York Times,* September 2, 1984.

27. Myron Magnet, "What Mass-Produced Child Care Is Producing," *Fortune* (November 28, 1983), 157–58.

28. Sheila B. Kamerman, *Parenting in an Unresponsive Society: Managing Work and Family* (New York: The Free Press, 1980), 58.

29. Interview, March 5, 1983.

30. Sheila B. Kamerman, "Child Care Services: A National Picture," *Monthly Labor Review* (December 1983), 36.

31. See discussion in Eugenia Kemble, *Starting Off on the Right Foot,* Publication No. 625 (Washington, D.C.: American Federation of Teachers, 1974), 12.

32. Kamerman, "Child Care Services," loc. cit., 37.

33. *Nation at Risk: The Imperative for Educational Reform* (Washington, D.C.: National Commission for Excellence in Education, April 1983), 32.

34. Interview with Michele Seligson, July 24, 1985. See also: *Employ-*

Notes

ers and Child Care: Development of the New Employee Benefit (Washington, D.C.: Bureau of National Affairs, 1984), 1.

35. Helen Blank, testimony of the Children's Defense Fund Before the Joint Economic Committee Concerning Child Care Problems Faced by Working Mothers and Pregnant Women, April 3, 1984.

36. Lynette and Thomas Long, *The Handbook for Latchkey Children and Their Parents* (New York: Arbor House, 1983), 174.

37. Interview, June 2, 1983.

38. *New York Times,* September 8, 1974.

39. Long, op. cit., 283.

40. Interview, March 1, 1983.

41. *Fact Sheets on Sweden* (Stockholm: The Swedish Institute, October 1982), 86.

42. National Plan of Action for Equality, *Step by Step* (Stockholm: 1979), 76.

43. Ibid., 76–105.

44. Olga Baudelot, "Child Care in France," paper presented to the Economic Policy Council, December 11, 1984. The cost data are from 1980–81. In this paper Baudelot draws on the research she did for the Kamerman-Kahn study. See note 47.

45. Sheila B. Kamerman, "Child Care and Family Benefits: Policies of Six Industrialized Countries," *Monthly Labor Review,* November 1980, 26.

46. Interview with Fabrizia Mauro, Ferrara, Italy, November 10, 1983.

47. Nicole Questiaux and Jacques Fournier, "France," in Sheila B. Kamerman and Alfred J. Kahn, eds., *Child Care, Family Benefits and Working Parents: A Study in Comparative Policy* (New York: Columbia University Press, 1981), 161.

48. *American Children in Poverty,* op. cit., 9.

49. *The Stake of the Public Schools in Early Childhood Education,* Publication No. 626 (Washington, D.C.: American Federation of Teachers, 1974).

50. See discussion in Marilyn Rauth, *A Review of the History, Current Conditions and Future Prospects of Child Care Programs in America,* Publication No. 630 (Washington, D.C.: American Federation of Teachers, 1974), 6.

51. Ibid.

52. Ibid.

53. *Wall Street Journal,* November 29, 1984.

54. *New York Times,* April 9, 1985.

55. *New York Daily News,* February 3, 1985.

56. *Nation at Risk,* op. cit., 5.

57. Ibid., 8.

58. Ibid., 17.

59. In 1982 the United States spent more per capita on education than Britain, West Germany, France, and Italy. Ruth Leger Sibard, *World Military and Social Expenditures, 1982* (Leesburg, Virginia: World Priorities, 1982), 30–32.

60. *Corporations and Two Career Families: Directions for the Future* (New York: Catalyst Career and Family Center, 1981), 15–16.

61. Dana Friedman, "Child Care in the US," paper presented to the Economic Policy Council, November 16, 1984.

62. Kristin Anderson, *Corporate Initiatives for Working Parents in New York City: A Ten-Industry Review* (New York: Center for Public Advocacy Research Inc., 1983), 74.

63. The Harvard School of Public Health found that the prenatal component of the woman, infant, and children's feeding program saves $3 in hospitalization costs for every $1 spent by reducing the number of low-birth-weight infants (*Wall Street Journal,* August 21, 1984).

64. Robert H. Bremner, ed., *Children and Youth in America: A Documentary History, Vol III, 1933–1973* (Cambridge, Mass.: Harvard University Press, 1974), 308.

65. *Wall Street Journal,* February 2, 1985.

66. Over $209 billion was projected to be spent by the federal government on the elderly in 1983. See: Select Committee on Children, Youth and Families, "Demographic and Social Trends: Implications for Federal Support for Dependent Care Services For Children and the Elderly" (Washington, D.C.: U.S. Government Printing Office, 1984), 63. In the same year federal spending on children and their families was projected at approximately $53 billion—$38 billion on entitlement programs (AFDC, Food Stamps, Medicaid, etc.), and $15 billion on appropriation programs (housing, education, etc.). See: Testimony of Dr. Alice M. Rivlin, director, Congressional Budget Office, to the Select Committee on Children, Youth and Families, April 28, 1983, 21–26.

67. *New York Times,* May 29, 1985.

68. John Betjeman, "Norfolk," *Collected Poems* (Boston: Houghton Mifflin, 1971), 211.

69. E. Nesbit, *The Railway Children* (London: Puffin Books, 1960), 9–10.

70. Betty Friedan, *The Second Stage* (New York: Summit Books, 1981), 100.

71. *Business Week,* January 28, 1985.

6: Image and Reality

1. *New York Times,* December 10, 1983.
2. R. W. Apple, Jr., "New Stirrings of Patriotism," *New York Times Magazine,* December, 11, 1983.
3. Quoted in Marvin Harris, *America Now: The Anthropology of a Changing Culture* (New York: Simon & Schuster, 1981), 76.
4. Ibid.
5. Eleanor Smeal, *Why and How Women Will Elect the Next President* (New York: Harper & Row, 1984), 26–32. When Eleanor Smeal was reelected to the presidency of NOW in the summer of 1985, she reaffirmed her prime commitment to the ERA and legalized abortion. *New York Times,* July 22, 1985.
6. Interview, March 7, 1984.
7. *New York Times,* July 22, 1984.
8. Quoted in the *New York Times,* November 5, 1984.
9. Ibid.

7: Equal Rights Versus Social Benefits

1. Bella Abzug, *Gender Gap* (Boston: Houghton Mifflin, 1984), 18.
2. William H. Chafe, *Women and Equality: Changing Patterns in American Culture* (New York: Oxford University Press, 1977), 24.
3. Quoted in Elisabeth Griffith, *In Her Own Right: The Life of Elizabeth Cady Stanton* (New York: Oxford University Press, 1984), 54.
4. Chafe, op. cit., 29.
5. Griffith, op. cit., XV.
6. As late as 1977 the national meeting to observe the International Women's Year convened in Houston, Texas, opened with the arrival of a torch carried by female runners from Seneca Falls. Seated on the dais was Susan B. Anthony's grandniece. The heroine of Seneca Falls, Stanton herself, had been lost to history (ibid., XV).
7. Quoted in Shulamith Firestone, *The Dialectic of Sex* (New York: William Morrow, 1970), 25.
8. William H. Chafe, *The American Woman: Her Changing Social, Economic, and Political Roles, 1920–1970* (New York: Oxford University Press, 1972), 59.
9. Consciousness-raising meeting, New York City, January 17, 1977.

Notes

10. Phyllis Chesler, *Women and Madness* (Garden City, N.Y.: Doubleday, 1972), 243–44.

11. Colette Dowling, *The Cinderella Complex* (New York: Pocket Books, 1981), 8.

12. Ibid., 21.

13. Ibid.

14. Ibid.

15. David Bouchier, *The Feminist Challenge: The Movement for Women's Liberation in Britain and the United States* (New York: Schocken Books, 1984), 45.

16. William O'Neill, *The Woman Movement: Feminism in the United States and England* (Chicago: Quadrangle, 1971), 31.

17. H. L. Mencken, *In Defense of Women* (New York: Alfred A. Knopf, 1922), 132.

18. Emily Blair, "Are Women a Failure in Politics?," *Harper's* (October 1925), 513–22.

19. Gayle Yates, *What Women Want: The Ideas of the Movement* (Cambridge, Mass.: Harvard University Press, 1975), 77.

20. Ibid., 102.

21. Carolyn Teich Adams and Kathryn Teich Winston, *Mothers at Work: Public Policies in the United States, Sweden and China* (New York: Longman, 1980), 132.

22. *New York Times,* November 3, 1975.

23. Anna-Greta Leijon, "Equality in the Labor Market, in Political and Trade Union Organizations, and in the Home" *Current Sweden* 75 (April 1975), 4.

24. Interview with Birgitta Karlstrom, foreign correspondent for Swedish Broadcasting, February 22, 1983.

25. Adams and Winston, op. cit., 116.

26. It should be pointed out that just after the Civil War an organization called the American Equal Rights Association (AERA) was formed to push for both black and female suffrage. But the rights of blacks took precedence over the rights of women. In 1868 the Fourteenth Amendment gave black men the vote but excluded black women from citizenship and voting rights. After this date the women's suffrage movement was self-consciously separatist (Griffith, op. cit., 118–25).

27. Adams and Winston, op. cit., 117. See also *Equality in the Labour Market: Programme Adopted by the Labor Market Board* (Stockholm: Avbetsmarknadsstyrelsen, September 1977).

28. Interview, Anna-Greta Leijon, March 7, 1984.

29. *The Guardian,* October 28, 1983.

30. Sheila Lewenhak, *Women and Trade Unions: An Outline History of Women in the British Trade Union Movement* (New York: St. Martin's Press, 1977), 60.

31. Norbert C. Soldon, *Women in British Trade Unions 1874–1976* (Dublin: Gill and Macmillan, 1978), 70.

32. Ibid., 75. See also Gladys Boone, *The Women's Trade Union Leagues in Great Britain and the USA* (New York: Columbia University Press, 1942).

33. Louise A. Tilly and Joan W. Scott, *Women, Work and Family* (New York: Holt, Rinehart & Winston, 1978), 173.

34. Bouchier, op. cit., 57.

35. Ibid.

36. Ibid., 37.

37. Interview, Ruth Spellman, National Economic Development Council, London, October 3, 1984.

38. See discussion in Anna Coote and Beatrix Campbell, *Sweet Freedom: The Struggle for Women's Liberation* (London: Pan Books, 1982), 143–49.

39. *The Guardian,* May 10, 1984.

40. Remato Giancola, ed., *Italy: Documents and Notes* (Rome: Presidency of the Council of Ministers, 1975), 401.

41. Daniela Colombo, "The Italian Feminist Movement," *Women's Studies International Quarterly* 4, 4 (1981), 467.

42. Giancola, op. cit., 421–27.

43. Interview, November 17, 1984.

44. Interview, March 1, 1984.

45. Interview with Fabrizia Mauro, Ferrara, Italy, November 10, 1983.

8: *Women's Liberation and Motherhood*

1. *American Women: Three Decades of Change* (Washington, D.C.: Bureau of the Census, August 1983), 4. In 1950 more than 20 percent of all forty-year-old women were childless.

2. See discussion in Chapter Two, especially Note 10.

3. Bureau of the Census, op. cit., 7.

4. Interview, January 28, 1985.

5. Paul Bagne, "High Tech Breeding," *Mother Jones* (August 1983), 23–27.

Notes

6. Interview, Roxanne Felshuch, IDANT Laboratories, January 4, 1985.

7. *Wall Street Journal,* May 21, 1985.

8. Elisabeth Griffith, *In Her Own Right: The Life of Elizabeth Cady Stanton* (New York: Oxford University Press, 1984), 184.

9. Shulamith Firestone, *The Dialectic of Sex* (New York: William Morrow, 1970), 73.

10. Ibid., 202.

11. Griffith, op. cit., 51.

12. Ann Dally, *Inventing Motherhood: The Consequences of an Ideal* (New York: Schocken Books, 1983), 133.

13. Ibid., 136.

14. Ibid.

15. Dolores Hayden, *The Grand Domestic Revolution: A History of Feminist Designs for American Homes, Neighborhoods and Cities* (Cambridge, Mass.: MIT Press, 1981), 189.

16. Dally, op. cit., 140–41.

17. Hayden, op. cit., 197–98.

18. Ibid., 281.

19. Ibid., 284.

20. Ibid., 286.

21. Valerie Solanis, "Excerpts from the SCUM (Society for Cutting Up Men) Manifesto," in Robin Morgan, ed., *Sisterhood Is Powerful* (New York: Vintage Books, 1970), 577.

22. "Redstocking Manifesto," in Morgan, op. cit., 598.

23. Ann Koedt, Ellen Levine, and Anita Rapone, eds., *Radical Feminism* (New York: Quadrangle Books, 1973), 219.

24. Quoted in Benjamin R. Barber, "Beyond the Feminine Mystique," *The New Republic* (July 11, 1983), 27.

25. Betty Friedan, *The Second Stage* (New York: Summit Books, 1982), 203.

26. Gloria Steinem, *Outrageous Acts and Everyday Rebellions* (New York: Holt, Rinehart & Winston, 1983), 131.

27. Ibid.

28. Betty Friedan, *The Feminine Mystique* (New York: Dell, 1963), 52.

29. Juliet Mitchell, *Woman's Estate* (New York: Vintage Books, 1971), 162.

30. Ibid., 156.

31. Firestone, op. cit., 15.

32. Morgan, op. cit., vii–xiii.

33. See account in the *New York Times,* November 21, 1977; Barbara

Howar, "Waxy Yellow Buildup at the Houston Women's Conference," *New York* (December 5, 1977), 39–42; and "What Next for U.S. Women," *Time* (December 5, 1977), 19–25.

34. National Commission on the Observation of International Women's Year, *Declaration of American Women* (Washington, D.C.: IWY Commission, 1977), 7.

35. Dally, op. cit., 177.

36. Interview, April 4, 1985.

37. Friedan, *The Second Stage,* loc. cit., 103.

38. Dally, op. cit., 174.

39. Ibid., 175. See also Suzanne Arms, *Immaculate Deception: A New Look at Women and Childbirth in America* (Boston: Houghton Mifflin, 1975), 25.

40. Interview, February 15, 1984.

41. Federation CECOS, D. Schwartz and M. J. Mayaux, "Female Fecundity as a Function of Age," *New England Journal of Medicine* (February 18, 1982), 404–06. See also L. Westrom, "Incidence, Prevalence and Trends of Acute Pelvic Inflammatory Disease and Its Consequence in Industrial Countries," *Epidemiology,* 138, 7 (December 1980), 880–92; Westrom explains increased infertility by "the current epidemic of sexually transmitted diseases."

42. Interview, January 6, 1984.

43. Quoted in Dally, op. cit., 179.

44. Firestone, op. cit., 188–89.

45. Friedan, *The Feminine Mystique,* loc. cit., 290.

9: The ERA: A Test Case

1. Barbara A. Brown, Thomas I. Emerson, Gail Falk, and Ann E. Freedman, "The Equal Rights Amendment: A Constitutional Basis for Equal Rights for Women," *Yale Law Journal* 80, 5 (April 1971), 980.

2. Elizabeth Pleck, "Notes on the Defeat of the ERA," Wellesley College Center for Research on Women, Working Paper No. 103, Wellesley, Mass. (1983), 9.

3. Carol Felsenthal, *The Sweetheart of the Silent Majority* (New York: Doubleday, 1981).

4. The distribution of half a million copies of Schlafly's book *A Choice Not an Echo* prior to the California primary was a major factor in Goldwater's victory (Phyllis Schlafly, *A Choice Not an Echo* [Alton, Ill.: Pere Marquette Press, 1964]).

Notes

5. Brown, Emerson, Falk, and Freedman, op. cit., 887.

6. Phyllis Schlafly, *The Power of the Positive Woman* (New York: Jove/HBJ, 1977), 93.

7. Ibid., 88–89.

8. As Lenore Weitzman points out, neither the extent of the obligation nor the level of support in relation to a man's income is defined by these laws so that the right to support means little more than the "privilege of living with a husband." See Lenore J. Weitzman, *The Marriage Contract: Spouses, Lovers and The Law* (New York: The Free Press, 1981), 40–41.

9. Felsenthal, op. cit., 237–38.

10. It should be pointed out that since 1973 the AFL-CIO has supported the ERA. The policy of the umbrella labor organization is that when a law is truly protective, it can be extended to both sexes; when it is discriminatory, it will be eliminated. But many rank-and-file union members are less than enthusiastic about the ERA. See discussion in Chapter Fifteen.

11. Paul A. Freund, "The Equal Rights Amendment Is Not the Way," *Harvard Civil Rights-Civil Liberties Law Review* 6 (March 1971), 234.

12. Schlafly, op. cit., 92.

13. Interview, December 11, 1984.

14. Schlafly, op. cit., 91.

15. For profiles of ERA opponents see David Brady and Kent L. Tedin, "Ladies in Pink: Religion and Political Ideology in the Anti-ERA Movement," *Social Science Quarterly* 56 (March 1976), 564–75.

16. Felsenthal, op. cit., 243.

17. Bella Abzug, *Gender Gap* (Boston: Houghton Mifflin, 1984), 50.

18. Felsenthal, op. cit., 247.

19. Ibid., 247–248.

20. Ibid., 251.

21. Ibid., 250.

22. A Sangamon County grand jury indicted a NOW field organizer on charges of bribery and solicitation, both felonies. The NOW volunteer was alleged to have offered a legislator a $1,000 campaign contribution to vote yes on ERA. In August 1980 an eight-woman, four-man jury found this NOW volunteer guilty of bribery but innocent of solicitation. Her attorneys filed an appeal. See Felsenthal, op. cit., 253.

23. Ibid., 256.

24. Lisa Cronin Wohl, "Phyllis Schlafly: The Sweetheart of the Silent Majority," *Ms.* (March 1974), 55.

25. Abzug, op. cit., 63.

26. Felsenthal, op. cit., 265.

27. Pleck, op. cit., 6. To take an example, in NOW's final push for ratification it spent $1 million a month nationally from January to June 1982. Schlafly spent $100,000 over the same time period, and even when you add in $300,000 in PAC donations by the STOP ERA movement, it is hard to approach the NOW figure. Jane O'Reilly, "The Big-Time Players Behind the Small-Town Image," *Ms.* (January 1983), p. 59.

28. Felsenthal, op. cit., 260.

29. *Eagle Forum Newsletter.* See also Jane De Hart Mathews and Donald Mathews, "The Cultural Politics of ERA's Defeat," *Organization of American Historians Newsletter* 10, 4 (November 1982), 13–15.

30. Wohl, op. cit., 55.

31. Ibid.

32. Betty Friedan, *The Second Stage* (New York: Summit Books, 1981), 100.

33. Felsenthal, op. cit., 289.

34. "What Next for U.S. Women?" *Time,* December 5, 1977, 22.

35. Ibid.

36. Felsenthal, op. cit., 290.

37. Ibid., 291.

38. Ibid., 292.

39. Judith A. Baer, *The Chains of Protection: The Judicial Response to Women's Labor Legislation* (Westport, Conn.: Greenwood Press, 1978), 77–79.

40. Alice Kessler-Harris, *Out to Work: A History of Wage-Earning Women in the United States* (New York: Oxford University Press, 1982), 206.

41. Ibid.

42. Ibid., 189.

43. Henry R. Seager, "Plan for Health Insurance Act," *American Labor Legislation Review* 6 (March 1916), 25.

44. Kessler-Harris, op. cit., 207.

45. Ibid., 208.

46. "Working Women Want Equality Not Blanket Laws," *Justice* (March 17, 1922), 3.

47. Kessler-Harris, op. cit., 212.

48. Joseph P. Lash, *Eleanor and Franklin* (New York: Norton, 1971), 71. See also Joseph P. Lash, *A World of Love: Eleanor Roosevelt and Her Friends, 1943–62* (Garden City, N.Y.: Doubleday and Co., Inc., 1984), 107.

49. David Bouchier, *The Feminist Challenge: the Movement for Women's*

Liberation in Britain and the United States (New York: Schocken Books, 1984), 18–19.

50. Kessler-Harris, op. cit., 286.

51. *New York Times,* December 31, 1983.

10: Ultradomesticity: The Return to Hearth and Home

1. Interview, May 3, 1983.

2. Lou Cannon, *Reagan* (New York: Perigee Books, 1982), 31.

3. John Russell Taylor, *Ingrid Bergman* (New York: St. Martin's Press, 1983), 90.

4. Ibid., 84.

5. Ibid.

6. Betty Friedan, *The Feminine Mystique* (New York: Dell, 1963), 52.

7. Ibid., 53.

8. Quoted in Carl N. Degler, "Revolution Without Ideology: The Changing Place of Women in America," in Robert Jay Lifton, ed., *The Woman in America* (Boston: Beacon Press, 1967), 193.

9. Fredrika Bremer, *Hertha* (New York: G. P. Putnam, 1856), iv.

10. Lucy Freeman and Herbert S. Strean, *Freud and Women* (New York: Frederick Ungar, 1981), 199.

11. Joanna Stratton, *Pioneer Women: Voices from the Kansas Frontier* (New York: Simon & Schuster, 1981), 57.

12. Degler, op. cit., 193.

13. Stratton, op. cit., 14.

14. Comparative figures obtained from Degler, op. cit., 194.

15. Alice Kessler-Harris, *Out to Work: A History of Wage-earning Women in the United States* (New York: Oxford University Press, 1982), 276–77. During the war years 4.7 million new women workers joined the labor force. Kessler-Harris estimates that 3.5 million women who might not otherwise have done so took jobs.

16. Ibid., 276.

17. Ibid., 275.

18. William H. Chafe, *The American Woman: Her Changing Social, Economic and Political Roles, 1920–1970* (New York: Oxford University Press, 1972), 170.

19. Degler, op. cit., 207.

20. Chafe, op. cit., 217.

Notes

21. Degler, op. cit., 202, and Alva Myrdal and Viola Klein, *Woman's Two Roles* (London: Routledge and Kegan Paul Ltd., 1969), 66.

22. John B. Parrish, "Professional Womanpower as a National Resource," *Quarterly Review of Economics and Business* 1 (February 1961), 58.

23. Myrdal and Klein, op. cit., 12.

24. Ibid., 13.

25. Employment rates for women increased during the 1950s, but the increase came from women over thirty-five returning to jobs when their children entered school. Employment rates for women under thirty-five actually declined in this period. See discussion in James P. Smith and Michael P. Ward, "Women's Wages and Work in the Twentieth Century" (Santa Monica: Rand Corporation, October 1984).

26. William Manchester, *The Glory and the Dream: A Narrative History of America, 1932–1972* (Boston: Little, Brown, 1974), 42.

27. Ibid.

28. Joseph Pleck, *The Myth of Masculinity* (Cambridge, Mass.: MIT Press, 1981), 159.

29. Alvin H. Hansen, *Economic Policy and Full Employment* (New York: McGraw-Hill, 1947), 19.

30. A. G. Mezerik, "Getting Rid of the Women," *Atlantic Monthly* (June 1945), 80.

31. See discussion in Alonzo L. Hamby, "Harry Truman and the Fair Deal," in Robert D. Marcus and David Burnet, eds., *America Since 1945* (New York: St. Martin's Press, 1977).

32. William E. Leuchtenberg, "Consumer Culture and the Cold War," in William E. Leuchtenberg, ed., *The Unfinished Century: America Since 1900* (Boston: Little, Brown & Co., 1973), 754.

33. *New York Times*, February 11, 1946.

34. Kessler-Harris, op. cit., 287.

35. Margaret Barnard Pickel, "How Come No Jobs for Women?," *New York Times Magazine* (January 27, 1946), 46.

36. Agnes Meyer, "Women Aren't Men," *Atlantic Monthly* 186 (August 1950), 33.

37. Quoted in Chafe, op. cit., 207.

38. Nell Giles, "What About the Women?", *Ladies' Home Journal* LXI (June 1944), 23.

39. Kessler-Harris, op. cit., 287.

40. Anna B. Mayer, "Day Care as a Social Instrument: A Policy Paper," Columbia School of Social Work (January 1965), 38.

41. Mezerik, op. cit., 81.

42. The provisions of the acts are summarized in *Servicemen's Rights*

Notes

and Benefits (Washington, D.C.: U.S. Office of War Mobilization, 1944), and in Charles L. Dearing and Wilfred Owen, *National Transportation Policy* (Washington, D.C.: Brookings Institution, 1949), 110. See also discussion in *Business Week* (November 4, 1944).

43. "The Roots of Home," *Time* (June 20, 1960), 15.

44. Betty Friedan, *The Second Stage* (New York: Summit Books, 1981), 100.

45. Christopher Finch, *Norman Rockwell's America* (New York: Harry N. Abrams, 1975).

46. See discussion in Leuchtenberg, op. cit., 741–57.

47. Dolores Hayden, *The Grand Domestic Revolution: A History of Feminist Designs for American Homes, Neighborhoods and Cities* (Cambridge, Mass.: MIT Press, 1981), 281.

48. Gilbert Steiner, *The Children's Cause* (Washington, D.C.: The Brookings Institution, 1976), 115.

49. Chafe, op. cit., 187.

50. Richard Nixon, *The Public Messages, Speeches and Statements of the President, 1971* (Washington, D.C.: Government Printing Office, 1972), 1178.

51. James J. Kilpatrick's column, reprinted in *Congressional Record,* December 2, 1971.

52. Nathan G. Hale, Jr., *Freud and the Americans* (New York: Oxford University Press, 1971), 304.

53. Paul Roazen, *Freud and His Followers* (New York: Knopf, 1975), 385.

54. Ferdinand Lundberg and Marynia F. Farnham, *Modern Women: The Lost Sex* (New York: Harper and Brothers, 1947), 235.

55. Ibid., 370.

56. Helene Deutsch, *The Psychology of Woman: A Psychoanalytic Interpretation* (New York: Grune & Stratton, 1944), 290–91.

57. Freeman and Strean, op. cit., 109.

58. Betty Friedan, "Smith College—Class of 1942, Questionnaires, 1957," Friedan Papers, Schlesinger Library Harvard University, Microfilm No 78-1.

59. Friedan, *The Feminine Mystique,* loc. cit., 52.

60. Ibid.

61. *Time,* op. cit., 16.

62. Mirra Komarovsky, *Woman in the Modern World* (Boston: Little, Brown, 1953), 258.

63. Friedan, *The Feminine Mystique,* loc. cit., 53.

64. Chafe, op. cit., 205.

65. Friedan, *The Feminine Mystique,* loc. cit., 51.

66. Lundberg and Farnham, quoted in Chafe, op. cit., 204.

67. Molly Haskell, *From Reverence to Rape: The Treatment of Women in the Movies* (New York: Holt, Rinehart & Winston, 1974), 141.

68. June Sochen, "The New Woman and Twenties America: Way Down East," in John E. O'Connor and Martin A. Jackson, eds., *American History/American Film* (New York: Frederick Ungar, 1979), 13.

69. Alain Silver and Elizabeth Ward, eds., *Film Noir—An Encyclopedia Reference to the American Style* (Woodstock, N.Y.: Overlook Press, 1979), 187.

70. Haskell, op. cit., 270.

71. Ibid.

72. Sochen, op. cit., 17.

73. Philip Slater, *The Pursuit of Loneliness* (Boston: Beacon Press, 1970), 62.

74. Kessler-Harris, op. cit., 302.

11: The Rise of a Cult of Motherhood

1. The article Beth referred to appeared in the *New York Times,* February 1, 1984.

2. Play group meeting, February 3, 1984.

3. N. I. Kugelmass, *Wisdom with Children* (New York: John Day, 1965), 292.

4. John B. Watson, *Psychological Care of Infant and Child,* 1928 (New York: Arno Press, 1972), 87.

5. Quoted in Christina Hardyment *Dream Babies* (New York: Harper & Row, 1983), 9.

6. Philippe Ariès, *Centuries of Childhood* (New York: Knopf, 1962), 38.

7. Quoted in Ann Dally, *Inventing Motherhood* (New York: Schocken Books, 1983), 28.

8. Winston Churchill, *My Early Life: A Roving Commission* (New York: Charles Scribner & Sons, 1930), 4–5.

9. Ronald Steel, *Walter Lippmann and the American Century* (Boston: Little, Brown, 1980), 1–12.

10. Sloan Wilson, *What Shall We Wear to This Party? The Man in the Gray Flannel Suit Twenty Years Before and After* (New York: Arbor House, 1976), 23–24.

Notes

11. Joanna L. Stratton, *Pioneer Women: Voices from the Kansas Frontier* (New York: Simon & Schuster, 1981), 145.

12. Willystine Goodsell, *A History of the Family as a Social and Educational Institution* (New York: Macmillan, 1919), 422.

13. Luther Emmett Holt, M.D., *The Care and Feeding of Children* (New York: D. Appleton and Co., 1900), 92.

14. See discussion in Dally, op. cit., 81.

15. Watson, op. cit., 87.

16. Ibid., 82.

17. Ibid., 83.

18. Erich Fromm, *The Sane Society* (New York: Holt, Rinehart & Winston, 1955), 38–39.

19. Philip Slater, *The Pursuit of Loneliness* (Boston: Beacon Press, 1970), 64.

20. See Sigmund Freud, *The Sexual Enlightenment of Children*, 1907 (New York: Collier Books, 1978). Interestingly enough, Freud himself had a nanny for the first three years of his life, and Freud's own children had a nanny and a nurse. See Lucy Freeman and Herbert S. Strean, *Freud and Women* (New York: Frederick Ungar, 1981), 48.

21. Interview with Jerome Kagan, April 1, 1985.

22. Jean Piaget and Barbel Inhelder, *The Psychology of the Child* (New York: Basic Books, 1969), 3. Piaget himself did not think it a good idea to hasten a child's development. In fact, he criticized Americans who were writing that one should accelerate development.

23. *Wall Street Journal*, August 29, 1984.

24. Interview, September 25, 1983.

25. Burton L. White, *The First Three Years of Life* (New York: Avon Books, 1975), 105.

26. Jerome Kagan, *The Nature of the Child* (New York: Basic Books, 1984), 108.

27. Dr. Benjamin Spock, *Baby and Child Care* (New York: Pocket Books, 1977), 286.

28. Selma H. Fraiberg, *The Magic Years* (New York: Charles Scribner's Sons, 1959), 93.

29. Ibid., 94.

30. Ibid.

31. Nancy Pottisham Weiss, "Mother, the Invention of Necessity: Dr. Benjamin Spock's Baby and Child Care," *American Quarterly* 29 (Winter 1977), 525.

32. Ibid.

33. Ibid.

34. White, op. cit., 100.

35. Ibid.

36. Weiss, op. cit., 526.

37. Spock, op. cit., 358.

38. Spock, op. cit., 2d ed. (1967), 570.

39. Spock, op. cit., 36.

40. T. Berry Brazelton, *Toddlers and Parents* (New York: Delacorte Press, 1974), 122.

41. Lee Salk, *What Every Child Would Like His Parents to Know* (New York: David McKay, 1972), 69.

42. Selma H. Fraiberg, *Every Child's Birthright: In Defense of Mothering* (New York: Basic Books, 1977). In this book Fraiberg stresses the dire consequences of maternal deprivation before eighteen months of age.

43. Burton White, "Should You Stay Home with Your Baby?," *Young Children* (November 1981), 3–5.

44. White, *The First Three Years of Life,* loc. cit., 104. The only child-rearing expert to show any interest in maternity leave is Berry Brazelton; recently Brazelton has advocated a four-month paid maternity leave (see *New York Times,* May 28, 1984).

45. Interview, March 1, 1983.

46. 1950 figure: U.S. Bureau of Labor Statistics, Series G 139–178. 1983 figure: Interview with Elizabeth Waldman, Bureau of Labor Statistics, January 29, 1985.

47. Claire Etaugh, "Effects of Nonmaternal Care on Children: Research Evidence and Popular Views," *American Psychologist* 35 (April 1980), 316.

48. Ruth E. Zambrana, Marsha Hurt, and Rodney L. Hite, "The Working Mother in Contemporary Perspective: A Review of the Literature," *Pediatrics* 64 (December 1979), 862–70.

49. Penelope Leach, *Babyhood* (New York: Alfred A. Knopf, 1983), 121–34. Polly Berrien Berends, *Whole Child Whole Parent* (New York: Harper & Row, 1983), devotes half of one page to the working mother. See the *New York Times,* August 29, 1984, for a list of the top sellers in child-care books.

50. Jerome Kagan, Richard B. Kearsley, and Philip R. Zelazo, *Infancy: Its Place in Human Development* (Cambridge, Mass.: Harvard University Press, 1978), 260.

51. Etaugh, op. cit., 312. In another survey Belsky and Steinberg find that middle-class children neither gain nor lose in the long run from day care, while disadvantaged children gain (Gay Belsky and L. D.

Steinberg, "The Effects of Day Care: A Critical Review," *Child Development* 49 [1978], 929–949).

52. Claire Etaugh, "Effects of Maternal Employment on Children: A Review of Recent Research," *Merrill Palmer Quarterly* 20 (1974), 85.

53. Ibid.

54. Kagan et al., op. cit., 165.

55. Kugelmass, op. cit., 292.

56. *New York Times,* September 3, 1984.

57. See "Population and Employment 1950–76," *Eurostat* (Luxembourg: Statistical Office of the European Community, 1977), 130; and *Statistical Abstract of the U.S., 1980* (Washington, D.C.: Bureau of the Census, 1985).

58. "Women in the Labor Markets," *OECD Observer,* May 1980, 4.

59. Slater, op. cit., 56. Anthony Trollope protested that "American babies are an unhappy race, they eat and drink as they please, they are never punished, snubbed and kept in the background as children are kept with us."

60. Quoted in Spock, op. cit., 12. See also discussion in David Riesman, *The Lonely Crowd* (New Haven, Conn.: Yale University Press, 1950), 42.

61. Interview, February 2, 1984.

62. Olga Baudelot, paper presented to the Economic Policy Council, New York, December 11, 1984.

63. Robert H. Bremner, ed., *Children and Youth in America: A Documentary History,* vol. III, *1933–1973* (Cambridge, Mass.: Harvard University Press, 1974), 704.

64. Spock, op. cit., 13.

65. Bremner, op. cit., 718.

66. Quoted ibid., 718.

67. Quoted ibid., 719.

68. Marian Wright Edelman, "A Political-Legislative Overview of Federal Child Care Proposals," in Nathan B. Talbot, ed., *Raising Children in Modern America: Problems and Prospective Solutions* (Boston: Little, Brown, 1974), 316.

69. Ibid., 305.

70. Interview, May 3, 1983.

71. Weiss, op. cit., 545.

72. Ibid., 520.

73. Interview, February 25, 1985.

74. Edelman, op. cit., 316.

12: *The Unraveling of the Fifties*

1. David Bouchier, *The Feminist Challenge: The Movement for Women's Liberation in Britain and the United States* (New York: Schocken Books, 1984), 31.

2. Interview, January 12, 1983.

13: *The Male Rebellion*

1. J. M. Barrie, *Peter Pan* (New York: Charles Scribner's Sons, 1950), 228.

2. C. Wright Mills, *White Collar* (New York: Oxford University Press, 1953), 282.

3. Arthur Miller, *Death of a Salesman* (New York: Viking Press, 1949), 22.

4. Herman Wouk, *Marjorie Morningstar* (New York: Doubleday, 1955), 47.

5. Ibid., 48.

6. Warren Farrell, *The Liberated Man* (New York: Random House, 1975), 74.

7. Sloan Wilson, *What Shall We Wear to This Party? The Man in The Gray Flannel Suit Twenty Years Before and After* (New York: Arbor House, 1976), 11.

8. William H. Whyte, Jr., *The Organization Man* (New York: Simon & Schuster, 1956), 306.

9. Charles A. Reich, *The Greening of America* (New York: Random House, 1970), 163.

10. Ibid., 209.

11. Wilson, op. cit., 183.

12. Bruce Bliven, Jr., "Life and Love in the Split Level Slums," *Reporter* (February 7, 1957); Anthony Winthrop, Jr., "The Crab Grass Roots of Suburbia," *New Republic* (February 11, 1957); "On the 5:19 to Ulcerville," *Newsweek* (August 17, 1959).

13. Quoted in Scott Donaldson, *The Suburban Myth* (New York: Columbia University Press, 1969), 14.

14. Philip Roth, *My Life as a Man* (New York: Holt, Rinehart and Winston, 1974), 169.

15. Ibid.

16. Morris Dickstein, *Gates of Eden: American Culture in the Sixties* (New York: Basic Books, 1977), 63.

17. Richard Yates, *Revolutionary Road* (New York: Dell, 1961), 12.

18. Ibid., 23.

19. Betty Friedan, *The Feminine Mystique* (New York: Dell, 1963), 261.

20. Betty Hannah Hoffman, "Through All My Housework in an Hour," *Ladies' Home Journal* (October 1960), 184–90. The portrait of Janice Crabtree featured in this issue was meant as a serious treatment of an efficient housewife, but it succeeded in stirring up a great deal of anger around the country. Irate readers wrote to the editor of the magazine complaining about Mrs. Crabtree. Housewives felt misrepresented, and men felt taken for a ride.

21. Bob Norman, "Miss Golddigger of 1953," *Playboy* (December 1953), 12–71. © Playboy.

22. Charles Perry, *The Haight-Ashbury: A History* (New York: Random House/Rolling Stone Press, 1984), 245.

23. Shulamith Firestone, *The Dialectic of Sex* (New York: William Morrow, 1980), 30.

24. Quoted in David Bouchier, *The Feminist Challenge: The Movement for Women's Liberation in Britain and the United States* (New York: Schocken Books, 1984), 52.

25. Dickstein, op. cit., 203.

26. Ibid., 207.

27. Marge Piercy, "The Grand Coolie Damn," in Robin Morgan, ed., *Sisterhood Is Powerful* (New York: Vintage Books, 1970), 483.

28. Robin Morgan, "Goodbye to All That," in *Going Too Far* (New York: Random House, 1977), 122–28.

29. Robin Morgan, "Take a Memo, Mr. Smith," in *Going Too Far*, loc. cit., 69.

30. Andrea Dworkin, *Right-Wing Women* (New York: Perigee Books, 1983), 91.

31. Ibid.

32. Ibid., 94.

33. "Redstocking Manifesto" in Morgan, op. cit., 598.

34. Herb Goldberg, *The Hazards of Being Male* (New York: Signet Books, 1977), 67.

35. Farrell, op. cit., 151.

36. Quoted in Joseph H. Pleck, *The Myth of Masculinity* (Cambridge, Mass.: MIT Press, 1981), 317.

37. The Playboy Report on American Men, *A Study of the Values, At-*

titudes and Goals of U.S. Males, 18–49 Years Old (New York: Louis Harris & Assoc. Inc., 1979), 59.

38. Dan Kiley, *The Peter Pan Syndrome: Men Who Have Never Grown Up* (New York: Dodd, Mead, 1983), xvi.

39. Interview, October 9, 1984.

40. Betty Friedan, *The Feminine Mystique* (New York: Dell, 1963), 363.

41. Frank Furstenberg, Jr., and Christine Winquist Nord, "Parenting Apart: Patterns of Childrearing After Marital Disruption," *Journal of Marriage and the Family* (November 1985), 874.

42. Nan D. Hunter, "Women and Child Support," in Irene Diamond and Mary Lyndon Shanley, eds., *Family, Politics and Public Policy* (New York: Longman, 1983), 206.

43. Eric Skjei and Richard Rabkin, *The Male Ordeal* (New York: G. P. Putnam, 1981), 72. See also Goldberg, op. cit., 162.

44. For examples of nurturing fathers, see Ari Korpivara "Play Groups for Dads," *Ms.* (February 1982), 43.

45. Donald H. Bell, *Being a Man: The Paradox of Masculinity* (Lexington, Mass.: Lewis Publishing, 1982), 97.

46. "Cat's in the Cradle." Music and words by Harry Chapin and Sandy Chapin. © 1974 Story Songs Ltd. Courtesy of the Chapin estate.

14: Contemporary Women: Two Hostile Camps

1. Marilyn French, *The Women's Room* (London: Jove, 1978), 267–68.

2. Grace Baruch, Rosalind Barnett, and Caryl Rivers, *Lifeprints: New Patterns of Love and Work for Today's Women* (New York: McGraw-Hill, 1983), 106.

3. Mirra Komarovsky, *Women in The Modern World* (Boston: Little, Brown, 1953), 108–110.

4. William H. Whyte, Jr., "The Wives of Management," in Sigmund Noscow and William H. Form, eds., *Man, Work, and Society* (New York: Basic Books, 1962), 548–55.

5. Philip E. Slater, *The Pursuit of Loneliness: American Culture at the Breaking Point* (Boston: Beacon Press, 1970), 74.

6. Sloan Wilson, "The Woman in the Grey Flannel Suit," *New York Times Magazine* (January 15, 1956), 15.

7. Alice Lake, "The Revolt of the Company Wife," *McCall's* (October 1973), 22.

8. Ibid., 24.

9. Interview with Greta Tullmann, September 9, 1984.

10. Midge Decter, *The New Chastity* (New York: Berkley Medallion Books, 1972), 78.

11. Quoted in Susan Lyndon, "The Politics of Orgasm," in Robin Morgan, ed., *Sisterhood Is Powerful* (New York: Vintage Books, 1970), 222.

12. Ibid., 219.

13. Simone de Beauvoir, *The Second Sex,* 1952 (New York: Vintage Books, 1974), 438.

14. Betty Friedan, *The Second Stage* (New York: Summit Books, 1981), 47.

15. George Gilder, *Sexual Suicide* (New York: Quadrangle Press, 1973), 6.

16. Phyllis Schlafly, *The Power of the Positive Woman* (New York: Jove/HBJ, 1977), 81.

17. In a recent study sociologist Kristin Luker points out that the pro-choice movement is populated by highly educated, well-paid career women with few children and a strong vested interest in their work roles, while women in the pro-life camp tend to be Roman Catholics with large families and low-paying or no outside jobs. The self-esteem of the pro-life woman tends to be derived from her maternal role. See Kristin Luker, *Abortion and the Politics of Motherhood* (Berkeley, Calif.: University of California Press, 1984).

18. Andrea Dworkin, *Right-Wing Women* (New York: Perigee Books, 1983), 69.

19. Schlafly, op. cit., 16.

20. Marabel Morgan, *The Total Woman* (New York: Pocket Books, 1975), 17.

21. Ibid., 60.

22. Ibid., 112.

23. Ibid., 113.

24. Ibid., 115.

25. Ibid., 116.

26. Ibid., 17.

27. Ruth Carter Stapleton, *The Gift of Inner Healing* (Waco, Texas: Word Books, 1976), 32.

28. Anita Bryant, *Bless This House* (New York: Bantam Books, 1976), 51.

29. Dworkin, op. cit., 72.

30. Nora Ephron, *Heartburn* (New York: Pocket Books, 1983), 104.

31. Beverly Lahaye, *To Manipulate a Housewife,* prepared by Concerned Women for America, San Diego, California, 1983.

32. Ibid., 2.

33. Arthur Miller, *Death of a Salesman* (New York: Viking Press, 1949), 134.

34. Morris Dickstein, *Gates of Eden* (New York: Basic Books, 1977), 27.

35. French, op. cit., 209–10.

15: What Can Trade Unions Do for Women?

1. Interview, March 26, 1985.

2. *Money, Income and Poverty Status of Families and Persons in the US: 1984,* Current Population Reports, Series P-60 (Washington, D.C.: Bureau of the Census, 1985).

3. *New York Times,* February 8, 1985.

4. Ibid.

5. Interview, November 5, 1983.

6. Larry T. Adams, "Changing Employment Patterns of Organized Workers," *Monthly Labor Review* (February 1985), 25.

7. Interview, September 7, 1984.

8. *Pay Equity on Trial* (Washington, D.C.: AFSCME, 1984), 2.

9. Ibid., 2.

10. *Winning the Fight for Pay Equity* (Washington, D.C.: AFSCME, 1984), 1.

11. Ibid., 11–12.

12. *Pay Equity and Comparable Worth: A BNA Special Report* (Washington, D.C.: Bureau of National Affairs, 1984), 73.

13. Ibid., 77.

14. William H. Chafe, *The American Woman: Her Changing Social, Economic and Political Roles 1920–1970* (New York: Oxford University Press, 1972), 77.

15. Quoted in Bettina Berch, *The Endless Day* (New York: Harcourt Brace Jovanovich, 1982), 41.

16. Cited in Alice Kessler-Harris, *Out to Work: A History of Wage-Earning Women in the United States* (New York: Oxford University Press, 1982), 153.

17. Berch, op. cit., 165.

18. Kessler-Harris, op. cit., 165–66.

19. Adams, op. cit., 30.

20. Interview, March 25, 1985.

21. Adams, op. cit., 25.

22. Ibid., 26.

23. *New York Times,* February 8, 1985.

24. Ibid.

25. *New York Times,* September 3, 1984.

26. Interview with UAW member at Ford assembly plant, August 28, 1984.

27. Adams, op. cit., 26.

28. Interview, November 23, 1983.

29. Gunner Quist, Joan Acker, and Val R. Lorwin, "Sweden," in Alice H. Cook, Val R. Lorwin, and Arlene Kaplan Daniels, eds., *Women and Trade Unions in Eleven Industrialized Countries* (Philadelphia: Temple University Press, 1984), 267.

30. Ibid., 264.

31. Ibid., 269. See also Annual Report of the Central Bureau of Statistics and various issues of *Allman Manadsstatistik,* Stockholm, Sweden. See discussion in Chapter Four.

32. Bianca Beccali, "Italy," in Cook et al., op. cit., 193.

33. "Equal Opportunity for Women," *OECD Observer* 97 (March 1979), 9, and *Eurostat,* "Hourly Earnings—Hours of Work," various issues, Statistical Office of the European Community, Luxembourg. See discussion in Chapter Four.

34. Chiara Ingrao, "Feminism and Trade Unions in Italy," mimeograph, New York, May 1981, 6.

35. Interview, February 11, 1984.

36. *Employment Gazette* 91, 1 (January 1983), 26.

37. See discussion in Peter J. Sloane, "The Trend of Women's Wages Relative to Men's in the Postwar Period in Great Britain," paper presented to the Economic Policy Council's panel on "Parents and Work: Family Policy in Comparative Perspective," Washington, D.C., June 12, 1984, 5.

38. *Wall Street Journal,* March 28, 1985.

39. Lindsay Mackie and Polly Patullo, *Women at Work* (London: Tavistock Publications, 1977), 166.

40. Catherine Bodard Silver, "France: Contrast in Familial and Societal Roles," in Janet Z. Giele and Audrey C. Smock, eds., *Women: Roles and Status in Eight Countries* (New York: John Wiley & Sons, 1977), 276.

41. Ibid., 277.

42. *Social Europe* (Luxembourg: Commission of the European Community, May 1984), 120.

43. Adams, op. cit., 21.

44. Interview, January 13, 1983. Joyce Miller is also president of CLUW, Coalition of Labor Union Women, a leadership group founded in 1974 to join "union women in a viable organization to determine first—our common problems and concerns, second—to develop action programs within the framework of our unions to deal effectively with our objectives."

45. CWA staff member (New York) interview, September 4, 1984.

46. Adams, op. cit., 28.

47. *New York Times,* July 31, 1984.

48. *Pay Equity and Comparable Worth: A BNA Special Report,* loc. cit., 89.

49. *New York Times,* April 2, 1985.

50. Interview, April 5, 1985.

16: *The Establishment Gropes for an Answer*

1. The Economic Policy Council (EPC) of the United Nations Association of the USA was founded in 1976. Its mission is to sponsor a systematic and constructive involvement in international economic problems by the American private sector. The EPC is committed to representing the views of both management and labor. Its membership comprises eminent individuals from the corporate, labor, and academic communities. The EPC is co-chaired by Robert O. Anderson, chairman of the Atlantic Richfield Company, and Douglas A. Fraser, president emeritus, United Auto Workers. Its steering committee consists of: Charles Barber (former chairman, Asarco, Inc.); Henry Kaufman (executive director, Salomon Brothers, Inc.); Ray Marshall (Bernard Rapoport Professor of Economics and Public Affairs, University of Texas at Austin); Jack Sheinkman (secretary-treasurer, Amalgamated Clothing and Textile Workers Union, AFL-CIO); Thomas A. Vanderslice (president and CEO, Apollo Computer Inc.); and Lyn R. Williams (president, United Steelworkers of America). The EPC has approximately 100 members.

EPC members are brought together in study panels to analyze important international economic issues. Every year the EPC branches out into two or three panels, each of which addresses a specific problem area.

The EPC both identifies critical policy questions and makes recommendations, which are then published and presented to officials within the executive and legislative branches of the United States government.

The EPC maintains a close working relationship with the executive branch and with leaders in Congress. Council members have regularly presented panel recommendations at hearings in the House of Representatives and in the Senate; cabinet-level officials attend the annual plenary sessions of the EPC to engage in an informal exchange of views; and several study panels have met with and advised presidential task forces.

2. The full titles of the other EPC panels running in September 1984 were "The Global Repercussions of U.S. Monetary and Fiscal Policy," chaired by Henry Kaufman (executive director, Salomon Bros.) and Peter B. Kenen (Walker Professor of Economics and International Finance, Princeton University) and "Jobs in the Eighties," chaired by John Filer (chairman, Aetna Life & Casualty Insurance Company) and Douglas Fraser (president emeritus, United Auto Workers).

3. Interview, December 11, 1984.

4. See discussion of the problems encountered by the panel in Sylvia Ann Hewlett, "Coping with Illegal Immigrants," *Foreign Affairs* 60 (Winter 1981–82), 358–78.

5. Statement of Albert Shanker, president, American Federation of Teachers, AFL-CIO, before the Senate Subcommittee on Children and Youth, June 5, 1975, 11.

17: Epilogue: Voices from the Post-Feminist Generation

1. *Wall Street Journal,* October 30, 1984.

2. Ibid.

3. *Fortune* (July 11, 1983), 58. In 1983 60 percent of these women were married and 46 percent had children. The average age of the women in this sample was thirty-seven.

4. *Wall Street Journal,* February 11, 1982. The average age of the women in this survey was forty-six, and most were vice-presidents.

5. Basia Hellwig, "The Breakthrough Generation: 73 Women Ready to Run Corporate America," *Working Women* (April 1985), 98–146. See also Mary Anne Devanna, "Male/Female Careers: MBA's a Decade into Their Careers," Center for Research into Career Develop-

ment, Columbia University School of Business Administration, 1983. Devanna sampled several hundred M.B.A.'s who received their degrees from Columbia University in the period 1969–72: "72% of men in the sample were married as opposed to 58% of women. . . . Less than 10% of the married men have no children, 22% of the married women are childless," 108. To round out one's picture of elite women, a study in the late 1970s of women scientists showed that 50 percent were unmarried, compared to 10 percent of their male counterparts; among married women scientists 33 to 50 percent were childless, again compared to 10 percent of the married men. According to this study, "women more than men must compromise their family lives for the sake of career." See Ruth E. Zambrana, Marsha Hurst, and Rodney L. Hite, "The Working Mother in Contemporary Perspective: A Review of the Literature," *Pediatrics* 64 (December 1979). For additional data, see Chapter 2, note 10.

6. Philip Blumstein and Pepper Schwartz, *American Couples* (New York: William Morrow, 1983), 146.

7. Interview, Roxanne Felschuch, IDANT Laboratories, January 4, 1985.

8. Germaine Greer, *Sex and Destiny: The Politics of Human Fertility* (New York: Harper & Row, 1984), 2.

9. Ibid., 29.

10. Ibid., 458.

11. Ibid., 2.

12. Quoted in Erica Abeel, "Dark Secrets," *Esquire,* June 1984, 262.

13. Quoted in Dolores Hayden, *The Grand Domestic Revolution* (Cambridge, Mass.: MIT Press, 1981), 197–98.

14. *Time,* May 27, 1985, 81.

15. *Barnard Alumnae* (Summer 1985), 9.

16. Warren Farrell, *The Liberated Man* (New York: Random House, 1975), 26.

17. Ann Critenden, "We 'Liberated' Mothers Aren't," *Washington Post,* February 5, 1985.

Afterword

1. *Ms.,* March 1986, p. 74.

2. *Baltimore Sun,* March 17, 1986.

3. *Time,* March 31, 1986, p. 62.

4. *Vanity Fair,* April 1986, p. 93.

5. *New York Times,* May 4, 1986.

6. *Vanity Fair,* April 1987, p. 118.

7. *Washington Post,* January 22, 1986.

8. *USA Today,* September 24, 1986.

9. Quoted in Letty Cottin Pogrebin, *Family Politics: Love and Power on an Intimate Frontier* (New York: McGraw Hill, 1983), p. 60.

Index

Index

Index

Index

Index

Index

Index

Index